# The Films of the Nineties

# By the Author

## Nonfiction

*The Fiction of John Fowles*
*The Films of the Seventies: A Social History*
*The Films of the Eighties: A Social History*
*Dickens and New Historicism*

## Fiction

*The Detective and Mr. Dickens*
*The Highwayman and Mr. Dickens*
*The Hoydens and Mr. Dickens*
*The Dons and Mr. Dickens*

# The Films of the Nineties
## The Decade of Spin

William J. Palmer

palgrave
macmillan

First published in 2009 by PALGRAVE MACMILLAN® in the United States—a division of St. Martin's Press LLC, 175 Fifth Avenue, New York, NY 10010.

Where this book is distributed in the UK, Europe and the rest of the world, this is by Palgrave Macmillan, a division of Macmillan Publishers Limited, registered in England, company number 785998, of Houndmills, Basingstoke, Hampshire RG21 6XS.

Palgrave Macmillan is the global academic imprint of the above companies and has companies and representatives throughout the world.

Palgrave® and Macmillan® are registered trademarks in the United States, the United Kingdom, Europe and other countries.

ISBN-13: 978-0-230-61344-7
ISBN-10: 0-230-61344-6

Library of Congress Cataloging-in-Publication Data is available from the Library of Congress.

A catalogue record of the book is available from the British Library.

Design by Scribe Inc.

First edition: March 2009

10 9 8 7 6 5 4 3 2 1

Printed in the United States of America.

*To my wife, Maryann, who has become my memory.*

# Contents

# Preface

A *New Yorker* cartoon by Stuart Leeds that, in four successive panels, parodied the famous *LOVE* sculpture of Robert Indiana helped generate the governing idea for this book. The first panel, labeled "The Sixties," contained an exact replica of the original *LOVE* sculpture. The second panel, captioned "The Seventies," portrayed the word LAME in the configuration of the original sculpture. The third panel, "The Eighties," read LOOT, and the fourth, "The Nineties," LESS. That cartoon, in the blending of a recognizable visual icon with a clear and simple verbal commentary and in the bringing together of history and cultural definition, posed the conceptual question upon which this book is based: if I were going to describe the nineties in one word, what word would it be?

In trying to arrive at an answer to that question, my first move was to isolate the dominant social issues (and icons) that defined the decade. Most prominent of all the forces influencing social history in the nineties was Bill Clinton, who was both icon and issue.

Also central to the evolution of nineties society was the communications explosion that took multiple forms, including

1. the ascendance of a totally wired and computerized society;
2. the burgeoning power of an electronic media based on a tabloid model that could make news as fast as they could cover it;
3. the emergence of a more aggressive investigative journalism that could find, dissect, and saturate society with any story of any type in any amount of time across any expanse of space;
4. the heightened involvement of the entertainment community and its "instruments of diffusion"[1]—movies, television, video games, music, theater—not only in the discourse surrounding the major social issues of the decade but also in the very definition and formation of those issues.

A third prominent force in the definition of the social issues of the nineties was the basic change in the decade's discourse communities. Evolving out of seventies and eighties academic discourse, by the nineties, social discourse had taken a new direction. As Jacques Barzun commented, "Deconstruction on a vast scale everywhere."[2] In other words, the philosophical theories that in the seventies and eighties had taken over the critical discourse of academia—Deconstruction, New Historicism, the postmodern ideas of thinkers like Michel Foucault, Mikhail Bakhtin, Hayden White, Jean Baudrillard, Jean-François Lyotard et. al.—were entering the mainstream and redefining the very nature and perception of reality by the nineties.

Finally entering the equation were the major nineties social issues themselves: the Clinton presidency, AIDS, gay rights, the New Sexuality, the attack media, new racisms/sexisms/ageisms, and the most vexing and dangerous issue of all, expanding global terrorism. But in the face of all these evolving nineties social forces, my question still remained: what one word, one nineties social force, could encompass and describe all these diverse issues?

While trying to answer this question, I was reading a book by Margot Norris on twentieth-century war where she writes, "My project is itself made problematic by its scope, its aim to function as a century book."[3] That statement gave me a sense of ambition to add to the sense of historical definition that the *New Yorker* cartoon had planted. I wanted to write a decade book that would capture the nineties the way that the public intellectuals of the past had caught the temper of their times: "The 'Me' Generation," "Generation X," "The Living Room War." I realized that if I was going to write a cultural history of the nineties, I had to capture its identity in the clearly defining way that the cartoon and those catchy slogans had caught the personality of their times.

Simultaneously, I was fully aware that my book was to be the third in a series of New Historicist social histories written from the perspective of the relationship between film and contemporary society.[4] Like so many movies of the seventies, eighties, and nineties, it was going to be a sequel of sorts (titled "The Films of the Nineties: A Social History" as its two predecessors on the seventies and the eighties had been titled). It was supposed to be the completion of a trilogy analyzing from a postmodernist, interdisciplinary perspective the relationship between contemporary film and late twentieth-century history. But as I perceived more and more how different the nineties were from the seventies and eighties, saw what powerful new forces were in play, like the computerized media and AIDS, my goals for this book grew more ambitious. I began thinking well beyond its original conception as a mere sequel and realized its kinship not only to those theorists who had called into question the nature of history (the New Historicists), but to another set of postmodernist philosophical thinkers (led by Jean Baudrillard and Jean-François Lyotard) who were calling into question the very nature of reality itself.

But even with these mini-epiphanic moments in place, I still set out to write this book in the same way I had written its predecessors, by isolating all the central themes (or cultural issues) of the nineties (like the tabloid fascination with the Clinton presidency or the "coming out" of the gay community) that seemed to repeatedly appear in the films of the decade. After all, these books were focused upon the way that the media, especially the movies, took the pulse of the times, monitored the heartbeat of the decade. But the nineties were different! That realization kept nagging at me as I began my research and started isolating the major issues of the decade. Only then did I realize what the times, the movies, and my book's arguments were really about. They were about spin.

## The Nineties and Spin

> This "atomization" of the social into flexible language games . . .
> —Jean-François Lyotard, *The Postmodern Condition: A Report on Knowledge*

In the nineties, contemporary social history and the media actually collaborated to define a shared metaphor for the age. That metaphor was the phenomenon of spin. Public intellectuals, media pundits, and cultural historians (as well as filmmakers) embodied the nineties leading up to the traumatic turn of the new century (the millennium a.k.a. Y2K) in the image of the vortex, the tornado, the centrifugal decentered creativity of the potter's wheel. Deconstruction, a central academic theory of the eighties with its emphasis upon decentering and marginalization, became the spinning force behind this metaphor. It all had to do with the age-old philosophical question: "What is the nature of reality?" By the nineties, reality had become such a slippery issue, such a babel of contesting narratives that the deconstructive metaphors were the only ones that made sense. Reality in the nineties leading up to all the dire predictions of Y2K, the very malfunction of time, was different from earlier decades. Nineties reality was centrifugally spun out of control, always in motion, always open to interpretation. The movies reflected this quandary better than any other media.

Reality took the form of a whole series of contesting narratives. Mapping the confluences of those narratives in the global society of the nineties makes the writing of history somewhat problematic. Make no mistake: this is a history. But the better question is, "What kind of a history?" Definitely, this is a film history. But it is also a social history, a political history, and a sexual history. More subtly, it is a rhetorical history that defines the relationship between Lyotard's "language games" and the politics, the media, the advertising, and the very mechanics of persuasion at the end of the twentieth century. Finally, it is a decade book, a history of the 1990s and how the decade's motion pictures mixed fact and fiction to create new realities out of what may have never been realities in the first place.

As one commentator writes, "Reality presents a random, infinite supply of details, and the job of writers—whether you consider yourself a historian, a biographer, or a novelist—is similar: to create a coherent narrative. You can't select everything, and in making choices, thus putting an emphasis here and diminishing it there, you invariably move into the realm of fiction."[5] This convergence of history and fiction was a major credibility issue in the nineties. Voltaire defined history as "nothing more than a tableau of crimes and misfortunes," and James Joyce called history "a nightmare from which I am trying to awake." For Napoleon, history was "a fraud agreed upon," while for Henry Ford, "history is more or less bunk."[6] Each of these famous gripers acknowledges the competing narratives of reality involved in trying to recapture the past, and each in turn discusses the historian's attempt as ill-considered, inadvisable, unethical, and futile. Nonetheless, history has always tried to order the chaos of reality. The only problem with doing this in the late twentieth century is that the chaos of reality has been totally spun out of control, like a centrifuge broken loose of its moorings or a tornado touching down in a Kansas cornfield.

Despite all this instability, the spinning realities of the nineties still offered historians attractive possibilities, and, by the beginning of that decade, historians were acquiring the tools to theoretically understand the constant spin and flux of nineties realities. Like a potter placing a lump of clay on a wheel, setting it spinning, and creating order out of its decentered reformation, the nineties historian takes a new approach to his material. The New Historicists eagerly embraced the interpretational possibilities of nineties spin, and one of their major allies and "instruments of diffusion" in their postmodernist attempt to write the narrative of this era of spin was the movies. The films of the nineties reread, rewrote, revised, and reenvisioned past and present history so often that the relationship between history and Hollywood actually became a History Channel TV show and a watercooler topic of debate. People were actually talking about history. Did it really happen that way? Is that how I remember it? How did that change us all? Most of all, what is the relationship between history and spin?

# CHAPTER 1

# Hollywood and History

This is history with a fucking flourish.

—Don DeLillo, *Libra*

At the 2000 Oscars, a short compilation film celebrated *History and the Movies*. It was appropriate for the millennium Academy Awards to look back at the film industry's engagement with the history of the tumultuous century just ending, but equally important was the recognition of the power of historical representation and interpretation that the motion picture industry gathered to itself in the last half of the twentieth century. From the sixties on, films became a looking glass through which cultures, nations, governments, societies, and individual historical figures saw themselves. Movies defined the history and culture of the latter half of the twentieth century by capturing it in a medium available and comprehensible to all. The movies became what Dominick LaCapra termed the major "instruments of diffusion"[1] for the historical consciousness of the second half of the twentieth century. This was a New Historicist consciousness that called into question not only the "Grand Narratives"[2] of the nineteenth century but also the sources, the methodology, and the very style of the voices of traditional twentieth-century academic history.[3]

The nineties in America will be remembered as the decade of Bill and Hillary Clinton, Monica Lewinsky (among others), O. J. Simpson, Gulf Wars and Desert Storms, hate crimes, children with guns, and, most of all, AIDS. If the seventies was the decade of Richard Nixon, Watergate, and Vietnam's aftermath, and the eighties was the decade of Ronald Reagan, terrorism, and Yuppie commodity culture, then the nineties was the decade of sex and death and alienation in so many different ways (the Clintons, the O. J. Simpsons, AIDS, and racial hatred).

The nineties also saw the discourse of postmodernism become a part of the discourse of everyday life.[4] The noun "deconstruction" and its verbal and adjectival uses, for example, became a commonplace in newspapers and on the nightly network news. It made no difference that Dan Rather, Tom Brokaw, and Peter Jennings had no idea what "deconstruction" really was; they used the term anyway. In tune with this popularized postmodernism, in the nineties rights became gay rights, gun rights, children's rights, and corporate rights, and texts became cultural texts, subtexts, intertexts, and metatexts.

But most important of all, eighties academia bequeathed a New Historicism to the nineties, a way of expanding the historical record to include what had been missed or repressed or ignored in the past. This New Historicism, so named by Stephen Greenblatt in the eighties,[5] drew its philosophical substance from the work of Michel Foucault and Mikhail Bakhtin and its theoretical methodology and definition from the work of Hayden White and Dominick LaCapra. The New Historicism became a discourse site for all who wanted to question, revise, or write contesting narratives to the accepted, power-centered histories of both the past and present.

In a 1994 speech, Steven Spielberg declared that film is "the most powerful weapon in the world" and threw out the challenge that "filmmakers have the responsibility not just to entertain but to be responsible, to inform."[6] That same year when Spielberg's *Schindler's List* (1994) dominated the Academy Awards, one media observer wrote, "With movies about AIDS and the Holocaust, maybe Ted Koppel should host."[7] Interestingly enough, the mainstream Spielberg's Aristotelian characterization of the power of film was echoed by America's most notorious historicist director. Talking about his own film, *Natural Born Killers* (1994), Oliver Stone said, "It was about capturing that mean season, from '92 to '94, when there was one bloody tabloid scandal after another."[8] In 1995 when presidential candidate Robert Dole, later to appear in Viagra TV commercials, attacked Hollywood for marketing "nightmares of depravity" and for "mainstreaming deviancy," film critic Gene Siskel answered that blaming movies for cultural problems "diverts the national agenda from the real problems. . . . 'Cancel the violent movies but let's make sure we have plenty of assault weapons.'"[9] What all these early nineties commentators realized was the power that had accrued to the movies.

That sociohistorical power is captured in one of the most oft-repeated journalistic pun/clichés of the nineties. In newspaper headlines, on magazine and tabloid covers, on the television network news, and on the most scurrilous trash-TV talk shows, the relationship between "reel life" and "real life" was constantly being trumpeted.[10] A whole television subgenre known as "reality TV" grew out of this pun/cliché. What had begun with the documentary filming of the dysfunctional life of the Loud family in the seventies' *An American Family* (1973) became a panoptic industry in the nineties.[11] Cameras focused on warring roommates (even to the point of watching one die of AIDS) and sitcoms like *Friends* (1994–2004) portrayed equally dysfunctional roommate relationships for laughs. Reality TV followed police into alleged criminals' homes and invaded those peoples' privacy before they were ever proven guilty. Then, in the best metatextual turnabout, reality TV became the subject late in the nineties of a group of films—*The Truman Show* (1998), *Pleasantville* (1998), *Ed TV* (1999)—satirizing the dehumanizing excesses of a surveillance mentality.

"History makes Hollywood nervous,"[12] a sidebar in *Entertainment Weekly* (the most widely read entertainment-focused magazine of the nineties and, in fact, a magazine conceived and developed specifically in and for the nineties that superseded the American Film Institute monthly journal, *American Film*, the major review and industry trend/news publication of the seventies and eighties)[13] declared in 1995 when *Braveheart* and *Rob Roy*, both Scottish historical period pieces, were in the theaters. But that declaration was hardly true. In fact, throughout the nineties, Hollywood found itself quite comfortable with history if *Titanic* (1997) and *Forrest Gump* (1994) are any indication. Perhaps Dean Devlin, producer of the mega-event blockbuster *Independence Day* (1996), defined the film/social history relationship best as he characterized Hollywood as harkening back to that great period of the disaster films of the seventies: "Trends are always a reflection of what's happening in the world."[14] Jerome Armstrong, the screenwriter of *Volcano* (1997), seconds that motion, saying, "We're coming up on a new millennium. Apocalyptic elements are in the air."[15]

While an Irwin Allen mentality from the seventies spawned a cycle of disaster films in the second half of the nineties—ranging from alien invasion films like *Independence Day*, *Mars Attacks* (1996), and *Men in Black* (1997), to natural disasters in *Deep Impact* (1998), and the appropriately titled for a decade approaching the millennium *Armageddon* (1998)—the reigning disasterousness of the nineties, which functioned as a continuing metaphor for the film/social history relationship across the whole decade, was that of disease and dysfunction stemming from excess. "Everybody in the '90s comes from a dysfunctional family"[16] a character in a nineties sitcom declared in 1999. Some of the films of that same year, particularly *The Truman Show* and *Pleasantville*, exposed how the dysfunctional life of the nineties deconstructed the placid TV-sitcom life of the fifties, sixties, and seventies. These films took television families, much like the Nelsons, the Cleavers, Donna Reed's brood, the Partridges, and the Brady Bunch (itself deconstructed in a brilliant 1995 satire, *The Brady Bunch Movie*), in which father did usually know best and mother always had a cake coming out of the oven to cut, and subjected them to the malaises of nineties domestic reality. For the nineties, the Simpsons (both on TV and in Los Angeles) were a typical family, and the most publicly dysfunctional family of all was the First Family.

But the most universal disaster, the most threatening dysfunction in American society in the nineties was AIDS. At the end of the eighties decade and throughout the nineties, humanity came to the realization that AIDS was the greatest social threat to life since the atom bomb. With the fall of the Soviet Union in 1989, the Nuclear Age came to an end and the age of AIDS began. America adjusted its historical gaze, stopped looking for death from the skies, and began looking within at the excess, dysfunction, and the single disease that became a metaphor embodying all the debilitation to which American society was no longer immune.

It was the mass media, especially television and movies via mainstream productions like *And the Band Played On* (TV; 1993) and *Philadelphia* (1993) that heightened the national and international consciousness of AIDS as a universal threat that could enter and decimate anyone's life. The power of Hollywood film as a social mechanism is, perhaps, nowhere more evident than in the propaganda strategy of *Philadelphia*. How does one educate a whole society to the dangers of AIDS? How does one make available to the whole society the clinical, social, and political realities of AIDS? One casts Tom Hanks—the Everyman, white bread, acceptably normal Jimmy Stewart of his generation of actors—as an AIDS victim. People tend to buy things from people they trust. Who better to warn America of the dangers of AIDS than Forrest Gump?

Mapping the historical, cultural, social impact of the films of the nineties involves the charting of the temper of the times as well as the history of the industry that produced those films. In the late summer of 1998, the word "history" was showing up quite frequently in the headlines of newspapers. When Mark McGwire of the St. Louis Cardinals hit his sixty-second home run on September 8, 1998, something as subtextual as "baseball history" asserted complete prominence over the primary text of American history. The next day's headlines all involved the historical significance of McGwire's mighty shot. One headline even punned playfully on the concept of "history": "McGwire makes Maris history."[17] That same day, writer Jonathan Yardley's column was headlined by a text that combined history and the movies into a commentary on the nineties generation that had so breathlessly followed McGwire and his happy warrior of a competitor, Sammy Sosa, through that glorious, exciting baseball summer: "History's field of dreams allows each generation its own home run chase."[18] History, the movies, baseball, generations—that headline covered all the bases. In the summer of '98, McGwire and Sosa's home run chase came to be a revivifying commentary on America, not just baseball America, but America. Its symbolism was not lost on either the American people or on the commentators on American history. The exhilaration of the summer was soon subsumed in the sludge and monotony and sordidness of the winter's impeachment proceedings, but for a few, brief months, nineties social history had risen above its dysfunctional nature.

## Historical Accuracy and the Media

Don't know much about history

—Sam Cooke, "Wonderful World"

In 1970, Ian Jarvie in his book *Movies and Society* argued, "There was something else that was vigorous and exciting about the American Cinema, something deeply entwined in the relation it bore to its society: its ability to portray every aspect of American society with almost clinical accuracy."[19] In 1995, at middecade, a nationally syndicated columnist wrote, "Oliver Stone's film *JFK* [1991] probably did more to create public suspicion of the government than anything in the last decade. An entire generation will grow up accepting Stone's distortions and outright lies as history."[20] In 1997 in an American Studies class at American University, Stone defended himself by arguing that his film *JFK* was intended to lead people to ponder how President Kennedy died. Later that same year in the *New York Times Magazine*, Stone, commenting on his historical films *JFK* and *Nixon* (1995), said, "I'm all for facts, but there's so much dispute about facts that the Kennedy murder to me borders on dream or nightmare."[21] While the historical presentations of Stone films have been a lightning rod for critics and defenders, the MTV generation has probably learned more about history from Stone's (and Spielberg's and others') films than from any other source or, as LaCapra would call it, "mechanism of diffusion."[22]

The fact of the matter is that the traditional historians have lost contact with their audience. In a Darwinian world, they have failed to adapt. The medium has outgrown their message, and, as a defense mechanism, they have chosen to revile the medium rather than adapt the presentation of their message to that new medium. The conventional medium of the academic history book has been superseded by the much more expansive mass media: television, the movies, and the Internet.

But another fact of the matter is that, by the late 1990s, many historians have indeed adapted. Or, if they haven't fully accepted that mass media is presenting much more history to many more people than they are, at least they have realized that they need to participate in the popular diffusion of history much more aggressively. As Karen Winkler in "History in Hollywood: The Way Films Present the Past" details, historians are becoming literary critics by filling the media niche of serving as commentators upon and reviewers of historical films, TV miniseries, History Channel cable offerings, and burgeoning Internet Web sites and discussion sites.[23] For example, Robert Brent Toplin, who began printing movie reviews in the *Journal of American History* in 1986, recalls that "there was a sense that this just wasn't something professional historians should be doing. We're light years ahead of that today."[24] Winkler goes on to describe just how far that evolution has come in the late nineties: "Today, more and more scholars are considering how films depict history. They are using movies in class, reviewing them, writing books about them. While documentaries are what probably interest the majority of historians, a growing number are turning to the analysis of feature films too."[25] Historian Mark C. Carnes argues that historians need "to capitalize on people's interest in film and engage them in a dialogue about history. It's not enough to say, 'Hey, they got it wrong in that film.' We have to figure out how to turn viewers into readers."[26]

The whole debate over the accuracy of history and its representation in motion pictures and other media "started in the late '60s or early '70s, when TV began to tie in topical events," Tim Brooks, author of *The Complete Directory to Prime Time Network and Cable TV Shows*, argues.[27] In a discussion of Terence Malick's *The Thin Red Line* (1998), which represents the Battle of Guadalcanal, historian Michael Gannon declares that "watching the film isn't going to help you pass a history exam" because James Jones's book upon which the film is based "took several liberties."[28] But Jones's daughter answers that *The Thin Red Line* is "a thinly disguised account of real experiences. In fact, the fight for a hill described in both the book and the film as 'the Dancing Elephant' is a recounting of an actual battle that took place in 1943 on a hill called 'the Galloping Horse.'"[29]

In an essay appropriately titled "World War II in Film: What Is the Color of Reality?" Thomas Doherty argues that while the black-and-white film footage of World War II seems "to glow with the aura of historical truth,"[30] nineties war movies, such as Spielberg's *Saving Private Ryan* (1998), shot in graphic color, help us "to see the Second World War as it truly looked."[31] Doherty, describing the difference between the war movies of the forties and fifties and those of the nineties, writes, "Yoked to black and white, the past seems fixed and distant. Arrayed in color, it seems dynamic and close."[32] A single change in the basic medium of representation, therefore, can function in offering a more accurate representation of history. Event to novel to film, black-and-white to color, the representation of history is constantly evolving, and yet, the debate over accuracy remains the major sticking point between historians and the media.

"The suspension of disbelief integral to the reading of fiction runs counter to the exacting demands one places upon testimony," Sara R. Horowitz writes.[33] Stone, Spielberg, James Cameron in *Titanic*, and any number of other filmmakers who have walked the thin line between fact and fiction in the making of a nineties movie have all had to submit themselves to this historical-accuracy litmus test, and, almost invariably, they have been found wanting.

But should they be?

Should they be blamed simply because their medium has more currency, more availability, and more mass immediacy than the more traditional print mediums that were the previous purveyors of history?

Don't historical films provide a service and reach an audience that traditional history could never envision even in its wildest dreams?

Arline Thorn writes, "As for Oskar Schindler, the 'lovable rogue,' he did in fact save the lives of 1,100 Jews and was recognized by Israel as a righteous gentile. Few individuals or organizations managed to do as much during the Holocaust."[34] Thorn argues that it is simply too easy to criticize a film for its failure of a rigid accuracy test because "in our cynical post-Holocaust world, it is worthwhile nevertheless, to contemplate the possibility and actuality of human goodness in the face of such an evil. It distorts history not to show that righteous gentiles, however few they were, have opposed genocide and slavery. Spielberg should be commended not castigated for taking on those 'big issues.'"[35]

Stone is, perhaps, a much more problematic case than Spielberg. Stone's historical reconstructions aren't softened by the sentimental aura of goodness discovered in the cesspool of evil that marks Spielberg's historical films. Stone's films aren't peopled with many conventional heroes like Speilberg's Robin-Hoodish Schindler or duty-bound Captain Miller in *Saving Private Ryan*. Stone's heroes are flawed, ironic, and sometimes despicable, and his films present a historical underbelly that seems to invite the fury of traditional historians. Stone often seems to welcome the controversy that the historical establishment tends to trigger on cue whenever another of his films is released. In other words, Stone knows that being castigated by the stodgy establishment is good publicity.

For example, one ruffled historian writes,

> That Oliver Stone believes he alone, among all others, knows definitively the facts behind the John F. Kennedy assassination and other events in recent American history speaks more to the hubris that exists in Hollywood than to the willful ignorance of the masses or the "power of corruption to rewrite history." It is truly sad, if not shocking, that an entire generation of young people will obtain their understanding of two seminal periods in U.S. history, the Kennedy and Nixon Administrations, from a man whose profession does not require, or even suggest, the use of documented sources in order to make an argument. . . . Would that the academy argued forcefully against such illogic and wrested the hearts and minds of young America away from Stone's tripe. But I fear that the academy may be no match for Hollywood, its money, and its MTV generation historical method.[36]

This overwrought condemnation of Stone as the Antichrist of history and its mournful whining over the impotence of the academy to deal with such an evil and powerful force is more inaccurate than the writer claims Stone's movies to be. Not only does it overestimate Stone's impact upon American historical consciousness, something that Stone himself minimizes, but it sorely underestimates and misrepresents the involvement of the academy with the evolution of historical method and media. The academic involvement in presenting history via new "mechanisms of diffusion,"[37] such as Ken Burns's documentaries or the History Channel on cable TV or historical CD-ROMs, certainly counters the image of academia as some pitiful ostrich with its head buried in its books while the brave new electronic, Internet, digital, and virtual worlds pass it by. In the nineties, history and Hollywood formed a tenuous relationship, often adversarial but always lively and complex. But one other aspect of this complex historical relationship that powerfully influenced the creative consciousness of Hollywood was its own nineties history.

## Hollywood's Nineties History

While the Oscars are intended to reward merit and present Hollywood's best face to the public, they are, above all, a calculus of the things Hollywood values socially, which then get transformed into artistic values.
—Neal Gabler, "To Pursue Youth, Even Mainstream
Tries to be Cool," *Los Angeles Times*

While Hollywood was making prestigious and often highly successful (in terms of both box office and awards) historical films in the nineties, it's sense of history, especially its cultural consciousness, was also being fueled by its own sinister, colorful, and competitive cultural and industrial history. In many ways the history of the Hollywood film industry in the nineties mirrored both the sociocultural history of the nation and the history being represented in the films produced.

If the movies during this particular historical period addressed the sociocultural/historical issues of greatest concern during this period—such as AIDS or attacks upon the American presidency or questions of widening social class—then within that history/film relationship, there was also a subtext of how Hollywood film represented that smaller more enclosed culture of Hollywood itself, much as Billy Wilder's *Sunset Boulevard* (1950) had done for the forties. Some films like Robert Altman's *The Player* (1992) and Joe Esterhas's *Burn Hollywood Burn: An Alan Smithee Film* (1998) approached this industry subtext frontally, but others, such as *Grand Canyon* (1991) or *Mulholland Drive* (2001), portrayed the industry more subtly, representationally, placing the evolution of the movie industry within the context of the changes taking place in the society at large.

*USA Today* newspaper in January 1992 ran an article titled "Decade-Defining Movies." The list of "decade-defining" films proved quite predictable: *Rebel Without a Cause* (1955) for the fifties; *The Graduate* (1967) for the sixties; *Saturday Night Fever* (1977) for the seventies; *The Big Chill* (1983) for the eighties. And, albeit only two years into the decade, *Grand Canyon* was chosen in the essay as the "decade-defining" film of the nineties because, as one of its characters declared, "We live in chaos. It's the central issue of everyone's life."[38] In the almost nine years of the nineties decade that followed *Grand Canyon* (and this *USA Today* essay), a number of other truly viable candidates for "decade-defining movie" appeared—certainly, *Philadelphia*, *Forrest Gump*, perhaps even *Pulp Fiction* (1994)—but *Grand Canyon* with its pervading sense of things falling apart, of centers that cannot hold, of urban worlds where no one is safe, was a rather good choice. *Grand Canyon* looks at all the different layers of Los Angeles society in the nineties and explores the constant tension between different classes, races, and views of the chaos of nineties life. But within *Grand Canyon*, in the characterization of an utterly corrupt yet highly philosophical movie director (of bloody horror movies soon to be the decade's most popular genre), played by one of the most ironic thinkers of the late twentieth century, Steve Martin, the film parallels its panoramic view of American society to a narrowly focused view of the film industry itself. Martin's director, like Shakespeare's fool in *King Lear*, raves about the state of his world, but what he says rings appallingly true. Chaos was the central issue in most Americans' lives in the nineties. Certainly, that chaos seemed the case in the history of Hollywood in the nineties. One commentator, writing in 1999, argues that "over the past century, the movies have done much more than provide us with entertainment. . . . The movies (as both art and commerce) have also served a symbolic role, as a sometimes polemical model of how our society functions."[39] If this is true, then it is also true that the movies also symbolically represent how Hollywood itself functions. In other words, movies offer a self-referential view of their own origins, motives, and industry history.

In 1992 film critic Michael Medved wrote, "America's long-running romance with Hollywood is over. . . . The real problem is that Hollywood no longer reflects—or even respects—the values of most American families. . . . On many of the important issues in contemporary life, popular entertainment seems to go out of its way to challenge conventional notions of decency."[40] Ironically, the rest of the nineties decade proved exactly the opposite of Medved's reactionary reading of the cultural landscape. If the box office successes of *Forrest Gump* and *Titanic* are any indication, America's romance with Hollywood was hardly over. But perhaps more tellingly, if the tabloid fascination for Hollywood's excesses are any indication, America's romantic fascination for Hollywood is no more dormant than is England's romantic fascination for royalty. When Hollywood made news, all of America paid attention. More interesting, however, is how often Hollywood news mirrored the subject matter of so many of the films that Hollywood was producing. Like the films of the nineties, Hollywood itself was violent, sexy, decadent, often stupid, frequently litigious, and universally materialistic. Murder, sex, drugs, stupidity, and lawsuits were the ruling categories of nineties Hollywood history, and all were subordinate to the one true grail of the Hollywood quest, materialist power.

No one could be more wrong than Medved in imagining that America had lost its fascination for Hollywood. The O. J. Simpson murder case and trial proved that. The O. J. event, with all its overtones of racism, injustice, the tragic fall from grace, and the ultimate (and ongoing) sense that the whole American justice system had been knocked off center, expressed every bit as much as the film *Grand Canyon* the chaos that lurked at the broken center of American life. The O. J. Simpson case was a big-event disaster movie right up there with *Twister* (1996), *Armageddon* (1998), and *Titanic*.

Also in the nineties, as the First Family and the White House were enduring repeated sex scandals, Hollywood was enduring its own sexual embarrassment. It began with the Heidi Fleiss prostitution scandal followed by the sheepish embarrassment of Hugh Grant's prostitution arrest on Sunset Boulevard followed by the bigamy case of New Line Cinema's executive vice-president Richard Saperstein. The Fleiss case, complete with police stings, high-level cover-ups and movie star decadence, was surely the stuff of movies (as films later in the decade like *L.A. Confidential* [1997] and *Showgirls* [1995] would prove). The similarities between Bill Clinton's, Grant's and the protagonist of *Pretty Woman*'s (1990) sexual dalliances are unmistakable. And over it all, in this age of AIDS and monogamy, floated the sense that Hollywood was the only remaining venue where sexual freedom in all of its squalor, immorality, and fantasy could still exist. Contrary to Medved's argument that moviegoers wanted old-time American family values in their movies, many of the box-office successes of the nineties proved exactly the opposite. Sexual promiscuity, experimentation, and humiliation were in rather than out, desired rather than abhorred. As one commentator wrote, "In *True Lies* [1994], as Arnold Schwarzenegger's wife, Jamie Lee Curtis accepted orders to dress like a hooker and strip for a man she didn't realize was her husband only to be thrillingly liberated by the experience."[41] In *Pretty Woman*, Julia Roberts triumphs as a Cinderella who is highly experienced at oral sex, and in *Disclosure* (1994), *Bitter Moon* (1994), *The Shawshank Redemption* (1994), *Natural Born Killers* (1994), *Showgirls*, *Lost Highway* (1996), *Basic Instinct* (1992), *Pulp Fiction*, *L.A. Confidential*, *Boogie Nights* (1997), *Eyes Wide Shut* (1999), and countless others, sexual humiliation serves as the driving force of plot, not just a sensational prurient sidelight. The society at large was extremely wary of sexuality, especially aberrant sexuality, in the nineties. Thus, the movies' explorations of aberrant sexualities become attractive outlets for curiosity, frustration, and fantasy.

But while Grant was cruising the Sunset Strip for prostitutes, others were cruising Hollywood for far more lethal entertainments. River Phoenix died in the street outside Johnny Depp's Viper Room on the Sunset Strip in October 1993. Chris Farley, in an eerie replay of John Belushi's death, died of a massive speedball overdose in December 1997. Producer Don Simpson died of a heart attack occasioned by a drug overdose in January 1996. Both Robert Downey Jr. and Christian Slater (reminiscent of Robert Mitchum and Sean Penn) were sentenced to prison terms for drug-related offenses in December 1997. From Marilyn Monroe to Belushi to the nineties "live fast, die young" crowd of the Viper Room, Hollywood history has always had its self-destructive cycles, from reefer madness to heroin chic, and the nineties seemed to be the latest resurfacing of Hollywood's dark side. Of the nineties, insiders "paint a searing portrait of a decadent new Hollywood in which everything from freshly created designer drugs to superpremium Persian heroin is there for the taking, just beneath the town's politically correct veneer of clean living and sober self-awareness."[42]

Pheonix's death did not serve as the wake-up call for the film industry that it should have. Judge Lawrence Mira, when sentencing drug-addicted actor Downey Jr. to six months in the Los Angeles County Jail for probation violations, partially blamed the Hollywood film industry: "It may be the very business you are in that is conducive to your continuing this lifestyle."[43] Indeed, drug abuse may have become occupational, not just recreational, in the film industry of the nineties. One actor attests, "I've done movies where people did coke [because] there was so much pressure to get it done that there was no time to rest. They were just using [it] like caffeine."[44] In the case of Don Simpson, who produced some of the biggest hit films of the eighties and nineties—*Flashdance* (1983), *Top Gun* (1986), *Beverly Hills Cop* (1984), *Crimson Tide* (1995)—the industry attitude "allowed him to indulge in substance abuse while using all the built-in excuses Hollywood reserves for the creative."[45] Ironically, on August 9, 1996, most of the cast and crew of Cameron's *Titanic* were hospitalized for a drug overdose. Someone put PCP (a.k.a. angel dust) into their lobster chowder. One of the film's caterers (in self-defense) charged that "it was the Hollywood crowd bringing in the psychedelic shit. I don't think it was purposefully done to hurt any body. It was done like a party thing that got carried away."[46] This identity of the Hollywood film industry's politically correct surface and drug culture subsurface mirrored the same deconstructive theme of "society without a center" that was so prevalent in the films of the nineties as well. It became so obvious late in the decade that the industry actually started making retro metamovies about itself and its drug habits: *Ed Wood* (1994), *54* (1998), *The Last Days of Disco* (1998), *Boogie Nights* (1997).

But drugs were not the only way that the young of Hollywood died in the nineties. Tupac Shakur and Notorious B.I.G. both were shot down as celebrity victims of the ongoing "gangsta rap" wars that began in the mideighties and escalated into the violent nineties. Then Brandon Lee, son of the legendary Bruce

Lee, was accidentally shot to death on the set of *The Crow* (1994). His death was just one of a number of crew deaths on Hollywood sets that marked the risk-taking, bigger-and-better-special-effects mindsets of nineties film. In the past, crew deaths had usually taken the shape of helicopter crashes, crane accidents, or heavy equipment failures, but Brandon Lee's death by gunfire in a world that is supposed to be pretend was another industry commentary on Hollywood's historical tendency to eat its young.

While the film industry of the nineties was a violent, decadent, dangerous place, it also found other ways of shooting itself in the foot. Two of its most self-destructive tendencies were toward duplicative competition and high profile litigation. By far the stupidest trend in the Hollywood film industry of the nineties was to make competing versions of the same movie. Hollywood managed to utterly defeat itself repeatedly by making two volcano movies—*Dante's Peak* (1997) and *Volcano*—two Dalai Lama movies—*Seven Years in Tibet* (1997) and *Kundun* (1997)—two Steve Prefontaine movies, two retro-disco movies, and way too many overblown monster movies—*Godzilla* (1998) and *Mighty Joe Young* (1998), among others. The other way that Hollywood fed on its own success was through lawsuits, most often for creative theft.

The 1997 plagiarism lawsuit over the origin of the story of *Amistad* (1997) was but one of a series of courtroom disagreements over rights in the Hollywood movie industry of the nineties. In 1996 Jodie Foster sued Polygram Pictures over her treatment as one of the principals in *The Game* (1997). Co-star Michael Douglas, despite their age difference, demanded that Foster play his sister, not his daughter, and the studio acceded to his wishes. One observer noted, "Believe me, it never would have happened if it were a man."[47] In January 1998, John Calley of Sony Pictures sued MGM for the right to make competing James Bond films. In July 1998, Francis Ford Coppola won an $80 million lawsuit against Warner Bros. for blocking his plans to film a live-action version of *Pinocchio*. "If it had been a movie, it would have been Francis Ford Coppola's third-most-profitable project," one Hollywood wag noted of the judgement.[48] Then, in October 1998 another lawsuit similar to the *Amistad* case surfaced as unknown writer Akusoa Busia sued Oprah Winfrey's Harpo production company and Disney Studios over the script credit for the film adaptation of Toni Morrison's Pulitzer Prize–winning novel, *Beloved* (1998), charging that two subsequent writers plagiarized her original script. "I felt as though two white men were picking over my bones," Busia couched her plagiarism charge in overtones of racism.[49]

But if the lawsuits over creative differences were prolific in nineties Hollywood, the litigations over money matters were ubiquitous. The nineties in Hollywood was the era of merger mania, executive power infighting, the rise of new studio players and independent production companies, and, above all, a bottom-line mentality so ruthless that it easily explained the hypocritical overlooking of the drug problems of the industry. One of the telling signs of the times was the institution by *Entertainment Weekly* of its annual "POWER 101" issue that ranked the 101 most powerful players in the entertainment industries. Michael Eisner of Disney spent much of the nineties at or near the top of this list.

The economics of the film industry was a kind of soap opera in itself, or perhaps Eisner's reign at Disney was the major vampire movie of the decade. He seemed to suck the blood out of everyone who worked with him. By far the biggest economic story in nineties Hollywood industry history was the formation of DreamWorks SKG in 1994, a new studio led by Spielberg, Jeffrey Katzenberg, and David Geffen. Katzenberg, driven out of Disney by Eisner's unwillingness to share power, teamed up with Spielberg and Geffen to form what many hoped would be a brave new world of enlightened film production. On the surface, each brings a specific expertise to the merger: Katzenberg's specialty is animation, Spielberg's is film creativity, Geffen's is music. But beneath the surface, Katzenberg brings the management skill, Spielberg the creative genius, and Geffen the salesmanship to the new studio. After a slow start, by the end of the decade DreamWorks SKG was a resounding success all across the board, especially while winning the Best Picture Academy Award for *American Beauty* in 2000.

Meanwhile, back at Disney, Joe Roth from Twentieth Century Fox took over Katzenberg's job in 1995, but by January 2000 he too had been drained by Eisner's power craving and also resigned his second banana role. Katzenberg certainly got the last laugh with *Shrek* (2001), his animated send-up of the Eisner era at Disney and its supplantation by the heavyweight power of Shrek (Spielberg), the ironic and comic sense of the Donkey (Katzenberg) and the great rock-and-roll soundtracks (Geffen) of DreamWorks SKG. But Disney's high-profile problems were more endemic than isolated in the movie industry of the nineties. Studio shake-ups and executive unrest made the Hollywood studio system an industry so much in flux that Mr. Potato Head might well have been the paradigm for studio management and the revolving door the model for studio architecture.

More serious economic concerns than personnel problems, however, plagued Hollywood in the nineties. The decade was an economic roller coaster that in the end installed a fierce bottom-line mentality that changed the whole nature of movies. Nineties Hollywood economic history can be clearly tracked across a treasure map leading right to *Titanic*. The decade began on the downside of an economic curve. "Tension mounts and budgets shrink as the movie business tries to come to grips with the recession," the headline of a 1992 article titled "Hollywood Squeeze" trumpeted. "After more than a year of falling box office, budget cutbacks, and diminished expectations, the movie industry has settled into one of its glummest moods in two decades."[50] By 1994 things had not improved. One magazine characterized the first quarter of that movie year "Springtime for Hitless," parodying the faux-hit Broadway tune from Mel Brooks's *The Producers* (1968). "Box office has been in freefall. . . . Hollywood is sinking slowly into a sea of red ink" was not a review of *Titanic*, but rather a lament for the flat condition of Hollywood economics at middecade.[51] Things were so bad that the studios resorted to padding their box-office figures to the point that reported opening weekend grosses were about as accurate as body counts during the Vietnam War. "What makes a blockbuster?" one writer asked, "creative genius or creative accounting?"[52]

Through middecade, Hollywood box office was down, but in 1996 it began to take off. Why this dramatic change in direction? Was it simply that the national economy was hitting an upturn? Was Hollywood making better movies? Or was Hollywood simply making bigger movies? In the summer of 1996, the tide started to turn with true hits: *Independence Day, Twister, Mission: Impossible, The Rock,* and *The Nutty Professor.* What did they all have in common? All were big-event movies dependent on eye-catching special effects.

When the dust settled on all the special effect explosions of 1996, one big-event movie, *Independence Day,* grossed more than a billion dollars worldwide. Two other big events, *Twister* and *Mission: Impossible,* grossed over $500 million worldwide. Thirty movies grossed more than $100 million. The compiler of these final 1996 box office figures predicted "given the current domestic, international and video outlook, it's no surprise Hollywood is releasing a dozen action movies and thrillers this year that will cost more than $100 million each (James Cameron's *Titanic* is reportedly nearing a record $180 million)."[53]

That prognosticator was on the money for 1997. In the spring quarter, led by the rerelease of *Star Wars* and the surprise success of *Scream,* film receipts rose 19 percent, but the towering stupidity of releasing two identical big-event movies, *Dante's Peak* and *Volcano,* tempered the economic optimism.[54] But the big-event, special effects blockbusters—*Lost World* (the sequel to 1993's *Jurassic Park*), *Air Force One, Batman and Robin, Con Air, Face Off,* and *Men in Black*—caused industry watchers to declare "it was the season of the Event Movie, with summer-movie budgets on nearly a dozen films reportedly hovering around the $100 million mark. . . . the studios embarked on their wildest spending spree ever" and to predict "the Event Era can't last forever."[55] But that prediction was as far out of the ballpark as McGwire's and Sosa's home runs that following summer. The Christmas season of 1997 launched Cameron's *Titanic,* and the rest, so to speak, was nineties film industry history. *Titanic* did indeed prove a rather hard act to follow. The summer of 1998 "will go down in history as the summer the blockbuster turned lackluster,"[56] one Hollywood wag quipped, but nonetheless, the big-event concept of moviemaking was definitely entrenched.

The big-event movie successes of the late nineties so overshadowed the equal number of big-event duds of the decade that Hollywood became quite comfortable with its new spending habits. Bigger did indeed become better. "Size counts," the advertising logo of 1998's *magnus flopus Godzilla,* and "Show Us the Money" from 1996's *Jerry Maguire* became the mantras of a new Hollywood moving toward the millennium. "You look at the numbers," an insider reasoned, "the syndication, the video sales, the print ads—you put everything into the salad. And you realize that you're better off making an Event Movie, because the upside is just so terrific."[57]

Not all big-event films of the nineties made money. Some flopped spectacularly (in the *Heaven's Gate* [1980]/*Cleopatra* [1963] class). But the euphoria in the wake of *Titanic* seemed to make all the dealmakers in Hollywood forget their past follies. Film critic Robert Sklar whined that "special effects disaster movies rule Hollywood. . . . [O]bservers inside and outside the movie industry still perceive Hollywood studios as no longer interested in, or capable of, marketing films with artistic ambition."[58] Sklar rightly argues that one spin-off effect of the late nineties big-event mentality was the surprising success of so many small, independent, comparatively low-budget films. The tremendous financial success, gauged by comparing gross box-office receipts to production budgets, of nineties independent films like *Pulp Fiction*, *Four Weddings and a Funeral* (1994), *Babe* (1995), *Trainspotting* (1996), *The Full Monty* (1996), *Life Is Beautiful* (1998), and a bundle of movies based on the novels of Jane Austen attest to one way in which the big-event mentality actually widened rather than narrowed the nineties film market. Seen as a hedge against the tremendous risk involved in producing a *Cutthroat Island* (1995) or *Waterworld* (1995)—the biggest of the big-event disasters of the nineties—the advantage of having at least one *Pulp Fiction* or *The Full Monty* on your distribution list became very attractive to many studios and independent production companies.

The other major hedge against big-event meltdown was the continuation of the major industry discovery of the eighties, the value of sequels and remakes (and, most tellingly, rereleases). "Re-releases are raking in surprising returns, and more tales from Hollywood's crypts are on the way," Steve Daly announced after the 1998 opening-weekend box-office performance of a reedited version of Orson Welles's 1958 *Touch of Evil*, a kinky black-and-white film noir. Hollywood "loves one kind of money better than any other: *found* money (something Fox discovered lots of with the *Star Wars* re-releases [*sic*] last spring)."[59] The rerelease phenomena all started with the twentieth anniversary rerelease of *Star Wars* on January 31, 1997, on a phenomenal (for a rerelease) 1,800 screens. Before the year was out, all three of the original *Star Wars* trilogy films were rereleased to rather astounding box-office success. The only franchise that ever had this sort of rerelease success before (in essence, introducing past films to a new generation) was Disney with its childrens' animation classics. What was even more startling about the *Star Wars* rerelease success was that it happened in the era of videotape when anyone could rent the three films at the corner video store anytime. People evidently wanted to see certain films on big screens with pristine sound systems, or, in other words, see great movies at the movies.

Of course, in typical Hollywood fashion, the success of the *Star Wars* rereleases stepped off a parade of other classic (and not so classic) rereleases. Later, in 1997 Francis Ford Coppola did a twenty-fifth-anniversary rerelease of *The Godfather* (1972). Next to be exhumed was Alfred Hitchcock. First, in 1997 came a meticulously restored new print of *Vertigo* (1958) that literally saved the movie for future generations: "Reel after reel of film materials was kinky, shrunken, torn, faded, mottled, or decomposing to vinegar. In a few more years what remained might have been *Vertigone*."[60] Three more Hitchcock rereleases followed: *Rear Window* (1954), *North By Northwest* (1959), *Strangers on a Train* (1951). Then, "Dial R for Remake"[61] kicked in as *Dial M for Murder* (1954) was remade as *A Perfect Murder* (1998) soon to be followed by Gus Van Sant's shot-by-shot remake (perhaps it might as well be a rerelease because nothing changed) of *Psycho* (1960). Martin Landau, commenting on the Hitchcock remake frenzy of the late nineties, said, "How is anyone going to make a Hitchcock movie better than Hitchcock?"[62] Four *Psycho* sequels had been made over the years, but no one had ever tried to remake Hitchcock's classic, and if the audience reaction to Van Sant's mirroring attempt was any indication, Landau's incredulity was borne out. Audiences stayed away from this remake because no one could understand why Van Sant even wanted to do it. It was, perhaps, understandable that the *Star Wars* trilogy, the *Godfather* trilogy, and four restored Hitchcock masterpieces could be rereleased and find some remarkable box-office success, but in 1998 the musical *Grease* (1978) was also rereleased for a new generation of John Travolta fans.

But if this rerelease phenomenon was one of the biggest economic stories of the late nineties, the decade was also driven by the continuing eighties trend of sequels. In the nineties, the dependable eighties (and in some cases, such as the James Bond films, earlier) sequel franchises continued to perform. The *Batmans, Die Hards, James Bonds, Lethal Weapons, Beverly Hills Cops* and *Aliens* all continued to pack audiences in, as did, of course, the long-awaited prequel to the *Star Wars* trilogy, *Star Wars I: The Phantom Menace* (1999). But all sorts of other films skewed the whole sequeling concept. Comic books were endlessly sequeled in the nineties in hopes of tapping the same mother lode that the *Batman* and *Superman* films of the eighties had mined. *The Rocketeer* (1991), *Captain America* (1992), *Judge Dredd* (1995), *Tank Girl* (1995), and *The Phantom* (1996) all failed to morph themselves off the pulp page and into live action. Radio sequels like *The Shadow* (1994) also failed, but the nineties found great success in making sequel movies of old TV shows, especially *The Brady Bunch Movie* and *A Very Brady Sequel* (1996), *The Flintstones* (1994) and *Viva Rock Vegas* (2000), and *The Mask of Zorro* (1998). In a sense, all these rereleases and remakes and sequels prove that, in the nineties, Hollywood still held to a very strong sense of its own history and realized that it could capitalize on that history as a predictable hedge against the tremendous risks of its big-event mentality.

The economic history of the film industry in the nineties was a roller coaster of box-office ups and downs. Production approaches ranged from foreign period pieces and American historical epics to gritty independent slices of life to the big-event, special effects mentality of the latter half of the decade. But the films that received the highest acclaim for their artistic accomplishment also displayed the diversity of the industry's evolving approach to moviemaking. Throughout the decade, films in Linda Hutcheon's "historographic metafiction" category[63] dominated the Academy Awards. Kevin Costner's *Dances With Wolves* in 1990, Clint Eastwood's *The Unforgiven* in 1992, and *Schindler's List* closely were followed by the sociohistorical AIDS drama *Philadelphia* in 1993, *Forrest Gump* in 1994, *Braveheart* in 1995, *The English Patient* in 1996, and *Titanic* in 1997. And even though the obscure little independent comedy *Shakespeare In Love* won in 1998, the film that everyone felt should have won the Best Picture Oscar as well as its acting awards was Spielberg's World War II historical film, *Saving Private Ryan*.

But despite this dominance of historical films and, toward the end of the decade, big-event, special effects historical epics (*Braveheart, The English Patient, Titanic, Saving Private Ryan*) at the Oscars, smaller independent films competed mightily for honors both as bottom-line financial successes and as artistic successes. While *Dances With Wolves* swept all the awards in 1990, Martin Scorcese's *GoodFellas* (1990) put a whole new spin on the Coppola-orchestrated *Godfather* romanticism of the seventies, as did Scorcese's other nineties mob film, *Casino* (1995). The historical underworlds of New York and Las Vegas of Coppola and Scorcese were two very different places in their evolution from Coppola's seventies to Scorcese's nineties. In fact, in the nineties Scorcese's artistic consciousness as a director, producer, sponsor, and conservator was matched only by that of Spielberg. While *Schindler's List* rightfully swept all the awards in 1993, an extremely important film like *Philadelphia* and a striking independent small film, *The Piano*, though highly acclaimed with award nominations, got lost in the shuffle. The same landslide effect buried other smaller, independent films in 1995 and 1996. When *Braveheart* won the Oscar in 1995, the independents (*The Usual Suspects, Sense and Sensibility, Il Postino, Babe*) actually dominated the nominations though they did not win. The same scenario played out in 1996 when the sweeping historical epic *The English Patient* swept all the awards. That year was the most competitive year of the decade for the wealth of high-quality, independent nominees—*Fargo, Shine, Sling Blade, Big Night*—and smaller studio movies—*Jerry Maguire, The People vs. Larry Flynt, Primal Fear*. In 1997, of course, *Titanic* swept everything, but in 1998 the heavily favored big-event historical film directed by the most honored filmmaker of the eighties and nineties, Spielberg's *Saving Private Ryan*, got nibbled to death by a gaggle of self-reflexive metamovies about the theater and television and creative imagination: *Shakespeare In Love, The Truman Show, Pleasantville*, and *Life Is Beautiful*. Thus, Hollywood seemed very conscious, at least in its most public evaluation of itself, the Academy Awards, of its double identity. While across the decade the greatest acclaim and the biggest awards went to big-event historical films, the smaller independent films were strongly acknowledged and broadly recognized. What *Titanic* and *Pulp Fiction*, the two most influential films of the decade proved, was that the industry could make significant profits on both big and little movies. Huge budget big-event blockbusters could make huge profits, but low-budget wit and creativity could also pay off big.

"What's the difference between recognizing history and clinging to nostalgia?"[64] Terrence Rafferty asked in 1997. "Academic approval does place cultural products within an established, structural vision of history," Rafferty argues. "The postmodern aesthetic which appears to celebrate the passing fancies of previous generations of pop consumers" is "just nostalgia with irony—an attitude that allows you to have your cake and deconstruct it too."[65] If the films of the nineties had attitude, that attitude was the ironic attitude of the academic, theoretical darlings of the eighties, New Historicism and Deconstruction. These two ways of reading and interpreting texts entered the consciousness of mass culture in the nineties. The overwhelming sense of the necessity to "thicken" the historical record and the seductive temptation to deconstruct—that is, examine the decentered nature of our culture and celebrate the existence of all that became marginalized when the center failed to hold—all the previously accepted meanings upon which our culture was based became central themes in the popular-culture representations of nineties society.

One of the more astounding accomplishments of the history/film relationship of the nineties was that it actually made the academic theories of New Historicism and Deconstruction available to a mass audience, comprehensible to normal people who don't have PhDs yet can still afford between $7 and $10 for the opportunity to not only go along on the last voyage of the doomed *Titanic* but participate in a discussion of class prejudice even as the great ship is sinking.

The movies and television participated in all the major cultural and historical discourse sites of the nineties decade, such as the deconstruction of the American presidency, the impact of AIDS upon nineties culture, the redefinition of sexuality, and the possibility for spirituality in such a decentered culture. All these discourse sites were repeatedly visited in the films of the nineties. For example, in the month of July 1996, the movies in the theaters of America represented either frontally or symbolically most of these discourse sites: *Lone Star* revisited the Kennedy assassination. The big-event film *Independence Day* carried a major subtext of the role of the American president in the global policy of the future. *Eraser* and *The Rock* both examined the theme of surveillance from a nineties cyber perspective. *Striptease* took a look at voyeuristic sexuality in the AIDS-threatened nineties. *The Nutty Professor* combined the race card with the new-age fitness craze. And *Twister* symbolically represented the whole decade as a big-event era of decentered spin. The major cultural issues of the nineties were all present in one form or another in these films, and Hollywood became a major participant in the decade's discourse of history.

# CHAPTER 2

# The New Historicist Films

In the age of the moving image, history on film is almost always more dynamic and influential that history in books.
                    —Thomas Doherty, "Televising the Cold War: the Problems
                                    and Promise of Video Documentary"

That fluid relationship between film and history in the late twentieth century leading up to the millennium drew the attention of postmodernist academics. The decade began with books like Tom O'Brien's *The Screening of America* and Mark Crispen Miller's *Seeing Through Movies* and ended with Robert Brent Toplin's *Reel History: In Defense of Hollywood* while, in between, offering other titles like *The World According to Hollywood, The Political Companion to American Film*, and *Hauntings: Popular Film and American Culture—1990–1992*.[1] What those books signaled was that the alliance between history and film was fully formed and the electronic version of history offered through motion pictures, television documentaries, and the Internet would be writing the historical narrative henceforth.

No longer, then, is it necessary to define, defend, or apologize for the power of film in the mass culture diffusion of history. What did become necessary and complicated about the history/film relationship in the nineties was understanding how the very nature of the presentation of history had changed and how film was an especially appropriate and accommodating medium for the imaging of history. But there were still problems involved with the basic issue of how history was represented or diffused to a mass audience. There were problems concerning accuracy issues, problems concerning the political exploitation of history, problems concerning the portrayal of certain kinds of violence in society (such as serial killings and terrorist attacks), and problems concerning the rewriting of the past in accordance with postmodernist themes, such as conspiracy and surveillance, but in the nineties, the most important history diffusion (and reality diffusion) problem of all was spin.

The thorniest issue related to the history/film relationship was not the questioning of the historical accuracy of specific films but, more importantly, the questioning of what "historically accurate" really meant and if it could ever be attained. Perhaps the accuracy issue drew the most attention in 2000 when it was raised concerning the films *The Insider* (about big tobacco), *Boys Don't Cry* (about a real hate crime), and *The Hurricane* (a biopic of a boxer). One commentator wrote then that the "accuracy issue is looming larger than usual of late, in part because so many recent films have dealt with emotionally charged true events. The debate—waged on radio talk shows and in newspaper and magazine articles—centers on fundamental questions about the limits of artistic license, the social obligations of film and importance of factuality in art."[2] Joseph Roquemore's book, *History Goes to the Movies*, also published, coincidentally, in 2000, "critiques films by how they measure up to their historical roots."[3] What is worth noting about this whole discourse on accuracy in films is not only that it existed in the nineties (because it has always existed in regard to historical representations), but that so many people cared about it, debated it, and paid attention to it as a mass culture issue. It was even debated on TV talk shows. Perhaps this issue of just what "is the artist's obligation to history"[4] reached its highest level of public discussion at the end of the decade, but all through the decade it had been energetically debated. The nineties saw consistent op-ed anxiety over the problem that the *New York Times* called "history contorted for dramatic effect."[5] The whole issue was most probably triggered in the mideighties and then sustained throughout the nineties by the historical films of Oliver Stone, beginning with his brilliant *Salvador* (1986) and being consistently raised in regard to his Vietnam films, his *JFK* (1991) and *Nixon* (1995), even his evisceration of American media society in *Natural Born Killers* (1994). In the same breath, Stone can be lauded as "the most undervalued of major American directors" and can be "branded a crackpot historian and conspiracy kook."[6] Stone himself "says repeatedly that the failure of *Nixon* ended his ability to make large-scale movies on subjects of contemporary history," and as a result, he has "turned from speaking of history to speaking of society"[7] as in his trashing of the world of professional football and corporate America in *Any Given Sunday* (2000).

But Stone was not the only director making big-event historical films and being criticized for it. *U-571* (2000), a riveting World War II submarine film, managed to ruffle the rudders of the British navy high command. *U-571's* transgression was that "in the process of translating real events to the screen, [it] rewrote history to make it more appealing to American audiences in the post-Cold War era" by changing "what the British regard as one of their greatest wartime accomplishments into an American triumph."[8] The film's writer and director turned a British destroyer into an American submarine, and the historic capture during World War II of an enigma decoding device by the British navy into an American adventure story. On the other hand, another navy story, the biopic of U.S. Navy diver Carl Brashear, *Men of Honor* (2000), was lauded by the navy: "The historicity and the gist of the film is accurate."[9] This discourse on historical accuracy throughout the decade in relation to a parade of big-event historical films, from *JFK* to *Apollo 13* (1995) to *Saving Private Ryan* (1999) and *The Thin Red Line* (1998) to *13 Days* (2001), perhaps all came together in the making of *The Patriot* (2000).

Though *The Patriot* is clearly a fictional rendering of the Revolutionary War as fought in the American South (only two real historical characters, George Washington and General Cornwallis, appear in the film), its writers and producers set out from the beginning to disarm the historical accuracy critics by seeking "a seal of approval from the august Smithsonian Institution. . . . Realizing that there was also the risk that the Smithsonian might be used simply to provide cover for a historically dubious Hollywood fiction, [the producer] Woodman distributed an early draft of the script to Smithsonian curators."[10] Nonetheless, the producers of *The Patriot* didn't just check for traditional sorts of historical accuracy; they were aware of New Historicist concerns as well. In demonstrating their concern "for the integrity of history. . . . It was not just a question of the accuracy of the uniforms, we wanted to make sure that the film captured the spirit of the times, the true feeling of the period."[11] While the lengths the producers and writers of *The Patriot* went to preempt the charge of historical inaccuracy is certainly commendable, historical films have always done their research. Stone, for example, is fanatical about research. For the accuracy critics, the problem with historical movies is involved much less with mise-en-scène authenticity than with historical interpretation or reinterpretation, or (worse) the repression of some of the facts or issues in favor of others.

*The English Patient* (1996), the Academy Awards Best Picture winner of 1997, is one of the decade's most visible cases of historicist repression. Set in the desert of North Africa in World War II, and based on the life of the Hungarian Count Almasy (Ralph Fiennes), though adapted from Michael Ondaatje's novel, Anthony Minghella's film forgot or neglected to tell its audiences one thing: the film's hero was very probably spying for the Nazi's in North Africa.

Michael Winterbottom's ultracontemporary historical film, *Welcome to Sarajevo* (1997), posed yet another problem for the accuracy critics. While the film was rightfully billed as "torn-from-the-headlines" and incorporated very real (and brutally graphic) news footage of the three-year siege of Sarajevo in Bosnia, its documentary war footage and its "save the children" theme was characterized as "advocacy filmmaking at its most inarguable" and an "impassioned howl."[12] This raises yet another issue between traditional historians and the New Historicists. No matter how contemporary or how close to the historical event a film may be (the cast and crew of *Welcome to Sarajevo* actually had to be evacuated from that city in 1996 due to dangers from uncleared land mines and the threat of the war re-igniting) or how accurate in its use of real news footage the film is, the question of the objectivity of its accuracy, the ethics of its argument, still arises. How can a fictional historical film be accurate if it clearly takes sides and pushes a thematic point—in this case "save the children"—that approaches propaganda?

Another major accuracy issue was leveled at the increasingly popular genre of the biopic, the biographical film, in the reality-obsessed nineties. It was, after all, the era of reality TV, of real cop chases, of funniest home videos compilation shows, all culminating in *Survivor*, the most-watched reality TV show. Biopics came under fire for either whitewashing their subjects (*The Hurricane*) or vilifying them (*Nixon*). Stone once again led the way in the biopic genre with his *Born on the Fourth of July* (1989), the life story of paraplegic Vietnam veteran against the war, Ron Kovic; his *JFK*, about the crusade of prosecutor Jim Garrison to find the truth of the Kennedy assassination; and his *Nixon*; but he was closely followed by Spike Lee's *Malcolm X* (1992), biographies of *Hoffa* (1992), *Chaplin* (1992), and *Cobb* (1994), two on distance runner Steve Prefontaine, two on the Dalai Lama, and, not to mention, films on Beethoven, *Immortal Beloved* (1995), and the Beatles, *Backbeat* (1994). This bombardment of the nineties biopics raised all sorts of accuracy problems as Owen Gleiberman noted in an article titled "Bios Debatable": "Big budget Hollywood biopics are alluring in about a hundred ways. In a single epic package they offer history and gossip, public spectacle and private psychodrama, true-life tales of fame, fortune, ambition, and ruin. Yet there are a hundred ways in which a biopic can go wrong."[13] While the real artistic problem that most biopics have is living up to *Citizen Kane* (1941), the more immediate problem is how to deal with a controversial (or just an interesting) life. One critic, for example, described *Immortal Beloved* as "passionately schlocky biographical melodrama,"[14] and the director of *The Madness of King George* (1994), Nicholas Hytner, claims rather cavalierly that his film is "pretty accurate—quite a lot of the ravings are taken from reports written at the time. Porphyria . . . does cause blue urine."[15] Ty Burr, writing of the biopic of the early Beatles, *Backbeat*, expresses perhaps the best way of answering the whole accuracy issue: "As with tales of all deities, the story needs to be told and retold to stay valid within the culture. So where your average rock legend is lucky to get one biopic—say, *The Buddy Holly Story* or *What's Love Got to Do With It*—the Beatles myth keeps being repolished for new audiences."[16]

But perhaps the most important issue to surface in the Hollywood and history discourse of the nineties decade was the postmodernist ascendance of New Historicism in the popular consciousness.[17] Historical consciousness exists in three dimensions. The traditional dimension of history foregrounds events, influential people, laws, political and social movements, timelines, all the basic factual components of history. The New Historicist consciousness, operating under the influence of postmodernist critical theory, revises and expands not just the subject matter of history but also the archival sources of history, the voices that had not previously been heard by traditional historians. The third dimension of nineties historical consciousness is the cultural studies phenomenon, the social dimension whereby history takes on a presentist as well as a historical significance. In the nineties, the cultural studies dimension of historical consciousness is strongly anchored in the movies as the major "instrument of diffusion" for postmodernist sociohistorical issues, such as gender, race, class, conspiracy, surveillance, the abuse of power, political exploitation, and, for the nineties, the one compelling force that forms all these specifically nineties themes, spin.

Historical films representative of each of these three dimensions of historical consciousness appeared all across the decade. The least interesting ones portrayed historical events only one-dimensionally—that is, only in terms of one of the three dimensions of historical consciousness. In 1992, predictably on its five-hundredth-year anniversary, two utterly traditional films about Christopher Columbus's discovery of America, *Christopher Columbus: The Discovery* and *1492: Conquest of Paradise*, appeared. One reviewer cut right to the heart of these two films' traditional one-dimensionality: "In each case the filmmakers have fallen into a similar trap. Out of some vague mixture of historical 'duty' and commercial myopia, they've presented Columbus as the same cardboard visionary we learned about in school. . . . Watching *1492* is about as exciting as doing your homework."[18] *Christopher Columbus: The Discovery* is characterized as "the bland, schoolbook version of Columbus" in which "historical revisionism is just a new mode of trash."[19] Ted Turner's *Gettysburg* (1994) took the same "schoolbook" approach "by staying true to military history" and took on "a trivializing, now-hear-this quality familiar to students of the John Jakes School of History Lite."[20] Rob Reiner's *Ghosts of Mississippi* (1996), purportedly about the assassination of civil rights leader Medgar Evers in 1963, suffers from the same monologic, power-centering compulsion that turned *Cry Freedom* (1987), supposedly about Apartheid in South Africa, into a white man's escape thriller, *Dances With Wolves* (1990) into a white man's flirtation with Native American culture and history, and *Mississippi Burning*'s (1988) indictment of the Ku Klux Klan into a white man's FBI procedural. *Ghosts of Mississippi* becomes a white man's courtroom drama in which the voice of the racist murderer, Byron De La Beckwith (James Woods), and the white prosecutor, Bobby De Laughter (Alex Baldwin), drown out any African American voices that might have been heard.

The more interesting historical films didn't just portray historical events one-dimensionally, but thickened their historical consciousness by engaging the metahistorical issue of the very nature and function of history itself. Michael Mann's *The Last of the Mohicans* (1992) did precisely this by foregrounding the Native American voices and motives of its complex Mohican and Huron characters. As didn't happen in *Dances With Wolves* (1990), the major Native American characters in *The Last of the Mohicans*, Chingachgook (Russell Means) and Magua (Wes Studi), are given multidimensional, complex characterizations that portray their history on an equal plane with that of the British invading army they are either trying to form an alliance with (in the case of the Mohicans) or taking violent revenge upon (in the case of the Hurons). One reviewer describes the historical multidimensionality of the film: "The French and British are battling for control of the colonies, the colonists are feeling the early stirrings of revolutionary fervor, and the various local Native American tribes have formed uneasy alliances with the Europeans. If this all sounds complicated, it is."[21]

A similarly interesting metahistorical film, John Sayles's *Lone Star* (1996), "layers history with heresy" and "throws in a lot of revisionist Mexican-American History."[22] Ambitious in his metahistorical vision in *Lone Star*, Sayles uses the mystery of the Kennedy assassination to examine the racial and class hatred between Mexicans and a small Texas town's sheriff who ends up mysteriously murdered. The film poses the questions, was he righteously murdered because of his personal racist evil? or was he murdered as part of a much larger national conspiracy? Whatever the answers, *Lone Star* does what postmodernist history tries to do. It asks interesting revisionist questions.

Other innovative attempts to portray history were much less successful. History as musical, for example, didn't work at all. *Evita* (1996; starring Madonna), the rock musical biopic about the first lady of Argentina, could have been an interesting examination of the seduction and exhilaration of power but, instead, chose to portray history as just another "fame is the name of the game" pop diva-of-the-week story. What *Evita* totally ignores are the voices of the people of Argentina under the rule of Juan Peron and his operatic wife, Eva.

### *Schindler's List* and *Forrest Gump*

> He is writing a history. . . . There is enough mystery in the facts as we know them, enough of conspiracy, coincidence, loose ends, dead ends, multiple interpretations.
>
> —Don DeLillo, *Libra*

Two of the most popular and highly acclaimed films of the nineties, Steven Spielberg's *Schindler's List* (1993) and Robert Zemeckis's *Forrest Gump (1994)*, represent in two very different ways the Hollywood and history liaison of the decade. These two films serve as exceptional examples of Hollywood bringing the complex, multilayered texts of twentieth-century history to a mass audience.

Of course the accuracy mavens chose films like *Schindler's List* as prime targets for their view of the acceptable nature of history. "The popularity of several 'historical' films has raised anew the question of whether scholars have an obligation to try to correct distortions," one traditional historian writes. "Does it really matter that Oliver Stone has created his own fictions about J. F. K., Vietnam, and President Johnson? Or that Steven Spielberg has played fast and loose with the historical record in *Schindler's List* and *Amistad* (1997)?"[23] What this accuracy proponent fails to acknowledge is the stated intent of these Stone and Spielberg films. What he fails to acknowledge are the clearly dramatized themes that bring to historical discourse a forum for those suppressed, other voices that the master narratives of traditional history (the Warren Commission, the U.S. Army and the U.S. government during the Vietnam War, a nineteenth-century slave-dependent American economy) have traditionally ignored, suppressed, or overlooked.

In an essay titled "Making History," Anne Thompson writes, "If the crowning achievement of *Schindler's List* is its authenticity, credit may belong to the Schindler Jews who offered their own experiences to the filmmakers."[24] In a historical film like *Schindler's List*, there are a number of different kinds of authenticity. There is, of course, the archival authenticity drawn from historical research and the shared memories of the Schindlerjuden. But there is a narrative and a stylistic authenticity as well that contributes mightily to the truth of *Schindler's List* as historical document.

In making the film, Spielberg was constantly confronted with difficult narrative and stylistic choices that balanced Hollywood against history. Thompson describes one scene in which Oskar Schindler (Liam Neeson) and Nazi Commandant Amon Goeth (Ralph Fiennes) play a game of cards for Goeth's maid, the Jewess Helen Hirsch: "I knew by the fourth setup that the scene was too entertaining and it would be cut. I did not . . . want this to be a Hollywood story in any way."[25] All indications are that Spielberg was acutely conscious of the necessity of historical authenticity from the very beginning of the ten-year journey from the film's conception to the screen. When Thomas Kenneally's book (from which Spielberg's film was adapted) first came out and was proposed as a film project, Spielberg's initial reaction was "It'll make a helluva story. Is it true?" And during the production Spielberg describes how he was plagued by historical doubt: "I said to myself, 'How can I bring truth to these impossible images?'"[26]

Perhaps the most important narrative choice in the service of historical authenticity, that of the film's point of view, shows the considerable theoretical instinct that Spielberg exercised in his conception of the film. When Steven Zaillian, who wrote the final version of the *Schindler's List* screenplay, presented an earlier version, he was told by Spielberg that it did not have enough Jewish faces: "I didn't tell the story from the survivors' point of view but from Schindler's."[27] Conversely, when *Schindler's List* opened, some critics complained that it told its story too much from the Germans' point of view. In reality, what Spielberg accomplished in *Schindler's List* was to immerse the audience in a nightmare of history, the Holocaust, by balancing the narrative between three different points of view: the omniscient narrative, which views the atrocities of the Nazis upon both victims and survivors; the third-person-limited narrative, which presents the view of Oskar Schindler through the eyes of his manager and partner in intrigue, Itzhak Stern (Ben Kingsley); and the psychological point of view, which focuses on the madness and degeneracy of the Nazis through the characterization of Amon Goeth. It is a classically postmodernist narrative that examines historical truth as a decentered, multidimensional phenomenon.

Another crucial choice that Spielberg made for *Schindler's List* in the service of historical authenticity was predominantly artistic, the decision to make the film in black-and-white rather than color. "Shot in a rich, subtle black and white that, for all its raw-satin beauty, evokes the authenticity of wartime newsreels and photographs," one critic wrote.[28] Another critic, analyzing why Spielberg picked then relatively unknown actor Liam Neeson for the part of Oskar Schindler, agreed that "Spielberg didn't have to worry about a colossal persona coloring his astringent black-and-white historical portrait."[29] Spielberg's choice of black-and-white to give his film a documentary or newsreel style accomplishes the precise distancing effect that traditional history values so much. Spielberg's black-and-white in *Schindler's List* captures the bloodless, doomed darkness of the Holocaust for both the Nazis and their millions of victims. Black-and-white transports the vividness of horror out of the realm of the melodramatic and into the realm of history.

Interestingly enough, later in the nineties, Spielberg made directly the opposite choice for his wrenchingly brutal filming of the invasion of Normandy in *Saving Private Ryan* (1998). In the case of *Saving Private Ryan*, Spielberg is more interested in the impact of history on the individual than the relationship of the individual (Oskar Schindler, Itzhak Stern, Amon Goeth) to history. In *Schindler's List*, history was the central focus, and the individuals were utterly subsumed in the horror all around them. In *Saving Private Ryan*, Spielberg wanted to show the bloody and beleaguered humanness of men caught in the juggernaut of history.

One critic captured the historical intensity of *Schindler's List* rather well: "*Schindler's List* is a film whose meanings are to be found . . . in its harrowing flow of images—images of fear, hope, horror, compassion, degradation, chaos, and death. Documentaries like *Night and Fog* and *Shoah* have detailed the workings of the Holocaust . . . but Spielberg . . . has allowed us—for the first time— to see it."[30] In one rather striking way, *Schindler's List* closely resembles Stone's Vietnam War masterpiece *Platoon* (1986). Both Spielberg and Stone relegate plot (Hollywood's most highly cherished and stringently demanded component for a film) to a secondary position. For Spielberg and Stone, the physical, psychological, and historical images of the true and the real are much more important than the frame stories that the films purport to tell. *Schindler's List* is clearly about the horrors of the Holocaust and not about the resurrection to humanness of Oskar Schindler and the descent into bestiality of Amon Goeth just as *Platoon* is about surviving the Vietnam War and not about two sergeants, allegories for good and evil, wrestling for the soul of an Everyman soldier.

Zemeckis's *Forrest Gump*, the nineties historical film seen by twice the number of people who saw *Schindler's List* and second at the box office among historical films only to *Titanic*, seemingly takes a radically different approach to history than Spielberg or Stone, yet his results are quite similar to theirs. *Forrest Gump* is an offbeat running tour through American history, circa 1950 to 1990.

Ironically, however, when *Forrest Gump* was released, none of the commentators viewed it as a historical movie. *Forrest Gump* became all the rage as a fable of political neo-Conservatism for the Newt Gingrich, "New Right," era of the early nineties. First Pat Buchanan, erstwhile unsuccessful presidential candidate and host of the cable TV political debate show *Crossfire*, "heralded Forrest Gump as a great conservative hero."[31] Another commentator headlined his essay "Mr. Gump Goes To Washington: The Story of How a Hollywood Film Forecast the Latest Political Shift."[32] William F. Buckley, editor of the venerable conservative magazine *The National Review*, applauded *Forrest Gump* as the "Best Picture Indicting the Sixties Counterculture."[33] In answer to these charges of political fabulation, producer Steve Tisch, accepting the Best Picture Oscar for *Forrest Gump*, declared that the film "isn't about politics or conservative values."[34] In fact, Tisch was right on both counts. *Forrest Gump* isn't about politics; it is about history. And *Forrest Gump* isn't about conservative values. If anything, *Forrest Gump* is about an innocent, wide-eyed liberalism that the Vietnam War, Watergate, and the cynicism of Reagan conservatism virulently opposed in the seventies and eighties.

A white man talking to a black woman whose feet hurt on the same park bench, how conservative is that? Teaching Elvis to bump his hips, how conservative is that? Not being allowed to sit down on the bus (a direct historical allusion to Rosa Parks), how conservative is that? Picking up a young black woman's notebook as she is integrating the University of Alabama right in front of Governor George Wallace, how conservative is that? Forrest's girl, Jenny, taking the stage name Bobbie Dylan and singing folk songs naked in a burlesque house, how conservative is that? In Vietnam, Forrest and Bubba, a black grunt, becoming brothers, how conservative is that? Voicing the truth of women's liberation ("He should not be hitting you, Jenny."), how conservative is that? Appearing with John Lennon on *The Dick Cavett Show*, how conservative is that? Being one of the first investors in Apple Computers ("some kind of fruit company"), how conservative is that? Like so many liberals after Vietnam and the Nixon betrayal of the seventies followed by the Reaganite cynicism of the eighties, Forrest finally finds himself "Running on Empty" as the soundtrack accompanist announces.

As he is running across America, the media bombard Forrest with questions:

> "Why are you running?"
> "Are you doing this for world peace?"
> "Are you doing this for the homeless?"
> "Are you running for women's rights?"
> "Or for the environment?"
> "Or for animals?"

Forrest's answer, "I just felt like running," signals what this immensely popular film is really about. Forrest is running away from history. History has chased him, dogged him, bullied him, and tormented him all his life just like those boys he used to have to run away from every day in down-home conservative Alabama. *Forrest Gump* is a film about all the people who the conservative right wing of American politics have forced to flee history, to abandon their idealism and take off running on empty. Near the end of this film, Forrest stops running and analyzes his own relationship with those forty years of American history that have chased him through life: "My mama always said you got to put the past behind you before you can move on, and I think that's what my running was all about." Pat Buchanan must have been hallucinating when he picked Forrest Gump, a simple-minded mama's boy who respects blacks and women, loves Elvis, and ends up an AIDS caregiver as his "conservative hero." In the end Forrest Gump simply outruns history so that the future can be born, and by sitting still and telling his story, he brings it into existence.

Forrest sits on a bus stop bench and tells his story to a succession of different auditors. "Why I thought that was a lovely story, and you tell it with such enthusiasm," one woman listener tells him as she gets up to board her bus. Forrest is a storyteller, the film's narrator, and the bench is the film's narrative frame, but the reason he tells his story with such enthusiasm is because it is not just his story but a history of the second half of the twentieth century. Forrest's narrated odyssey through history serves as a vehicle for the movie audience to contemplate where we in America were forty years ago, where we've been in the last forty years, and how far we have come in the nineties.

The accuracy issue that traditional historians always raised about Stone's and Spielberg's historical films didn't seem to bother anyone when it came to *Forrest Gump*. Why? Because Forrest, the narrator, was so innocent, so trustworthy (so Tom Hanks), that the historians didn't even recognize this film as a history.[35] If anything, the movie and its narrator capture the nineties pop culture view of history quite well. The narrative structure and style presents history anecdotally: history as sound bite, history as bumper sticker, history as aphorism. Forrest Gump the character and Forrest Gump the narrator both become a darling of nineties media and culture because he keeps history short, sweet, and simple.

Yet Zemeckis's *Forrest Gump* is very much like Stone's *JFK* and Spielberg's *Schindler's List*. All employ black-and-white simulations[36] (as defined by Jean Baudrillard) to align their narrator's life to the historical life of the age. In *Forrest Gump* and *JFK*, those images are television reports of assassination, the repeated historical event that punctuates the second half of the twentieth century more than any other. In *Schindler's List*, television not being available, those black-and-white images are omnisciently narrated views of Nazi atrocities.

But what all three of these films most intimately share is the conviction that history is not destiny, is not determined, and that the individual does not have to be subsumed by history. A Jim Garrison, an Oskar Schindler, a Forrest Gump can be threatened by history but can still triumph in the face of history's power. One of the most powerful visual images of *Forrest Gump* occurs at the very end of the Vietnam War section of that film. Carrying his friend Bubba on his back, Forrest literally outruns a friendly fire napalm air strike. This scene is Forrest at his fastest outrunning the technologized power of late twentieth-century American history.

In *Forrest Gump* history truly is as mobile as the flight of a feather or as random as one's choices in a box of chocolates. Though history tries to control peoples' lives, peoples' perceptions of reality, the individual can still influence history, can still divert the juggernaut of history. It is those individuals that nineties historical filmmaking chose to focus upon: Jim Garrison, Oskar Schindler, Forrest Gump, and Cinque.

### *Amistad* and Historical Voice

In a courtroom whoever tells the best story wins.

—John Quincy Adams in *Amistad*

Cinque was the leader of forty-four African slaves who in 1839 carried out a mutiny on the Spanish slave ship *La Amistad*, and he is one of the voices of history in Spielberg's *Amistad*. In fact, the central theme of *Amistad* is that of the participants in the court trial that followed in the wake of the shipboard mutiny finding their voices, entering into the discourse of history. Spielberg focuses his film on the marginalized voice in particular, the racial voice, the voice of colonially oppressed people of color.

Throughout *Amistad*, Spielberg dramatizes Cinque's finding of his voice. As John Quincy Adams (Anthony Hopkins) prepares himself to address the Supreme Court of the United States in the *La Amistad* trial, he talks to Cinque (Djimon Hounsou), who tells him that he will invite all of his ancestors to come back through time and accompany him into the courtroom because "at this moment I am the only reason they existed at all." Subsequently, when he addresses the Court, John Quincy Adams, as Cinque has done with his ancestors, invokes all of American history, all the names of a young America's presidents, including his own father John Adams, in a plea for the court to uphold the Bill of Rights and the Declaration of Independence in their decision. "Who we are is who we were," John Quincy Adams powerfully argues. *Amistad* is not only a film about the power of history but also about the necessity of history.

All through the film, the central theme of giving the marginalized people of history a voice is dramatized. All the voices of power-centered, master-text history are marshaled against Cinque and the forty-four Africans who survived the *La Amistad* mutiny. Isabella II, the teenage queen of Spain, sends her ambassador to lodge her protest and stake her claim to her "property." President Martin Van Buren, on the campaign trail, sends Secretary of State Forsythe to handle this annoyance. Senator John Calhoun speaks for the American South and threatens civil war if the mutinous slaves are not executed and slavery upheld. Joadson (Morgan Freeman), a composite character representing a black abolitionist, speaks for the American antislavery movement. Roger Baldwin (Matthew McConaughey) speaks for the law, the legalistic concept of "property" upon which the whole trial (and the greatest irony of the film) hinges. The only one who doesn't get to speak out through much of the film, first because he does not know the language (English) of the power structure and later because everyone else is speaking in a babble of voices that drown his voice out, is Cinque.

A linguistic professor is brought into the prison to learn the Mende language of the Africans and teach it to lawyer Baldwin so that he can communicate with his clients one-to-one rather than through an interpreter. In the first courtroom hearing, the very first issue raised is that of language as Baldwin challenges the "property" claims of Spain, the military salvage officers, and the slave traders: "How can they be Cuban-born plantation slaves," Baldwin asks, "if they can't speak any Spanish at all?"

This theme of language combines with the theme of history as the trial gets underway. *Amistad* is a metamovie, a "historiographic metafiction," to use Linda Hutcheon's term,[37] whose central self-referential focus is upon examining how history is written. "This story is about American history, not just African history," Spielberg insists.[38] In the film, when, early in the trial, Joadson, the black American abolitionist, comes to John Quincy Adams for advice, Adams answers,

> *Adams:* When I was an attorney, a long time ago, young man, I realized after much trial and error that in a courtroom whoever tells the best story wins. . . . What is their story, by the way?
> *Joadson:* Sir?
> *Adams:* What *is* their story?

In this speech John Quincy Adams is taking a very postmodernist approach to history. Echoing the theory of simulation of Baudrillard and the concept of reality as narrative of Jean-François Lyotard,[39] Adams portrays history as narrative, a fictional simulation of the distant reality. Then Adams counsels Joadson to find out who the Africans are and to devise a way to let them tell their own story.

In court later, after Cinque (through an interpreter) has told the Africans' story of their capture and sale at the slave fortress in West Africa, of the "Middle Passage" across the Atlantic in the hold of the slave ship to Cuba, and of the mutiny, the prosecuting attorney compliments Cinque on his version of history from the slave's point of view: "Like all good works of fiction it was entertaining, no more." Ah, but it is much more that Spielberg's film is proclaiming. *Amistad* is exploring one of the basic principles of New Historicism. It is these voices in American history that need to be heard, these stories in American history that need to be told. As one critic described Spielberg, "he's no fool: he knows a great story when he sees one."[40]

In *Amistad,* "Spielberg will try to do for slavery what he did for the holocaust," Jonathan Alter writes, "to bring a vast audience face to face with the subtlety of the crimes of history."[41] History as fiction, the need for history to listen to the repressed voices of the marginalized other, Spielberg's New Historicist version of American history did not go unchallenged. Once again, as with *Schindler's List,* the traditional historical establishment raised its usual "accuracy" objection. University of Alabama history professor Howard Jones wrote the book upon which Spielberg's film was based: "Spielberg's dramatic portrayal of the 1839 incident strayed from the facts,"[42] Jones stated. But they were Jones's facts, and one might ask how far his version, a traditional history written in 1987, 148 years after the fact of the "real" *La Amistad* trial, strayed from the original reality.

Another southern historian complained, "What they call dramatic license, I call historical error."[43] But the champion historical nitpicker of all was Eric McKitrick of the *New York Review of Books,* who based his accuracy charges on the presence of facial hair on the characters in the film. Luckily, McKitrick was probably the only person in America who cared about this trifling nonissue.[44]

Other conservative popular historians, principally Joseph Sobran and Michael Medved, thought they had found a "smoking gun" in the whole *La Amistad* affair when they seized on the historical rumor that, after Cinque was freed in the *La Amistad* trial, he returned to West Africa and became a slave trader. Jones quickly refuted this charge and traced its provenance to a mistake promulgated since the fifties in traditional historical textbooks emanating from a detail in a novel that supposedly "factual" historians as eminent as Samuel Eliot Morrison and C. Vann Woodward promoted into fact from fiction.

An even stronger charge in the form of a $10 million plagiarism lawsuit came from historical novelist Barbara Chase-Ribaud, who claimed that Spielberg got the story of *La Amistad* from her novel *Echo of Lions*. But Bert Fields, attorney for Spielberg's DreamWorks productions and *Amistad*, countered with the legal argument that *Amistad* "is entirely based on history. You can't monopolize history."[45] When asked if he had read Chase-Ribaud's novel before writing the initial screenplay draft of *Amistad*, David Franzoni asserted that he purposely did not read *Echo of Lions* because "he didn't want to put himself in a *JFK* situation—an inextricable tangle of history and fiction."[46]

But the accuracy mavens did not lean nearly as hard on *Amistad* as they had upon *Schindler's List* and *JFK*. Begrudgingly affirming the power of Dominick LaCapra's "instruments of diffusion" theory, almost all historians acknowledged that Spielberg's *Amistad* did indeed bring a repressed episode in American history to the attention of a vast audience. Jones acknowledges that the film "introduced millions to an episode that had been largely ignored."[47] Alter dismisses the accuracy issue comparatively: "The film takes some literary license. . . . Even so, *Amistad* stays more true to the facts than most big-budget historical dramas."[48] One important scene in *Amistad* addresses this central historicist issue: historical accuracy versus dramatic representation. After the abolitionist Joadson, in a plea for John Quincy Adams's help in the *La Amistad* trial, recites the whole history of Adams's own actions in abolitionist causes, Adams replies, "You're quite the scholar, Mr. Joadson, quite the historian. Let me tell you something about that quality, if I might. Without the accompanying mass of at least one/tenth its measure of grace such erudition is useless, sir." History needs strong voices telling their own stories. History cannot simply consist of perceived "facts" collected long after the event by historians tied to a traditional mode of discourse. That is what Spielberg's *Amistad* is about.

It is no coincidence that two of the three most important historical films of the nineties—*Schindler's List* and *Amistad*—were directed by Spielberg. He and Stone are Hollywood's most historically conscious producer-directors. But there are others who brought the discourse of history to the forefront in their films. While Zemeckis's *Forrest Gump* has its eccentric narrative spin, its postmodernly Shakespearean tale told by an idiot, others engaged the complexities of historical discourse within the context of established film genres: the war movie, the spy thriller, the biopic. Two of the most genre-heavy historical years of nineties film history were 1995 and 1998 and both were dominated by different kinds of war movies. In 1995, Scottish history became the focus of historical discourse in the movies, and in 1998 World War II was the historical *cause celebre*. In the case of 1995's *Braveheart* and *Rob Roy*, thirteenth- and eighteenth-century guerilla warfare was examined as a bloody revenge tragedy of the sort that would make Webster and Tourneur proud. *Saving Private Ryan* turned the Normandy Invasion of World War II into a celebration of fatherhood and family, and *The Thin Red Line* portrayed the World War II Pacific theatre Battle of Guadalcanal as a violation of an edenic pastoral ecology. What all these epic war films portrayed was the inability of the individual to survive (no matter how heroic or courageous or duty bound) in the face of the bloody chaos of history.

Spielberg's Captain Miller, again played by that nineties icon of duty, morality, and normality Tom Hanks, and Mel Gibson's William Wallace both are doomed isolatoes caught up in and run over by the juggernaut of history. Both are technically competent in a very nineties computerized way—Miller can calibrate the range to a German gun emplacement through a mirror and Wallace can fashion homemade weapons that can defeat a heavily armed professional army—but ultimately, Wallace is literally torn limb from limb, and Miller's whole platoon is run over by lumbering machines of war.

The message of both *Saving Private Ryan* and *Braveheart* is that the chaos of history cares little for the quests of individual men, whether that quest be to save a family for the future or to revenge the loss of a family in the past. Both films were praised upon their release for their realistic simulation of their central historical events. Spielberg's twenty-five-minute bloody recreation of the invasion of Normandy at the beginning of *Saving Private Ryan* and Gibson's shockingly visceral Battles of Stirling Bridge and Bannockburn in *Braveheart* are historicist wonders due to the sheer research that went into the production of their gore. "There are many amazing things about *Braveheart*," *New Yorker* critic Anthony Lane wrote. "There are horses thundering into a thicket of extra-long, supersharp staves. There is every kind of mortal blow: one guy loses his head, another is stretched out like human chewing gum, a third has a leg slashed off by a single slash of a sword."[49] Of *Saving Private Ryan*, David Ansen of *Newsweek* wrote, "Steven Spielberg has taken Hollywood's depiction of war to a new level. He does it right at the start of *Saving Private Ryan*, in a 25-minute sequence depicting the landing of American forces on Omaha Beach in 1944. This is not a triumphant version of D-Day we're used to seeing, but an inferno of severed arms, spilling intestines, flying corpses, and blood red tides."[50] Staff Sergeant Robert Slaughter, then age nineteen, was actually there at Omaha Beach in 1944. "It was chaos," Slaughter remembered as he watched a special History Channel screening of *Saving Private Ryan*. "There was screaming, and men drowning, and bullets flying everywhere." But after seeing Spielberg's recreation of that battle at the opening of the film, Slaughter confirmed that the only thing missing is "the odor of cordite and the sickening stench of death."[51] Slaughter's testimony affirms how far the act of simulation has come in the nineties recreation of history.

What the graphic battle scenes of *Saving Private Ryan* and *Braveheart* really affirmed for nineties audiences was that "history is at last being told not from the perspective of the White House or Whitehall but from the foxholes and hedgerows."[52] *Braveheart* was similarly acclaimed as "a movie in which torsos get impaled, crotches gouged, and heads smashed like melons, each action accompanied by the savage thwack! of exploding bodily fluids. . . . you feel the pulse-quickening rush of war."[53] Both Spielberg and Gibson preceded the filming of their battle epics with meticulous historical research, but that research wasn't directed at getting the facts of the respective events straight (the dates, the times of day, the weather, the names of generals), it was aimed at capturing the look, the feel, the sound of battle, the visceral detail that could actually bring history to life (or as close to life as a film simulation could come). "This is how you die. When a bullet hits you on a field of battle, your knees buckle. Your stomach contracts. If the slug hits your brain, you flop to the ground like a mannequin. You don't throw your arms in the air like a Broadway dancer. You don't die, says Steven Spielberg 'in slow motion' with a bloody bag coming out of the front of your chest and a huge fireball behind you."[54] Making an obvious dig at Stone's version of death in *Platoon*, Spielberg reveals his real visceral intention in *Saving Private Ryan* to show history as chaos and death in all of its ugliness and evil. Both Gibson's vision in *Braveheart* and Spielberg's vision in *Saving Private Ryan* are nihilist visions defined by their battle sequences and unmitigated by the futile nobility of their warrior heroes. "History is violence and death not sentiment and honor," these films are saying.

The two Scottish historical recreations offer one other motive for action that rarely enters the traditional historical accounts of the lives of their real central figures, sex. Both Gibson's Wallace and Michael Caton-Jones's Rob Roy McGregor (Liam Neeson) take up the claymores of history as instruments of sexual revenge. Wallace's one true love is murdered by the sexually intimidating British who revel in asserting their right to deflower their Scottish tenants' new wives on their wedding nights. McGregor's wife is raped by a hateful British bounty hunter sent to kill her husband. In these films, the result is a version of history that is much more personalized, more psychologically motivated, more human. Gibson's Wallace, Caton-Jones's Rob Roy, and Spielberg's Captain Miller are all heroes more confused than historically driven, more isolated from the traditional historical stereotypes of command than earlier representations of historical warriors in the John Wayne mold. What one critic wrote about *Saving Private Ryan*, that "more than Coppola, Stone, or Kubrick . . . Spielberg has captured the hair-trigger instability of modern combat,"[55] describes all three of these tortured historical characters. Earlier historical films attempted to find order in the chaos of war, nineties historical films celebrate that chaos and look inside the human heart for ways to survive it. They are affirmations of Lyotard's assertion "of the decline of the unifying and legitimating power of the grand narratives" of nineteenth-century history.[56]

Terence Malick's *The Thin Red Line*, however, is different. It counters the chaos-driven, nihilist visions of history articulated in *Braveheart*, *Rob Roy*, and *Saving Private Ryan* with a nostalgically romantic (almost Wordsworthian) vision of war as a violation of nature. "What's this war at the heart of nature," *The Thin Red Line*'s voice-over narrator opens the film, and the natural world becomes the central character. In this war film, the characters, mostly nameless, mostly doomed, move like fleeting shadows across the edenic landscape of Guadalcanal.

*The Thin Red Line* has all the chaos of hellish battle and the same unrelenting parade of young men's deaths as does *Saving Private Ryan*, and its simulation of the battle of Guadalcanal is from the bottom up, the grunt's eye view, but its vision of history is different, more metaphysical. Only one character, a cynical top sergeant (Sean Penn), makes any attempt to counter the pastoral romanticism of the film. "Don't you understand? Property. The whole goddam thing's about property," the top sergeant tries to convince his charges, all of whom are trying to find meaning in this chaos.

*The Thin Red Line*, though based on a novel by James Jones, is a historical film that focuses upon the real battle for Guadalcanal, but it is nothing like the other major historical films of the nineties. Shot with long pans of the green landscape and still offering the romantic cliché of slow motion battle, Malick's film views history as a disaster in nature. The film is "an aestheticization of World War II. . . . a kind of Buddhist tone poem about the timeless spirit of war: men and their guns, their machines of violation, ripping the sacred heart out of 'nature'."[57] Malick's history is nineteenth-century history, history that turns war into nature poetry and death into metaphysical passage. Unfortunately, that is a romantic vision incompatible with a postmodernist New Historicist sensibility. As a historical film, James Cameron's *Titanic* has the same problem.

## *Titanic*

Things fall apart; the center cannot hold.
—William Butler Yeats, "The Second Coming"

*Titanic* succeeds brilliantly in turning historical disaster (meticulously simulated) into romantic soap opera. Though the film went overboard in its historical research and reconstruction of the physical setting of history, the reason *Titanic* triumphs as the most-seen movie of all time is the doomed romance between Jack Dawson (Leonardo Di Caprio) and Rose DeWitt Bukata (Kate Winslet). The starstruck, young lovers and the engaging present/past flashback narrative (reminiscent of *Citizen Kane*) that director Cameron places them in shine so brilliantly that the film's strong sociohistorical consciousness often gets lost in the glare. As one article put it, "From the tides of history, James Cameron mates romance with catastrophe in the astounding *Titanic*."[58] Romance may indeed be the mastertext of *Titanic*'s universal appeal, but the subtexts of historical representation carry every bit as strong a message as does the *Romeo and Juliet* love story.

Romance and history find a luxurious comfort zone aboard the *Titanic*. As Owen Gleiberman describes the film, it is a monumental reconstruction of history punctuated by the deconstructive consciousness of the nineties world: "With extraordinary physical verisimilitude, Cameron re-creates the sinking of the *Titanic* in the North Atlantic on April 15, 1912. . . . In *Titanic*, he restages the defining catastrophe of the early 20th century on a human scale. . . . By the time that Rose and Jack are floating in the icy sea. . . . the two have left the 19th Century behind, here then is a new world, one in which the center will not hold."[59] The decentering of all our romantic, modernist confidence in industrialism and technology is the postmodernist nineties theme of *Titanic*. The greatest ship to ever sail the seas, the triumph of the Industrial Revolution, ripped in half, broken in two at its center, the sinking of the *Titanic* is a tremendously serviceable metaphor. "Organized by tiers, each of which houses its own social class, the *Titanic*, though a product of a new era's technology, is also a kind of floating version of the 19th Century, the last mighty bulwark of a Victorian world that has no idea it's literally about to perish."[60]

The one problem that Cameron and *Titanic* did not have to face was the challenge to historical accuracy. There was some half-hearted nitpicking: Would a woman like Rose smoke at the dinner table? Give the finger in public? Did all of the ship's four funnels belch smoke? Could a charcoal drawing survive eighty-five years underwater? But overall, "Cameron's attention to detail—including the set's 90-percent-scale re-creation of the ocean liner and carpets made from original patterns—has by and large impressed historians. 'It was incredibly accurate especially compared to previous films about the *Titanic*,' says Steven Biel, author of 1996's *Down With the Old Canoe: A Cultural History of the Titanic Disaster*."[61] Cameron took great pride in the film's historical accuracy: "If you went back in a time machine to the ship, this is exactly how it looked."[62] Ironically, however, as one commentator argued, "it is theoretically possible, of course, that *Titanic*'s success has nothing to do with . . . all that lavish attention to historical detail."[63] What this argument overlooks is whether the doomed romanticism of Jack and Rose's love works if not set on such a large scale and utterly believable historical stage. As a number of commentators have pointed out, "while the principals are pure fiction, several supporting characters are taken from history"[64]: *noveau riche* Molly Brown; ship's architect Thomas Andrews; Charles Joughin, the drunken baker; Bruce Ismay, the director of the White Star Line; Benjamin Guggenheim; and John Jacob Astor.[65] Even the fictional history has a physical referent in the grave in a Halifax, Nova Scotia, cemetery of one J. Dawson (really James Dawson) who was a worker in the real *Titanic*'s engine room and went down with the ship.[66]

*Titanic* definitely was an accurate historical movie, but *Titanic* was also, quite consciously, a movie about history itself. Cameron's inventive narrative frame employs eerie nineties footage of the submerged wreckage of the *Titanic* in the way that Orson Welles employed the images of Charles Foster Kane's gothic mansion, Xanadu, at the beginning of *Citizen Kane*. This frame sets up a Hitchcockian McGuffin, the blue diamond necklace, "The Heart of the Ocean," just like Welles's "Rosebud." The temporal counterpoint between the salvaging of the *Titanic* wreckage off Nova Scotia in the 1990s and the flashback history of the sinking of the great ship underscore that Cameron wanted to bring together time and history, the nineties and the accurate reality of April 14, 1912. The result would be a history in which the present attempts to salvage the past.

For the salvage crew working on the wreckage of the *Titanic* at the beginning of the film, the salvaging effort is not about history, not about myth, but only about one thing—money. "It's payday, boys!" one of the salvagers gushes as they raise an ancient waterlogged trunk from the ocean floor. "Shit, no diamonds!" he exclaims in disappointment after the trunk is opened. For them, the sunken *Titanic* exists merely as a commodity. The huge diamond, "The Heart of the Ocean," that they see around the neck of the beautiful nude woman in the drawing that they find (perfectly preserved in its leather case after eighty-five years under water) means nothing more to them than its monetary value. But to Rose Calvert, née Rose DeWitt Bukater, 101-year-old *Titanic* survivor, that diamond necklace means much more than its mere commodity culture value. "For you see, the woman in the picture is me," the nineties Rose declares, thus triggering a historical flashback to the fateful voyage of the *Titanic* in April 1912. "Are you ready to go back to the *Titanic*?" 101-year-old Rose asks. "It's been eighty-four years, and I can still smell the fresh paint."

With these words, the movie audience actually does enter Cameron's time machine and the nineties Rose becomes our historian of one of the defining events of the early twentieth century. Similarly, when the movie audience first meets Jack Dawson, the young artist who will fall in love with the radiant nine-teen-year-old Rose, he is engaged in a very commodity culture situation, a poker game in which he wins his third-class ticket aboard the *Titanic*. But it is this poker game that introduces the other major theme of the film, that of social class. Jack is playing cards with Fabricio, Sven, and Olaf, all immigrants, all going to America in pursuit of the commodity culture dream. The theme of social class will be Cameron's counterpoint to the dominant romantic theme of the love of Jack and Rose.

"The ship of dreams," 101-year-old Rose reminisces. "To me it was a slave ship, taking me back to America in chains." While the *Titanic* was hardly *La Amistad*, Cameron's theme of social class does bear some striking resemblances to Spielberg's simulation of the "middle passage" of an African slave ship. Both Rose and Jack are imprisoned by the prejudices and commodity culture realities of their respective social classes. When the *Titanic* strikes the iceberg and the "abandon ship" is given, the third-class passengers are kept locked behind gates to drown just as the chained slaves on *La Amistad* were cast into the sea to drown because they were a stress upon the commodity culture.

Cameron's theme of class is flogged across the whole three hours of the film. The ship is a virtual "Upstairs, Downstairs" of space defined by social class: the above decks' staterooms verses the below decks' class cabins, the bridge versus the engine room, the black-tie ball versus the below decks' Irish dance. Only Jack Dawson, because he is an artist, and Rose, because she is a "new woman," are able to cut through these class restrictions, break down the barriers, and move through the rigidly classed world for which the *Titanic* is a metaphoric microcosm.

The whole relationship of Jack and Rose is consistently punctuated by the rhetoric of class. "I don't have to leave. This is my part of the ship. Why don't you leave? Are you an artist or something?" Rose interrogates Jack. "A person of lim-ited means," Jack answers. "I'm a poor guy." When Rose introduces Jack to her mother, "my mother looked on him like an insect." When Molly Brown dresses Jack up in an elegant tuxedo, she says, "You shine like a new penny" and the steward in the ship's main ballroom addresses him as "sir." Jack himself imitates all the gestures and affectations of the rich. "It's amazing. He could almost pass for a gentleman," Rose's fiancee pronounces. Jack turns himself into a simulation of social class, but the old money forces him to fight a rearguard action against the onrushing twentieth century. Unfortunately, that iceberg inexorably bearing down on this rigidly classed ship signals the immensity and power of nineteenth-century class prejudice that won't allow Jack's simulation to become reality. "Mr. Dawson is joining us from the third class," his simulated status is made clear, and later he is dismissed with "you hold a third class ticket and your presence is no longer appropriate."

Once the iceberg hits and the passengers are ordered to the lifeboats, social class becomes the measure of who shall live and who shall die. In order to keep the ship from flooding, the doors to the engine room are locked, imprisoning the crew. Orders are given to lock the gates to the third-class section of the ship so that the decks will not become overcrowded as the lifeboats are loading. "When they finish putting the first-class people in the boats, they'll be ready for us," one third-class passenger tells another when they are stopped by the gate. "Will the lifeboats be seated according to class?" one first-class gentleman asks the mate who is supervising the loading. Cameron has made his ship a vehicle for this examination of the demise of the nineteenth-century class structure in the same way that Jean Renoir in *Le Grand Illusion* (1937) made his prison camp a vehicle for the playing out of the death of the old aristocracy in the face of the rising middle class.

At the end of *Titanic*, history does not win out. "He exists now only in my memory," 101-year-old Rose says. Her whole existence, her telling of her story of the sinking of the *Titanic* to this gang of rapacious commodity culture salvagers, has come down to one important truth, the value of historical consciousness. As for historical films, what Cameron's *Titanic* proved was that no matter how Hollywood, how big-event, or how record-setting at the box office a film may be, it can still be historically accurate and meaningful. *Titanic* is a film about a significant historical event that served as an important watershed metaphor for the decentering of a rigid class system. That class system had been passed on from the Victorian age and was ripe to be exposed as out-of-date in the brave new post-industrial era of the twentieth century.

# CHAPTER 3

# The Decade of Spin

The '50s were boring, the '60s rocked, and the '70s, oh my God, they obviously sucked.

*—Dazed and Confused* (1993)

eyond Hollywood's strong sense of history (and New Historicism) in some of its big-event films of the nineties decade, there was something else happening that took the mainstreaming of academic critical theory into a whole new dimension. Defining the nineties as an identifiable historical epoch isn't as easy a task as, perhaps, it has been for earlier decades. For example, if the Eisenhower fifties was the decade of stability and expansion, the rise of suburbia and the building of the interstate highway system, is the nineties the decade of chaos and gridlock on the information highway? If the sixties passionately rocked and saw everyone get involved, is the nineties the decade when everyone stopped reaching out to help others, went slack? If the seventies was the decade of the introduction of the computer, the corporate structuring of the American dream, and the loss of confidence in the moral ascendancy of America itself, is the nineties the decade of the Internet and the cyber-isolation of the individual? If the eighties was the decade of Reagan and neoconservatism, is the nineties the decade of Clinton and out-of-control liberal promiscuity? While the nineties may have been all those things—the decade of cyber-isolation and information overload, the decade of the slacker, the decade of an ethics-challenged liberalism, the answer to all those questions is a resounding "no." More than anything else, the nineties is the decade of spin.

The twentieth century moved toward the new millennium like a tornado bearing down on history, spinning dizzily out of control around its empty center. One of the most popular movies of the nineties, *Twister* (1996), could also serve as a symbol of the reigning agenda of the decade, the irresistible impulse to spin both reality and truth. Metaphorically, *Twister* represented how, in the nineties, conventional accepted reality (the cow calmly chewing in the field) could be lifted and spun and launched violently into space and time in a way that would never allow us to look at it as simply a harmless reality (or cow) again. One magazine wag sensed the philosophical quality of *Twister's* special effects in the headline: "If a Cow Falls In a Forest."

A similar cultural symbolism had formed in the seventies when the disaster film genre made a surprising resurgence. At the time, with the Vietnam War and Watergate on everyone's mind, the concept of disaster (and how to survive disaster) was uppermost in the public consciousness. The very ethical center of America's national and international reputation was being questioned. The movies simply provided a symbolic representation of those troubling social, political, and moral issues. In fact, the success of *Twister* spawned a late nineties return of the big budget disaster film subgenre. Special effects extravaganzas about erupting volcanoes (*Dante's Peak*, *Volcano*) and approaching meteors (*Armageddon*, *Deep Impact*) ultimately culminated in the most profitable disaster film of all time, *Titanic*, which is, in an eerie way, a remake of the granddaddy of the seventies disaster genre, *The Poseidon Adventure* (1972).

Other films of the nineties also symbolically represented the spinning nature of contemporary reality. *Casino* (1995), for example, begins with a scene that might have been an outtake from *Twister*. A Las Vegas gambler, Sam Rothstein (Robert De Niro) is car bombed and sent spinning through the air like one of *Twister's* flying cows. Throughout the rest of *Casino*, the visual imagery of spinning—from the ever-present roulette wheels to Martin Scorcese's dizzying overhead shots of the gamblers on the casino floor—forms a motif that represents the constant motion of the Las Vegas milieu. For Scorcese, the casino in Las Vegas is a microcosm of American life. The city itself is an illusion, a huge scam, the biggest pickpocketing operation ever conceived. Ironically, the Las Vegas economy is the epitome of postmodernist pickpocketing in which (by skimming) even the pockets of the pickpockets get picked. By the end of *Casino*, reality has spun so far out of control that all that is left is the most brutal violence imaginable (filmed by a camera warily circling it), the desert baseball bat murder of Nicky Santoro (Joe Pesci).

Another film, *Apollo 13* (1995), is the story of the 1970 Apollo mission crippled by an in-flight explosion that spun the astronauts Jim Lovell (Tom Hanks), Jack Swigert (Kevin Bacon), and Fred Haise (Bill Paxton) out of control 205,000 miles above the globe. But for all of its heroism and docudrama historical accuracy, Ron Howard's *Apollo 13* is still tinged with a very nineties irony—until the explosion onboard occurred, nobody in America or on Earth really cared because it wasn't on television. Neil Armstrong had walked on the moon barely a year before on the Apollo 11 flight, and that had sated the world's romantic inclinations toward the space program. Apollo 13 might as well have been three guys going out for beers for all anyone cared, . . . until the explosion. At best, in Hollywood terms, it was a sequel to Neil Armstrong's moonwalk. Early in the film, using a futuristic (for 1970) video camera, the three astronauts take TV pictures of themselves floating weightless around the cabin of the space-ship, but unbeknownst to them no one is watching back on earth. "The major television networks, picking up on the nation's collective lack of interest, have all gone with their regularly scheduled programming, stranding Lovell and his comrades—without their even knowing it—in a broadcast void. The year before the trip was a religious experience: now it's a rerun."[1] This media irony draws an interesting parallel for the film. From being stranded in this broadcast void, the astronauts quickly go to being stranded in the void of the universe and, like E.T., trying to get home.

In one sense, Howard's *Apollo 13* works very hard to create "history in all its verisimilitude."[2] But, in another sense, the film is about gyro-spin, about the center giving away and normality spinning out of control. The scenes within the Apollo capsule were shot in what the actors called, "the vomit comet," a "pad-ded, windowless jet officially known as the KC-135."[3] This plane is used to give real NASA astronauts training in weightlessness. In order to film *Apollo 13* in all its authenticity, director Howard built a space capsule set inside the KC135 and spun the actors free of earth's gravity. Basically, "it's a great big roller coaster in the sky" a NASA executive described the experience.[4] Like the computer-gener-ated tornado in *Twister* or the spinning overhead camera in *Casino*, the careening weightlessness scenes in *Apollo 13* visually represent reality suddenly, unexpect-edly, losing its center and finding itself, to quote that old song, "caught in the spin, that wonderful spin I'm in."[5]

But unlike the imagery of spin in *Twister* and *Casino*, in *Apollo 13* there is a center that contends with the out-of-control gyro-spin of the disabled spacecraft. That center is appropriately named "Mission Control" and manned by NASA Flight Director Gene Kranz (Ed Harris). Harris's powerful portrayal of Kranz as the center, the unflappable controller steadfast against all the forces of spin and chaos, becomes the most important characterization in the film. But there is irony inherent in Kranz's symbolic control function as well. He exerts his control through the limited reality of television. Just as everyone in America in the fifties and sixties followed the space program through television and held their collec-tive breath over the grainy blurred TV images of men walking on the moon, so also does Kranz guide the three astronauts back to earth while never taking his eyes off the TV and computer screens that dominate the control room. As the speculative movie *Capricorn One* (1978) posited in the seventies and as reality became virtual in the nineties, *Apollo 13* ironically demonstrates what happens when television actually does become our only window on reality. What hap-pens is that reality is taken over by the power of media spin and that spin has the power to change the very nature of truth. As *Capricorn One* originally speculated, how do we know that the TV images of men landing on the moon are real? How do we know that they aren't just a TV show done in a studio, like Orson Welles's radio broadcast of *War of the Worlds* in 1939?

## The Principles of Spin

We have reconstructed the Tower of Babel and it is a television antenna.
—Ted Koppel, quoted in Casey Davidson's "Grad Tidings," *Entertainment Weekly*

The concept of spin is based on two major principles that are themselves modeled on a metaphorical reading of the principles of particle physics. After all, wasn't Albert Einstein the twentieth century's greatest nature poet? The two major principles of nineties spin are

1. Decentered loss of monologic control;
2. Relativist power to manipulate reality.

Those two basic social principles, reality and truth, collided with these two major principles of spin and found themselves under severe attack in the nineties. It became the decade in which most people would believe anything, some people realized that they could believe nothing, and the rest settled for defining belief as a constantly ongoing dialogue with versions of truth. It was the decade when society reached a state of ethical impasse where lies and truth became corespondents. It was the decade of Bill Clinton, spin doctor par excellence.

The first principle of spin, the decentered loss of monologic control, posits that reality and truth can no longer be defined as just one thing. For example, Jean-François Lyotard argues that "realistic representations can no longer evoke reality" and, therefore, ours is "a world in which reality is so destabilized" that what remain are diverse "realisms."[6] Spin rejects the idea of a solid core or center and opts instead for a circular, constantly moving path around the margins of reality. However, unlike the patterned circling or orbiting of the atom or planets in the universe, nineties spin was the out-of-control circling of Lyotard's "realisms" around a void.

The second principle of spin, the power to manipulate reality, is more sinister. Jean Baudrillard calls this "the universal simulacrum of manipulation."[7] Based on the idea that reality and truth is relativist (many views of the same subject), spin becomes the act of extending the power of interpretation to the point that truth and reality can be broken down and reconfigured into whatever shape the master of the centrifuge desires to serve a multitude of agendas. Baudrillard creates an analog to this idea when he defines his central principle of simulation as "a strategy of the real, of the neoreal and the hyperreal."[8] Baudrillard's simulation strategies that result in a "holographic reproduction" that is "no longer real, is already *hyperreal*"[9] resemble Lyotard's "language games" (a term appropriated from Ludwig Wittgenstein) or "language 'moves'" or "language strategies,"[10] which already have replaced the obsolete "grand narratives"[11] in postmodern culture. And both Baudrillard's "simulacra" and Lyotard's "language games" resemble the power of spin in the late stages of the twentieth century. Baudrillard even uses the metaphor of spin to describe this "whole discourse of manipulation." He sees it as "gigantic circumvolution"[12] and "the circularization of power, of knowledge, of discourse" that results in "the spiraling effect of the shifting of poles, the effect of circularity."[13]

But spin is not just a nineties phenomena. "The roots of spin"[14] began to grow quite early in the twentieth century when large corporations, such as the railways and AT&T, realized that they needed to manipulate advertising to make over their images to a public strongly influenced by muckraking journalists, to the government trustbusters, and to the rising labor organizations. Cultural historians have tracked the history of spin from its origins (in a book like *The Father of Spin: Edward L. Bernays and the Birth of Public Relations* by Larry Tye). Spin began quite early in the twentieth century—"Take George Baer, a Pennsylvania railway president, who was incensed when 150,000 coal miners struck in 1902. . . . Four years later when the miners threatened to walk out again, Mr. Baer hired America's first public-relations professional to leak information on negotiations to the press."[15]—but only in the nineties did the cultural concept of spin permeate the whole of society.

While philosophers like Lyotard and Baudrillard explored how "language games" and simulacra were replacing a reality that had never really existed, advertising set the tone in postmodern commodity culture. The advertising industry, Madison Avenue, invented the masters of spin, plotted the agendas of spin for the nineties. For example, in October 1989 the Energizer Bunny made its appearance. The bunny became "an op-ed cliché (everyone from Bill Clinton to Saddam Hussein is compared to the durable pink guy), but has spawned an era of postmodern, self-aware advertising."[16] The Energizer Bunny commercials, in which the little pink battery-operated toy went relentlessly marching and drumming through all sorts of other staged parody commercials, defined the "spin" that made nineties spin different from all the decades of advertising spin that had come before. The metacommercial approach (a commercial within a commercial) of the Energizer Bunny signaled the decade's concept of reality spinning out of control to the bunny's relentless beat that just keeps on "going and going." After the Energizer Bunny, nothing was sacred in advertising, not even advertising itself.

If the decade of spin, the nineties, began with advertising, it got its theory and its vocabulary from academia. For example, in an article about one of the eighties' most notorious advertising figures, the following academic theoretical language spins the dark reality into cultural iconography: "Heroin addiction, lesbianism, bad '80s fashion, if ever a life was primed for deconstruction in the latter half of the '90s, it's that of Gia, the gay supermodel whose bad girl beauty, sexual bravado, and scandalous behavior provided the blueprint for Heroin Chic before her death of AIDS in 1986."[17] Whatever Gia was, that sentence spins her so far out of control that she becomes a cultural symbol for the excesses of the eighties and the nineties. But what is most interesting is the appropriation of Jacques Derrida's academic theory of deconstruction to the spinning of this cultural icon.

By the late nineties, the word "deconstruction" had entered the popular idiom (newscasters, moviemakers, spin doctors were all using it) even though very few of its users actually understood what it meant. Certainly, few (if any) of its popular users had ever read the arcane academic theory upon which the concept of deconstruction was based. Yet, they used the term with abandon. Dan Rather especially, on the CBS news, gloried in deconstructing everything that beeped across his teleprompter. By the end of the eighties, what advertising had learned from academia was a well-established discourse of spin based upon a decentered view of reality that allowed for a wide range of interpretations of the truth of any given event, situation, or idea.

## The Academic Discourse of Spin

*We need theory to organize our observations and make sense of our experience.*
—Gilberto Perez, "In the Study of Film, Theory Must Work Hand In Hand
With Criticism," *Chronicle of Higher Education*

For twenty years, during the seventies and eighties in academia, the theoretical concept of spin had been growing out of the writings of Jacques Derrida, Michel Foucault, Mikhail Bakhtin, Lyotard, and Baudrillard. All of their voices explored the relativist nature of reality to the point that there was "the problem of cacophony."[18] This problem of cacophony is, in popular culture, the Tower of Babel as television that Ted Koppel asserts. It is also the decade of out-of-control, decentered spin that is the 1990s. Baudrillard, as characterized by Bradley Butterfield, is one theorist acutely aware of the excesses of runaway nineties spin. "Now that Princess Diana has been sacrificed by her public to the 'Universe of simulation,' literally driven to death by the very media that immortalized her," he writes, "Jean Baudrillard readers no doubt expect to be told that in some real sense the princess never died, that the real tragedy was somehow lost in the hyperreal hype."[19] Baudrillard's theory of simulacra argues that, in a media-dominated society such as that of the nineties, "slowly simulations begin to displace their originals."[20] When this happens, spin has taken over and the center of reality and truth has been sucked out and whirled away. Baudrillard sees how the temper and technology of the times are systematically obliterating reality and creating substitutes for it.

Lyotard approaches the same problem in different terms. He writes, "The grand narrative has lost its credibility, regardless of what mode of unification it uses, regardless of whether it is a speculative narrative or a narrative of emancipation. The decline of narrative can be seen as an effect of the blossoming of techniques and technologies since the Second World War, which has shifted emphasis from the ends of actions to its means."[21] For Lyotard (and for Hayden White),[22] this replacement of the failed grand narratives of the nineteenth century with the "dissemination of language games"[23] is "what the postmodern world is all about . . . their knowledge that legitimation can only spring from their own linguistic practice and communicational interaction."[24] Thus, for Lyotard, the hyperreality of the postmodern condition makes it "necessary to posit the existence of a power that destabilizes the capacity for explanation."[25] At the end of the twentieth century, that destabilizing power is the power of spin. In his popular essay that attempts to answer the question, "What is postmodernism?" Lyotard characterizes realism as the attempt "to preserve various consciousnesses from doubt." He goes on to discuss "the fantasies of realism" and the realism "whose only definition is that it intends to avoid the question of reality."[26] Spin is directly the opposite of this fantastical illusion of realism that both Lyotard and Baudrillard mock. Spin destabilizes. Spin embodies what Lyotard characterizes as the postmodern "realism of 'anything goes.'"[27]

To all appearances, this decade of spin would seem a very unhealthy time, a very confusing space. If reality has no center and truth can be constantly manipulated, how can there be any order or reason or definable meaning? That was much the same criticism that Albert Einstein faced when he first put forth the theory of relativity and what the particle physicists faced when they first theorized about splitting the atom. It is all a question of speed and energy and motion and time and space. In other words, it is all a physics of persuasion, a relativist theorization of rhetoric. In this case, the decade of spin is the nineties and the space is the electronic media of movies and television and the cyber media of the Internet. The speed is that of the modem and the digital camera. The energy and the motion is that of centrifugal spin. But above all, this era of spin is not the unsettling, sinister, threatening, confusing, antireal, antitruth time of excess and manipulation that nostalgic thinkers argue it to be. It is simply the latest evolutionary adaptation of theory to historical hyperreality.

The very character of the nineties demands this adaptation. One critic, Shawn Rosenheim, defines this late twentieth-century adjustment of the cultural mindset in terms of cryptography and what he calls "the cryptographic imagination." Here is how it works: "Codes unlocked the secrets of the late 20th century. Think of the four-digit number that gains access to a cash machine. The genetic code that makes up DNA. Or the algorithms that allow software writers to translate huge amounts of information into a microchip the size of a thumbnail. . . . Language theorists argue that meaning is unstable. Don DeLillo, Thomas Pyncheon, Paul Auster and other novelists write metaphysical detective stories, in which getting to the bottom of one mystery only opens another."[28]

This metaphor of encoded reality works well for the concept of spin. In fact, the first decoding machine, invented by Thomas Jefferson, involved a series of spinning wheels with the letters of the alphabet on them. The concept of spin turns on the acknowledgement that within history, language, and meaning itself, there are all sorts of encoded competing meanings. As Lyotard has argued, reality is a constantly moving, changing, infinitely interpretable experience.

Spin is a belief in the power of interpretation. Nineties spin became a way of altering the direction of history. Spin is what all the president's men and Hilary do when Bill Clinton turns into Humpty Dumpty. Spin is what drives the NAS-DAQ high-tech economy as stock prices in companies that have never shown a profit skyrocket. Spin is what utterly redefines sexuality (for example, making condoms a featured, front-counter item) in the era of AIDS.

This discourse of spin proved most appropriate for dealing with the uncertain realities of nineties life. In 1998 at the very height of the impeachment proceedings against President Bill Clinton over the Monica Lewinsky affair, the ad for a new movie, the political satire *Wag the Dog* (1998), trumpeted, "The action starts with a crisis in the White House!" When asked about the eloquent exclamation point in the movie ad, which implied that the film was piggybacking on the whole Clinton/Lewinsky affair, a New Line Cinema spokesman answered, "We change our ads and headlines all the time. . . . We did it to keep our creative advertising and print campaign fresh."[29]

The movies developed a whole level of spinmasters whose sole responsibility was to figure out how to sell a movie as something that would put bodies in the seats. For example, the history of the *Star Wars* franchise in the nineties demonstrates the tremendously seductive power of spin. First, Hollywood convinced the movie-going public that in order to enjoy the new trilogy of *Star Wars* prequels, they had to see the old *Star Wars* films all over again. People flocked to the theaters. Then, when the trailer (not the film itself, only the trailer) for *Star Wars: Episode I—The Phantom Menace* premiered on the front of the opening reel of an otherwise undistinguished Brad Pitt film, *Meet Joe Black* (1998), people lined up around the city blocks for tickets, watched the two-minute teaser, then left before the feature attraction began.[30] At the same time, one million users downloaded the trailer of *The Phantom Menace* in its first twenty-four hours of availability on the Internet. The real "force" of the nineties *Star Wars* phenomena was the power of spin.

Another strong nineties aspect of movie spin (akin to prostitution) was the ubiquity of product placement in films. The major fast-food chains, McDonald's, Burger King, Taco Bell, etc., all struck huge marketing tie-in deals with the latest blockbuster movie. Even James Bond, after thirty years of driving his legendary heavily armed and comically gadgeted Aston Martin sports car, changed to a BMW for very lucrative advertising (not performance) reasons.[31] The spin doctors of Madison Avenue infested the movie industry through product placement and merchandising tie-ins so thoroughly that the clarion call of the nineties, from the brilliantly spin-sensitive film *Jerry Maguire* (1996), became "Show me the money."

The title character of *Jerry Maguire* (Tom Cruise) is a sports agent at the very center of a global marketing bonanza. He represents the fictional equivalents of the Michael Jordans and the Tiger Woods of the nineties. He is the guy who makes all the deals, the Midas Touch or Rumpelstiltskin guy who takes ignorant jocks and turns them into gold, spins them into multimillion-dollar advertising commodities. One critic characterizes the nineties setting of *Jerry Maguire* as "the greed decade" and its central character as a man "on a merry-go-round that won't stop."[32] In other words, a decade of spin.

Jerry realizes early in the film that his world has spun out of control, that he lives in a decade of dysfunction. His first act is to compose a manifesto that exposes how the dysfunction of out-of-control greed has taken over the profession of the sports agent and damaged the client-agent relationship. His agency colleagues respond to his manifesto with a collective yawn and immediately go after his clients by persuading them that he has lost his cutthroat interest in making them all the money they can get.

In fact, as a sidebar to *Jerry Maguire*, Cruise's roles in the nineties are all representations of the decade of dysfunction. Besides the disillusioned sports agent *Jerry Maguire*, Cruise played a betrayed Vietnam vet in *Born on the Fourth of July* (1989), a betrayed superspy in *Mission: Impossible* (1996), a betrayed lawyer in *The Firm* (1993), a betrayed physician/husband in *Eyes Wide Shut* (1999), and culminated his nineties roles with the most dysfunctional of all, Frank T. J. Mackey, the male supremacist con man in *Magnolia* (1999). But *Jerry Maguire* was Cruise's decade-defining role as it established the equation "SPIN + GREED = DYSFUNCTION." The "Show me the money" clarion call of *Jerry Maguire* really began with Gordon Gecko's (Michael Douglas) "Greed Is Good" speech from Oliver Stone's eighties film *Wall Street* (1987) and was reiterated throughout the nineties in films like *Blue Chips* (1994) where college basketball players are given money by corrupt coaches and agents, and *Greedy* (1994) where a whole family lines up to inherit a dying millionaire's fortune. The "SPIN + GREED = DYSFUNCTION" theme of the decade culminated in the 1999 media frenzy over the TV game show *Who Wants To Be a Millionaire* starring Regis Philbin and the even tackier (verging on TV pimping and prostitution) *Who Wants To Marry a Multi-Millionaire* in which fifty women strutted their wares for the chance to marry a man they never really met, knew nothing about, and who turned out to be nobody's Prince Charming. *Who Wants To Marry a Multi-Millionaire* was *The Dating Game* spun completely out of control.

While advertising, television, and movies were taken over by spin in the nineties, academia was totally absorbed with studying it. "Just because it's time to go back to school doesn't necessarily mean it's time to stop visiting the local multiplex or watching TV," one wag characterized the nineties academic love affair with "cultural studies."[33] Academic discourse actually "crossed over" (a music industry term) into the mainstream. The arcane language of postmodernist critical theory—Derrida's "deconstruction," Foucault's "panoptic surveillance," Bakhtin's "heteroglossia" and the "carnivalesque," Lyotard's "language moves," Baudrillard's simulacra, and above all, the concepts of New Historicism and "cultural studies"—became the language and philosophical agendas of the print and electronic media, the movies, and the Internet in the nineties.

Some critics, such as British playwright David Hare, attacked the "'relativising' effects of media and cultural studies—with their tendency to have students study soap operas alongside Shakespeare."[34] Cultural studies professor Simon Frith also expressed some doubts about the socializing of academic discourse in the nineties: "I find some bad faith in what we know as cultural studies. Some scholars treat popular texts only for their ideological significance, without addressing the question of value. They leave it to sales figures to determine what matters."[35] While some academics found the new academic curriculum threatening, for the first time in the century, the society at large found the discourse of academia engaging. The integration of the academic discourse of the seventies and eighties into the mainstream proved a major breakthrough as the millennium approached. It was academic theories of interpretation that laid the groundwork for the decade of spin.

## The Ethics of Spin

Ethics has gained new resonance in literary studies during the past dozen years, even if it has not—at least yet—become the paradigm-defining concept that textuality was for the seventies and historicism for the 1980s.

—Lawrence Buell, "In Pursuit of Ethics"

In the nineties, the concept of spin began to assert itself so aggressively that its power became confusing and threatening and raised a number of basic ethical questions:

Is spin good or evil?
Does it matter?
Is spin's ethical value as relative as everything else in life?

Whether spin is good or bad depends on two defining aspects: its motive and its effect. If spin sets out to confuse reality, to put the best light on something that is overwhelmingly dark, such as arguing that O. J. Simpson is innocent because the LA cops are guilty, then perhaps spin is evil. But conversely, if spin tends to obscure one reality, it tends to illuminate other realities, for indeed the LA cops *were* guilty (and racist and corrupt).

Spin is Faustian, the making of a pact with the devil, and the devil is reality itself. By the end of the twentieth century, by the cyber-virtual nineties, the nature of reality had drastically changed. No longer was it possible to find a single meaning in the events of reality. If reality no longer exists, as Baudrillard controversially argues, and has been replaced by simulacra, "the substituting the signs of the real for the real,"[36] the result is "the neoreal and the hyperreal"[37] culminating in "an omnipresent fourth dimension, that of simulacrum."[38] For Baudrillard, "the real is no longer real"[39] but "is a total simulacrum that links up with 'reality' through a complete circumlocution"[40] that "does not put an end to this vertigo of interpretation."[41] Notice Baudrillard's metaphorical uses of the terms "circumlocution" and "vertigo," both varieties of spin. If in another sense, as Lyotard argues, reality has been subsumed by language games, "Not: I can prove something because reality is the way I say it is. But: as long as I can produce proof, it is permissible to think that reality is the way I say it is."[42] The games or language "moves" Lyotard calls "narratives" bear a striking resemblance to the nineties concept of spin. As Lyotard argues, "Lamenting the 'loss of meaning' in postmodernity boils down to mourning the fact that knowledge is no longer principally narrative. Such a reaction does not necessarily follow."[43]

Because spin is a language game or a simulation of reality, its ethical function is rarely a central concern of the spinmaster whose major goal is the reconstitution of reality, the realignment of the atoms of reality to create new compounds or reactions, new realities. The question of whether spin is good or evil is much too simplistic and static a question. That question might better be posed in terms of the deconstructing function of spin in the social operation of truth and reality. Spin can create deceptions, illusory realities, twisted truths, but it can also create new ways of viewing reality, new truths that had hitherto been repressed due to prejudice (against gays, for example), political suppression, monologic power, or new necessary behavior in the face of threatening reality (such as the AIDS epidemic).

Postmodernist reality is a moving, changing, and spinning vortex of events, possible meanings, and contending interpretations. Spin is the interpretive act of trying to express, from the multiple meanings of reality, the one that best serves the spinmaster's purpose. The motives of spin are like the motives of Mephistopheles. Emanating from the interpretive reconfiguring that academic critical theory formulated in the seventies and eighties,[44] spin injected postmodernist interpretation into the mainstream discourse of the nineties.

Spin, for example, significantly affected the nineties approach to history. A wide range of cultural commentators offered a different, more hostile view of history. "To hell with history!" novelist John LeCarre declares in his novel *Our Game*.[45] Mudrooroo, Australia's foremost aborigine writer, said, "History is just a gigantic whitewash after all, and we shouldn't accept it."[46] And American filmmaker Stone said, "Never, never underestimate the power of corruption to rewrite history."[47] What all of them were saying was that history has always been written under the aegis of spin. As Wallace Stegner once said, "history is an artifact . . . [that] does not exist until it is remembered and written down."[48] Stegner's definition of history as artifact held up pretty well until the nineties when his last point, that history had to be "written down," began to spin off into other media. J. Hillis Miller argued in 1994 that "already the sensibilities, the ethos, the politics, the sense of personal identity of many of our citizens, including college students and faculty members, are determined more by television, cinema, and video than by printed books."[49] He went on to reiterate that our study of language in the nineties must, by necessity, be "the study of those media that mix language with other visual and auditory materials, media such as cinema, television, and video."[50] In other words, in the late twentieth century, the masses were getting their history via the media not from the traditional sources of history, books by professional academic historians. Lyotard describes a similar shift in the sources of narratives when he writes of the "discovery of the 'lack of reality' of reality, together with the invention of other realities."[51] For the New Historicist, Lyotard's "other realities" take the form of alternate narratives or contesting narratives or unexplored interpretations that deserve a voice.

## Spin and Textuality

*I'd like to leave a legacy that I was a good historian as well as a good dramatist.*
—Oliver Stone, quoted in "Stone's Sixties," *USA Weekend*

Spin is about the wide-ranging possibilities for interpretation. Under the aegis of spin, all the texts of supposed historical or cultural reality are fair game. The movies provide an excellent example. One critic, analyzing a Disney animal romance, *Mighty Joe Young* (1999), puts the following spin not only on that movie but on all the movies of the decade: "Is there a movie of the late '90s that *isn't* about finance?"[52] That critic has managed to spin a monkey movie into a film about global economics. Two other monster/disaster movies, *Godzilla* (1997) and *Deep Impact* (1997), were characterized as films that "examine the struggles of women trying to get ahead in the all-consuming world of news."[53] But it is not as if *Deep Impact*, whose star is a megaton meteor, or *Godzilla*, whose star is a megaton saurian monster, are movies like *The Front Page* (1931, 1974) or *His Girl Friday* (1940) or *All The President's Men* (1976) or even *Up Close and Personal* (1996). They are monster movies being spun into girl-power newspaper or media movies as a means of broadening their audience. In the same manner, Jeffrey Katzenberg of DreamWorks SKG attempted to spin one of the fledgling studio's first animation films, *Antz* (2000), as both a parable of the studio's own corporate identity—"on one level, *Antz* celebrates a healthy leftist balance of individual initiative and cooperative teamwork"—and a movie about spin—"on another level, the movie is about the apolitical joys of perspective busting."[54] Later, Katzenberg could give the same kind of insider textual interpretation to his animated film *Shrek* (2001), a hilarious send-up of Michael Eisner and Disney Studios. Eisner had forced Katzenberg out of Disney in the major film industry power shift of the nineties.

But perhaps the most predictable focus of nineties spin is also the most time-honored, the creation of celebrity, of fame itself. Jay McInerney, author of 1984's *Bright Lights, Big City*, was the decade-defining novelist of the druggy eighties, but he was, if anything, adaptable to the nineties. As one critic characterizes his 1998 novel *Model Behavior*, "different decades, different themes. The club-hopping, powder-snorting excesses of the '80s have been replaced with a more '90s-style obsession: the celebrity culture. Fame is the drug everyone in these pages is hooked on."[55] This particularly nineties concept of celebrity as "the apex of consumer society"[56] is, perhaps, the ultimate goal of spin in a society in which everyone is constantly watching everyone else.

Woody Allen's 1998 *Celebrity* focuses on "that desirable display space where talent and buzz converge."[57] The film places celebrity journalist (read: spinmaster) Lee Simon (Kenneth Branagh) at the center of a celebrity universe where he is spying on the bits and pieces of the lives of all the models, writers, movie stars, hookers, and clubbers of nineties celebrity culture. *Titanic* icon Leonardo DiCaprio plays a hot, bratty, and very destructive young star who "juices *Celebrity* with a power surge. . . . Woody knew this and used Leo's celebrity magic. Leo knew of the cachet of a Woody Allen production and used Woody's celebrity magic."[58] The language of that evaluation is telling: two celebrity magicians spinning their imaginative powers around one another, using one another.

In the nineties, everyone is a user and spin is the user's magic. This nineties obsession with fame, with the Andy Warhol-cursed fifteen minutes of celebrity, is the reason so many films of the nineties are subtextually populated by journalists, photographers, media news anchors, and reporters—*Natural Born Killers, L.A. Confidential* (1997), *Up Close and Personal, Mad City* (1997), the aforementioned *Godzilla* and *Deep Impact*, and *The Insider* (1999).

But if the movies embraced the celebrity scramble of the spin-dominated nineties, so did all the other spin-susceptible media of the culture: TV, politics, journalism, the Internet, and even the academic bastions of traditional, reality-based narrative, such as history. Television, perhaps more than any other media, held the most self-reflexive view of its relationship to the concept of spin.

A major late nineties TV sitcom, starring eighties icon of Reaganomic conservatism Michael J. Fox (former star of TV's *Family Ties* and the movie *Bright Lights, Big City*), was titled *Spin City*. The main comic premise of the sitcom was language and how language could be spun and manipulated in order to make the city work. As Lyotard acknowledges, "in the computer age, the question of knowledge is now more than ever a question of government."[59] Late in the decade (1999), a much more serious TV series, *The West Wing*, built much of its drama on this same theme of the spin of language in the day-to-day functioning of the American presidency. But by far the most spin-conscious and language-conscious TV show of the nineties was *Seinfeld*.

*Seinfeld* was the decade-defining TV series for two very deconstructive reasons. First, it was a show about nothing, about the decentered nothingness around which nineties life revolved. Second, the show was almost completely dialogue. As one of the show's supporting actors said, "It's a show where people sit around and talk. . . . it's a show about language."[60] And the language that *Seinfeld* spoke was the language of spin. Every motive, every interpretation, every angle, every sound, smell, taste, and gesture of body language was endlessly analyzed, interpreted, and spun in the ongoing game of language that Jerry Seinfeld and his three morally challenged friends, George, Elaine, and Kramer, played. *Seinfeld* graced TV screens with thirty minutes of nineties spin on nineties life every Thursday night.

Strangely enough, an ongoing deconstructive symbiosis between TV and the movies developed all through the nineties decade and was expressed in the campy trend of the made-from-TV movie. In almost every instance, these big screen reinventions deconstructed their TV originals. In the case of *Mission: Impossible* (1996) the movie, the memorable tag line, "this tape will self-destruct," from the 1966 to 1973 TV show might well have been revised to "this concept will deconstruct."

In the movie, the new Impossible Mission Force (IMF) team are no longer the emotionless operatives of the TV show but are a new breed of hip misfits. The villain is no longer a cold war dictator or organized crime gangster as in the original TV series but Jim Phelps himself (Jon Voight), the leader of the IMF team. And the plot is no longer the working out of a flawless detailed plan as occurred each week in the TV series, but a convoluted series of capers gone bad, of betrayals within betrayals, of losses of nerve and failures of the best laid plans. "With the Cold War ancient history, the new *Mission: Impossible* updates super-spy hanky-panky to the Aldrich Ames era, locating the enemy inside the IMF. And the story line, as well, turns in on itself. *Mission: Impossible* is structured as a Rubik's Cube that keeps on twisting," one critic characterizes the film's deconstructing, "studiously labyrinthine" plot about "setups within setups."[61] Another notes how "the realities of a post–Cold War world add a level of LeCarrean disenchantment that the series never envisioned. . . . A key plot development trashes the series' memory."[62] Despite all this overprotectiveness for the old TV series, the *Mission: Impossible* movie spins that clunky, contrived TV series into the edgy, confusing, unpredictable nineties and retools it to the times.

A myriad of other made-from-TV movies were produced in the nineties, but perhaps the most successful and the most entertaining were *The Brady Bunch Movie* (1995) and *A Very Brady Sequel* (1996). What made them so popular with nineties audiences was "the absurd wholesomeness of the Bradys, the quality that made them such an enduring icon for the generation that grew up in the '70s, has now been turned inside out. . . . *The Brady Bunch Movie* is a sly and witty surprise, a mainstream comedy that's savvy enough to celebrate American pop kitsch by deconstructing it."[63] While more serious films like *Boogie Nights* (1997) and *Dazed and Confused* (1993) examined the seventies decade with a cultural seriousness, the two Brady Bunch movies portrayed the seventies "with a postmodern smirk."[64]

Late nineties films, however, like *The Truman Show* (1998) and *Pleasantville* (1999), more graphically portrayed the strident clash of nineties dysfunction with fifties sitcom innocence, complacency, and moral superficiality. The striking color imagery of *Pleasantville*, a black-and-white world suddenly bursting into glossy colors, especially red, perhaps best represented the changing cultural spin of television at the very end of the twentieth century.

One TV critic, writing about the late nineties TV obsession with reality-based programming, wrote that "such programming concepts suggest that the excesses forecast in the 1976 film satire *Network* have in essence come to pass."[65]

## Dialogic Discourse and the Movies

> The test of a first-rate intelligence is the ability to hold two opposed ideas in the mind at the same time, and still retain the ability to function.
> —F. Scott Fitzgerald, quoted in Mark Krupnick,
> "Diagnosing Trilling: Why the Critics Are Wrong"

This dialogic capability that F. Scott Fitzgerald affirms is one of the most prominent characteristics of nineties popular culture. The ability to see two sides to every question, two possible ways of solving every problem, gained credibility all across the diverse mind-set of nineties culture. "Official stories are suspect in a postmodern world," one commentator observed. "Any effort to sum up and declare this is how it is, this is how it was, usually gets tweaked, undermined, or turned inside out, according to the style of the day."[66] The philosophical voice that defined this particular "style of the day" of the postmodernist nineties was that of Bakhtin. For Bakhtin, the dialogical sensibility could be either complementary or antagonistic, but never monologic. Bakhtin's theory of language always posits a relationship or dialogue between discourses.[67] If Albert Camus's myth for the second half of the twentieth century is Sisyphus, then Bakhtin's myth for the postmodern era is Janus of the two faces, the dialogic smile. For example, the nineties president is either a good guy (a normal everyday McDonald's-eating Bubba) or a bad guy (a lying bimbo-chasing sleaze). The nineties villains, especially lawyers and corporate executives like Bill Gates, are both good and bad depending upon what (in the case of lawyers) their cause is or how well (in the case of CEOs) their stock is doing. Nineties children can be either angelic like little Elian Gonzalez or demonically murderous like the gun-toting schoolchildren that consistently plagued nineties history. Nineties sex could be either liberating or degrading, or (in the age of AIDS) lethal. This dialogic temper of the times served the concept of spin extremely well. In order for reality to be spun, there must be more than one possible way to interpret that reality. Spin builds on such possibilities.

One of the major indicators of the power of dialogic thought in the nineties is the movies. One commentator wrote,

> It is often said that the movies are a mirror held up to America. . . . the movies locate the fault lines in our culture and dramatize our differences and shared beliefs. . . . And you don't need to have seen the movies in question to take part. Powered by multimillion-dollar ad campaigns and endless publicity, Hollywood's latest products are inescapable. . . . While only a fraction of the U.S. population actually has seen *JFK*, 200 million more feel as if they have, and can argue passionately whether Stone is a hero who single-handedly pulled back the seal of government secrecy covering up a military coup—or an irresponsible sleight-of-hand artist who obscures history with deliberate fabrication.[68]

This 1992 commentary previews the whole nineties decade's thralldom to spin and the debates that spin inevitably touches off. The films of the nineties catalyze this dialogic energy, capture the different ways that reality can be interpreted.

By the end of the decade, the movies had presented a whole series of metaphoric representations of the decentering nature of nineties life from the natural elemental forces of tornadoes and volcanoes and meteorites (*Twister*, *Dante's Peak*, *Volcano*, *Deep Impact*, *Armageddon*) to past (*Saving Private Ryan*, *The Big Red One*) and future (*Independence Day*, *Mars Attacks*, *Starship Troopers*) wars to *Titanic*. In films like these, the present reality of nineties life is always deconstructing in some apocalyptic way that needs to be balanced by some antidote. Ironically, one of the most powerful filmmakers of the eighties and nineties, Steven Spielberg, was criticized for not being dialogic enough: "One ambition of art is to get people to think what they did not already think, or what they thought without really understanding, and the profound trouble with Spielberg as a film-maker is that he does not allow his audience to think at all."[69] This critique of Spielberg, however, fails to take into account the postmodernist approach to history that films like *Schindler's List* and *Amistad* took. Spielberg, like Stone, consciously in the nineties made films that served as discourse sites for the discussion of how history is composed. In other words, both made historical films about the writing of history.

In fact, a great many nineties movies, in their plots and characterizations, examined the ruling doubleness of late twentieth-century life. Two prominent examples of the postmodernist movie are *Groundhog Day* (1993) and *Sliding Doors* (1998). The plot premises for both films posit a world in which life can go in multiple directions at the slightest tilt of reality. In *Groundhog Day* time proves to be multidimensional and perpetually repetitive though fraught with possibilities. In *Sliding Doors* time functions in two parallel streams. A third film, *Clean Slate* (1994), does yet another variation on this time warp theme. Its hero, a detective named M. L. Pogue (Dana Carvey), is afflicted with a rare form of amnesia: whenever he goes to sleep, he forgets everything. For Pogue, as for Phil Connors (Bill Murray) in *Groundhog Day*, history starts anew each morning when he wakes up.

In *Groundhog Day* TV weatherman Phil Connors is sent to Punxsutawney, Pennsylvania, to cover the annual ceremonies. Connors is an experienced TV spinmaster, bored, cynical, and looking for a spinable gimmick for his Groundhog Day feature, and he finds one—with a vengeance. He becomes caught in a time warp in which the same twenty-four hours of Groundhog Day keep playing over and over again. Where M. L. Pogue in *Clean Slate* forgets everything and begins history anew each morning, Phil Connors is condemned (or blessed) to repeat history and change it, play with it, or rewrite it, if he wants. What Connors realizes is that there is no center and he can do anything he wants because the next morning he will start all over. The question that *Groundhog Day* poses is, if reality has no center and history offers endless possibilities, what choices would humankind make? Or, if everyday life was endlessly the same, what possibilities can humankind grasp to change life's boring repetitiveness?

*Groundhog Day* could not have made a better choice of actor to play Phil Connors than Bill Murray. The role demands a persona willing to constantly spin, manipulate, exploit, undermine, and turn inside-out the possibilities of reality. "Bill is a social anarchist . . . there's this little fear of anarchy that surrounds him,"[70] one of Murray's directors describes him. But that description might also describe *Groundhog Day*'s Phil Connors as well. Once he realizes that he can spin the reality of this single day any way that he wants, his boring, repetitive life becomes a highly intriguing and ultimately redemptive Lyotardian game.

"Parallel Whirls" reads the headline of a magazine review of *Sliding Doors*. "Gwyneth Paltrow, a lovesick Londoner, lives twin lives in the doubly romantic fantasy *Sliding Doors*," reads the subhead.[71] As these rather perceptive headlines signal, *Sliding Doors* is a consciously structured film about spin. Parallel worlds in time spin themselves simultaneously out in this contemporary love story. Helen, a young Londoner, runs down the underground platform to catch her train, but she is a moment late, and the doors slide shut on her. This imagery of sliding doors, which recurs throughout the film, triggers the "what if" structure of Helen's life. What if she had caught her train? What if she had missed her train? Helen's life spins out in two parallel versions triggered by these two "what ifs."

As *Groundhog Day* explored the creative power that spin can exert upon the boring repetitiveness of day-to-day life, *Sliding Doors* explores the "mysterious metaphysics" of "the merge and morph of every possibility, converging in the one road down which each soul inevitably travels."[72] *Sliding Doors* reveals the dialogic possibilities of reality. Helen is "real" in both versions of her life, but time or fate spins her into different possible "realities." In *Sliding Doors*, chaos theory meets dialogic spin. Time spins Helen's life down two parallel yet divergent yellow brick roads, but the question is a tantalizing one that, right up to the very end, maintains its dialogic structure before succumbing to the monologic Hollywood necessity: the two lovers somehow must get together in the end, the two parallel worlds must ultimately converge, the "what if" question must ultimately be resolved as they were in earlier parallel-universe films like *It's A Wonderful Life* (1946), *Heaven Can Wait* (1978), and *Ghost* (1990).

But while *Groundhog Day* and *Sliding Doors* offer comic and romantic dialogic structures, other nineties films offer much more sinister parallel worlds. David Mamet's *The Spanish Prisoner* (1998) is one of those films that explores the threatening aspects of spin. Described as a "Rubik's Cube of a suspense film" about "a con game that sheds layers like an onion"[73] and possessed of a "plot that twists and twists again,"[74] *The Spanish Prisoner*, like other game movies, such as *Zorro* (1975, 1999) or *The Game* (1997), where everyone operates under a double identity in order to deceive, coerce, or scam the world, is a movie in the best Mamet style about the running of an elaborate con game—in other words, an exercise in spinning reality via the vehicle of elaborate double identities and parallel worlds. In *Zorro*, L. Q. Jones of mythic *The Wild Bunch* (1969) fame, describes the world of the film as a metaplay, a play within a bigger play: "I am the master of the opera. It is all a play that they play." In *The Spanish Prisoner*, while the author/director is the ultimate spinmaster, his spinmaster inside the plot is the mysterious businessman Jimmy Dell (Steve Martin) who creates a phony, constantly shifting world, a labyrinth, in which he entraps naïve scientist Joe Ross (Campbell Scott) as a means of stealing a very secret and lucrative process. "Spielberg makes movies about the clash of alien creatures. . . . Martin Scorcese likes stories about Italian Americans. . . . I like telling stories about confidence games,"[75] Mamet places himself as a nineties director in relation to his peers. From *House of Games* (1987) to *Glengarry Glen Ross* (1992) to *Oleanna* (1994) to *Wag The Dog*, all of Mamet's movies are about spin, about the potential to skew reality to one's advantage. The salesmen of *Glengarry Glen Ross*, the movie people of *Wag the Dog*, the con men of *House of Games* and *The Spanish Prisoner* are all masters of the art of spin, the art of selling their versions of reality to a selected, carefully researched, eternally susceptible audience. Perhaps Mamet was one of the earliest to perceive the overarching truth of the nineties decade of spin, that indeed a sucker is born every minute.

Though written by John Guare, *Six Degrees of Separation* (1993) could well be another Mamet spin movie. A young, black man named Paul (Will Smith) talks his way into the lives of a rich Fifth Avenue couple by claiming to be a classmate of their son and the son of Sidney Poitier. The young man is brilliant, charming, and well-mannered, and these middle-aged New York liberals fall for his elegant spin. But there is more than one side to Paul just as there are two sides to the prized Kandinsky painting that hangs symbolically in their living room and that Paul analyzes so perceptively.

Another very Mamet-like spin movie is David Fincher's *The Game* in which Michael Douglas plays Nick Van Orton, a powerful business tycoon who "finds his daily existence being manipulated from every direction" when he becomes involved in an elaborate game given to him by his brother as an unusual birthday gift. Once Nick enters the game, "the whole thing begins to spiral out of control."[76] The plot of *The Game* is very much like the plot of John Fowles's play-within-a-play-within-a-play novel, *The Magus* (1965). Van Orton seems to be caught in a violently spinning universe out to destroy his whole life, which proves, in the end, to be out to save his life. One commentator captured the metatextual spinmaster spirit of *The Game* when he wrote, "Like David Mamet's *House of Games*, this is a movie in which everything we see is an elaborate ruse and in which everybody but our hapless protagonist is playing a role."[77] Movies solely about spin are truly vortextual. Like the very texture of nineties life, everything is constantly set spinning until it finally whirls out of control.

However, individual con men (or salesmen or movie producers) are not the only vehicles for exploring the doubleness of spin. Even in the post–cold war age of the nineties, governments mount elaborate con games for the purposes of either eliminating their rivals in the quest for power or covering up their crimes committed in the quest for power. Following in the tradition of *Three Days of the Condor* (1975), *Capricorn One, All the President's Men*, and *The Star Chamber* (1983), which focused on conspiracies within the government, secret agencies within government agencies, and metagovernments, nineties films like *Conspiracy Theory* (1997), *The Enemy of the People* (2000), *Absolute Power* (1997), and, especially, *L.A. Confidential* examined the violent techniques that governmental spinmasters use to cover up their crimes.

One of the most highly praised and artistically satisfying films of the nineties decade, *L.A. Confidential*, brilliantly adapted from James Ellroy's novel, works on many levels of interpretation. It is classic film noir in the best Hollywood genre style, offering a femme fatale who turns out to be good not evil, violent cops who turn their violence away from racist injustice to existential justice, and a plot with so many twists, turns, and surprises that it makes films like *The Maltese Falcon* (1941) and *The Big Sleep* (1946) seem like one-finger exercises. On another level, it is a textbook New Historicist film in its accurate recreation of its fifties Los Angeles milieu coupled with its presentist relevance in terms of real nineties LA police corruption. But, parallel to these central themes, *L.A. Confidential* is the nineties' most complete film about spin. *L.A. Confidential* relentlessly descends into the underworld of both fifties and nineties spin, and encounters the media, the government, the sexual fantasy hucksters, and the dream machine of the movies, all the scrambling purveyors of spin, on its spiraling journey.

*L.A. Confidential* descends into the spinning circles of a modern Dante's *Inferno* in its attempt to find the ultimate spinmaster, Rollo Tommasi, "the man who gets away with it." Ironically, Rollo Tommasi does not even exist. In *L.A. Confidential*, Rollo Tommasi is the grail, the McGuffin, the Rosebud, of young Edmund Exley (Guy Pearce). Exley is the political yet honorable good cop in a whirling plot in which the good cop/bad cop double identity exists within single characters, constantly spins back upon itself. The good cop can spin Janus-like into the bad cop at the drop of a phrase, a smile, a taunt, the flash of a flashbulb, or the mere mention of Rollo Tommasi.

Another powerful film about spin, *The Usual Suspects* (1995), also turns on a nonexistent, off-stage character like Rollo Tommasi. Keyser Sose, the mythical Hungarian gangster mastermind, in one way or another, controls the whole fabricated narrative of that film. Keyser Sose in his double identity as a clubfooted small-time crook is the reigning spinmaster of this film. He literally makes up the narrative as he goes along, finding direction in his surroundings: the interrogation room, the bulletin board, even his coffee cup.

But the one film to which *L.A. Confidential* is most consistently compared is *Chinatown*.[78] "Like *Chinatown*, the 1974 classic of Los Angeles depravity," Owen Gleiberman writes, *L.A. Confidential* "is the rare night-world thriller that understands what bad impulses can do to good men. Even the heroes have to get down in the muck to take on the devil."[79] *L.A. Confidential* is the nineties version of *Chinatown* neo-noir. As Gleiberman notes, it catches the dialogic nature of its characters and the Dantesque descent-into-the-Inferno quality of its plot the way that *Chinatown* spun Jake Gittes (Jack Nicholson) through his doomed and confused journey. Even the central imagery of *L.A. Confidential*, that of eyes, of seeing clearly, of spying and voyeurism, of photography, is directly lifted from *Chinatown*.[80]

*L.A. Confidential*'s ironic theme of spin asserts itself from the opening credits montage of idyllic southern California scenes, played to the song *Accentuate the Positive*:

> Accentuate the positive
> Eliminate the negative
> Latch on to the affirmative
> Don't mess with Mr. In-Between.

This spin song plays beneath the voice-over narration of Sid Hudgens (Danny DeVito), fifties paparazzi reporter for *Hush* magazine, a precursor of the nineties tabloids. Sid, the ironic hipster, smarmily smirks that LA is "paradise on earth. That's what they tell ya anyway. Because they're selling an image," and he goes on to ask, tongue in cheek, "How could organized crime exist in the city with the best police department in the world?" This opening credits montage combines the images plus the ironic song plus the voice-over narrative to create a layered effect that embodies the concept of spin.

Throughout the film, music and Sid's voice-over narration provide ironic counterpoints to the images that often only show the uncomplicated surface of LA life. Later in the film, the ironic song "Look For the Silver Lining" plays in the background of the bar as LAPD Captain Dudley Smith (James Cromwell) returns Officer Bud White's (Russell Crowe) badge to him because of "your adherence to violence as a necessary adjunct of the job. . . . You follow my drift?" And White replies, "In technicolor, sir." Even the cops use movie metaphors to express themselves.

In another montage of gangland assassinations orchestrated from prison by off-stage spinmaster Mickey Cohen, the jivey tune "Bye, Bye, Baby, Time to hit the road to Dreamland" plays in comic counterpoint over the gruesome images of blood and murder much as did "Singin' In the Rain" over the rape scene in Stanley Kubrick's *A Clockwork Orange* (1971). The whole film is filled with these double ironies. Perhaps the most ironic of all is the title of the fifties TV show that portrays the LAPD, *Badge of Honor*. The whole film is a study in the dynamic of how honor is lost and found, how the badge is tarnished and given back its shine. At the end of the opening sequence, Sid, at his typewriter, signs off with his tagline "Remember, dear readers, you heard it here first, off the record, on the Q-T, and very Hush-Hush"—and claims his place as one of the reigning spinmasters of the world of the film. But then, everyone is a spinmaster in *L.A. Confidential*.

This theme of spin is most obviously represented by the LA media. While Sid and *Hush* magazine occupy the lowest, sleaziest circle of media hell in the LA of the fifties, the headlines of the *L.A. Times*, a supposedly legitimate family newspaper, "BLOODY CHRISTMAS" and "NITE OWL MASSACRE," are every bit as sensational as Sid's. Sid shows that by means of blackmail, setups, and even creative camera angles (he sets his photography up to catch the marquee of a movie premiere in the background of a drug arrest and headlines it "MOVIE PREMIERE POT BUST"), he can create his news, his image of LA, and spin it any way he wants. In a conversation with celebrity cop Jack Vincennes (Kevin Spacey), Sid glories in the tremendous potential for spin in the media galaxy of fifties LA:

> *Vincennes:* I'm the technical advisor [to *Badge of Honor*]. America isn't ready for the real me.
> *Hudgens:* Once you whet the public's appetite for the truth, there's no telling where it can go.

Sid expresses one of the major texts of *L.A. Confidential*, the spin potential of everyone—of the sensational press, of police corruption and city politics, of organized crime, of the sexual underground—in the tremendously corrupt society of fifties (and nineties) LA. This film's version of Los Angeles is of a city not only lacking a center, but coming apart at the seams. Ironically, the center that LA had, crime boss and social butterfly Mickey Cohen, has been sent away. Without him keeping order via crime and violence, even worse disorder and violence has arisen in the wake of his departure. Everyone is trying to fill the void left by the arrest of Cohen, some wishing to take his place as the center of LA's dark world, others hoping to survive and prosper in the violent decentered world that Cohen has bequeathed to them all.

*L.A. Confidential* pulls no punches in its portrayal of LA as a lost world. It is all image, all spin, and beneath the glossy images and the slick spin lies violence, degradation, corrupt power struggle, and chaos. The film's mixmaster of a plot involves at least five major cases under investigation. Count 'em—the Nite Owl coffee shop massacre, the gang rape of a Mexican girl, the *Fleur de Lis* pornography/sex ring, the Cohen mob hits, the political corruption surrounding the building of a new freeway—plus other assorted drug busts and blackmail shakedowns and wife-beating rousts, not to mention the major internal affairs problems of the LAPD itself, including police brutality, racism, media payoffs, and mob involvement. All these plot circles ultimately spin around the antiheroes of the film, Bud White and Ed Exley, with Jack Vincennes and Sid Hudgens serving as bystanding ironic narrators caught up in observing and surviving in the decentered world that White and Exley are trying to put back together. White and Exley are, in a sense, like the two sergeants in Stone's film *Platoon* (1987), good and evil in the midst of the chaos of the Vietnam War. However, where Stone's two characters were one-dimensional allegorical figures, White and Exley are more complex characters within whom good and evil is constantly contending. As one critic wrote, "*L.A. Confidential* shows us what it takes to find your honor in a world that's lost its soul."[81]

What Ellroy's novels, all set in the fifties, imply and what *L.A. Confidential* eerily prefigures is the biggest police scandal in LAPD history, the Rampart Division's special gang unit scandal of 1998. That scandal involved all the elements that Police Captain Smith in the movie includes in his three-question test of the fitness of a man to lead the LAPD:

1. Would you be willing to plant corroborative evidence on a suspect you know to be guilty to get an indictment?
2. Would you be willing to beat a confession out of a suspect you know to be guilty?
3. Would you be willing to shoot a hardened criminal in the back?

Smith's three little questions exactly describe the methods of the Rampart Division's officers that were exposed in the 1998 LA police scandal. It is almost as if they used Smith's questions as a textbook for their own unconstitutional joyride in municipal corruption.

But all sorts of other ironies are involved in these three questions as well. All three describe methods of spinning reality in the policeman's favor with the abstract concept of justice being the only casualty. Exley, early in the film, adamantly answers "no" to all three of Smith's questions. Then, as the film unwinds, Exley fulfills each question's prophecy culminating in shooting the questioner, Smith (the behind-the-scenes spinmaster, the "wizard" of this perverted Oz), in the back. By shooting Smith and fulfilling the Macbeth-like (or, perhaps, oedipal) prophesies of the three questions, Exley, in effect, maintains the decentered world that Cohen's absence has created, thus offering the possibility that a future new center of good might replace the old center of mob evil and the present decentered void in the history of LA.

One other major question is posed throughout *L.A. Confidential*. "Why did you become a cop?" is asked of all three of the film's principals. Each answers it in his own soul-searching way. White answers that he wants to protect women as he couldn't protect his own mother who his father beat to death with a tire iron. Exley answers "Rollo Tommasi," the imaginary criminal who got away with killing his police officer father. But Vincennes has the most deconstructive answer to the core question. When Vincennes is asked why he became a cop, he stops to think and then answers regretfully, "I don't remember."

Vincennes's answer signals the LAPD's fateful decentering (in both the fifties and the late nineties), which those on the inside can't deny despite all the contrary images that they try to spin for the unsuspecting public. For example, an LAPD recruitment billboard trumpets "A GREAT FORCE IN A GREAT CITY—JOIN THE FORCE," a message quite different from what all the newspaper headlines are trumpeting. After a disciplinary hearing for the officers involved in the "BLOODY CHRISTMAS" beatings, the police commissioner comments in a wry aside, "Not exactly the image of the new LAPD that we're trying to create." Despite all their attempts to spin an image of the police force and its officers as guardians of public trust, they all realize that the LAPD is decentered and empty at the core. They all are trying to fill up that void at the center of existence just as so many different factions are trying to fill the void that the departure of Cohen has left in the center of the LA underworld. This micro/macro relationship between the existential lives of the characters and the sociocultural life of the whole city of LA finds its expression in one brief exchange between White and pimp/pornographer/blackmailer/freeway contractor Pierce Patchett (David Straithairn):

> *White:* You wanna go downtown and discuss this officially?
> *Patchett:* Is that what this is? Official? Somehow I have the feeling this is more personal with you Mr. White.

All the characters in *L.A. Confidential* lead this double existence. Their real life and their fantasy life, their political life and their personal life, are constantly at odds. Lynn Bracken (Kim Basinger), one of Pierce Patchett's "whores cut to look like movie stars," is, perhaps, the best symbolic example of the double spin needed to survive in the decentered universe of LA. Lynn's house, where she entertains her rich and influential johns, fulfilling their movie star fantasies as Veronica Lake, is an opulent movie star's home complete with screening facilities for the movies whose plots she and her customers will initiate on the white satin sheets of the platform bed. But Lynn keeps one bedroom of her house for her real self, the little girl from rural Arizona who came to Hollywood with big dreams. That is the room where she takes White.

Patchett's stable of double-identitied hookers—Veronica Lake, Rita Hayworth, Marilyn Monroe—are emblematic of all the doubled existences that plague all the characters in the film. They are simulacra of simulacra, surgically designed simulations of Hollywood celebrity. They represent holographic layers of simulation. Lynn of rural Arizona has become Lynn of LA, a high-priced prostitute who resembles Veronica Lake who is, herself, a creation of the Hollywood spin machine. Everyone in *L.A. Confidential* spins fantasies off of their realities. All the major characters are Janus-like, double-faced, and dialogical in their relationships with others, themselves, and the social world of the film.

White, ultraviolent police detective, spins himself into St. George, protector of all women. Exley, college boy cop, spins himself into the ultimate political animal in the police department. Vincennes spins himself into one of the stars of the hit (*Dragnet*-like) TV cop show *Badge of Honor* and then tries to spin himself back into real life as an honorable cop. Smith tries to spin himself from the position of one of the most powerful police officers in LA into the most powerful gangster in LA as he tries to take over the absent Cohen's underworld enterprises. Like Patchett's hookers, each of these cops plays out the good cop/bad cop scenario within their very own existences. Perhaps the only truly comic scene in the whole dark plot of *L.A. Confidential* deconstructs this whole sickness that infects the film. Exley and Vincennes go to confront Cohen thug Johnny Stompanato in a bar and find him having a drink with a woman who looks suspiciously like Lana Turner. Vincennes just stands back and watches utterly amused as Ed Exley tells the woman to get lost, calls her a whore, accuses her of being just another of Patchett's hookers cut to look like a movie star, and catches her martini with his face. Only at that point does Vincennes step in and inform Exley that "she really is Lana Turner." As this hilarious scene slowly builds, the discourse of the whole movie turns back on itself. The fragility of the line between fantasy and reality deconstructs. What this scene intimates is that when the spin of fantasy versus reality becomes so powerful that one can, like Vincennes answering the question of why he became a cop, no longer remember which is which or distinguish between the two, then the center of existence has truly disappeared.

The controlling imagery of *L.A. Confidential* also supports the interwoven themes of spin, and *Chinatown*-like illusionary irony. Throughout the film, the imagery of eyes, seeing clearly, lenses, photography, spying, and voyeurism constantly recurs as a commentary upon the central discourse problem within the decentered world of LA: no one can see reality clearly. Reality has become an illusion consistently mediated, filtered, spun through distorting lenses, such as the press with their posed photos and political cover-ups with their staged press conferences. Everyone seems to be on the outside looking in, separated from the reality they are seeing. In the very first scene of the film, after the Hudgens LA illusion opening montage, White is found looking through the window of a neighborhood house as a woman is beaten by her recently paroled ex-con husband. Throughout the film, this scene of a spy or voyeur recurs: White peers through the window of Patchett's car at the bandaged face of a young woman, Hudgens's *Hush* photographer shoots photos of the two young aspiring actors high on marijuana in front of the Christmas tree through the window. Exley watches through the one-way mirror as Vincennes is offered the deal to testify that Exley has orchestrated. Bud spies on Bracken entertaining her tricks through the round window of her house. White and Exley stare through the window of the morgue at the dead hooker's body. The LAPD bigwigs observe through the one-way glass as Exley interrogates the three young Negroes accused of the Nite Owl murder. Hudgens photographs Exley and Lynn in flagrante again through the window of Lynn's love nest.

In fact, flashbulbs are constantly going off. They are the transitional triggers that fire *L.A. Confidential's* mixmaster of a plot. As a tribute to the noir style that Orson Welles used to such powerful effect in *Citizen Kane* (1941) and that Roman Polanski so tellingly appropriated in *Chinatown*, Curtis Hanson structures his information-dispensing montages around an exploding flashbulb (the trigger), cut to the photograph(s) themselves (the spin on reality), cut to the photographs morphing into life (a return to reality after it has been spun). Actually, almost as many flashbulbs go off in the course of the film as do gunshots to the point that one wonders whether the film's characters should be more gun-shy or camera-shy.

Indeed, everyone is extremely photo-conscious in *L.A. Confidential*. Echoing the adultery photos that open *Chinatown*, black-and-white photographs are constantly being passed around in *L.A. Confidential*: the bondage pornography photos that the vice squad passes around, the blackmail photos that force the city councilman to change his vote on the freeway, the forensics photos of the Nite Owl Massacre, and the photos of Exley and Lynn that Smith sets up White to find in the trunk of Hudgens's car. This photography motif is so prevalent that, at one point, a young street cop says in disgust to Vincennes and Exley, "The two of you guys should bring along a photographer." The LAPD is more publicity conscious (a kind of spin) than justice conscious is the upshot of this offhand sarcastic remark.

But besides the socially conscious motifs of spying, voyeurism, and photography, the imagery of ways to see also takes a much more philosophical turn in *L.A. Confidential*. This aspect of the motif hinges on Exley's eyeglasses. Early in the story, he is solemnly advised by his superiors, first Captain Smith and then the police commissioner, to "lose the glasses." In the street in front of the Nite Owl Coffee Shop when a *Los Angeles Times* photographer asks for a picture of him and Smith, Exley takes off his glasses and strikes a pose. The flashbulb goes off, and he has succeeded in spinning his new image. The only problem is that when Exley takes off his glasses, he can't see clearly enough or far enough to either shoot straight or distinguish the nature of reality.

Just as the eye imagery in *Chinatown* emphasized a theme of flawed sight, so too does this eye imagery in *L.A. Confidential*. The only one smart enough and, as his star rises in the police department, powerful enough to see through the complex web of interwoven crimes and cover-ups that Smith (who fills the role of Exley's imaginary Rollo Tommasi, "the one who gets away with it") weaves is Exley. For political reasons, Exley obscures and distorts his own vision and takes off his eyeglasses. Late in the story, however, as Exley gets closer and closer to the object of his quest, his Rollo Tommasi, he starts wearing his glasses again so that he can see better.

Lynn Bracken, the Veronica Lake look-alike prostitute who falls in love with White, becomes the voice of clear sight who convinces Exley to put his glasses back on. Ironically, sitting in the dim light of a police station with two black eyes from a beating, Lynn talks to Exley about the value of seeing a person clearly: "You're afraid of Bud because you can't figure out how to play him. . . . I see Bud because he can't hide the good inside of him. . . . I see Bud because of all the ways he is different from you." While Lynn is making a play on the word "see" throughout this speech, she is also stating the case for anti-spin as opposed to Exley's very powerful commitment to political spin. Lynn sees White clearly because she looks for the honesty in a person while Exley only looks at people as potential objects for his own games of spin. In the last scene of the film, after everything has been resolved and Exley, the district attorney, and the police commissioner have spun Smith into a dead hero and Exley himself into a live one. Lynn, with a twinkle in her eye, says goodbye to Exley on the steps of City Hall:

> *Lynn:* You just couldn't resist. . . .
> *Exley:* They're using me, so for a little while I'm using them.

What Lynn sees and Exley admits is that he just couldn't resist the chance to spin the violent reality that he, White, and Vincennes finally saw clearly to his own political purposes and profit. "The king is dead, long live the king," this final scene says; when Exley kills Smith, the reigning spinmaster of this dark and violent LA version of Oz, he becomes the new wizard, capable of interpreting reality in whatever way is the most valuable to him.

*L.A. Confidential* is a neo-noir mock epic of spin. Vincennes, White, and Exley are a quixotic triumvirate, and Hudgens is their down-to-earth Sancho Panza. Late in the film, as Vincennes tries to get Hudgens to expose Patchett, Sid turns him down saying, "He can't help me in my quest for prime sinuendo." In *L.A. Confidential,* the flashbulbs are constantly going off. The sensational headlines are constantly being written. The "sinuendo" is constantly being spun by Hudgens, *Hush* magazine, and all the other spinmasters in the film's world. The film presents a fifties world that has already mastered the intricacies of nineties spin.

When Vincennes, near the end of *L.A. Confidential,* goes to Smith, he says that he is there "to dig up the past." Smith's reaction to Vincennes's little historical foray is to kill him on the spot. Smith has spun much too complex an image to allow Vincennes to tarnish it with the truth. *L.A. Confidential* is a New Historicist reinterpretation of fifties LA history. What New Historicism does is take the spin off history and expand the historical record to include what has been missed or repressed or ignored by the spinmasters of the past. New Historicism is a project very similar to the project that the three quixotic detectives of *L.A. Confidential*—Exley, White, and Vincennes—undertake with the help of their bottom-feeding Sancho Panza, Hudgens.

# CHAPTER 4

# Politics and Spin

History is written for the victors and what they leave out are the losers.
— Arthur Drexler, quoted in "Preparing a 'Conquest,'" *Los Angeles Times*

The story goes that David Geffen, then CEO of Asylum Records and soon to be one of the founding partners of DreamWorks SKG, "spent 45 minutes in the pre-Monicagate Oval Office of 1994 lecturing President Clinton on how to spin the press."[1] Scary as that scenario may be considering the epic hustler reputation of Geffen, it demonstrates a rather powerful street savvy and sense of what is important in his time, the nineties, on the part of Bill Clinton. The political world of the nineties can safely be triangulated as the very epicenter of spin. First, the Congress of Newt Gingrich and then the Whitewater/Monicagate/impeachment proceedings White House of Bill Clinton became accustomed to playing every public policy and public pronouncement *only* to the press and not to the people. In consternation in 1999, *Newsweek* magazine announced that for "the first time politicians displayed the serious bipartisanship befitting a constitutional crisis . . . last week when senators met in the old Senate Chamber with the TV cameras off. A timeout from the 24-hour-a-day cycle of speculation and spin gave them a chance to apply some order to the chaos."[2] If there was ever any question that the nineties was the decade of spin, politics answered that question with a vengeance.

An excellent example occurred when "Rep. Lindsey Graham, R-SC, spun a web of intrigue during the House Judiciary Committee hearing, accusing President Clinton of abusing his power as president in an organized effort to discredit Monica Lewinsky," and Maxine Waters answered, "I would like to say that every member of this committee should be offended by the spin, the wild spin, that was just put on."[3] By the end of the nineties decade, this era of wild political spin actually acquired a name that was provided by Hollywood and the movies. In January 1998, when President Clinton was wriggling under the sexual allegations of his affair with Monica Lewinsky plus the sexual harassment trial of Paula Jones plus his previous lying about an affair with Gennifer Flowers, the president decided to attack Iraq and Saddam Hussein. TV anchor Matt Lauer on NBC's *Today Show* used the term "the Wag the Dog Syndrome" to describe the whole situation.[4] In the same vein, James P. Pinkerton wrote in *Newsday*, "it was the Year of the Dog, as in *Wag the Dog*. That 1997 film, about the staging of a phony war to distract attention from a presidential sex scandal had already entered the popular consciousness even before Bill Clinton ordered air strikes against Iraq on the eve of the impeachment vote. . . . No Hollywood film of 1998 had really as much politico-cultural impact."[5] A newswire release also headlined "'Wag the Dog' revisited," which stated, "Those three little words kept cropping up Thursday as news spread that the United States had bombed suspected terrorist installations in Afghanistan and Sudan. . . . On Thursday, life again imitated popular culture, except the confrontations were real."[6]

*Wag the Dog* (1997) may, indeed, be the most decade-defining film of the nineties, not because of its timely, ripped-from-the-headlines relevance, but rather because of its clear and present representation of a world taken over by spin. Some people may have thought the premise of *Wag the Dog* was a bit farfetched, but it was nowhere near as farfetched as it was thought to be once reality stepped in, taking the form of Bill Clinton's air strikes, or once historians started comparing it to the Gulf War of George Bush. One critic described *Wag the Dog* as "a satire of political manipulations in the era of media run amok. . . . To divert the nation's attention [from a Presidential sex scandal], Conrad Brean (Robert De Niro), the President's spin-control guru, calls in a veteran Hollywood producer named Stanley Motss (Dustin Hoffman), and the two end up collaborating on the ultimate political-advertising boondoggle. Using the mass media as their stage, they create, through an elaborate series of technological tricks and public relations dupes, a 'war.'"[7] But *Wag the Dog* is much more than just a political satire or a reel-life-mirrors-real-life happening. *Wag the Dog* is a truly decade-defining film because it captures the amoral nineties as a decade caught in the g-forces of spin.

*Wag the Dog* is a classic three-act screenplay comprised of a fast-talking, dialogue-focused setup (act 1); a techno-marvel execution of the plan, the caper (act 2); and a final twist, an obstacle-to-be-overcome conclusion (act 3), followed by the briefest of ultracynical epilogues. The opening setup, however, is where the theme of spin is asserted. This first section of the film presents an analysis of the relationship between history and spin. Once Conrad Brean, the White House's spinmaster (affectionately known as "Mr. Fixit"), learns about the president's sexual liaison with a FireFly girl in the anteroom to the Oval Office and realizes that he has to create an eleven-day diversion (until the election is over), the roller coaster of spin takes off. Brean decides that he needs to create a war as his diversion and no one does wars better than Hollywood. Brean goes straight to Stanley Motss, one of Hollywood's most powerful producers (in this case based on a bravura impersonation of producer Robert Evans by Dustin Hoffman), to create not a war but "the appearance of a war," a high-tech simulacra.

The initial planning session for this disinformation campaign is a complete history and anatomy of spin:

> *Brean:* "Remember the Maine." "Tippecanoe and Tyler Too." They're all slogans, Mr Motss. We remember the slogans; we can't remember the fuckin' wars. You know why? That's why we're here. Naked girl covered in napalm. (cut to picture) V for Victory. Five marines raising the flag on Mount Surabachi. (cut to picture) You remember the picture fifty years from now but you've forgotten the war. The Gulf War. The smart bomb falling down the chimney. 2500 missions a day, 100 days. One video of one bomb. The American people bought that war. War is show business. That's why we're here.

This back and forth conversation defines and analyzes the process of creating political spin and manipulating history:

> *Motss:* They gotta know at some point.
> *Brean:* Who?
> *Motss:* Who? You know . . . the, the . . . American public.
> *Brean:* They gotta know?
> *Motss:* Yes.
> *Brean:* Stan, bear with us. Who killed Kennedy? I read the first draft of the Warren Report. Says he was killed by a drunk driver. You watched the Gulf War. What did you see day after day? The one smart bomb falling down the chimney. The truth. I was in the building when they shot that shot. We shot it in a studio in Falls Church, Virginia. 1/10 $^{th}$ scale model of the building.
> *Motss:* Is that true?
> *Brean:* How the fuck do we know? You take my point.
> *Motss:* Yes, OK, and you want me to do what?
> *Brean:* We want you to produce.
> *Motss:* You want me to produce your war?
> *Brean:* Not a war. It's a pageant. We need a theme, a song, some visuals. You know. It's a pageant. It's like the Oscars. That's why we came to you.

In the world of Brean and Motss and American politics in the postmodernist computer/digital age of the late twentieth century, reality has no relationship to spin. Spin is "a pageant," a movie, and because the American public has reached a state in which they are totally susceptible to accepting movies or television as reality, spinmasters like Brean and Motss can engineer whatever reality they can invent. Plus, their major accomplice, the entrenched network that makes it all work in this whole dynamic of spin, is the Fourth Estate, the press and the electronic media.

One of the primary visual motifs of *Wag the Dog* is the continuous ironic intercutting of television images into the flow of the story: TV political commercials, TV news broadcasts, TV roundtable political discussions, TV coverage of White House press briefings, and TV talk show monologues. Once movie producer Motss puts together his production team—assistant producer, songwriter, costumer, digital effects editor, and technical and camera crew—all of these media outlets become sitting ducks for the spin that he leaks to them. Act 2 of *Wag the Dog* consists of spellbinding montages that chronicle how spin is created. How the sensory vehicles of spin (images, songs, slogans) are brought to life dominates act 2 of *Wag the Dog*. Pretty soon spin has taken over and reality recedes. Winifred, the presidential aide (Ann Heche), reports to Brean and Motss, "the *Times* has got the Firefly girl in the *Style* section. The *Post* has it on page 12."

Meanwhile, the president's opponent, Senator Neal (Craig T. Nelson), tries to set up a campaign of counterspin. He makes attack commercials with their own theme song: "Thank heaven for little girls." He has the effrontery to call a press conference and declare the war over. When candidate Neal makes this spin move, Motss, in his anger, directly echoes Charles Foster Kane's spinmaster position on the Spanish-American War:

*Motss:* What has he done?
*Brean:* He's just ended the war.
*Motss:* He can't end the war. I'm the producer.
*Brean:* The war is over. I just saw it on TV.
*Motss:* The war isn't over until I say it's over.

When Neal's counterspin foray of ending the war starts to take hold, Motss and Brean have to spin that counterspin back into the president's favor:

*Motss:* Our guy *did* bring peace.
*Brean:* Yeah, but there wasn't a war.
*Motss:* All the greater accomplishment.

Finally, the whole back and forth game of spin and counterspin is described by Brean with utter cynicism: "This is politics at its finest."

This cynicism rules *Wag the Dog* as it did not rule earlier films on the same subject. In *Mr. Smith Goes to Washington* (1939), Jimmy Stewart's title character embodies the triumph of simple, straightforward Capra-esque political and moral values over entrenched political cynicism. But there is no such victory in *Wag the Dog*. It belongs in the same cynical category as Orson Welles's *Citizen Kane* (1941; remember Charles Foster Kane saying, "I'll provide the war"), Sidney Lumet's *Power* (1986) starring Richard Gere as a corrupt political spinmaster, and Michael Ritchie's *The Candidate* (1972) in which naïve Bill McKay's (Robert Redford) political campaign is ruthlessly orchestrated by a professional political spinmaster (Peter Boyle). What all of these films say is that politics in the seventies of *The Candidate* and the eighties of *Power* is more and more being run by political professionals and controlled by the press and electronic media. The ultimate extension of their quite realistic theme culminates in the postmodernist satire of *Wag the Dog*. What *Wag the Dog* says, taking this theme of political manipulation to an even more cynical level, is that the professionals are no longer even political and the press is merely a duped vehicle for a much more cynical game of spin the candidate.

In *Wag the Dog* the terrible absurdist truth of the power of media spin comes out after the plane carrying Brean, Motss, Winifred, and Schumann (Woody Harrelson), the psycho convicted of raping a nun who they are all trying to spin into a war hero, crashes. They all survive the crash, as does a single functioning TV set, which Winifred, in frustration, throws her shoe at:

> *Brean:* Leave it alone. What did television ever do to you?
> *Winifred:* It destroyed the electoral process.

In a film that so rigorously denies the possibility of truth in deference to the power of spin, small kernels of dark truth (like Winifred's frustrated answer) sometimes surface in the film's sea of cynicism.

At the very beginning of *Wag the Dog*, when Winifred first tells Brean about the president having sex with the Fire Fly girl just off the Oval Office, the concept of truth is rejected out of hand:

> *Brean:* Who's got the story?
> *Winifred:* Don't you want to know if it's true?
> *Brean:* What difference does it make if it's true. It's a story and if it breaks they're going to run it.

Truth has no place in the nineties political equation: TRUTH = TV/SPIN. The only number that truly crunches is the effect of the spin factor on TV ratings. One SCUD stud plus one smart bomb down one chimney equals the "truth" of the Gulf War. Like everything else in the nineties, truth, has been taken over by the power of spin.

But the cynicism of *Wag the Dog* makes the political operatives of *The Candidate* and *Power* look like naïve Pollyannas. *Wag the Dog*'s political cynicism is aligned with two much more sinister films about the evil potential for spin, *Capricorn One* (1978) and *The Parallax View* (1974). In these two earlier films, truth becomes exactly the kind of "pageant" that Brean describes to Motss in *Wag the Dog*. In *Capricorn One* corrupt Space Agency executives fake a moon landing by shooting it as a studio TV show. In *The Parallax View*, journalist Joe Frady (Warren Beatty) becomes the fall guy in an elaborate political assassination conspiracy. What both of these films share with *Wag the Dog*, however, is one essential truth: a TV image can be used to convince anyone to believe anything.

One of the most compelling scenes in *Wag the Dog* could be a scene out of Michelangelo Antonioni's *Blow-Up* (1966) or Francis Ford Coppola's *The Conversation* (1974) or Brian De Palma's *Blow Out* (1981) or Richard Rush's *The Stunt Man* (1980). What all of these films have in common are extended scenes in which technology attempts to simulate reality[8] as a means of learning or understanding some truth, constructing some reality out of a series of images or sounds. *Blow-Up*, *The Conversation*, and *Blow Out* are all essentially the same movie, and in their pivotal techno-simulation scenes, their protagonists all try to reconstruct the commission of a crime out of fragmentary images and sounds. In

*The Stunt Man,* an all-powerful film director cuts and recuts a scene in which a stunt man supposedly dies resulting in so many different versions that no one has any idea what really happened.

The compelling techno-simulation scene in *Wag the Dog* involves the making of a phony news bite that depicts a young Albanian girl running through her burning, bombed village carrying her kitten. The whole scene is created by the digital overlay of visual and audio effects. First, the special effects technicians have the actress playing the Albanian girl run toward the camera in front of a blue screen. She is given a bag of *Tostitos* corn chips to carry as she runs so that, when they add the white kitten later, her arms will be in the right carrying position. Then, the blue screen image is taken into the digital editing room and the village, a bridge for her to run across, and the kitten are added digitally to the image. "Give me some flames," Motss orders the digital editor. "Now the sound of screaming, and the Anne Frank sirens."

The creation of this news bite is the making of a movie within the movie, a metamovie. *Wag the Dog* becomes a movie about making movies, only in this case the movie that is being made is not to entertain the American people but to politically and historically deceive them, to cynically spin their sympathy (the kitten, puhleeze!) toward believing in this nonexistent Albanian war. Winifred, the president's aide, takes one look at this finished news bite that Brean and Motss have created and rejoices: "We can leak that to the press and they can download it."

Immediately upon finishing and leaking their masterpiece to the press, Brean and Winifred are detained and interrogated by CIA Agent Young (William Macy), who, using CIA satellites and on-the-ground sources as proof, insists that "there is no war!" Nonplussed, Brean answers, "Of course there's a war. We're watching it on television." The appearance of war, the TV image, is everything, and the truth is nothing compared to the power of media spin. Brean even cites unimpeachable authorities (though not exactly) to support his version of truth: "As Plato once said, 'It don't matter how the fuck you get there, just so you get there.'"

In *Wag the Dog*'s second act, which focuses completely on the techno-magic and delivery of spin, Motss consistently uses movie imagery to describe the process of creating this "pageant" of spin. As the spinmasters face one last obstacle, how to sell their convict nun-raper to the American public as a hero, Motss spells out both the medium and the message:

> *Motss:* Big Mistake. Big Mistake. You gotta bring him in by stages. Big mistake to reveal Schumann before the election.
> *Winifred:* How so?
> *Motss:* Sweetheart, Schumann is the Shark. OK? Schumann is Jaws. You know. You have to tease 'em. You don't put Jaws in the first reel of the movie. . . . Vote for me Tuesday. Wednesday I produce Schumann.

Earlier when Brean made his definition of spin, all of his allusions were to contemporary history: the Gulf War, Grenada, Vietnam, Iwo Jima. Here, as Motss discourses on the technique of spin, all of his allusions are to film history. He uses *Jaws* (1975), but he could have used rosebud or the incest revelation in *Chinatown* (1974) or the unveiling scene in *The Crying Game* (1992) or Keyser Sose in *The Usual Suspects* (1995). The reason there are two major protagonists in *Wag the Dog*, Brean and Motss, and the reason the audience never sees the president's face or ever learns the president's name is because Hollywood intentionally set out to make an academic study of the theme of nineties spin. Brean is the theorist of spin, Motss is the applied technician of spin, and the president is a nonentity. He doesn't make any difference. If they wanted, Brean and Motss could spin this whole affair in exactly the opposite direction and get Senator Neal (whose name and face the audience ironically, and very cynically, does know) elected president.

In fact, they hold the president, the object and subject of their spin, in complete contempt. They even hate his "Don't get off a horse in midstream" TV commercials. In a totally decentered world in which the president of the United States is a child molester who answers to the code name "Big Bird," Brean and Motss know all along that all they are doing is playing a creative game that (thanks to the power of spin) allows them to create their own fictional worlds and fictional history. Then (thanks to the ravenous appetite of the news media), they can turn those fictions loose on the world as if they were real and true, not simulacra or "language games." At the end of *Wag the Dog*, after the president has been reelected, a political analyst sums up the cynical truth: "89% favorable is based not on the events, just on the spin given to those events."

In the nineties, spin took over, culture became virtual and lost any sense of center, and truth utterly disappeared. History became a feeble attempt to understand events already obliterated by conspiracies and cover-ups. Stanley Motss, at the end of *Wag the Dog*, with a catch in his voice, sums up the ultimate result of the triumph of spin (and Hollywood) over America's political system: "That is a complete fucking fraud and it looks 100% real! It's the best work I've ever done [pause] because it's so honest." The creative energy of spin has completely captivated Stanley, and he decides that he wants to take credit for his masterpiece. Of course, the powers that be can't let him take that credit, so they send the CIA to kill him.

As Motss repeatedly declares in his signature phrase of the film—"This is nothing!"—the power of spin can overcome any obstacle that reality places in the way of its creative energy. Spin is the ultimate metafiction of the nineties, the triumph of the deconstructive imagination. Perhaps Hollywood producer Robert Evans, the man upon whom Hoffman's characterization of Motss is supposedly based, can validly have the last word on *Wag the Dog*. In an interview in 1994, four years before *Wag the Dog*, Evans said, "There are three sides to every story. Yours, mine, and the truth. No one is lying."[9]

## The Press and Spin

This is the way the effects of reality, or if one prefers, the fantasies of realism, multiply.

—Jean-François Lyotard, *Answering the Question: What is Postmodernism?*

But Hollywood wasn't the only spin factory responsible for creating the simulations of history. Willing coconspirators in the ascendance of spin as the dominant cultural force and in the deceptions of power in the nineties were the media, both print journalism and TV news. The days of Ernie Pyle, Edward R. Murrow, and Walter Cronkite were forever over. The days of heroic newsmen filing battlefield reports, of serious public spokesmen examining social injustice, or of just plain, trustworthy voices were things of the past. The romance of the Fourth Estate became no more than a nostalgic memory. Perhaps that romance never really existed. The seriousness and integrity of *All the President's Men* (1976) had always been offset by the cynical satire of the many incarnations of *The Front Page* (1931, 1974), and *His Girl Friday* (1940), full of stupid, venal, uninvolved, sensationalistic, and corrupt newspaper reporters. But in the nineties, the men and women who wrote "the first draft of history" were no longer romantic, serious or funny.

The Fourth Estate had lost its credentials, but so had the network news. "Accurate Reporting. Responsible Coverage," a local nightly news show in 2002 blew their own horn, but before the nineties and the triumph of spin, TV news outlets would not have needed to do that, to protest too much. Their credentials would have been taken for granted. The nineties saw the cynicism of *Network* (1976) and *Broadcast News* (1987) finally fully kick in. One harsh critic of the nineties press charges them with "compassion fatigue" and laments how "the editing of reality goes on at every stage of the news-delivery process."[10] This is not a new or revolutionary perception, but it does underline how the nineties media became accomplices in the spinning of reality set in motion by the decade's power brokers and spinmasters. Were the print and TV media news reporters simply dupes of the spinmasters or were the newspapers and the networks putting out their own form of sensationalistic spin? This is a question that a whole cluster of nineties films attempt to answer.

The answer that surfaced, however, was "that reporters and editors simplify news reports and hype them with flashy headlines and dramatic images to keep audiences interested."[11] This whole portrayal of nineties journalism harks back to the early twentieth-century journalism of William Randolph Hearst and to the subsequent characterization of Charles Foster Kane as a journalist—"I'll take care of the war." John LeCarre in *The Tailor of Panama* offered the same sort of characterization for the nineties: "The Hatry press broke the story. The Hatry press gave it its spin. Hatry television networks spun it a bit harder. Soon every British newspaper across the spectrum had its own Abroxos story."[12] In 1998, this whole process of media spin was never more evident than when the President Clinton/Monica Lewinsky sex scandal broke.

In an article appropriately titled "Spin City," the "media's insatiable appetite for the White House sex scandal (a.k.a. Tailgate, a.k.a. Fornigate, a.k.a. Clinterngate, etc.)," with its clever word plays and leering headlines ("Sex, Lies and the President"),[13] proved the coconspirator charge against the nineties media. And the big winners in this particular episode of "Spin City" were the twenty-four-hour cable news networks, which had only come into existence in the nineties: "CNN's ratings rose more than 40 percent, MSNBC's numbers doubled, and FNC drew six times its usual audience."[14] The news media became the vehicle for Lyotardian "language games" out of which the new narratives of the age of Baudrillardian simulacra were crafted. It was this comfortable symbiosis between the spinmasters and the media that made the nineties the decade of spin. That symbiosis found representation in nineties films that set out to expose, satirize, vilify, and even, once in a while, compliment the media's functioning.

By far the dominant characterization of the nineties media as spinmasters or accomplices to the spinmasters was negative. In the many films that portrayed print or TV journalists at work, the characterizations were overwhelmingly cynical, venal, and even sometimes sinister. Journalists were no longer the searching-for-truth, well-meaning, innocent victims like Joe Frady (Warren Beatty) in *The Parallax View* (1974) or the investigative reporter (Elliott Gould) in *Capricorn One* (1978) or Kimberly Welles (Jane Fonda) in *The China Syndrome* (1979), news men and women trying to see the truth hidden behind elaborate spinmaster frauds. In the nineties, journalists were much closer to the Sid Hudgens (Danny DeVito) of *Hush* magazine model in *L.A. Confidential* (1997).

*Natural Born Killers* (1994), for example, is one of the most poisonous indictments of TV journalism ever. While most critics agreed that the primary text of Oliver Stone's film was a graphic "vision of violence in America," most also recognized its competing subtext, its placing of the blame for this culture of violence upon "the pervasive barbarity of the shock-mongering mass media."[15] Stone took the basic story line and folk heroization theme of a whole subgenre of earlier road films—*Bonnie and Clyde* (1967), *Bad Lands* (1973), *The Sugarland Express* (1974)—and turned up both the stylistic and the textual voltage. *Natural Born Killers*, if it was an op-ed article rather than a movie, would have a subheadline that might shout in the best tabloid style, MURDERERS AND THE MEDIA. One critic duly noted how "the O. J. Simpson case was fortuitously coming into full flower when the movie was released" and its "mass murderers who become media superstars" theme seemed strikingly appropriate.[16]

However, Stone's film is no more than a crazed nineties version of *The Front Page* (which has sensation-seeking newspaper reporters hiding escaped murderers in a rolltop desk or a copy machine) or, even more appropriate, 1976's *Network* in which the first great tabloid TV guru, Howard Beale (Peter Finch), is ultimately assassinated on his own out-of-control network news show. If *Natural Born Killers* fed upon the American obsession with the O. J. Simpson murders, *Network* had its own role model in the Patty Hearst kidnapping by the Symbionese Liberation Army. But while *Natural Born Killers* escalated a historical cynicism toward an increasingly tabloid press in America, it also played off of some very nineties influences.

The nineties was the decade of true-crime TV with shows like *Most Wanted*, *Cops*, and *Greatest Police Chases* garnering huge audiences and sustained popularity. Wayne Gale (Robert Downey Jr.) in *Natural Born Killers* is one of those true-crime TV, Howard Beale-like journalists on a show titled *American Maniacs*, whose whole intention is to spin dysfunctional misfits, deviates, and murderers into folk heroes and media celebrities. "We're satirizing the tabloids," Stone argues. "But it's part of a larger *canvas* of America and crime and the media."[17] Similar to the over-the-top, high-voltage approach of Stone to the theme of the press and the media in America was the similarly over-the-top loopiness of *To Die For* (1995), the network news satire that took the true romance anchorwoman of *Up Close and Personal* (1996) and turned her into a celebrity-driven killer. If Tally Atwater (Michelle Pffiefer) could sleep her way onto the network news, then *To Die For*'s wacky weatherwoman (Nicole Kidman) could kill her way to the top of the TV ranks.

In the nineties, the media set out to spin the news in such a way that it generated large audiences and huge advertising revenues. This strategy worked so well that the spin sometimes spun out of control. The result was not only the idealization of violence but the actual generation of violence itself in the form of copycat crimes and the assassination of on-air personalities. An earlier Stone mediafocused film, *Talk Radio* (1989), perhaps best predicted the nineties fascination with shock media as opposed to the legitimate news media of the preceding decades as in *All the President's Men*'s ideal world. In *Talk Radio*, the belligerent, badgering, aggressive style of its shock-jock central character (Eric Bogosian, who also wrote the original play and script) results in his own assassination as punishment for his hateful tirades.

Less over the top than *Natural Born Killers* or *To Die For* or *Talk Radio* and, therefore, more disturbing because it rings more of truth is the characterization of Max Brackett (Dustin Hoffman) in *Mad City* (1997). A great deal has changed since Dustin Hoffman played Carl Bernstein in *All the President's Men*. In *Mad City*, Hoffman's Brackett has abandoned print journalism and abdicated to the nightly news, which is in the process of abandoning him. When a distraught security guard, Sam Baily (John Travolta), takes a museum curator and a class of schoolchildren hostage, Brackett finds himself in a scoop situation right out of *The Front Page*, *His Girl Friday*, or *Ace in the Hole* (1951). But *Mad City* doesn't play that situation for laughs. It is deadly serious. It portrays TV reporters as "soulless, opportunistic bastards"[18] and offers the "spectre of a powerful medium run amok" and "makes its points with the kind of grim intensity that has always been a Costa-Gavras trademark."[19]

What is unnerving is how *Mad City* makes Brackett, a neurotic, self-serving, heartless weasel, more attractive as a human being and media reporter than the suave, slick, utterly soulless news anchor (Alan Alda) and his amoral, mediawhore, woman intern (Mia Kirshner). Brackett, who spins the Baily hostage story for all of its sensationalistic tabloid exploitation, is supposed to be the good guy, or at least the least bad guy, in this rogue's gallery of nineties media bottom-feeders. *Mad City* is not at all about Baily getting mad and taking hostages in the vain hope of getting his job back. It is not even so much about Brackett's mad scramble to cover the story that has fallen into his lap. It is about the madness of an American media that is hungry to spin every small event into a big event that, for a few hours or a few days, will captivate a TV audience in the way that the Kefauver hearings into organized crime did in the fifties, the coverage of the Kennedy assassination did in the sixties, the Watergate hearings did in the seventies, and the O. J. Simpson and Monica soap operas did in the nineties.

While in *Mad City* the text of the social unfairness of contemporary American society is totally subsumed in the powerful text of media voraciousness and spin, *The Insider*'s (1999) primary text of the crimes and cover-ups of Big Tobacco is counterpointed by the equally self-serving and hypocritical machinations of the scions of *CBS News*, including the seemingly credible *eminence grise* of that network, Mike Wallace of *60 Minutes*. As one commentator writes, "TV journalists aren't repugnant enough to be big villains on screen, but they're serving quite nicely as punching bags."[20]

However, in the James Bond film *Tomorrow Never Dies* (1997), the larger-than-life villain is very much a media man. William Carver (Jonathan Pryce) is a power-crazed media mogul who, in the tradition of William Randolph Hearst and Charles Foster Kane, attempts to start a world war as a way of elevating the ratings for his global news network. Carver is truly a villain of the New World Order. He has invested everything in the premise that power lies only in words and images. His is a very *Wag the Dog* approach to postmodernist life, an approach in which presidents and corporate CEOs and royalty are far outstripped in the halls of power by those who rule the media: the newspapers, radio, television, and computer screens. This approach is postmodernist because it recognizes that power lies in words and images and that power is gained through the ability to spin those words and images to one's advantage. Carver is a refreshingly inventive James Bond villain in that his hardware is less military and more media. Instead of fighting with the guns and tanks and bombs and airplanes of the early Bond films, Carver in *Tomorrow Never Dies* sees the possibility of ruling the world with TV screens, something that Aldous Huxley in *Brave New World* prefigured five decades before.

What so many of these media-focused nineties films have in common is their realization of the utterly failed illusion of objectivity in journalism and the mass media. The spinmasters of global corporatism and political power reinterpret the fragile truth of reality so quickly that, by the time the media writes "the first draft of history," any truth that might have been included has long since been spun out.

## Spin and Counterspin Strategies

You can't tell any story without a message in it. Not that you get up on a soapbox and talk about it.

—Robert Wise, quoted in "'Storm' Breaks the Calm," *Los Angeles Times*

Though the concept of spin ruled the corporate, political, and media representations of reality in nineties culture, Hollywood also realized that motion pictures could serve as an antidote to the power of spin. On December 3, 1997, Vice President Al Gore, soon to be running for president himself, met with representatives of Hollywood's creative community and asked them to stop glamorizing the act of smoking cigarettes in motion pictures. In reply, Screen Actors Guild (SAG) President Richard Masur promised to stress "realistic and thoughtful and not thoughtless or arbitrary" smoking scenes in movies.[21] The strong antitobacco message underlined in the 1999 film *The Insider* was one of the first and most powerful responses to this promise, a case of Hollywood attempting to unspin a harmful message it had promulgated. Across the decade, films would commit their characterizations and story lines to a number of spin and counterspin strategies that would confront, comment upon, educate about, and ultimately take a stand on the major cultural and social issues of the times, like the American presidency, AIDS, or sexual orientation.

But also throughout the decade, from *Basic Instinct* (1992) to Robert Altman's *Short Cuts* (1993) to Paul Thomas Anderson's *Magnolia* (1999), movies presented bleak postmodernist visions of nineties life that emphasized the breakdown of reality and the emptiness of existence in the world of cultural, political, and media spin. The message that so many nineties films present is that of a troubling loss of identity in a world coming apart at the seams. The characters are plagued by the instability of their culture, the dizzying spin of their ambient reality. Writing about Altman's *Short Cuts*, one critic noted that "Altman is more willing than ever before to see America as a society wallowing in confusion, loss, fatally missed connections."[22] If Stone defines the postmodern nineties as a society shattered by violence and conspiracy, Altman defines the nineties in *Short Cuts* as a society that has gotten off the track, has tried to take a shortcut through life, and has gotten lost as a result. By the nineties of *Short Cuts*, peoples' lives are in such disarray and reality has become so totally resistant to the ordering impulses of story that all that is left is improvisation, finding shortcuts from one story line to the next. *Short Cuts* ends with an increasingly common Los Angeles apocalypse, an earthquake. It is LA's constant reminder that, at any moment, the world can split open and fall apart.

Anderson's *Magnolia* also ends in apocalypse, albeit a much less familiar one—a plague of frogs—than Altman's earthquake. Strikingly similar in its structure to *Nashville* (1975), *The Big Chill* (1983), *Grand Canyon* (1991), *Short Cuts*, and the 2006 Best Picture Academy Award winning *Crash*, *Magnolia* turns up the volume and catapults its ensemble of nineties San Fernando Valley misfits, pathetic losers, wasted celebrities, suicidal wives, and degenerate sex exploiters into unreal suspension similar to that of the scuba diver found dead in the top of a tree in the film's opening. *Magnolia*'s characters are all isolated, all plagued by guilt, loneliness, and the inability to love. Therefore, is it such a stretch that the trajectories of their lives should end in one of the biblical plagues of Egypt: torrential frogs?

The lost worlds of films like *Basic Instinct*, *Short Cuts*, *Magnolia*, and *Mulholland Drive* (2001) are further omens of what W. B. Yeats prophesied in his poem "The Second Coming." So many nineties films portray worlds in which "things fall apart; the center cannot hold," worlds in which the individual has lost all identity and wanders in confusion and loneliness.

# CHAPTER 5

# The American President

In a year when post election quibbling reduced our respect for politics to the size of a solitary chad, the Oval Office ironically proved to be an inspiring ground for entertainers. From comics aping real presidents, to an actor conjuring a fictional one, to a standing President playing himself, it's impossible to single out one performer-in-chief.

—Neil Gabler, "The Year That Was," *Entertainment Weekly*

At the end of the nineties decade, only months before the demise of the two-term Clinton presidency, Neal Gabler described what the American presidency had become under the influence of the spin that Bill and Hillary Clinton and Kenneth Starr, assisted by an accommodating American media, created. First describing how Lee Atwater (as campaign manager for the elder Bush whose son would succeed the Clintons as a result of the contested 2000 election) commissioned Clotaire Rapaille, a medical anthropologist, to hold therapy sessions with groups of voters to analyze their most primal associations with the American presidency, Gabler goes on to write, "What he [Rapaille] discovered is that Americans see their president as a kind of 'movie character' whose primary function is to provide 'cheap entertainment' for the country. . . . But the idea that the office of the presidency would become a provender of entertainment, the idea that one of the president's key functions would be to provide the public with a few voyeuristic thrills is a relatively new phenomenon."[1]

What Gabler observed, and what the *Saturday Night Live* mimics mocked during the 2000 election, and what Bill Clinton himself hilariously (and self-reflexively) parodied in his Academy Awards ceremony video portraying the home life of an ex-president complete with packing his wife's brown bag lunches, was the same spin that the Clintons, nineties films, and the American media put on the presidency throughout the decade. Gabler stresses that "the presidency itself has been transformed into a long-running soap opera that the media believe the public want to follow."[2]

Seeing that this particular spin of the president of the United States as our "entertainer-in-chief"[3] was credible, nineties films proved an excellent barometer of the many different degrees of spin that the presidency took during the Clinton era:

> Harrison Ford and Bill Pullman played him as an action hero. Jack Nicholson depicted him as a sniveling Martian appeaser. Michael Douglas portrayed him as the world's most powerful boyfriend.
>
> There's John Travolta's Clinton clone in *Primary Colors*, Jeff Bridges' zestful chief executive in the current *The Contender* and Martin Sheen's no-nonsense boss on *The West Wing*, among dozens of portrayals.
>
> Whatever the reason—saturation news coverage, an obsession with celebrity, President Clinton's personality, White House scandals—the past eight years have been a fertile time for Hollywood explorations of the presidency.[4]

This listing of the various simulations of the Clinton presidency underscore both Jean Baudrillard's and Jean-François Lyotard's discomfort with and ultimate rejection of the slippery concept of reality in the late twentieth century.[5] Even before these film and television simulacra of Clinton appeared, the Clinton presidency and Clinton himself had already been spun out of reality. The "language games"[6] of the political spinmasters had found in Bill Clinton a marvelously malleable subject. And so, when the movie and television media started creating Bill Clinton characters, those characters were already doomed to be simulations of a simulation.

Why did Americans spend so much money at the box office during the nineties to see movies about presidents? Writer-director Rod Lurie speculates that "before Clinton came around, there was a certain mystification of the president. . . . Clinton has demystified it,"[7] and Gilbert Robinson, of the Center for the Study of the Presidency, agrees with Gabler that "when you get all that news coverage, some of it is like soap operas."[8] Some historians compare the Clintonesque regular guy/soap opera spin to the similar spin of the John F. Kennedy era "by family and friendly historians to manufacture a hero. . . . 'An awful lot of people don't want to know the truth,' [historian Thomas C.] Reeves says, 'They desperately want heroes.'"[9] In the case of Bill Clinton, what America desperately wanted was a president who was just one of the guys.

Introducing a complete magazine issue whose theme was titled "Person and Persona: The Presidential Balancing Act," editor Kerry Temple writes, "Leader of the free world. The most powerful man on earth. Able to launch missile attacks around the globe. Whose every move (almost) is accompanied by 'Hail to the Chief,' stage-directed by Secret Service agents, photographed by chroniclers, explained by spin doctors, analyzed by pundits and investigated by special counsel, only to be dredged up later by old friends and enemies and historians."[10] Thus Temple eloquently lists the many layers of spin that an American president endures daily, but this special magazine issue also maps the past history of presidential persona spinning—George Washington as the general on horseback, Old Hickory Andrew Jackson, William Henry Harrison as a log cabin dweller, Honest Abe Lincoln, Roughrider Teddy Roosevelt, heroic family man JFK—until it arrives at the unique (very postmodernist) personas of Ronald Reagan and Bill Clinton. In the eighties of Reagan and the nineties of Clinton, the idea of "entertainer-in-chief" arises: "For Ronald Reagan, being the president was, indeed, playing a role—a public performance that advanced his administration's agenda. His 'big picture' priorities often seemed to come from the reassuring, good-defeats-evil scripts of the big screen."[11] Bill Clinton encounters the same situation. David Maraniss in *The Clinton Enigma* describes a very Baudrillardian president: "With Clinton, the tension between reality and image, between what he is and what he wants to be, is so relentless that over the years it became habitual for him to withhold information—justifiably or not."[12] The American president "playing a role" and operating "between reality and image" captures well the postmodernist dislocation from reality of both Reagan and Clinton.[13]

The Reagan and the Clinton dilemmas (or solutions) of the real person being subsumed in the persona was one of the major contributors to the evolution of nineties culture into the decade of spin. As Robert Schmuhl writes, "Today the best a president and his staff can try to do is 'spin' or manipulate their version of events in the most favorable way, with the results of such efforts enormously unpredictable. . . . Language functions as both shield and sword, defensive and offensive weapons, as he tries to protect himself politically and personally."[14] While this commentator seems to view presidential spin as some sort of instinctual defense mechanism or protective coloration, a weapon of panic or reaction, the presidential deployment of the mechanisms and strategies of spin were really much more sophisticated and polished by the nineties, based on commissioned demographic (extensive polling) and psycho-anthropological (like Rapaille's) research. Again, Gabler analyzes why and how the phenomenon of spin became the governing force in American presidential politics: "One can understand why Americans, having gotten their bread, now want their circuses. . . . Now, by the new politics of entertainment, the presidency has become the circus, the media are the ringmasters and we all sit in the bleachers clapping, stamping and cheering for the show to go on."[15]

While Gabler employs a Roman metaphor, the world of the Bill Clinton presidency can be even more accurately represented by a more contemporary, postmodernist metaphor—that of the Bakhtinian carnivalesque. The carnivalesque is that magical time of excess when the public persona can be shed and a persona of anonymity can take to the crowded celebratory streets in search of adventure.[16] As the master of spin, Bill Clinton as president wrapped himself in the identity-obscuring domino of the medieval carnival as a means of simultaneously indulging, concealing, justifying, and denying his personal sexual license while reserving the right to continually return by the light of day to the power suits and limousines and waving, smiling, speechmaking conventions of the American presidency.

## The Presidential Carnivalesque

This campaign confirms that Clinton, while unique, was not a one-time deal. He is the forerunner and pioneer of a slick, cynical new age in which politics is dominated by hired gun hucksters, the ad salesmen who run television stations and networks and an overly complacent, self-regarding media . . .

While this campaign spun, terrorists blew up an American warship, oil prices soared, a small war raged between Israel and Palestine, Europe's unified currency swooned, Indonesia unraveled further, democracy broke out in Serbia. The candidates avoided discussing any of these events in detail or substance.

—Jim Hoagland, "Clinton's legacy? Campaigns by spinmeisters for empty suits," *Washington Post*

Jim Hoagland's *Washington Post* column on the 2000 election campaigns of George W. Bush and Al Gore, headlined "Clinton's legacy? Campaigns by spinmeisters for empty suits," was one of the more prophetic commentaries on that campaign—in the receding Clinton world and the wannabe worlds of Bush and Gore, the American presidency was the centrifuge that spun out all the various versions of nineties reality.

While the nineties was a decade of spin, it was also a decade of dysfunction, the dance of chaos masking the breakdown of integrity. America had always been fascinated with the kinds of family, marital, and sexual dysfunction acted out in its afternoon soap operas, but, in the nineties, dysfunction became a multimedia carnival. America's voyeuristic hunger for dysfunctional human beings and families was fed by *The Roseanne Show* on TV, the O. J. Simpson trial, *Real People* and all the subsequent so-called reality-TV shows leading up to the incredibly grotesque ABC game show *Who Wants to Marry a Multi-Millionaire* and cable-TV's *The Osbournes*. Ultimately, the public dysfunction of the nation's first family, headed by "a President who proudly confesses his own and his family's shortcomings with a candor (and compulsiveness) never before seen in a White House occupant,"[17] took center stage.

Not only did the Clinton White House admit to and constantly spin its dysfunction, creating a very fluid reality for its media mystified audience, it constantly courted the presence and approval of those American symbols of spun reality, the biggest stars of the Hollywood community. Barbra Streisand became such a frequent visitor to the Clinton White House that the press gave her the nickname "Beltway Barbra." Television producers Harry Thomason and his wife Linda Bloodworth-Thomason were the Hollywood insiders closest to the Clintons. Steven Spielberg, Billy Crystal, Sam Waterston, Liza Minnelli, Michael Douglas, Richard Dreyfuss, Sarah Jessica Parker, Warren Beatty, and Annette Bening all visited Clinton in Washington. Waterston and Douglas would actually play the American president in nineties films, and Dreyfuss and Beatty would play presidential candidates. Since the very beginning of his campaign for office in the early nineties, Clinton had confessed his admiration for John Kennedy and had emphasized the similarities between JFK and himself. However, when President Clinton in 1993 dined with reigning nineties blond sex symbol Sharon

Stone, the *déjà vu* qualities of the Kennedy/Clinton simulacra became painfully obvious.[18] But Bill Clinton just didn't seem to care. That disregard for convention, that indulgence in sexual license, was the one quality of his presidency that linked it most closely to the paradigm of the carnivalesque.

For a Bill Clinton, a "Bubba" from a poor, southern, rural background who had jumped through all of the Georgetown, Yale, Oxford political hoops to rise to the powerful yet totally surveilled and thus restricted position of president of the United States, the enticements of the carnivalesque—the anonymity bestowed by the domino, the uncritiqued feasting, the total sexual freedom—provided that other world where he could function as a human being rather than as the leader of the free world. Spin became the vehicle that transported Bill Clinton between his two worlds, allowing him to move in and out of the surveillant light and the carnivalesque shadows. Bill Clinton's time in office was much like that which Dickens created in his novel *Hard Times*. There, the world of the circus (read: Hollywood stars, bimbo eruptions, saxophone solos) served to balance the relentless public duty and responsibility of Gradgrindian Utilitarianism (read: Kenneth Starr and the watchdogs of the Christian Right).

Dominick LaCapra defines the carnivalesque in terms of its doubleness: "'carnivalization' is an engaging process of interaction through which seeming opposites—body and spirit, work and play, positive and negative, high and low, seriousness and laughter—are related to each other in an ambivalent, contestatory interchange that is both literally and figuratively 're-creative.'"[19] Each of those oppositions can be applied to the relentlessly spun persona of President Clinton. His indulgence of his bodily appetites, his playfulness and quickness with a smile or a laugh, and his low birth and common-man tastes were all aspects of Clinton that made him attractive to the American people as their "performer-in-chief." Yet he was the president of the United States. He held the highest position in the land, and he engaged it with a positive can-do spirit, a rigorous work ethic, and a seriousness that made him a quite successful chief executive. These contradictory elements in the Clinton persona are exactly the qualities that made him such a fascinating and attractive subject for Hollywood portrayal. Movies are the art form that consistently attempts to recreate the fluid, ever-changing carnival of modern culture. George Bush the elder was also the president of the United States in the nineties, but no movies were made during the decade with a presidential character resembling him. George Bush the elder never exhibited the complexity of the Clinton persona, didn't possess the performative talent necessary in a postmodern president to entertain the American people, and wasn't qualified to star in a vehicle that could be described as *The Presidency: The Movie*.

But, if Clinton did have the presidential star power that JFK and Ronald Reagan had first brought to the White House, the presidential persona that the movies brought to the American people was still a diverse and multidimensional figure. Nineties film presents a montage of presidential personas. As spin constantly circumvents one text for the temporary emphasis upon another, or chooses between competing texts or even creates fantasy texts out of real texts, so too do the movies of the nineties create images of the American presidency in terms of a wide variety of diverse texts. "Hail to the Chiefs," one headline remarked on the abundance of actors playing presidents in American movies in the nineties.[20] But above all, it was Clinton who succeeded (by virtue of his ability to master the power of spin) in carnivalizing the office of the American presidency and fulfilling the social desire for a consistently entertaining performer-in-chief starring in an ongoing national soap opera.

Nobody was, perhaps, more qualified to comment upon the performative role of the American president in the nineties than Jack Valenti, chairman of the Motion Picture Association of America (MPAA) and former speechwriter for President Lyndon Johnson. Valenti describes the American presidency in terms very similar to those that Gabler uses: "Hollywood and Washington spring from the same DNA. Both attract those who like the glamorous life, are always on stage, and are willing to read from scripts written by someone else."[21] In the Clinton presidency, as in the afternoon soap operas, those scripts were mostly about sex.

The year 1998 was the most climactic year, so to speak, for the subject of the American presidency and sex. The publication of the *Starr Report*, which graphically described President Clinton's West Wing affair with White House intern Monica Lewinsky, stirred up interest in four opportunistically reissued books on presidential sex (including the foibles of the standing president). That year, the Lewinsky affair also stimulated the box offices for two eerily Clintonesque movies, *Wag the Dog* and *Primary Colors* (1998). With titles like *White House: Confidential, Sex Lives of the Presidents, The Dysfunctional President,* and *Presidential Sex,*[22] this flood of tabloid-like presidential sex exposés clearly signaled the voyeuristic feeding frenzy that the Lewinsky scandal (and all the other scandals of the Clinton history) had triggered. No less than six women—Gennifer Flowers, Paula Jones, Monica Lewinsky, Kathleen Willey, Dolly Kyle Browning, Juanita Broaddrick—had gone public with accusations against President Clinton of sexual misconduct ranging from groping to oral sex to sexual assault and even to rape. Certainly, the media fed this frenzy, but both Kenneth Starr and the Clinton White House also fed the media. On the topic of the president's sex life, in 1998 the phenomenon of spin was in full whirl. With every "bimbo eruption" that was reported, the Clinton attack dogs struck back at the accusers to deflect the mud from hitting the president and splatter it back upon its slingers. Flowers had been accused of taking "cash for trash," Paula Jones was "trailer trash," Monica Lewinsky a "stalker," Kathleen Willey a liar, and Dolly Kyle Browning a cheater on her income tax (imagine that!). The basic spin strategy of the Clinton White House was a lot like the grade-schooler's taunt, "I'm rubber and you're glue. Everything bounces off of me and sticks to you." When *Primary Colors* was released, one commentator wrote, "Current events may end up taking control of the movie . . . there really is no way *Primary Colors* can distance itself from the tawdry real-life White House allegations currently running amok in the media."[23]

*Primary Colors*, Mike Nichols's and Elaine May's film based on a 1996 *roman à clef* novel by Anonymous (a.k.a. Joe Klien), is the one film that best understood the dynamics of spin and carnival in the Clinton presidency. It has Bill and Hillary, all the staffers, the press, and even the American people in that zany and troubling moment in political history down pat. But it is much more than a triumph of mimicry or historical accuracy. *Primary Colors* is a complex and holographically layered[24] construction of issues, images, and ideas that comment on the state of American presidential politics at the dawn of the twenty-first century. *Primary Colors* is an anatomy of spin set in the continuously carnivalesque world of public and private performativity that characterized the 1992 Clinton run for the presidency.

Early in *Primary Colors*, southern Governor Jack Stanton (John Travolta), running for the Democratic presidential nomination, visits an adult literacy program. After listening to the touching story of a black short-order cook who has just learned to read, Jack takes the stage and performs. He tells the equally sad story of his World War II war hero Uncle Charlie who became a useless recluse after the war because he couldn't read and he didn't want anyone to know it. Ironically, when new campaign staffer Henry Burton (Adrian Lester), a conservative young yuppie idealist (based on Clinton staffer George Stephanopoulos) and the grandson of a great black sixties civil rights leader, walks into the campaign party moments later, the second person he meets (after Jack's media consultant) is a smiling Uncle Charlie who laughs and winks, "Well, I'm Uncle Charlie. Whatever else he says, he's the master." Jack's story was a pure fiction spun to fit the situation and performed to sentimental perfection.

That is what *Primary Colors* repeatedly does so well; it takes real issues, like adult literacy, and uses them as a stage upon which Jack can perform. Jack is not averse to using his Uncle Charlie, his mama, or anything he can spin in his favor out of his personal experience to get people to like him, to give him their votes. In a barbecue restaurant, Susan Stanton (Emma Thompson), Jack's lawyer wife and campaign partner (based on Hillary Clinton, of course), looks on in disgust with Henry as Jack and his cronies indulge in what she calls a "mamathon." Echoing a line from *Citizen Kane*, she puts husband Jack in quite clear perspective when she tells Henry, "Your grandfather was a great man. Jack Stanton could also be a great man if he weren't such a faithless, thoughtless, disorganized, undisciplined shit!" Yet despite her clear-sightedness about her husband's flawed character, she nonetheless accepts his rampant infidelity and soldiers on as the foulmouthed architect of his campaign and career.

Besides adult literacy, *Primary Colors* gives Jack the issues of factory closings, the loss of jobs, education for people stuck in dead end jobs, and negative political campaigning to use as stages for his performances. At the very center of the movie is a quiet night scene in a donut shop where Jack sits talking to the counter man and eating donuts after jogging (typically Clintonesque). The scene emphasizes Jack's understanding for the plight of the working poor, the under classes, "the folks" as he calls them. Unlike all the phoniness of the persona that Jack and Susan are trying so hard to create, Henry sees a glimpse of the real Jack in this donut shop meditation. Nichols's direction and May's script use occasional scenes like this one to define the double natures of Stanton and Clinton and probably all politicians in the nineties. The spun persona and the real human being contend for space within the candidate. In the end, the spun persona must inevitably take over and evict the real person. "Keep the folks in your mind. It's about them," Henry pleads to Jack in the donut shop. "It's about history." Henry had made the same plea earlier to Susan when she asked him, in a similar night scene, "So, why are you here? Tell me. It's four in the morning. Let's just tell the truth."

Henry's answer is thoughtful, idealistic, and politically incorrect in the sense that, given the ascendant arc of spin in political life, the possibilities of telling the truth are slim to none:

> *Henry:*  OK. Well, I was always curious about how it would be to work with some-
> one who actually cared about people. I mean, it couldn't always have been the
> way it is now. It must have been very different when my grandfather was alive.
> Well, hey, you were there. You had Kennedy. I didn't. I've never heard a Presi-
> dent use words like "destiny" and "sacrifice" without thinking *bullshit*! And,
> OK, maybe it was bullshit with Kennedy too, but people believed it. And, I
> guess, that's what I want. I want to believe it. I want of be a part of something
> that's history.
> *Susan:*  History's what we're about too. What else is there?
> *Henry:*  I've never helped run a Presidential Campaign before.
> *Susan:*  Neither have we, but that's how history is made, Henry, by first timers.

Jack in the donut shop and Susan and Henry in their late night soul searching show a clear understanding of the poles between which they and their campaign are spinning, but the sad reality of this film is that they can't do anything about it. They are caught in the vortex of political spin, and all they can do is try to control it because they can never escape it. "You can't run for President of the United Fucking States without CNN," Jack screams when his campaign front man rents a motel room without cable TV. After Henry burns his tongue on some hot tea, Susan pointedly says, "That's the real thing experience teaches you, isn't it? How not to get burned." Susan's reflection signals another whole dimension of political spin that *Primary Colors* dissects—damage control. Spin, as a Lyotard-ian "language game" or as a targeted political strategy, can be either proactive or reactionary. In the case of Jack in *Primary Colors* and Clinton in the sad, real life of American politics, it was almost always reactive to some damaging disclosure of past or present sexual transgressions.

In *Wag the Dog*, the elaborate damage control of creating the illusion of a war distracted from a president's statutory rape of a girl scout. In *Primary Colors* the damage control is in reaction to events less sensational but equally more human, tawdry, and stupid, mainly Jack's Clintonesque "bimbo eruptions." The main assertion of the overwhelming power of spin in American political life in *Primary Colors* is the character of Libby Holden (Kathy Bates), based on Clinton troubleshooter Betsy Wright, whose job it is to investigate Jack's past and find out what the opposition might have ready to throw at him so that Jack and Susan and all the Stanton political strategists can figure out how to spin the mud back

at the mudslingers. Richard Gemmings (Billy Bob Thornton), Jack's main political strategist (a dead-on-portrayal of Clinton's James Carville) calls for Libby
when he advises, "We need to hire an operative to do research . . . to investigate
everything. Everything anybody can make an allegation about." Libby, tongue
in cheek, characterizes herself as a comic book superheroine: "Call me the dustbuster. I'm stronger than dirt." But Richard is not amused. He knows that Libby's
special kind of personal research is essential to the effectiveness of spin and warns
Jack and Susan: "You're putting the whole campaign in her hands." In other
words, spin is everything.

When the first crisis hits the Stanton campaign, the revelation that Jack had
his arrest at the Democratic National Convention in 1968 covered up by no less
a villain than Mayor Richard Daley, the whole campaign team sags in despair.
"We're fucked," Richard laments. "Now they're all gonna come after us. It's gonna
be the war thing, the drug thing, and the woman thing" (the exact map of the
Clinton secret history). But Libby, the dustbuster, rides in to the rescue toting a
huge handgun, intimidating everyone with her ingeniously creative foul mouth,
and finding out the truth so that it can be skillfully spun into a tissue of lies that
will benefit the Stanton campaign. When the first bimbo, with the great name of
Cashmere McCloud (based on Flowers), erupts, Libby declares, "She's the tip of
the iceberg. He's poked his pecker in some sorry trash bins."

In fact, from this point on, the bulk of *Primary Colors* is made up of scenes that
can only be characterized as spin sessions, debates in which all the different possibilities for spinning the simple factual reality are explored and a final spin strategy
is decided upon. In these scenes, the participating strategists are no more than
screenwriters scripting a performance for a movie actor. Actually, these scenes are
reminiscent of the writing sessions of the joke staff on the old Dick Van Dyke
TV show of the sixties, only these meetings are no joke. They are deadly serious
efforts at changing the nature and meaning of reality and manipulating the moral
significance of human action for political gain. In other words, these spin sessions
are clearly dedicated not to making history but to controlling history.

As *Primary Colors* proceeds, the Stanton campaign registers a number of spin
victories, but then the fickle gods of spin turn upon Jack, Susan, and the campaign's clever spinmasters. As the campaign proceeds toward election day, the
film's whole discourse of spin changes from a playful game of dirty tricks (like
tapping Larry King's cell phone and making a phony incriminating tape of him)
to a life-and-death (literally) moral battle within Jack. The chosen vehicle for
the film's exploration of the dangers of spin when it gets out of control is the
very real nineties political discourse issue of negative campaigning. At first, Jack
is totally against going negative in any way: "I'm not going to go negative. Any
jackass can burn down a barn." When he is criticized by his staff for not hitting
back at the negative campaigning of others, he argues, "I don't want to give that
son of a bitch the power to make me the son of a bitch." But as the campaign
progresses and Jack is attacked more and more, as Libby has to bust more and
more dust, Jack's attitude changes. When his opponent falls behind in the Florida
primary and starts running anti-Stanton ads that carry the slogan "It's All About

Character," Jack, to the cheers of his assembled staff, declares belligerently (and, unbeknownst to all of them, prophetically), "I'm gonna kill him." So, when the opponent calls in to a radio talk show to ambush Jack on the air, Jack strikes back with his first personal negative attack of the campaign. Unfortunately, the opponent, still holding the phone, has a massive heart attack and dies. Spin has turned lethal.

Ironically, despite their chagrin at this death and their withdrawal of all the negative ads from their campaign, Jack and Susan don't learn any lessons about the destructive power of spin. The lesson to be learned is, instead, delivered by a new voice that enters the discourse of the film at this point, Governor Picker (Larry Hagman) who takes over for Jack's dead opponent at the widow's request. On *The Larry King Show*, Picker shocks the political world by declaring, "I'm not gonna do any TV spots. I'm not gonna pay any pollsters." Then, in his first major campaign speech, Picker delivers the first half of *Primary Colors*'s message about spin and American politics. He quiets the cheering, chanting crowd, then thoughtfully says,

> I really mean it. I wish everyone would just calm down. This is a terrific country and sometimes we go a little crazy, and that is part of our greatness, part of our freedom. But if we don't watch out and calm down, it all just spins out of control. You know, the world is getting more and more complicated and politicians have to explain things to you in simpler terms so that they can get their little oversimplified explanations on the evening news. And eventually, instead of even trying to explain things, they just give up and start slinging mud at each other. And it's all to keep you excited, keep you watchin', like you'd watch a car wreck or a wrasslin' match. As a matter of fact, that's exactly what it's like, professional wrestling. It's staged and it's fake and it doesn't mean anything. And that goes for the debates. We don't hate our opponents. Hell, half the time we don't even know them. But it seems it's the only way we know to keep you all riled up. So what I wanna do in this campaign is to quiet things down and start having a conversation on what we want this country to be in the next century.

Delivered by a new and different, quieter voice amidst the contending voices in the film, what this speech does is not only define the mastertext of the film as an anatomy of spin but also defines America and American politics as a textbook carnivalesque society of staged, fake, phony, yet infinitely lively, entertaining, and watchable spectacles in which the president is the entertainer-in-chief. Picker's speech, coming near the end of the film, is comparable to Gordon Gecko's (Michael Douglas) greasily powerful and venally moving "Greed is good" speech near the end of Oliver Stone's *Wall Street* (1987). Picker's speech portrays America, Americans, and American politics with truth and accuracy. In the guise of a good and moral man (and candidate), he exposes the huge conspiracy of spin that has taken over American politics and he resolves to take that phony spin out of his campaign. But he can't do it.

Unfortunately, the second half of *Primary Colors*'s message about spin and American politics is delivered by Jack and Susan. They send Libby out to get the goods on Governor Picker, and she does. "But this has every fucking thing, sex, drugs, corruption," she reports back to the spinmasters, hoping that they won't use the dirt that she has dug up. But they don't even hesitate:

*Jack:* (reading Libby's file) This is remarkable. How on earth did he ever think he was gonna get away with this? Now what do we do with this?
*Susan:* The Times. No. *The Wall Street Journal*, maybe more authoritative in a way. Through an intermediary. Certainly no one associated with the campaign.

The tragedy of Jack and Susan's unhesitating embrace of this dirty information lies in their chilling nonchalance. The fact is that there is no question whatsoever about what they are going to do with this devastating dirt, no discussion at all about any of the moral issues it raises, just the cold logistical details of how it is going to be spun out into the cesspool of American politics. As one commentator wrote, "There is one implicit message in the movie that is ultimately disheartening: At this point in the evaluation of American politics, every likely candidate has a dark past just waiting to be revealed. It is only a question of when and by whom."[25] As Jack says to Governor Picker when he tells him that they have the goods on his past life, "if they think it will sell one newspaper, yes," the press will print it no matter how sordid or destructive.

When Jack and Susan deliver *Primary Colors*'s message about spin, it portrays spin as a reality so powerful in American politics that everyone involved must live with it, practice it, try to control it, rise, or fall with it. As critic Lisa Schwarzbaum recognizes, "In the syncopated rhythms of Stanton's morally chaotic pace and Picker's statesmanlike amble lies a really deep and subtle political story."[26] In American politics, in the spinning vortex that lies between idealism and pragmatism, persona and person, morality and winning, the first things to get lost are truth and honor.

The last words of the film characterize a president much like Clinton who really cares little for history, who has trained himself, steeled himself, persuaded himself that he can live and survive in the nineties world of morally decentered spin, and has found a way (to paraphrase Joseph Conrad's *Lord Jim*) to "immerse" himself "in the destructive element." The only problem with being comfortable within the centrifugal spin of American politics is that the more you spin, the more your hold on reality breaks down. Jack captures this breakdown in the last speech of *Primary Colors*: "This is hardball. . . . This is it, Henry. This is the price you pay to lead. You don't think that Abraham Lincoln was a whore before he was a President? He had to tell his little stories then smile his shit-eating, backcountry grin, and he did it just so that he would one day have the opportunity to stand in front of the nation and appeal to the better angels of our nature. And that's where the bullshit stops." And that is also why, ultimately, *Primary Colors* is such a sad story—because it is true, because it is accurate, and because it understands the sad reality. Spin has completely taken over the world of American politics and changed it forever. In an essay titled "The Faking of the President," Benjamin Svetkey asks, "What happens when life starts to look a lot like art?"[27] *Primary*

*Colors* presents an extremely clear-sighted, cynical, and true answer to that question: that's when you know that spin has taken over.

*Primary Colors* is the utterly cynical, slick, polished culmination and lexicon of a distinct grammar of visual images, motifs, scenes, characters, and spin strategies that evolved throughout the nineties for the articulation of the American political situation. One commentator referred to the Clinton years as the "Postmodern Presidency."[28] At least two important films preceded *Primary Colors* that contributed to the visual grammar of that definitive film, the D. A. Pennebaker/Chris Hegedus behind-the-scenes documentary of the 1992 Clinton campaign, *The War Room* (1993), and the potentially perceptive but ultimately trivial *Speechless* (1994). From *The War Room*, *Primary Colors* got two of its most riveting characters, James Carville (Richard Gemmings as played by Billy Bob Thornton) and George Stephanopoulos (Henry Burton as played by Adrian Lester), its most dominant recurring scene (the staff spin session), and its recurrent imagery (TV screens, fast food, hand shaking). From *Speechless*, *Primary Colors* got its insomniac drive, its emphasis upon issues and gimmicks as vehicles for candidate performances, and all the same visual imagery of spin that *The War Room* had introduced as the reigning grammar of nineties politics.

*Primary Colors* opens with a series of extreme close-ups of the presidential candidate shaking hands. It is a clearly symbolic opening, representing the ideal political goal of connecting with the voters, reaching out to them, and touching them in a way that will make them believe you, trust you, and vote for you. Throughout the film, the first image of almost every scene in which presidential candidate Jack Stanton appears in public is a handshake. Ironically, as the marriage of Jack and his wife Susan progressively deteriorates due to the revelations of his infidelities, this opening imagery of hands touching becomes a fake, a lie, a mere empty image performed for the manipulative purposes of spin. In a televised news conference to deny the sexual allegations of Cashmere McCloud, the married couple sits together on the sofa holding hands, but as soon as the red light on the camera blinks off, Susan rips her hand out of her husband's and stalks angrily off the set.

Perhaps the most ubiquitous recurring image in *Primary Colors* (as it was in both *The War Room* and *Speechless*) is that of television screens, often shown in close-up prior to a widening or expanding out of the shot to reveal the campaign staffers eagerly watching to gauge the results of their efforts. The TV screen is the ultimate projector and arbiter of political spin. Thus, it is no wonder that all the candidates and campaign staffers in these films are perpetually glued to their TV sets in campaign headquarters, in rented motel rooms, in airports, in bars, in hotel lobbies. The evening news and the talk shows are the infrastructure, the streets and highways of spin that the politicians must travel every day.

One of the funniest, smallest, imagistic touches in both *Primary Colors* and *The War Room* is the Clintonesque appetite for donuts. Throughout the film, Jack never meets a donut he doesn't like. One of the pivotal scenes of the film takes place in a donut shop late at night right after Jack has finished jogging.

The recurring presence of the donuts represent wife Susan's (and presumably Hillary's) major complaint about her husband's character, his lack of discipline. It is this flaw, when it takes form in terms of another appetite, Jack's sexual proclivities, that poses the greatest challenge to the powers of spin in the campaign.

One commentator, however, notes an aspect of spin in *The War Room* that *Primary Colors* fails completely to portray. The spinmasters in *Primary Colors* spend all their time creating reactive spin to deflect the negative effect of Jack's sexual infidelities, but, as Owen Gleiberman notes, "Carville emerges in *The War Room* as a star and, indeed, a hero . . . because the feisty intensity of his desire to *get* George Bush—to string him up in public by his own failed presidency—redefines spin control as a genuinely democratic act."[29]

*Speechless* is a different kind of nineties spin movie from both *Primary Colors* and *The War Room*. Though it is the first film to represent the Clinton spin world and is based on the real-life romance of James Carville and Mary Matalin (who actually coined the phrase "bimbo eruptions" and were the competing spinmasters for Clinton, the Democratic candidate, and Bush, the Republican incumbent president in the '92 campaign), *Speechless* never attains the believability or the credibility to make any sort of real social statement about the phenomenon of spin and its effect on American politics. Instead, *Speechless* opts to be a weak imitation of the political screwball comedies of the forties like *His Girl Friday* (1940) and *Adam's Rib* (1949). Like all the other campaign films, *Speechless* has its spin strategy sessions, its debate performances, its TV screens eagerly monitored, but it has no real issues like adult literacy or jobs, no real politicians like Bill and Hillary Clinton to portray, and no powerful spinmasters who really know what they're doing. *Speechless* is aware of the dark side of political spin but simply doesn't want to descend into that particular heart of darkness.

Kevin Valek (Michael Keaton) and Julia Mann (Geena Davis) are the two competing speechwriters who meet during the New Mexico senatorial campaign. There lies the first problem with *Speechless*. Not much is at stake. The film doesn't attempt to make a national statement on the presidency even though its plot is inspired by a presidential campaign. A second problem with *Speechless*'s credibility is that its vehicle issues for the campaign are fake and ill defined, unlike the very real issues discussed in *Primary Colors*. The main issue of *Speechless* is something called the Mexico Ditch. "Our guy's for it. Don't bring it up in the barrio," Annette (Bonnie Bedelia), the campaign manager and also Kevin's ex-wife, tells him when he joins the speechwriting team. "I'll bet our opponent does," Kevin protests, having already discussed the Mexico Ditch issue with Julia though he doesn't know that she is also a speechwriter for the opposing camp. "Interesting," Annette answers. "Spin it our way. Garvin'll [their candidate] love ya." That, however, is about as complex or in depth as any discourse about or representation of theme of spin in *Speechless*.

One thing that *Speechless* does contribute to the discourse of these presidential spin movies is the importance and imagery of television screens as the main visual grammar of political success or failure. In a well-conceived comic montage, the film crosscuts from Kevin and Julia writing the words in the isolation of their rooms to the candidates delivering the speeches and totally botching the words on the television screens as the writers watch and cringe. Ironically, after one of these badly delivered speeches, Annette, judging her candidate the winner in the exchange, jumps off her barstool and shouts, "Yes! Doctor Spin!" as she gives Kevin a high five and introduces him to the rest of the staff with the words, "Our resident genius. Great speech, Kevin." At another point in the film, the head speechwriter on Julia's team says, "Julia, okay, it's time for happy hour with the press. Listen, Wannamaker [her candidate] wasn't sounding too good on the debate issue. We've gotta spin it." But though the concept of spin is mentioned a number of times in this film, it is never really explored, its intricate workings never engaged, and its use and effect never judged.

The closest thing to a critique of the political process in *Speechless* comes in an exchange between Kevin and Julia on how they got into the political speechwriting business in the first place. "I was a speechwriter before, but then I found that I believed in my words more than the candidate did," Kevin says. In response to Kevin's argument that "campaigns are about one thing and one thing alone. Winning," Julia disagrees: "No. They're about changing the world. I hate that. I hate how people treat it like it's a game. Like it's all some race with winners and losers. What we do affects people and people who do anything to win will do anything to keep on winning." Julia's stance here objects to the cynical pragmatism of Kevin and occasions a very typical reaction in terms of the grammar of nineties spin politics. "I haven't heard anyone talk like that in a long time," Kevin answers. Like his counterparts in *Primary Colors*, Kevin reverts nostalgically to a lost golden age of past political idealism.

The last scene of *Primary Colors* defines the dark, cynical vision that the Clinton spin machine brought to his postmodern presidency. In the last scene, Jack and Susan, the supposedly happily married president and First Lady, he in his tuxedo and she in her red designer ball gown, dance gracefully through the red, white, and blue balloons at their inaugural ball to the Tennessee Waltz, victorious, triumphant, and therefore justified. When you have seen *The War Room* and *Primary Colors* and have come to know how the Clinton spin machine manipulated reality and changed American politics forever, this dance scene causes a sort of sick, sinking feeling, triggering the realization that these candidates lied and treated the American people with utter contempt and yet WE STILL VOTED FOR THEM and THEY STILL WON! The dance at the end of *Primary Colors* isn't a symbol of victory and honestly earned celebration, but rather an ironic image of the triumph of cynicism. That dance isn't a graceful whirling of a beloved partner, but the symbol of the skillful spinning of a successful tissue of lies.

## The Clinton Apologists

Director Rob Reiner and screenwriter Aaron Sorkin [of *The American President* (1995)] . . . have devised a very '90s concept, a love story for the age of spin control.
—Owen Gleiberman, "Executive Action," *Entertainment Weekly*

In 2000, a new network TV show, *The West Wing*, caught on immediately. Set in the White House and created by Aaron Sorkin, it was a drama series cut almost wholly out of the extremely popular cloth of Sorkin's 1995 movie *The American President*. Even some of *The West Wing* actors, principally Martin Sheen playing liberal President Jed Bartlet and later Joshua Malina playing Bartlet's speechwriter, were carryovers from the movie as were also the main Oval Office set and almost all the characters and their characterizations. It even got its title from the film's central character, who at one point says, "I'm more of a West Wing President." Coming on the television scene contiguously with the disputed Gore-Bush election of 2000, *The West Wing* became a positive Wednesday night refuge for Americans discouraged by the fallen state of American politics post-Clinton and circa Bush the younger. As one *West Wing*er put it, "Every Wednesday night they can pretend they have a real President," and as the show's promo pitched, "watch the critically acclaimed show that has the one President we all agree on."[30] *The West Wing*, coming at the turn of the millennium, and the earlier *The American President* were so popular and touched such a sensitive chord for American audiences and because they both gave America the kind of president that Clinton could have been. As apologias for the Clinton White House, *The American President*'s Andrew Shepherd (Michael Douglas) and *The West Wing*'s Jed Bartlet (Martin Sheen) were honest, intelligent, moral, and faithful parents and presidents dealing daily with the nineties dilemma of sustaining their humanity while continuing to function as a politician in the age of spin. In other words, Sorkin offered two fictional presidents trying to balance their human personness against the demands of their presidential personas.

Though Douglas ultimately played Andrew Shepherd in *The American President*, the part was originally offered to Robert Redford. Ironically, Redford's reason for turning it down—he "wanted to do a love story, but [Rob Reiner] wanted to do something that was ultimately about politics"[31]—became the film's greatest strength. Its perceptive political consciousness raised the film above the limitations of being just a love story to being a Capraesque commentary upon the American political scene in the nineties much like *Mr. Smith Goes to Washington* had been for an earlier generation. In fact, Sorkin and Reiner, early in the film, make clear exactly what they are trying to do. When the film's heroine, Sydney Ellen Wade of the Commonwealth of Virginia (Bening) stops to savor her first business visit to the White House with her jealous co-worker, she says to the security guard,

*Sydney:* Forgive me, this is my first time at the White House. I'm trying to savor the Capraesque quality.
*Susan:* He doesn't know what Capraesque means.

*Security Guard:* Yes I do. Frank Capra. Great American director. *It's a Wonderful Life, Mr. Smith Goes to Washington.* Sydney Ellen Wade of Virginia, knock them dead!

It is a stilted and transparent exchange, but it leaves no doubt of the major influence on the filmmakers and the governing positive idealistic tone that the film is going to take. The cynical, dismissive, classist, and racist (the security guard is African American) coworker is summarily put in her place. Sydney's (and the film's) Capraesque potential is signaled. From the very beginning, *The American President* asserts itself as an apologia for the sorry state of American politics in the age of spin.

But *The West Wing* wasn't the only presidential text that Capra and *The American President* influenced. The first date for President Shepherd and Sydney is a state dinner at the White House, the centerpiece of which is the moment when the president and his new girlfriend get up to dance. It is a graceful, romantic moment that, unfortunately, the newspapers the next morning will spin into a major American issue. Reiner, the director of the *The American President*, also has a bit part as a radio talk show host in *Primary Colors*. Thus, it is probably no coincidence that *Primary Colors* ends with a graceful dance scene almost visually identical to that earlier scene in *The American President*. Two presidential films, same scene, yet there is a major difference. While the dance scene in *The American President* is romantic and celebratory and the two lovers talk to each other about their relationship, the dance scene in *Primary Colors* is cynical and celebratory only of a hard-won dirty political victory about which the dancing new president and his First Lady have absolutely nothing to say to each other. Their silent victory waltz is a sad commentary on what it takes to win in American politics in the decade of spin. Whereas *Primary Colors, Speechless,* and *The War Room* portrayed the Clinton presidency with a hard edge as a ruthless game played by cold, calculating, cynical, and morally challenged politicians, films like *The American President* and *Dave* (1993) and the TV series *The West Wing* took, to paraphrase Bush the elder, a kinder, softer approach to the Clinton years. These films represent the issues, the politics, even the human foibles of those years more hopefully and even idealistically in a more Capraesque fashion. Nonetheless, no matter what tone these films choose to take, they cannot ignore the power of spin in the world of the nineties American presidency.

The innocent dance scene in *The American President,* for example, is immediately subjected to the force of spin when it appears as a front-page picture in every newspaper in America the next morning. This spinning of a first-date dance into the beginning of an American soap opera romance embodies the carnivalesque presidency. *The American President* explores how the American voter is more interested in the human drama of the presidency (read: the president's love life, or in the case of Bill Clinton, his sex life) than in the issue-driven (often things that neither the press nor the American public can fully understand), decision-making duties of the leader of the free world. When Andrew Shepherd decides to court a girlfriend, he enters by choice the carnival world where he is just like everybody else when it comes to dancing with his girlfriend, ordering flowers, and finally standing up for her virtue when the black knight of conservatism attacks it. Shepherd is the kind of president for the nineties that everyone hoped Clinton might become because he never loses track of the issues of the American presidency—like the environment and global warming, gun control, crime, terrorism, airline strikes—and the reigning power of spin that governs how any president, no matter how good or bad a guy he is, must deal with them in order to both serve and get reelected.

Like the other films representing the Clinton presidency, *The American President* is filled with spin session scenes that acknowledge the power of that reality-morphing phenomenon within the poll-driven universe of American political life. *The American President* begins with the morning briefing of the Shepherd inner circle (as seen later on TV's *The West Wing*) composed of the president; A. J. McInerney, his chief of staff (Martin Sheen); Robin, his press secretary (Ann Deavere Smith); and Lewis, his political strategist and speechwriter (Michael J. Fox); all of whom have just found out that the Shepherd presidency has reached an all-time high, 63 percent approval rating in the polls. Exhilarated and over-confident, they discuss how they are going to spin their popularity into policy:

> *President:* But the poll also tells us what we already know. If we don't get our crime bill through Congress, those numbers are going to be a memory. So starting today we're shifting it into gear.
> *Robin:* Can I tell my morning press gaggle that gun control is . . .
> *A. J.:* "Crime control," Robin. "Gun control" means we're wimps and we're soft on crime.
> *Lewis:* Well hang on, are we not . . .
> *A. J.:* Lewis, please . . .
> *Lewis:* Are we not putting back the hand gun restrictions?
> *A. J.:* No, we're leaving them out.
> *Lewis:* Mr. President, we campaigned on this issue. I understand we took them out when we were in the low 40s, but we could push it through now.
> *President:* After the elections, Lewis.
> *Lewis:* We may never have an opportunity like this again, so let's take the 63% out for a spin and see what it will do.
> *President:* We can't take it out for a spin. We need it to get reelected.

The whole plot of the film will eventually hang on the competing spins given to President Shepherd's crime bill and lobbyist Sydney Ellen Wade's environmental bill. Both are real issues and the film realistically explores them while simultaneously using them as a vehicle for the romantic love story.

"Meeting cute," for example, is a revered convention of the Hollywood love story. In *The American President*, Shepherd enters the room silently behind Sydney in the midst of a lobbying meeting as she rants about his environmental record and his reelection plans. "Let's take him out back and beat the shit out of him," Shepherd suggests, to the utter embarrassment of Sydney, who realizes that he has overheard her harsh criticism of him. Attracted to her, however, he invites her into the Oval Office, "the greatest home court advantage in the modern world," and makes a deal with her that pits his crime bill against her global warming initiative. The filmmakers of *The American President* have taken a traditional Hollywood convention and used it as a vehicle for a somewhat in-depth discussion of the issues of the availability of assault weapons and the threat of global warming, both subjects that rather infrequently appear in Hollywood love stories.

It is nice that a mainstream Hollywood love story like *The American President* takes the time to dwell on critical American issues, but the real focus of the film is a much more crucial issue, the one issue that would become *the* issue of the nineties and the Clinton presidency, the character issue, or, as it is called in this film, "the Sydney issue," christened thus when the president's press secretary spin-consciously asks, "How do you want me to handle the Sydney issue?"

Around the White House pool table, the president and his chief of staff and close friend, A. J., begin by discussing how to spin the crime bill but quickly turn to discussing the Sydney issue:

> *President:* Did she say anything about me? . . . When she called?
> *A. J.:* Did she say anything about you? . . .
> *President:* She didn't say anything about me?
> *A. J.:* (sarcastically) Well, no sir, but I could pass her a note during study hall.
> *President:* Well, tell me this, hypothetically . . .
> *A. J.:* I feel a nightmare coming on.
> *President:* What would happen if I called Sydney Wade and asked her to be my date for the State Dinner on Thursday evening.
> *A. J.:* You're not serious.
> *President:* Don't I sound serious?
> *A. J.:* The President can't just go out on a date.
> *President:* Well, why not? Jefferson did. Wilson did. Wilson was widowed during his first term. He met a woman named Edith Gault. He dated her, courted her, and married her. And somewhere in there he managed to form the League of Nations.
> *A. J.:* Mr. President. This is an election year. If you're looking for female companionship we can make certain arrangements that will insure total privacy.
> *President:* I don't want you to get me a girl, A. J. What is this? Vegas? . . . I'm a single adult. I met a woman who I'd like to see again socially. How is that different from what Wilson did?
> *A. J.:* The difference is he didn't have to be President on television. You've said it yourself a million times. If there had been a TV in every living room 60 years ago, this country does not elect a man in a wheelchair.

Sydney's boss calls her in and points to the picture of her and the President dancing on the front page of *The New York Times* and asks,

> *Boss:* Did you sleep with him?
> *Sydney:* Leo!

*Boss:* Did you sleep with him?
*Sydney:* That's none of your business, Leo.
*Boss:* Yeah, it is Sydney.
*Sydney:* You wanna tell me how my personal life . . .
*Boss:* Yeah, because when it's the President it's not personal. I hired your reputation Sydney. I hired a pit bull not a prom queen. . . . . Politics is perception.

As soon as opposing presidential candidate Senator Bob Rumson (Dreyfuss) sees the front-page picture, he calls his troops together for a spin session as well:

*Rumson:* You're overthinking this. Voters aren't interested in how to achieve economic growth. And they don't want to hear our plans to strengthen foreign policy.
*Politician #1:* So it comes down to character?
*Rumson:* . . . For all the bitching we do about the liberal bias of the press, when it comes down to a good character debate . . .
*Politician #2:* . . . the press is an unwitting accomplice.

Rumson wants a completely carnivalesque election campaign scenario, a down-in-the-gutter, soap opera, national character debate (which is exactly what nineties postmodern politics became for the Clinton administration). Even Sydney warns Shepherd against the perils of political spin: "If I were on your staff, I would tell you that the absolute worst thing you can do coming into an election year is to open yourself up to character attacks and the quickest way to do that is to prance around like the playboy of the western world."

But no matter how well informed on the perils and prerogatives of spin a nineties president or presidential candidate can be, the whole issue of character always comes down to the one spin strategy that both *The American President* and *Primary Colors* share with equal avidity, negative campaigning. Rumson's stump speech to the, naturally, Conservative Coalition of America takes negative campaigning even lower than Jack Stanton in *Primary Colors* ever ventured to go:

*Rumson:* I'm glad to see the President has a girl friend. Never mind that she's the hired gun of an ultra liberal political action committee. Never mind that the President takes the fifth any time that a reporter has the temerity to ask him a question about a woman in the position to exert enormous influence over a huge range of issues. Never mind that this woman's idea of how to unwind after a hard day is to get together with some of her ACLU pals and set American flags on fire.
*Robin:* (watching TV) No reaction from the White House.
*President:* Because it doesn't need to be dignified with a response. There's no upside so I'm leaving it alone.

Despite his romantic, good guy characterization, it is still somewhat ironic that the reason President Shepherd doesn't choose to defend the love of his life from these scurrilous attacks is because "there's no upside." In the nineties political arena, everything is judged by its spin potential, its ability to generate "upside" numbers in national popularity polls. No wonder that when, at five o'clock one morning, Sydney tells Shepherd that she wants "to leave the building before the press corps gets here," he answers, "I have those same thoughts every day of my life."

*The American President* is a truly earnest movie that works hard to make apologies for the Clinton presidency in midterm. As Shepherd says, "I have one election left. I don't have the luxury of losing my patience." But the one thing that this movie or any other cannot defend no matter how idealistically they try to spin it is the growing character issue of midterm President Clinton's presidency. The question that *The American President* really asks is, if I'm Bill Clinton, and I am the president, then why don't I act like one? Instead, Clinton opted for the donuts and the soap opera promiscuity that turned his presidency into a frantically spinning media carnival on a downward spiral.

Even earlier than *The American President*, one other film, *Dave* (1993), also realized the necessity to apologize for the transgressions of the Clinton presidency and its spinmasters. In *Dave*, President Bill Mitchell has a totally debilitating stroke at the moment of climax atop one of those "bimbo eruptions" that Bill Clinton made so famous. This time, however, the president's chief of staff and press secretary don't hesitate to take criminal action. They cover up the president's total incapacity and replace him with his stand-in, a look-alike, provided by the Secret Service, a nice small-town guy named Dave Kovic (Kevin Kline). Capraesque as the plot premise may be, this film is infinitely less believable than *The American President* and utterly incredible when compared to the realistic spinmastering of *Primary Colors*. But *Dave*'s plot, in a sense, expresses the same apologetic yearning that *The American President* will two years later. Both films ask, why can't we have a good president rather than a flawed or undisciplined or uncaring or phony president? Why can't we have a regular everyday good guy for a president, rather than a lying, spinmastering, bimbo chasing, ineffective chief executive? Ironically, when Dave replaces President Mitchell, even though he is committing a federal crime, things start to get better, the country finds some leadership and direction. Even Mitchell's wife, who hated her husband, falls in love with this new version of her presidential spouse.

*Dave* is a fun movie that falls somewhere between *Wag the Dog*, the most extreme satire of the lengths spin will go to cover up presidential transgressions, and *Primary Colors*, the closest to a realistic example of the arc of the Clinton spin machine. In *Dave*, the visual narrative grammar of the nineties political movies is already in place, complete with its spin sessions, its TV screens, its speeches, and its performances. But this time the spin isn't just trying to reconfigure a presidential romance or a marital infidelity, rather it is dealing with the federal crime of actually replacing the president with an imposter (even if that imposter turns out to be a much better president). It is a very Baudrillardian film as its title character becomes a simulation of the actual president and his simulation is so successful that the simulacra replaces the reality so seamlessly that the whole country accepts it.[32]

Stroked-out President Mitchell's spinmasters tell Dave, his look-alike replacement, just how their little conspiracy is going to be spun:

*Chief of Staff:* We'll tell them it was a stroke, but, just a mild stroke. He'll be up and around soon, you know.

*Dave:* Is this legal?

*Press Secretary:* Dave, have you ever driven through a red light? You know, on an empty road when there's nobody around and you know its safe.

*Dave:* I'm not sure. I might have.

*Press Secretary:* Say your mother is in the car and you have to get her to the hospital. You'd do it then for sure, wouldn't you?

*Dave:* Yes. I guess I would.

*Press Secretary:* Now, let's say the whole country is in the car. The entire United States of America.

*Dave:* The whole country in the car? I see what you mean.

*Press Secretary:* Dave, the country is sick.

*Chief of Staff:* And you're gonna get her to the hospital.

What *Dave* does is reverse the carnivalesque situation of the American presidency by thrusting a common, anonymous man into the performative public position of the presidency. When the commoner, Dave, gets totally caught up in the performance of being the president, the film then asks, how can he possibly escape back to the anonymity of the carnivalesque world? Dave is the nineties version of a metapresident, a person performing the role of the president so convincingly that he actually becomes the president. Dave represents the presidential potential of anyone who manages to attain the position of presidency.

But *Dave* is actually a critique of the carnivalesque presidency. Dave the imposter performs the role of the president both inside and outside the White House. His inside simulation of incapacitated President Mitchell is so successful that everyone who observes it—his wife, the leaders of Congress, the press, the American people—begins to believe that the president and his presidency have been reborn. But late in the film, Dave takes his presidential impersonation out of the White House and into the streets seeking the anonymity of the carnivalesque world once again. This scene takes place when he and the First Lady, who have fallen in love, decide to run away. They escape into the anonymity of the Washington DC night through the fabled White House steam tunnels, get sandwiches at a convenience store and have a picnic on the banks of the Potomac, but their little night of carnival comes to an abrupt end when they are pulled over by the Washington police. However, Dave the performer rescues them by putting on a metaperformance, a performance within a performance, in the streets for a gathering crowd complete with a terrible rendition of "The Sun'll Come Out Tomorrow" from the Broadway musical *Annie* as a means of convincing the police and the crowd that they are really not the president and First Lady but merely celebrity look-alikes impersonating the president and First Lady.

*Dave* tries hard to make its audience believe in its comic conspiracy premise. It brings on a succession of talking-head cameos of famous politicians from Tip

O'Neill to Tom Harkin to Christopher Dodd to comment on the revived Mitchell presidency. The real McLaughlin Group meets for a roundtable discussion of the new President Mitchell, and, in one of the film's finest comic touches, Oliver Stone appears on *The Larry King Show* charging that it is all a conspiracy and President Mitchell has been replaced by an imposter.

But all these high jinks notwithstanding, Dave still has to find a way to get out of his felonious impersonation of the incapacitated president. He calls a press conference and declares that he is going to talk absolutely straight to the American people, no spin, and then he performs the greatest spin trick of all. He fakes a debilitating stroke that allows him to change places with the already stroked-out real president and then disappear back into the DC night. He puts on, once again, the anonymity of the carnivalesque world outside of the glare of the TV cameras.

What these Clintonesque political films of the nineties did was present a number of different critical readings not only of the Clinton presidency but also of the phenomenon of spin that became the Clinton legacy to the political life of the twenty-first century. But other films about Clinton's illustrious presidential predecessors focused on another aspect of spin, what novelist Don DeLillo calls "the spin of history."[33]

In the nineties, though films like *Primary Colors* and *The American President* (and even *Dave*) explored how caught up in the spin of history the American presidency had become, one would like to think that it wasn't always this complicated, that the presidency wasn't always at the mercy of a ravenous press; professional spinmasters; lying, scheming, power-hungry, and even criminal staffers and politicians; and conspiracies to cover up, manipulate, and even rewrite history before the events themselves have even cooled. Stone's wonderful cameo as a conspiracy theorist on *The Larry King Show* in *Dave* is, perhaps, the one great metahistorical satiric comment in that film. In the world of the most outrageous criminal conspiracy imaginable in politics that *Dave* creates, Stone, an obsessive, over-the-top nineties conspiracy theorist, is the most rational voice in the whole discourse over the Mitchell presidency. Significantly, in the nineties, Stone is that alternative historical voice that reminds how, at least in the recent past going back to the fifties, the American presidency has always been at the mercy of spin, the spinmasters, and their elaborate (or more often amateurish or sophomoric) conspiracies.

Stone's *JFK* (1991) was the first major film foray into the historical representation of the American presidency in the nineties, but it wasn't really about President John Kennedy at all. Its title was deceptive packaging. *JFK* was really Stone's first major expression of his conspiracy theory obsession since *Salvador* (1976). He would become the poster boy for conspiracy theorists who would end up being so pointedly and hilariously spoofed in *Dave*. Stone's other major (and equally controversial) early nineties film about spin was *Natural Born Killers* (1994), his brutal critique of the tabloid media of the late twentieth century. Yet neither *JFK* nor *Natural Born Killers* explored the phenomenon of spin in the kind of analytic depth that the other nineties films like *Primary Colors* or

*The American President* did. While *Natural Born Killers* spotlighted the sensationalistic tabloid TV media, it did little more than represent its ruthless pursuit of sensation. There were clear examples of the discourse of spin in *JFK*. Late in the film, New Orleans District Attorney Jim Garrison (Kevin Costner) goes to Washington DC to interview a former CIA "Black Ops" agent played by a sinister Donald Sutherland. As they walk the Capital Mall from the Lincoln Memorial to the Washington Monument with the Capital Building gleaming in the background (all the public symbols of the American presidency), the ex-spy tells the conspiracy-enmeshed district attorney about the stories that the government was already spinning out about Lee Harvey Oswald and the assassination before President Kennedy's body was even cold. But the clinching detail of this description of conspiratorial spin was that the ex-spy read these stories in newspapers halfway around the world across the international dateline in a time frame that was impossible unless the stories had been prepared for release to the press before the actual assassination ever happened.

But Stone's major contribution to the nineties discourse on the American presidency and on the power of political spin in American society came in a film generally considered one of Stone's few failures in the historical film genre, his epic biopic *Nixon* (1995). Unfortunately, the only problem with analyzing *Nixon* as a major contributor to the nineties discourse on the American presidency is the sad fact that in *Nixon* Stone derailed his exploration of the Richard Nixon presidency and all the fascinating characters involved in that constantly grinding spin machine and sent his movie crashing back into the twisted wreckage of the Kennedy assassination conspiracy. Stone allowed *Nixon* to become a subtextual sequel to his *JFK* four years earlier. According to Stone, Nixon not only knew about the Watergate break-in, the existence of the secret "plumbers" cell within the executive branch, and the secret slush fund for the Watergate burglars, but, and this was the greatest sin of all, he also had foreknowledge of the conspiracy to assassinate John Kennedy, the president of the United States, the one position that Nixon so hungrily lusted to attain.

About two-thirds of the way through Stone's *Nixon*, a young protestor, camped out at the Lincoln Memorial the night before a huge rally against the bombing of Cambodia, confronts Nixon (Anthony Hopkins), who is making an impulsive, unscheduled, late night visit to his idol, the great president who also led a terrible divided country during a time of war. The teenage protestor, just by looking at him face-to-face, realizes that Nixon can't stop the bombing, can't end the war, and that though he is the most powerful man in the world, it has all spun totally out of his control. She asks Nixon point blank, "Then what's the point? What's the point of being President?" That question is a critical one when we consider the worlds of nineties American politics that all these films create. If the American presidency, as represented in *Primary Colors*, *The American President*, *Dave*, and *Nixon* resembles anything even approaching the reality of life in the office, then Don DeLillo's and Dave's accountant friend Murray's (Charles Grodin) advice, "Get out as fast as you can," certainly ought to be heeded. But no president or presidential candidate ever does.

"What's the point of being president?" For Stone in *Nixon*, the whole point of being president is entering, trying to control, and finally surviving within "the spin of history." Stone portrays Nixon as a president obsessed with achieving more than his TV-image nemesis, the dead thus canonized John Kennedy, and living up to the historical records of those other presidents who he idolizes: Washington, Lincoln, Roosevelt. In other words, for Nixon the point of being president is earning space on Mount Rushmore. The iconography of the presidency and its historical record is all over Stone's film from the portraits of the presidents that hang ubiquitously throughout the White House and are lovingly caressed by Stone's camera to Nixon's visit to the Lincoln Memorial in the dead of night in 1970 to the long shadow of John Kennedy that always hangs over Nixon and his presidency. This placing of Nixon, a small and petty man, within the daunting, larger-than-life historical past of the office makes this film as much about the office as it is about the man. In Nixon's case, that young protestor's ironic reading of the president's lack of power, his impotence, hits home because even Nixon sees its truth. He is at the mercy of his handlers, the press, the horrible spin of history of his times.

Even though *Nixon* is set mostly in the seventies, the one scene that dominates more than three hours of screen time is the spin session, as in all the other political films of the nineties. Over and over again, in all sorts of locales and situations, Stone sits Nixon down with his political staff—Bob Haldeman (James Woods), John Erlichman (J. T. Walsh), Henry Kissinger (Paul Sorvino), Ron Ziegler (David Paymer), John M. Mitchell (E. G. Marshall), J. Edgar Hoover (Bob Hoskins), Alexander Haig (Powers Boothe), John Dean (David Hyde Pierce)—not to ask the question, "What are we going to do?" but to connive about how are we going to sell what we are doing to the press or cover up what we've already done so that we can stay in office rather than go to jail.

The film begins with a scene of a movie within a movie, a Department of Labor instructional film on salesmanship:

> *Boss:* Sure you've got a great product, but you have to remember what you're really selling. Yourself.
> *Salesman:* So it's not necessarily what I say, as how I say it.
> *Boss:* That's right, Earl. A good salesman can sell anything. And remember Earl. Always look them in the eye. Nothing sells like sincerity.

This is Stone's way of tipping off what Nixon and his staff of hucksters are really intent upon doing, selling themselves to the American people (and to history) as great leaders when really they are simply a gang of slick, self-interested salesmen.

In the true spirit of the power of spin, Nixon and his cronies really did believe that they could sell anything. Listen to his sales pitch for the massive bombing attacks on Cambodia in 1970: "This is not an invasion of Cambodia. We take this action not for the purpose of expanding the war into Cambodia, but for the purpose of ending the war in Vietnam." That incredible, self-contradictory speech came out of a mammoth spin session held right before the bombing of Cambodia was given the green light. In Stone's version, everyone was there—Haldeman, Erlichman, Kissinger, Haig, Zeigler, and others—and Nixon invoked one of his historical models, Teddy Roosevelt, as the main selling point for his decision: "You see, your people in the State Department, they don't understand. You gotta electrify people with bold moves. Bold moves make history. Like Teddy Roosevelt rushing up San Juan hill. Small event but dramatic. People took notice. . . . We'll bomb the hell out of those people."

Unfortunately, the result of Nixon's "bold move" in bombing Cambodia is simply the major acceleration of political protest and unrest at home in America and, worst of all, Kent State. However, once again (as represented by Stone in an executive branch spin session on the presidential yacht on the Potomac), the issue isn't dead college students at all. It is really all about spin.

> *Nixon:* Jesus Christ, dead kids! How the hell could we give the Democrats a weapon like this.
> *Haldeman:* Well, one way or the other, Kent State is not good. We have to get out in front of this.
> *Erlichman:* Maybe we could have a National Prayer Day?
> *Haldeman:* Never complain, never explain, John.
> *Nixon:* Now if we keep our heads, we'll win this thing. . . . What we can do is drive a stake through the hearts of the Communist Alliance. Henry is getting strong signals from the Chinese, how they fear the Vietnamese more than the Russians. . . . Now if we stick it out, we'll end up negotiating separately with both the Chinese and the Soviets. And we'll get better deals than we ever dreamed of from both. That is triangular diplomacy, gentlemen.
> *Kissinger:* Exactly Mr. President. That's what geopolitics is about. The linking of the whole world for self-interest.
> *Nixon:* So, you tell me Ron, how the hell I can explain that on TV to a bunch of simpleminded reporters and weeping mothers.
> *Ziegler:* Yeah, but what am I telling the press about Kent State?
> *Nixon:* Oh, tell them what the hell you like. I don't care. They don't understand anything anyway.

For Nixon and his brain trust of spinmasters, America's children dead on the grass at Kent State weren't the issue at all. All Nixon and his cronies were interested in was how they were going to avoid that issue and sell a more complicated one. The president just didn't care about "dead kids," rather, his concern in bombing Cambodia was to "give history a nudge."

The whole discourse of spin in Stone's *Nixon* would be oppressive (as much of this darkly lit biopic is modeled quite closely on *Citizen Kane*) if at other times the Nixon brain trust's attempts to either sell Nixon's presidency or cover up its crimes weren't so funny. Some of their spin sessions evolve strategies that are so bizarre, paranoid, and Byzantine that they verge on the hilarious and push the envelope of the ridiculous. When Nixon wants to contest the 1960 election loss to Kennedy and call for a recount, Haldeman scoffs (ironically and prophetically in light of the Bush-Gore Election of 2000), "Don't be ridiculous. No one has ever contested a national election." And another of Tricky Dick's political advisers laments, "They stole it from us fair and square."

But Stone's funniest spin scene involves Nixon's realization of just how much he curses on the tapes that have been typed up as transcripts to be delivered to Sam Ervin's Watergate Investigation Committee. Ziegler, the press secretary, comes up with the solution of inserting the words "expletive deleted" for all the swear words. This was their way of spinning Nixon's incredible foul mouth to a public that probably doesn't know what an expletive is but would easily recognize the obscene words Nixon was using. But there are just too many. Actually, Stone has set us up for this ironic, comic scene by making the very first word that Nixon utters in the whole film the expletive "Cocksucker!"

In fact, in Stone's biopic, which unfolds as a nineties parable for the age of spin, it was the tapes that ultimately made this political salesman resign his presidency. Echoing the advice of the opening informational movie, Nixon just didn't want anyone to hear what he actually said or how he really, replete with expletives, said it. He knew that, if the tapes became public, there was no way he could spin what he actually said and the obscene and racist words he used. In the end, *Nixon* is much like *Citizen Kane*. Kissinger actually echoes that film in an aside to Haig: "He could have been a great man if only he'd ever been loved." Nixon's final bitter lament about his failed presidency is a mournful realization of how he has dragged the executive branch down into the carnival atmosphere of the real world. "You know, they sell tickets," Nixon shakes his head at the novelty of it. "They sell tickets to an impeachment. Just like a damn circus."

But the original sin of the Nixon presidency, according to Stone, is hidden in those missing eighteen-and-a-half minutes of the Nixon tapes. Unfortunately, Stone chooses to hitch the mystery of those eighteen-and-a-half minutes to the one mystery and conspiracy that Stone had already hitched himself to in the nineties, the Kennedy assassination. The dead horse that Stone is beating in *Nixon* is whether or not Nixon had foreknowledge that there was an assassination plot on Kennedy in motion and chose to do nothing about it. Thus, the voice-over words on the TV that open the first dark scene in the White House where we meet Stone's cursing Nixon for the first time, "The White House continues to deny any involvement," become expansively ironic. "Involvement" in what? In the Watergate break-in? In the Watergate cover-up? In the bombing of Cambodia? In the Vietnam War? In the assassination of John Kennedy?

Unfortunately, for this biopic film, that last conspiracy is all Stone really cares about. Nixon as a biographical subject simply becomes a vehicle for Stone to make a sequel to *JFK*. Thus, Stone puts his own spin on the original sin of the American presidency, on the ultimate measure for contesting an election, political assassination. There is a definite reason why it was necessary for Stone to place a bizarre disclaimer (unlike any disclaimer that had ever come before) at the beginning of *Nixon*: "This film is a dramatic interpretation of events and characters based on public sources and an incomplete historical record. Some scenes and events are presented as composites or have been hypothesized or condensed." Before his film even starts, Stone is deconstructing it. For a film heavily populated by real historical characters using their real names and mouthing their authentic recorded words, Stone begins by immediately spinning its New Historicist credibility in the direction of fiction rather than fact. Yet the film is presented as hard fact right down to its brilliant editing that incorporates real news footage seamlessly into the narrative. By the end of Stone's film, the question, "Did Nixon know?" has been planted and even Nixon isn't quite sure of his own culpability in the assassination of Kennedy.

Stone hangs his whole argument that Nixon knew on the fact that the Watergate burglary was done by Cubans under the command of Howard Hunt, the *éminence grise* of Track Two, an Eisenhower-era CIA political assassination secret cell, and by Gordon Liddy, who Hunt (Ed Harris) describes as thinking he is Martin Bormann. When the Nixon handlers propose that the White House bribe Hunt to take the fall for Watergate and pass the money through the CIA, Nixon replies,

> *Nixon:* Play it tough. That's the way they play it, and that's the way we're going to play it. Don't lie to Hubbs and say there's no involvements. Just say that this is sort of a comedy of errors, bizarre, without getting into it. Say the President believes this is going to open up the whole Bay of Pigs thing again. Tell Hubbs he should call the FBI, call Pat Gray, and say that we wish for the sake of the country, that they don't go any further into this hanky-panky. Period.
>
> *Haldeman:* Bay of Pigs? That was Kennedy's screw up. Why would that threaten us?

Good question, Bob.

Stone's argument is that the Bay of Pigs, the Kennedy assassination, and Watergate were all done by the same people at the order of the same people and that the different presidents were all somehow culpable. Stone's conspiracy theory, as it shakes out in *Nixon*, posits that the leftover CIA assassination team from the Eisenhower administration—"Kennedy didn't even know about it," Nixon says, but, as Ike's vice president, he did—formed the plot to kill Castro. When that failed and Kennedy became president and betrayed the Cubans at the Bay of Pigs by withholding air cover, they assassinated him—all of which is fine, or as Haldeman says, "was Kennedy's screw-up," yet Nixon is nervous about it. Why? Because Nixon was meeting with a group of rich right-wingers in Dallas the day before Kennedy was assassinated. He characterizes them on the phone to Hoover as "really strange, extremists, Birchers." Stone lingers on Nixon's long evening of partying in the presence of (but not with) call girls in this Dallas mansion listening to these shadowy figures talking as if they know something is going to happen to Kennedy the next day. This is Stone's conspiracy contribution to the presidential discourse of the nineties, and it is pretty thin, clearly fictionalized, and ahistorical. The whole scene ends with Nixon at the Dallas airport the next morning walking to board his plane and looking ominously up at the sky as Kennedy's plane is coming in to land.

Finally, Stone's *Nixon*, as idiosyncratic of a historical biopic as it may be, does share one theme with all the other political films of the nineties. All of these films that explore the inner workings of the American presidency, where the first thing on everyone's mind is not the country, not truth, but simply getting elected or reelected, focus on the theme of negative campaigning. "Bobby's a mean little son-of-a-bitch, Edgar," Nixon tells Hoover. "I wanna fight just as dirty, Edgar." Hoover advises, "His women, use his women." Nixon actually enlists the FBI to do the research (as Libby did for the Stantons in *Primary Colors*) for his negative campaigning against Bobby Kennedy. Yet despite all the lies and the negative campaigning and even Watergate, Nixon still gets reelected in 1972 because, as Haldeman puts it, "we got the press this time." Finally, however, Nixon is undone by the damning tissue of lies that his administration has become. He ends up doing something that no other president was ever forced to do, resign in disgrace, or, as one critic puts it (citing the earlier biopic that Stone used as his model), "by the end of the movie, he is standing alone, like Charles Foster Kane."[34]

The nineties produced one other film that placed the Kennedy brothers front and center. *Thirteen Days* was in one stage or another of production all through the nineties and was finally finished and released in 2000 right in the middle of the Bush-Gore contested election fiasco. Whereas *Thirteen Days* had some connection to Stone's *JFK* and *Nixon* conspiracy theory films of earlier in the decade (Kevin Costner is its star, the Kennedys its heroes), it is a much different sort of nineties political film. *Thirteen Days* is a thriller, scrupulous in its historical accuracy and unflinchingly positive in its representation of the leadership qualities of the American presidency. *Thirteen Days* actually plays as a film about two political leaders, Jack and Bobby Kennedy, who saved the world in 1962. As one commentator wrote in 2000 about the film, "Leadership . . . is the missing presence, the great ghost, in our current oversaturated frenzy of political/legal/media noise," but the film "is a gripping glorification of what real leadership is all about . . . and there's virtually no way to experience the movie—at least in the present climate—without wondering what either of the two current candidates [Bush or Gore] might have done in the same situation."[35]

Coming at the end of the decade of spin, when political cynicism marked the Clinton years and the very concept of the truth became ephemeral mirage, *Thirteen Days* is a throwback political film. There are no shadowy conspiracies lurking in its closets as in Stone's films. There is not a succession of spin session scenes as in *Primary Colors, The American President, Nixon,* and all the decade's political films that preceded it. There is one crucial moment during the thirteen-day missile crisis when Kenny O'Donnell (Kevin Costner), President Kennedy's appointments secretary and main political adviser, needs to get the president back to Washington from a fund-raiser in Chicago and calls in Pierre Salinger, the press secretary: "All I can tell you now," O'Donnell confides, "is that the president may have to develop a cold tomorrow." In the world of spin of the Clinton magnitude, O'Donnell's little ruse to keep from tipping off the press to the crisis that is building seems noble and innocent by comparison. *Thirteen Days* "emphasizes a political heroism almost forgotten in today's coolly ironic age,"[36] one commentator writes, and Kevin Costner agrees that "this movie offers us an opportunity to drop some of our cynicism and see one of the moments when

Jack and Bobby Kennedy became golden."[37] Whereas Costner, playing District Attorney Jim Garrison, had been Stone's third-person-limited point of entry into the Kennedy assassination conspiracy, once again Costner's O'Donnell, like Nick Carroway in F. Scott Fitzgerald's *The Great Gatsby*, is *Thirteen Days*' doorway into the top-secret deliberations of the Cuban Missile Crisis, one of the defining moments of the Kennedy presidency. But even though everyone knows that both Bill Clinton and the Kennedys had a taste for extramarital affairs with high-profile women, were masters of Hollywood-style image building, and had no qualms about spinning the truth to their own political advantage, *Thirteen Days* takes one brief shining moment in presidential history when all those superficial concerns were shoved aside and Kenny O'Donnell says, when he, Jack, and Bobby realize what they are seeing on the CIA U-2 spy plane photographs of the nuclear missile sites in Cuba, "Jesus Christ almighty, it's just us."

*Thirteen Days*, coming at the end of the nineties decade and at the beginning of the millennium, could be characterized as nostalgia for a better, more innocent, more heroic time in White House history, or it could be another exercise in wish fulfillment (as *Dave* was) signaling a desire to reinstill confidence in the American presidency. Michael DeLuca, president of New Line Pictures, which produced *Thirteen Days*, describes it as a cure for the disease of the Clinton era: "It's an uplifting story that makes you nostalgic for an era where there were real heroes. I think it's a great antidote to the times we live in now, where it seems like everything is about cynicism and corruption."[38]

The one aspect of *Thirteen Days*, other than its positive nostalgic representations of the presidency, that sets it apart from almost all the other films of the decade on the subject, is the total absence of the public spectacle of performativity in the representation of the American presidency. All the action and deliberation that takes place during the Missile Crisis is behind closed doors, is not dramatically orchestrated for public consumption in the press. Another historical film of the nineties about a soon-to-be president learning how to be president, *Jefferson in Paris* (1995), focuses directly upon this performance trap that can be the downfall of so many national leaders, whether they be the king of France or Bill Clinton.

*Jefferson in Paris* is an epistolary film as befits its late eighteenth-century setting and the reigning style of that century, as in the novels of Samuel Richardson and Tobias Smollett. The very first image of the film is Thomas Jefferson writing a letter on his own ingenious invention, the letter-copying machine. After those opening credits run over the camera's close-up fascination with the letter-writing machine, letter writing and receiving (often accompanied by Jefferson's or his paramour's voice-over reading of what is being written) becomes a motif employed for the dispersal of Jefferson's observations of the world around him, the things he is learning, the fuel for his insatiable curiosity about how the world works. Ironically, one such scene, presented in voice-over as Jefferson writes a letter on his machine, could be a commentary on the nineties American presidency as well as on the French court of Louis XIV and Marie Antoinette. Jefferson observes,

Sunday last I went as a private citizen accompanied by my daughter to Versailles. We joined the crowd admitted . . . to view the King and Queen on their way to Mass. I meant to impress upon my daughter the vainglory of these spectacles. May we Americans never emulate them, nor burden our taxpayers with such useless splendors. . . . Daily life at court is still ruled by an etiquette so rigid that the most private pursuits of the King and Queen are converted into public ceremony. It is like watching actors, fantastically painted, bewigged and bejeweled desporting themselves on a stage, the leading actress, though never a popular one, is the Queen, whose extravagance is blamed for the desperate financial situation of France.

Jefferson's epistolary observations of the French court in the years immediately prior to the French Revolution describe the identical performativity that the American presidential election process and the Bubbafied Clinton White House took on in the nineties.

The world of the president as performer in a national soap opera found a telling echo in the portrayal of the French court in *Jefferson in Paris*. One of the best scenes occurs when the film takes to the streets of Paris to observe a puppet show in which the queen is portrayed as a whore being graphically bounced up and down on an impressively phallic representation of the king's brother.

While the major films about the American presidency in the nineties were closely based on cultural fact (and sometimes history) and the lives of real presidents, like Clinton or Nixon, and portrayed the political realities of the decade of spin, the parade of fictional presidents represented in Hollywood movies in the nineties also worked out a number of political scenarios that represented the growing sense that the people and many public intellectuals and media artists shared, that the decade needed a political makeover. The movies expressed that need through nostalgic wish fulfillment of the most exaggerated kind.

## Presidents as Superheroes

Bold moves make history.

*—Nixon*

If Jack and Bobby Kennedy, as portrayed in *Thirteen Days*, actually saved the world during the 1962 Cuban Missile Crisis, then they deserve to be ranked right up there with the presidential superheroes of a cluster of other nineties films who also take action to save the world. This "President as Superhero" text adds yet another dimension to the American wish list for leadership. These films represent presidents who actually get out of their chairs and do things (other than have extramarital affairs).

*Independence Day*'s young, baby boomer fighter pilot President Bill Whitmore (Bill Pullman), who is at first indecisive but finally heroic and can lead a wing of F-16s against an alien spacecraft as big as the Grand Canyon, and *Air Force One*'s mature, always decisive, two-fisted and machine-gun-packing President James Marshall (Harrison Ford) present a totally different image of the American presidency opposed to the cynicism toward and the disappointment in Bill Clinton.

These wish-fulfillment, comic book superheroes are all that conservative Americans could want in a president. Both are loving, dedicated, and, above all, faithful family men willing to go to any lengths and brave any threats or danger to save their wives and daughters (and, of course, by implication, the larger family that they lead, the American people). Both are brave, cunning, inventive former war heroes, and pilots, who are at home with violence and hand-to-hand or plane-to-plane combat. Both are moral and conscientious leaders of the free world. Both can fire off a quotable and belligerent one-liner in the best Schwarzenegger or Eastwood style. But, most important of all, both are not what Bill Clinton was perceived to be—draft dodger, womanizer, liberal avoider, and appeaser.

There is a kind of irony, a sort of incestuous relationship between these films and the earlier, more Clintonesque films. *Independence Day*, for example, was filmed on the set used for *The American President* and *Nixon* before its alien spaceship's lasers blew the White House to smithereens. Both presidents, as did Nixon in his biopic and Shepherd in *The American President*, have daughters that they want to shield from the press and other intrusive realities of being president in the dangerous nineties, a protective parental stance that Bill and Hillary Clinton never wavered from in all their years in the White House. But the bottom line for Hollywood is that the American moviegoers paid huge amounts of money, record-breaking amounts of money, to see these presidential superhero movies. Why? One commentator remarks that *Independence Day* is "an emblem of American cinematic sensibility in the late 1990s,"[39] a sensibility that clearly recognized the desire for wish fulfillment at-large in a country grown sick of the sordid scandal of the Clinton presidency.

*Independence Day*'s young President Whitmore is much like Clinton in personality and baby-boomer image but not like Clinton in background and character. He is a decorated Gulf War fighter pilot who, when push comes to shove, declares, "I'm a fighter pilot. I belong in the air," and takes off to lead his attack squadron of misfit pilots against the huge hovering spacecraft. He is Luke Skywalker all grown-up and riding out against the Death Star once again. *Independence Day*'s plot takes off very quickly with very little time for character development. The alien spacecraft appears in the sky as a huge all-enveloping shadow and the battle begins. Symbolically, in sync with the film's all-American title, the spacecraft's shadow, starting at the Lincoln Memorial, moves slowly over Washington DC engulfing the major icons of the American government—the Washington Monument, the Capital Building, the White House—as it goes. In New York, the shadow engulfs the Statue of Liberty and darkens the whole skyline of Manhattan. This shadow triggers a scenario right out of both H. G. Wells's and Orson Welles's *The War of the Worlds*, panic in the streets and traffic jams as everyone tries to evacuate the great cities. But President Whitmore is in heroic mode from the very beginning. He sends the vice president and the cabinet to safety in the bunkers at NORAD, but he refuses to abandon ship: "I'm not leaving. I'm staying. I don't want to start a general panic that might cost lives."

After the aliens attack and the outcome looks unbelievably grim—the cities in flames, huge laser fireballs everywhere, the enemy ships indestructible, refugee camps all over the country, all the icons of America, even the White House, blown up—President Whitmore looks for consolation to his past as a warrior. "That's the advantage of being a fighter pilot," he declares. "In the Gulf War we knew what we had to do. It's not so simple anymore." But actually, in the comic book, one-liner rhetoric of the film, it really is pretty simple. "Let's kick the tires and light the fires," one warlike pilot exults in the opportunity to play with war's sophisticated toys. "Lock and load," another alliterates. "Let's kick E.T.'s ass." And even the president gets his chance to emulate the Schwarzeneggerian wit: "Nuke 'em. Let's nuke the bastards!" he orders. At another crucial juncture, he gives the tense order, "Let's do it!" Then, in the climactic battle scene, he twirls off a whole succession of one-liners like Dirty Harry on speed: "Hold on, Command. I want another shot at him," then, "Let's take it out before it takes us out," and, finally, to his fighter wing, "Gentlemen, let's pave the road." Clearly, there is a much different Hollywood mindset at work in these comic book films than there was in the much more sophisticated, cynical, and ironic Clintonesque films. No subtle irony here, just decisive presidential action.

Yet despite the great difference from the other presidential films, these super-hero films still are conscious of the cultural elements that defined the American presidency in the nineties in films like *Primary Colors*, *The American President*, and *Dave*. Both *Independence Day* and *Air Force One* are aware of the American public's desire for a president who can perform, who can offer a narrative that can entertain the nation and capture its attention. The difference is that, in *Independence Day* and *Air Force One*, a different kind of performance is represented. The performative narrative that all the Clintonesque films took was that of the sordid, melodramatic, sexually active afternoon soap opera. The presidential performances of *Independence Day* and *Air Force One* are old-fashioned, heroic, American Western narratives out of *High Noon* (1952) and *The Gunfight at the OK Corral* (1957). In fact, it is almost as if these films are answering the prayer of Jack Stanton's political aide in *Primary Colors* who, watching an old western on TV, begs, "Come back, Shane. Run for President."

But these superhero films are also aware of the carnivalesque qualities that the nineties American presidency had taken on. In *Independence Day*, for example, the First Lady is rescued from a crashed helicopter by a stripper. That is an example of the White House meeting the carnival world of the streets with a vengeance. After the White House is blown up, the president ends up in the post-Holocaust world of the survivors and, at one point, becomes one of the guys with a bunch of ragtag misfits right out of *The Dirty Dozen* (1967). And, of course, there is always the ever-present press. Even when the world is coming to an end, they continue to stick their microphones in peoples' faces and report what they think is going on. *Independence Day* gleefully steals from the worlds of every sci-fi movie that ever preceded it. Its most fully articulated thefts come from *Dr. Strangelove*, *Star Wars*, *Alien*, and *War Games* with *War of the Worlds* serving as the *éminence grise* ruling over the genre references that appear in *Independence Day*.

*Air Force One* is a much less rowdy, much more mature, somber, interiorized, and politically acute film than *Independence Day*, but it is still, despite its gravity and the much more presidential bearing of Harrison Ford, no less a superhero comic book. On a scale of unbelievability, it ranks right up there with *Independence Day*. Actually, the one film that *Air Force One* most resembles is *Die Hard* (1988). President James Marshall exhibits all the same instincts as John McCain does in those popular terrorist thrillers of the late eighties and nineties, except that instead of trying to reclaim a skyscraper or an airport (plus his wife), President Marshall must defeat the terrorist usurpers on the biggest, most sophisticated airplane in existence.

When *Air Force One* was released, ex-President Gerald Ford (no relation to Harrison Ford) consented to review it and wrote, "*Air Force One* is great entertainment, with great action and great performances. Just like politics."[40] While ex-President Ford noted the presidential performativity of his namesake, other critics consistently emphasized the discourse of wish fulfillment that Ford's performance and the script offers: "Harrison Ford as the President of the United States is such a perfect piece of casting. . . . As President James Marshall . . . Ford is the chief executive as red-blooded liberal superjock—a Bill Clinton who served in Vietnam and has never waffled since. . . . Here, at last, is what America has yearned for in a leader: the heart and mind of Franklin Delano Roosevelt joined with the *cojones* of Clint Eastwood."[41] At times, President Marshall even sounds like Eastwood, such as when he delivers the great one-liner "Get off my plane!" as he knocks his terrorist nemesis into kingdom come from ten thousand feet. But at no time does he ever sound like Clinton or act like Clinton.

Perhaps the strongest subtext that both *Independence Day* and *Air Force One* share is the theme of family. The presidents in both films are unequivocally devoted family men, and family becomes a metaphor for country as the thing most worth fighting to preserve and protect. Time and again the one thing that President Marshall places above his country is family. First, he refuses to leave the plane in the special president's escape pod when the takeover begins. Once he gains control of enough weapons and men to retake the plane from the terrorists, he refuses to push his advantage because his wife and daughter are still held hostage. When he finds a way to parachute all the hostages to safety, he refuses to go for one simple reason: "I'm not leaving without my family." And when the terrorist leader (Gary Oldman) holds a gun to his daughter's head and asks him if now he is ready to negotiate, his immediate answer is, "I'll do it. I'll do it. Just leave my family alone."

The other subtext that both *Independence Day* and *Air Force One* share is an unintended yet uncannily prophetic one. The imagery (skyscrapers on fire and planes exploding) and the terrorist threats of both films are visually predictive of the September 11, 2001, terrorist attacks on the World Trade Center and the Pentagon. These films may be comic books, but their vision of the world order in the late nineties is frighteningly accurate. In fact, President Marshall's reaction to the threat of world terrorism could have been a template for Bush's reaction following the 9/11 attack and his subsequent rhetoric in regard to the rogue government of Saddam Hussein in Iraq. *Air Force One* opens with a tough talking, root-out-the-evil-and-destroy-it speech that Bush wishes he had given: "Atrocity and terror are not political weapons and to those who would use them, your day is over. We will never negotiate. We will no longer tolerate and we will no longer be afraid. It is your turn to be afraid." President Marshall keeps things simple. When his political adviser, after this speech, cautions that "it might come back to bite us in the ass in November," Marshall simply replies, "It is the right thing to do." When his wife asks him why his political advisers disliked his hard-line speech, he answers, "They're afraid we won't have the guts to back it up." Again, this political reaction to terrorism rather eerily predicted the Bush administration stance post-September 11.

The world of *Air Force One*, with its heroic president, its female vice president, its hard-line antiterrorist view, and its clear morality at the top, is a brave new world for representation of the American presidency. Until *Independence Day* and *Air Force One*, the nineties film representations of the presidency had all emphasized the corruption, the unfaithfulness, and the moral vacuum created by the powerful phenomenon of spin. While the war hero-pilot presidents of these two films may be utterly unbelievable, they reflect what American moviegoers wanted to believe and wished for, despite the fact that reality in no way resembled this representation. At one point in *Air Force One*, the air force chief of staff tells the vice president, "Let's not forget that the President is a Medal of Honor winner. In Vietnam he flew more helicopter rescue missions than any other man in my command. He knows how to fight. . . . The element of surprise is a formidable advantage in combat. If he's up there, he's the best chance we've got." How could any 1997 moviegoer not wish that the real president could match up to this fictional one?

Harrison Ford, actually a personal friend and supporter of President Clinton, made it very clear when *Air Force One* came out in 1997 that "I didn't base my performance on President Clinton or on any other President, living or dead."[42] He may be protesting too much, but he is right. Presidents aren't physical superheroes, except perhaps for Teddy Roosevelt. The war heroes who become president are more likely to be brilliant administrators like Dwight D. Eisenhower or aging warriors with bad backs like John F. Kennedy. Yet the reason the American public longs for the kind of superhero president portrayed in *Independence Day* and *Air Force One*, and the reason Harrison Ford didn't base his characterization on any single, real president, is because, as President Marshall's chief of staff (Paul Guilfoyle) put it in *Air Force One*, "the Presidency is bigger than any one man." Americans may long for presidential superheroes, but our history predicts that real presidents are always going to have their flaws, yet more often than not the office itself will help them to grow in sometimes heroic ways. From a wheelchair, Franklin D. Roosevelt led a nation at war, and a shopkeeper from Missouri ended that war by declaring, "the buck stops here." Two college boy millionaires from Massachusetts faced down the Russians in Cuba, and a serial philanderer from backwoods Arkansas led the American economy to the highest level it ever reached. Who says that just being president can't spin an ordinary man into a superhero of sorts?

*Independence Day* and *Air Force One*, with their themes of the American president at risk in the air, are similar to two other nineties movies, *Passenger 57* (1992) and *Executive Decision* (1996), films that could be characterized as *Die Hard (1988, 1990, 1995)* at 30,000 feet movies. In *Passenger 57*, the superhero in the air is a former Secret Service agent who used to guard the president. In *Executive Decision*, the movie's title refers to the choice the American president is faced with making: either shoot down a planeload of American citizens or risk a terrorist Armageddon. Ironically, that very decision may have formed a scenario for President Bush on September 11, 2001, when the fourth terrorist-hijacked plane was still in the air over Pennsylvania and reportedly on course for an attack on the White House. How that plane ultimately crashed in Pennsylvania has fueled conspiracy theories worthy of Stone ever since that day. Did the "Let's roll" passenger uprising cause the terrorists to crash it, or did the president order air force jets to shoot it out of the sky? But in the glare of the fireworks and gunfire of all these presidential, high-flying, superhero films, one other movie that portrays the American presidency over three full administrations keeps the feet of its unlikely presidential superheroes planted solidly on the ground until the very end when they climb aboard two Washington DC police horses to ride to the rescue of the country. That movie is *My Fellow Americans* (1996), and its superheroes are two senior citizen ex-presidents who are both morally and physically flawed but every bit as inventive and ultimately heroic as their counterparts in *Independence Day* and *Air Force One* (and much wittier than either). One media wag described ex-Presidents Russell Kramer (Jack Lemmon) and Matt Douglas (James Garner) as "Grumpy Old Presidents."[43]

While *Independence Day* and *Air Force One* fly high with their pilot-president superheroes, *My Fellow Americans* presents two ex-presidents that are so down-to-earth that they could serve as poster boys for the carnivalesque. For Bakhtin, the pure carnivalesque situation occurs when a person of power leaves their established identity behind and goes down into the crowded streets of carnival, embraces the anonymity that the domino provides, and indulges in all the action, excitement, sexual license, danger, and freedom of the carnival atmosphere. *My Fellow Americans* presents exactly that kind of scenario. Ex-Presidents Kramer (the Republican, played with a kind of George Bush Sr. and Felix Unger fastidiousness) and Douglas (the Democrat, played with a Clinton and Oscar Madison moral looseness) leave the White House and are forced to enter the real world in all its diversity and chaotic irrationality, all its potential free market and sexual license.

After leaving the office, President Kramer spends his time giving ridiculous motivational speeches at corporate sales events. At one such outing, much to his dismay, he ends up dancing with a huge panda bear: "Tomorrow morning there's gonna be a picture of me dancing with a giant dog in every newspaper on the planet. . . . Did Jefferson dance with a bear? Did Lincoln? Did Reagan foxtrot with a friggin' Panda?" His dismay is understandable. What he has become in the real world isn't very presidential. But then neither is the post–White House life of ex-President Douglas. He spends his time sleeping with every bimbo he can get his horny presidential paws on. One of his girls rolls over and says, "I can't believe I just did it with Matt Douglas. He was the leader of the free world. My mother has a commemorative plate with your face on it." No, not very presidential. At a state funeral, as they stand over the coffin, Kramer and Douglas (like little boys) obscenely mock each others' fall into reality:

> *Douglas:* You're a whore. Admit it. You're a big whore. Go ahead.
> *Kramer:* Name three women from the District of Columbia that you didn't bang when you were in office.
> *Douglas:* Screw you!
> *Kramer:* Blow me!

This language sounds like Burgess Meredith's hilarious outtakes from *Grumpy Old Men* (1993), not the language that ex-presidents would use. But it is very much the vulgar language of the carnivalesque world that these two have entered.

As the film progresses, these two salty ex-presidents descend further and further into the carnival world. After an assassination attempt ordered by the standing president to cover up a Whitewater-like crooked kickback deal, Kramer and Douglas are forced to make a cross-country journey to reveal the truth and save the presidency. In a Kentucky railroad station restroom at a urinal next to a redneck who recognizes him and wants to shake his hand, Douglas answers, "I can't shake right now. Have to keep my hands on the First Penis." On a party train headed for the NCAA finals, an Elvis impersonator marks them as president impersonators and insists they share tips while a Marilyn look-alike brags that she slept with the real President Douglas when he was in the White House. "How was he?" ex-President Douglas's curiosity pushes him to ask. "He was a lot like his Presidency," she answers. "There was a lot of talk leading up to it, but then he didn't do much." They hitch a ride with a truck driver who gets stopped by a helicopter and are forced to flee with about fifty illegal aliens who jump out of the back of the truck. They end up in a station wagon with a factory worker and his family who, after getting in an argument with them about the state of the nation, charges, "Both of you. You ignore the voice of the people." This charge turns Kramer apoplectic: "The voice of the people! There's no such thing. There are 240 million voices all yelling for something different. The only thing you can agree on is you don't want higher taxes. The voice of the people, my fanny." Welcome to the heteroglossia (many voices) of the American carnival, Mr. President. Finally, these two geriatric presidents, trying to become superheroes and save the country, end up in a West Virginia parade celebrating gay power from which they are forced to flee when the evil president's agents crash the party. Luckily, they are whisked away on Harleys by their newfound allies, "Dykes on Bikes." As they work their way back to Washington, the two ex-presidents become more adept at the etiquette of survival in the carnival world of America outside the beltway.

One of the major obstacles that ex-Presidents Kramer and Douglas encounter in trying to reveal the truth about the most recent Washington scandal is that no one will believe them. The era of spin in nineties politics has engendered a deep-set disbelief and cynicism toward the office of the president. "The people will believe us because we're Presidents," Kramer declares confidently, but when Douglas rolls his eyes and gives him a who-are-you-kidding look, he has to admit, "OK, they won't believe us." The abusive truck driver who gives them a ride looks them right in the eye and says, "That's the trouble with you boys in Washington. You wouldn't know the truth if it jumped up and bit you in the butt." Finally, the moment comes as it does for all superheroes when they have to act, take that decisive step to save the country, and gain back historical respect for the presidency. Interestingly enough, Kramer uses exactly the same phrase that President Whitmore in *Independence Day* uses at the defining moment:

> *Douglas:* Somewhere out there . . . there's some idealistic sucker who still believes in us. After all the scandals and the party politics and all the bull, there's somebody out there that still believes that we care, that we would do what we promised to do.
> *Kramer:* All right. Let's do it!

What Douglas is saying is that in the era of spin, when confidence in the presidency has all but been destroyed, someone has to ride in and rescue the office from the spinmasters, and that is literally what these two unlikely cowboy heroes do. In the presidents of *Independence Day*, *Air Force One*, and *My Fellow Americans*, there are superheroes for every generation.

## Presidents as Villains and Victims

The difference in golf and government is that in golf you can't improve your lie.
—Governor George Deukmajian of California

If the most prominent wish-fulfillment text of the nineties film discourse on the American presidency is that of the comic book superhero, then there are also other more sinister and disturbing presidential texts represented. For every representation of a two-fisted, flyboy, gun-toting president, there is an equal number of movie presidents who either criminally abuse the power of the office or are threatened by the danger and responsibilities of the office to the point that they are unable to act. Again, in reaction to the total lack of confidence in the American presidency, nineties films portrayed presidents as both villains trying to cover up their abuses of power and victims intimidated by threats of terrorism, assassination, kidnapping, public persecution of loved ones, or blackmail.

*Absolute Power* (1997) is such a film, and it offers a window into the very kinds of abuses that its title signals. In *Absolute Power*, the president of the United States, Alan Richmond (Gene Hackman), is a sadomasochistic philanderer who causes the death of his best friend's wife with whom he is having an affair and then tries to cover it up. Here, the president is actually a murderer and his weapon of choice is the Secret Service. When the film was released, the critics recognized that "Hackman's Alan Richmond is obviously meant to be a hyperbolic takeoff on Bill Clinton and his fabled promiscuity."[44] This film even steals the trademark Clintonesque dance scene from *Primary Colors* and *The American President* and plays it with a cynical, hypocritical, comic spin. Richmond and his loyal Chief of Staff Gloria Russell (Judy Davis), who is in charge of the cover-up, dance at a White House reception. As they twirl around the floor, dipping and spinning, they are all smiles, but beneath those smiles, through clenched teeth, Richmond is asking why she is wearing the dead woman's diamond necklace, and Gloria is realizing that a witness to the murder, Luther Whitney (Clint Eastwood), is playing both of them. *Absolute Power*'s dance scene accomplishes something that the visually identical scenes in *Primary Colors* and *The American President* don't. It captures the physical embodiment of spin in all its irony. Richmond can smile and laugh uproariously as he is cursing his partner for her stupidity. Gloria can gaze adoringly into the president's eyes even as she is desperately defending herself against his berating anger. Immediately following this set-piece dance scene, the president takes Gloria into the Oval Office in the West Wing of the White House and orders the murder by the Secret Service not only of Whitney but of Whitney's daughter as well (who they surmise also knows about the president's involvement). Richmond may be a hyperbolic Clinton, but this film's plot makes Watergate look just like the third-rate burglary that it was.

Clinton's groping fingerprints are all over Hackman's characterization of President Richmond. As the adulterous assignation that opens the film begins, the first thing that Richmond does is push the soon to be dead woman's head down to perform oral sex on him. After the murder, as Gloria tells Richmond that she will cover it all up, she reassures him that the Secret Service agents who shot the woman "are no strangers to scandal." And Richmond's wife, the First Lady, never even appears in the film. The presidency in *Absolute Power* has all the details of Clinton's morally challenged White House years, yet it blows those scandals up into the unthinkable.

Richmond is the president of the United States and yet he tosses off the death that he has caused as if he had done nothing more than swat an annoying fly: "I apologize for my behavior. It won't happen again. Consider it a blip on the screen." Not only does he refuse to acknowledge the consequences of immoral action, he doesn't even see that he's done anything wrong despite the dead woman lying in the morgue. And he is so hypocritical that he calls a press conference to rail against violence in America and to embrace his closest friend (whose wife's death he has caused) and share his mourning on national TV. When Whitney sees this astounding display of hypocrisy, he literally talks back to the president on the TV screen: "You heartless asshole. I'm not about to run from you." Thus, Richmond's hypocritical attempt to spin this murder into political opportunity mobilizes the only witness to the crime into righteous action.

But the main premise of *Absolute Power*, Whitney's inadvertent and unwilling witnessing of the sexual liaison and the killing of the president's bimbo, comments on America's reaction to all the Clinton revelations of hanky-panky in the Oval Office. *Absolute Power* is a film about voyeurism. Whitney is a brilliant jewel thief, a master of disguise and a cat burglar, much like Cary Grant in

Hitchcock's *To Catch A Thief* (1955). While looting the secret vault (complete with an entrance through a sliding two-way mirror) of a Washington suburban mansion, he witnesses through the mirror the rough sexual liaison and the death by Secret Service gunfire of a young woman. He realizes that the victim's husband had created this special room in order to watch his wife have sex with other men. This film's theme of voyeurism serves as an ironic commentary on the nineties fascination of the American people with the tawdry, melodramatic, soap opera, sexual scandals of the American presidency. Who needs to watch *Passions* or *Days of Our Lives* in the afternoon when you can look through the keyhole of the White House and watch the president's sex life on the evening news? *Absolute Power* and a similar film that followed, *Murder at 1600* (1997), both emphasize surveillance as the government's primary means of control.[45] In both films, surveillance becomes an ever-present motif employed by the Secret Service to cover up the crimes committed in the White House. In *Absolute Power*, the Secret Service bugs the police detective in charge of the investigation in order to target what they need to cover up.

Perhaps of all the presidential spin movies of the nineties, *Absolute Power* is the most cynical. President Richmond is an irredeemable villain who never exhibits a single spark of humanity or remorse. But even worse than that heartless and soulless characterization of the Leader of the Free World is the manner in which spin triumphs at the end of the film. President Richmond is given the honorable way out by his best friend whose wife he has caused to be killed, and he commits suicide in the Oval Office. At least the Clinton administration never left blood spatters on the West Wing walls, though the suicide of attorney Vincent Foster came uncomfortably close to the White House. But the most disturbing scene of the film is the press conference following the president's suicide. Lying to the press, the husband of the president's dead bimbo sustains the cover-up and allows this guilty president to go to the grave unexposed. Once again spin triumphs, and, in the films of the nineties, the president as "supersleaze" becomes the flip side—the president as superhero.

*Murder at 1600* is no better. This time the murdered bimbo, having just had sex in the Oval Office before being multiply stabbed, becomes the subject of cover-ups in layers, cover-ups within cover-ups within cover-ups to the point that the powers of spin are taxed to their ultimate limits. Like *Absolute Power*, *Murder at 1600* was immediately recognized as a narrative based on the realities of the Clinton White House. One critic quipped, "Bill Clinton may be up to his keister in troubles, but this takes the biscuit for Hollywood-style political paranoia."[46] In this film, the whole First Family (father, son, First Lady, and even the family dog) is implicated in the various cover-ups. In an interesting twist, however, by the end of the film the whole conspiracy somersaults and the First Family becomes the victim rather than the villain.

From the opening scene, there is no doubt that this story is modeled after the Clinton presidency. *Murder at 1600* opens with a Washington bureaucrat (much like White House lawyer Vincent Foster) threatening suicide in the shadows of the Washington Monument and the Capital Building, cut to sex in the Oval

Office beneath the portraits of Washington and Jefferson and right on top of the presidential seal, cut to the body of a beautiful young woman found in a White House restroom, cut to the White House Press Secretary briefing the staff: "I'd like you to avoid using two words if you give any statements to the press. The words are 'woman' and 'murder.'" By the end of this quick-cut opening, the full power of spin is in control as it was all through the Clinton years. This, however, isn't a mere "bimbo eruption," but rather a full-scale murder inside the White House.

When the press learns of the murder, the feeding frenzy begins. "Was the First Family involved?" is the first question that the press mob asks of DC Police Detective Harlan Regis (Wesley Snipes). Soon, he finds out that they are more involved than even the most far-fetched soap opera could imagine. Both President Jack Neal (Ronny Cox) and his son Kyle are having sexual affairs with the murder victim. "'Jack, Kyle and Carla, The Oval Office Threesome,'" Regis predicts the tabloid headlines. "Will Carla Towne be Jack Neal's Chappaquidick?" a TV news anchor asks the nation. Even venerable *Time* magazine's cover reads, "Murder in the White House," and as the president looks at it he asks his advisers, "How can I defend the country when I can't defend my own house?" As Detective Regis quickly realizes, his whole investigation is going to progress at the pace of the press. One of the first things he asks of the tight-lipped White House Chief of Security Nick Spikings (Daniel Benzali) is, "I guess I'm supposed to get my briefings from CNN?" When Regis asks Spikings what it would take to get a look at the White House surveillance tapes for the night of the murder, the answer is, "Not much. Only an act of Congress." Regis and his Secret Service liaison officer, Nina Chance (Diane Lane), quickly realize that the full power of White House spin control is being beamed at their investigation.

The main tool of that spin control is surveillance. Everything functions under the controlling, information-gathering eye of surveillance in this film. Everyone is spying on everyone else, through surveillance cameras, binoculars, photographic enhancements, electronic bugging devices, and peepholes. What all this surveillance finds under the rocks that it turns over isn't pretty. The son of the president's "one mission in life is to get laid in every room in the White House," and he even brags about "sharing a mistress with his father." But this is a much deeper conspiracy and cover-up then just a presidential sexual liaison. Nina and Regis, the two detectives trying to find out what really happened that night in the White House, find themselves under full surveillance by the Secret Service who have been enlisted in the cover-up. The Secret Service even pursues them in government helicopters. What *Murder at 1600* is thematically exploring in this steamy, melodramatic, soap opera plot is the theme of how spin and surveillance are completely out of control in American politics. "I think Washington is drowning in a sea of its own bull shit" is Regis's despairing assessment of the state of the union.

As it turns out, the First Family is not guilty of murder at all in *Murder at 1600* (though they are guilty of a number of other unsavory things), and the murdered girl "wasn't killed to protect the First Family. She was killed to destroy it." It is all a plot by the president's national security adviser, Alvin Jordan (Alan Alda), to get the president to resign because he is too much a dove. The film ends with a clumsy series of lectures on the presidency delivered by Jordan (in a rhetoric recognizable from all the other nineties films) about the sorry state of the American presidency in the decade of spin. Jordan intones, "The President is not to be involved. . . . You're not questioning the President. The Presidency is an institution not a person. An institution will be protected at all costs." And, later, Jordan accuses the president, right inside the Oval Office, of failing in his duties to that institution: "Any President who serves up his country as appetizers for the enemy isn't fit for this office. So the choice is yours. You can resign, say it's due to your health, and tour the best golf courses in America." These speeches, especially coming in this potboiler of a conspiracy plot, are a preachy motive for an ill-conceived and clumsily executed conspiracy.

But the most unappetizing aspect of *Murder at 1600* isn't the unbelievable plot or its clichéd preaching about the presidency as institution. The most disturbing aspect of the film is the characterization of the president himself. President Neal is a total nonentity, an indecisive, international wimp as well as a Clintonesque womanizer. When Jordan reveals the whole conspiracy to him and orders him to resign, he just meekly goes along. He signs off on Jordan's dirty little conspiracy even though it includes the murder of an innocent young woman. It is the weakest characterization of an American president in any of the films of the nineties. This particular presidential soap opera is even more disheartening than the cynicism at the end of *Absolute Power*. Spin triumphs here as well. Wimpy President Neal covers up the whole conspiracy for the good of the country and all is forgotten (except perhaps the dead woman in the White House restroom).

In the wake of *Absolute Power* and *Murder at 1600*, a colorless, gray-power-suited array of presidents as villains appeared in the films of the nineties. This parade of negative presidential representations (often supported by equally villainous aides, Secret Service agents, cabinet members and even First Family members) portrayed the White House as a den of thieves and a pit of cover-ups. President Bennett (Donald Moffat) in the Tom Clancy government conspiracy thriller *Clear and Present Danger* (1994) is "a character who is part Reagan (the supposedly kindly, selectively deaf old man), part Bush (the well connected preppie), and part nostalgic throwback to a Nixonian era of righteous public outrage about government crimes and cover-ups."[47] John Carpenter's *Escape From L.A.* (1997) is a sequel to his own *Escape From New York* (1981), and both are films in which the presidents of the future are shown to be just as unpresidential and villainous as are the present president (Clinton) and all the past presidents (especially Nixon and Reagan). In *Escape From New York*, set in a futuristic 1997, the president (Donald Pleasance) is a wimpy weasel who needs to be rescued from Manhattan, which has become an island penal colony for the postapocalyptic world. In the sequel, *Escape From L.A.*, set in 2013, Snake Plissken (Kurt Russell) is forced back into action by "the most conservative President in history"[48] to rescue the First Daughter, a radicalized sexpot named Utopia. She has stolen a world-threatening scientific device and fled morally righteous America for the place that the ascendant Christian right wing sends all who disagree with its rigor, in other words, all the theologically deviant. Where else? LA, now an island thanks to a huge earthquake.

Equally common as all these "presidents as villains" in nineties films were the representations of "presidents as victims." These films mainly involved assassination plots but also had their share of kidnappers and blackmailers. In *My Fellow Americans* ex-President Douglas asks the Secret Service agent assigned to guard him if there has ever been an assassination attempt on an ex-president. When the agent answers in the negative, Douglas says, "Take a night off. Go rent *In the Line of Fire* again." Eastwood's presidential assassination movie is second only to Stone's *JFK* in portraying the president as victim in the complex spin of American political life. *In the Line of Fire* (1993) is not really about the presidency at all, rather it is about the Secret Service, the president's bodyguards. The Secret Service has been portrayed (mainly as villains) in almost all these nineties presidential films. If their role goes beyond merely following the president around, they are usually represented as assassins in the service of some White House initiated conspiracy. *In the Line of Fire* is the first film to focus on the single true mission of the Secret Service, that of protecting the president (not covering up his crimes or killing his enemies). In *Absolute Power*, the two Secret Service agents are totally corrupt; one is a stone-cold killer and the other commits suicide out of guilt for his involvement in the conspiracy. In *Murder at 1600*, the Secret Service bodyguards become so confused that they don't know who to take their orders from until female agent Nina Chance reaffirms their mission by actually taking a bullet for the president. In *Dave*, the president's Secret Service agent remains loyal to the office even though he knows that a stand-in has been substituted for the president in violation of a myriad of federal laws and constitutional imperatives. But *In the Line of Fire* rights all these diverse Secret Service wrongs.

Like Nina Chance in *Murder at 1600*, Frank Harrigan (Eastwood), veteran Secret Service agent, would like nothing better than to throw himself in front of his president and take an assassin's bullet. He had his chance to do just that thirty years earlier in 1963 in Dallas, but he was too slow to react and it has haunted his edgy psyche ever since. *In the Line of Fire* is the story of how one Secret Service agent gets his own and his profession's mission back on line in the age of spin. While in most of these films the Secret Service agents are mere bric-a-brac, bland satellites of manipulative, sometimes criminal, presidents, the president in *In the Line of Fire* is no more than a target, a Hitchcockian McGuffin, there simply to attract psycho-assassin Mitch Leary's (John Malkovich) and eager-agent Frank Harrigan's long sought bullet. *In the Line of Fire* sets the bar for a whole string of Secret Service films throughout the nineties, none of which reach its high standard of portraying the strangely masochistic ethos of a person whose sole mission in life is to serve as a human target for a presidential assassin's bullet.

If *In the Line of Fire* is the best film portrayal of the Secret Service in action, *First Kid* (1996) has to be the worst and *Guarding Tess* (1994) the most boring. A nineties take on *The Ransom of Red Chief*, *First Kid* has a Secret Service agent guarding the president's bratty elementary school-age son. *Guarding Tess*, similarly, has agent Doug Chesnie (Nicholas Cage) guarding widowed former First Lady Tess Carlisle (Shirley MacLaine) in a film that more closely resembles *Driving Miss Daisy* than any sort of political thriller. In the wake of *In the Line of Fire*, *Guarding Tess* is pretty weak stuff and Chesnie dealing with a cranky and lonely ex-First Lady doesn't really stack up very well with Frank Harrigan dealing with a psychopathic, extremely intelligent, would-be presidential assassin who, in his most twisted scene, literally fellates the barrel of Harrigan's astounded and befuddled gun, taking it all the way into his mouth in a psychosexual moment of *doppelganger* identification. Malkovich's Leary is such a riveting sicko, such an intelligent psychic tormentor of strong, silent Harrigan that he becomes the driving force of the film.

Whether the president is a villain or a victim, whether the Secret Service loyally guards or allows itself to be used as a criminal tool of political conspiracy, the noirish political thriller was back in business in the nineties. These thrillers, like the Clintonesque films about our performer-in-chief and the historical films about the paranoia of conspiracy and surveillance, ultimately do not explore the lives or worlds of the individual presidents who they portray. Rather, they examine the presidency itself as caught in the whirl of nineties spin.

## Political Satires

> Robbins captures the dizzying surface—and grisly underbelly—of American televisual politics.—Forget infotainment—Robbins has captured the disorienting spectacle of poli-tainment.
>
> —Owen Gleiberman on *Bob Roberts* (1992),
> "Running on Empty," *Entertainment Weekly*

In the era of spin, American films about politics and the presidency did indeed capture two main truths. First, all the major political films of the nineties acknowledged the Kennedy-Reagan legacy of presidential performativity spun out of control. The American public wanted a president who was a performer-in-chief and whose life in office could have the sort of melodramatic or sexually titillating entertainment value of an afternoon soap opera. Hence, a Bill Clinton appears on the late-night *Arsenio Hall Show* in dark glasses playing a jazz saxophone and all the candidates for the presidency make their appearances on *Oprah*, *The Tonight Show*, and *Saturday Night Live* every bit as frequently as they appear on *Meet the Press*. Gleiberman's characterization of the 1992 election year political scene (in his review of *Bob Roberts*) as "televisual politics" and "poli-tainment" is accurate. Gleiberman's word coinages and Tim Robbins's (both director and lead actor as was Orson Welles in *Citizen Kane*) movie both capture the dizzying spin of the nineties political ethos in which nationally visible politicians are brazen entertainers, chamelion-like performers.

Second, the presidential satires of the nineties dramatize the strong carnivalesque impulses of contemporary American presidents who have been previously dramatized in films like *Primary Colors*, *The American President*, and *Dave*.

*Bulworth* (1998) represents this text of the presidential carnivalesque more dramatically, satirically, and hilariously than any other political film of the decade. But the one truth that every one of these nineties political satires stresses is the powerful and corrupt influence of spin on the American political process. *Bob Roberts* and *The Distinguished Gentleman* (1992) demonstrate the total cynicism of both the politician and the voter. Nineties politics has become a world that exists outside of any normative or recognizable reality, all "dizzying surface" and "poli-tainment." As early as the 1992 election year, spin was already in full control of American politics.

"*Bob Roberts* is at its acrid best when it's observing the process of modern political packaging,"[49] one commentator identifies its cynical satirical mastertext. It is a film about spin and political performance, about a country singer twanging and plucking his way into the United States Senate. Roberts (Tim Robbins), the candidate, instead of giving boring speeches engages the issues and audiences at his rallies with poli-tainment folk songs like "The Wall Street Rap" and "Drugs Stink" and the reactionary anti-Dylan anthem, "Times Are Changin' Back." Critic Gleiberman captures how the style of *Bob Roberts*—the mockumentary—mirrors the satirical message—"political packaging"—of the film: "Satire, even at its most merciless, is powered by the comic rush of discovery. . . . It's this quality that made the mock rockumentary *This is Spinal Tap* so exhilarating. . . . Robbins, having parodied the phony surface of politics, now reveals the "truth" below. . . . He doesn't seem to realize that though the right wing (via Reagan) may have perfected the politics of image, by now it's everyone's game."[50] This statement is in many ways prophetic. Written when Clinton was just taking office in 1992, it acknowledges the utterly bipartisan, apolitical identity of nineties political spin. Republican, Democrat, right winger or leftist, conservative or liberal, Reagan or Clinton, actor or saxophone player, it just doesn't make any difference; all politicians have been caught in the power of spin, have fallen in love with its possibilities, constantly use it, try to control it, rise and fall with it. The theme song of nineties politics might well be that great old jazz standard "The Old Black Magic":

> Caught in the spin,
> That wonderful spin I'm in.

*The Distinguished Gentleman's* satire takes aim at the performance requirement for public office in a way quite similar to *Bob Roberts*. Where *Bob Roberts* is a satire in the *This is Spinal Tap (1984)* vein, *The Distinguished Gentleman* is a satire of all the smug idealism and Pollyanna innocence of the Frank Capra school of political commentary (read: *Mr. Smith Goes to Washington* from 1939 and, the neo-Capraesque *The American President* to come in 1995). The days of Capraesque satire and gently comic politicians are over forever in the nineties. When *The Distinguished Gentleman's* con man-turned-Congressman finds religion near the end of the film, the sea change sinks the whole movie and rings utterly unbelievable because everyone knows that the film's earlier cynicism was the true picture of nineties politics. Politicians are damned to spin in their self-made, Dantean circle of hell from the moment they throw their hat in the ring for their first campaign.

But by far the most powerful, most bizarre, best written, and funniest of all the nineties political satires is *Bulworth* (1998). This film combines the American desires for both a performer-in-chief (how about a rap-singer president?) and a Bakhtinian carnivalesque president (as at home in a South Central LA after-hours club as on national TV). It is a film like *The Wizard of Oz* (1939). Here, a politician is catapulted out of the charcoal-gray-suited world of political spin into the colorful, rap-spinning, turntable world of ghetto life in search of the truth about politics. But when he returns to his original political office, he is assassinated for violating the only hard and fast rule of nineties political spin—never ever tell it like it is, never ever allow the truth to enter the "language games" of nineties politics.

What would happen if politicians actually used the contemporary language of the people, the real people, not the corporations, not the lobbyists, not the spinmasters and political handlers, but the language of the ethnic minorities, the workers, the poor, the disenfranchised, the marginalized? What if, in using that language, they actually told the truth, told it like it is, sans spin, straight? That is the bizarre scenario that forms the mastertext of Warren Beatty's hip political satire, *Bulworth*.

Jay Billington Bulworth (Beatty) is a California senator running for reelection, a crooked Democratic machine politician who will take bribes from any lobbyist and will tell anyone who donates big money to his campaign war chest exactly what they want to hear. In other words, he is a nineties politician who has totally immersed himself in the pull of political spin. Personally befuddled, Bulworth does whatever his team of political handlers tells him to do. Dennis Murphy (Oliver Platt), his chief of staff, orchestrates his every move and puts all his words into his mouth. Bill Feldman (Joshua Malina) writes his speeches and Davers (Jack Warden) handles all his day-to-day problems. Graham Crockett (Paul Sorvino), a lobbyist for the insurance industry, hovers over him ready to give him anything he wants for the right corporate legislation. All of these spinmasters generate the vortex in which Bulworth exists. They spin him through his days and nights on an endless whirl of campaign speeches, photo ops, interviews, fund-raisers, and strategy sessions. But Bulworth, wildly successful nineties politician, a shoo-in for reelection, is not happy living in his spinning world. In fact, he is suicidally depressed, so depressed he can neither sleep nor eat, so depressed that all he can do is sit in his darkened office watching TV commercials of himself and sobbing uncontrollably. All is not well in Spinville.

The opening of *Bulworth*, a sarcastically written text, sets this typically nineties political premise for the film:

Mid-March 1996.
The time of the California Primaries.
Robert Dole has secured the Republican nomination.

President Clinton runs unopposed by other Democrats.
The populace is unaroused.

After that uninspiring establishing statement, the credits roll over the film editing of a "Jay Billington Bulworth for U.S. Senate" campaign commercial in which the candidate intones, "We stand on the threshold of a new millennium," over and over from different angles and in different inflections as the spinmasters attempt to capture just the right sales pitch. Finally the film begins with a pan over photos of a young Bulworth on the campaign trail with Bobby Kennedy to the real present-day Bulworth sobbing uncontrollably in the darkness.

Bulworth sobs in the darkness because he realizes that he no longer exists, that he is no longer in touch with any idealistic political reality (a.k.a. the Kennedy years), and that he is nothing more than a mouthpiece, a talking head, a vehicle for the same old political spin. His handlers, Murphy, Davers, and Feldman, manage to put him back together for one more day on the campaign trail, but, at their first stop in a South Central LA African American church, he unravels again. He takes the pulpit, starts to mouth the words of his "Doorway To The New Millennium" meaningless stump speech, and just can't go on with it. To the utter horror of his spinmasters, he starts to tell the truth. In answer to the first question about promises of federal funding to help rebuild after the Watts Riots of 1992, Bulworth answers, "Well what happened was that we all knew that was gonna be big news for awhile so we all came down here. Bush. Clinton. Wilson. All of us. Got our pictures taken. Told you what you wanted to hear. Then we pretty much forgot about it." In answer to the second question of why he won't vote for better insurance rates for the poor, he answers, "Because you haven't really contributed any money to my campaign, have you?" By this time, his handlers are apoplectic. He is saying things so straight and true that his answers are unspinable. Murphy pulls a fire alarm to clear the building and stop Bulworth's fatal truth telling.

The same thing happens at his next campaign stop, a Clintonesque fundraiser with the Hollywood set in a Beverly Hills mansion. Again, he starts to give his canned speech but quickly discards it. He proceeds to tell the movie people how all their films are just "crap." The funny thing is, though, that when Bulworth is telling the truth, saying exactly what he is thinking, he feels good about himself. In stepping outside of the power-centered vortex of spin, he reclaims his voice, his humanity, and his political integrity. At this point, *Bulworth* becomes truly postmodern. When Bulworth flees the Beverly Hills fund-raiser and heads down into the hip-hop world of South Central, this film becomes the spinmasters' worst nightmare. Bulworth discards his stiff political suit, loosens his power tie, dons the domino of anonymity (a bartender first thinks he's Clint Eastwood, then thinks he's George Hamilton) of the South Central night world, hangs with the brothers, walks the streets, and talks in the language of pure sexual freedom. He descends into the nocturnal celebration of the hip-hop carnival and finds a whole new identity for himself (or, as the TV news tags it and as his handlers try to spin it, a new "campaign strategy").

Fleeing from Beverly Hills in his limousine with two hookers and a young black activist, Nina (Halle Berry), added to his entourage and being filmed by CNN (*à la* the mockumentary *Bob Roberts*), Bulworth starts to talk differently. He enters the nineties version of Oz by first indulging his curiosity about the sexual license that the language of rap offers and then by starting to speak in tongues (after meeting a homeless wino who will appear throughout the film as a magic realism chorus figure much like the good witch in *The Wizard of Oz*), and, finally, by totally embracing that language and becoming a rap-singer political candidate. Pinstripe-suited, talking head, spinmastered political candidate Jay Billington Bulworth becomes Rapmaster JB and his political campaign is really "not in Kansas anymore, Toto."

Although an equally bizarre take on nineties politics as *Wag the Dog*, both that film and *Bulworth* share the Reagan legacy, the nineties demand that the presidency and the president are driven by the phenomenon of public performance. In *Wag the Dog*, the spinmasters create a national spectacle, a pageant, out of thin air as a diversionary ploy in a presidential campaign, while in *Bulworth* a potential presidential candidate takes his message to the people by becoming the most outrageous political performer that anyone can imagine. One can imagine an actor like Reagan or a saxophone player like Clinton or a conservative folk singer like Bob Roberts actually becoming president of the United States, but a gangsta rapper, whoa?

For Bulworth, this change in identity, this new language, this newfound freedom in telling the truth, gives him something to live for and he decides to cancel the mob hit he has put out on himself. Remarkably, or unremarkably considering that this is the decade of spin, the press, the national media, the tabloids, and talk television pick up positively on the new Bulworth and report the "sudden change in [his] campaign style" as a refreshing new spin on American politics. It is almost as if the telling of the truth does set them all free. Bulworth, who began the film suicidal because he had become a pure "simulation" mouthing only "language games" of power politics, suddenly transforms himself into a simulation of a rapper and launches himself into a new hip-hop language game. In a sense, he swaps simulations in his quest to find himself, which, of course, has been lost forever in the spin of postmodern simulation. Larry King (who seems to pop up in all of these political movies like some goggle-eyed finger puppet representing the national media) puts it best as he talks to Murphy, Bulworth's head spinmaster, about the candidate: "Are you kidding? This guy is on a roll. They want someone like this. People are sick and tired of all this baloney. I want him on my show."

That conversation with King signals to Murphy that he can, indeed, spin this manic-depressive episode to his candidate's advantage. Suddenly, Murphy realizes that he is back in the game and he doesn't hesitate to start spinning the new Bulworth for all he's worth. Whereas Murphy had only moments earlier shut off the electricity in the TV studio where the debate was being held, Murphy now accuses the head of the network: "You turned off the electricity because you knew [Bulworth] was telling the truth. You could put that debate back on the air, but you didn't want the American people to hear what he had to say." The spinmaster starts spinning Bulworth's newfound truth-telling style as the new *realpolitik.*

What this comically deconstructive political satire asks are the crucial questions of spin: Who says you can't make chicken salad out of chicken shit? Who says you can't fall into a cesspool and come out smelling like a rose? Who says you can't sell a political candidate who raps the truth? That is the beauty of spin. It always spins back. For Murphy, in mere moments, Bulworth goes from being a political handler's worst nightmare to being the newest flavor on the menu of spinmastering. The grand finale of Bulworth's political makeover occurs when he is asked on election eve to appear with Bob Dole and Bill Clinton on the national TV American elections special. He shows up in full hip-hop gear from his knit hat to his dark sunglasses to his basketball shorts to his basketball shoes. The interviewer sits him down on national TV and asks, "Senator, why this new campaign style? Why this new manner of dress and speech? Your ethnic manner of speech? Your clothes? The use of obscenity?" This question is interesting because it is all about style rather than substance. It is all about Lyotardian language games. It is all about the only thing that the media is interested in and can handle. The nineties media aren't interested in issues and ideas. All they care about is the performance, the entertainment value of the candidate.

Ironically, however, the end of that interviewer's question, the word "obscenity," triggers a reaction in Bulworth that sets in motion one of the great political speeches of all of these nineties films. Bulworth's manic "obscenity" rap is a speech that rivals the "Greed is good" speech in *Wall Street* and the "I *am* the President" speech in *The American President* and demonstrates just how far the concept of the presidency has been spun in the nineties. But, despite its rap rhythm and its ghetto lyrics, *Bulworth's* climactic speech actually does address a broad range of nineties political issues in a fairly sophisticated way. It is a presidential State of the Union address delivered by a gangsta rapper, and, beyond its style, it is worth listening to for its substance:

> Obscenity!
> The rich is gettin' richer and richer, and richer,
> While the middle class is gettin' more poor
> Obscenity!

While the original question was about the obscenity of Bulworth's new *realpolitik* vocabulary, the truth-telling, gangsta politician redefines "obscenity" in terms of the blight on America's political landscape.

> But we got babies in South Central dying as young as they do in Peru.
> We got public schools that are nightmares.
> We got a Congress that ain't got a clue.
> We got kids with submachine guns.

We got militias throwin' bombs.
We got Bill just getting' all weepy.
We got Newt blaming teenage moms.
We got factories closin' down.
Obscenity!
. . . Oh shit, fuck, cocksucker!
That's the real obscenity black folks livin' with every day,
tryin' to believe a motherfuckin' word Democrats or Republicans say.

For Bulworth, the real obscenity isn't the rude words of the hip-hop generation, but the sad state of the nation that American politics has created.

And who does Bulworth, the rapper politician, point to as the villain in this obscene political scenario? Who else but the mass media, the purveyors of spin:

I got a simple question that I'd like to ask
if this network pays you for doin' your task.
How come they get the airwaves?
They're the peoples', aren't they? . . .
It's hopeless you see
if you're runnin' for office without no TV . . .
You been taught in this country there's speech that is free,
but free do not get you no spots on TV . . .
Telecommunications is the name of the beast,
that-that-that-that's eatin' up the world from the west to the east.
The movies, the tabloids, TV and magazines.

For Bulworth, late twentieth-century American history has been hijacked by the spinmasters and their willing accomplices, the media.

Bulworth's long rap monologue strikes out at every issue, racial group, special interest, and political faction in American life with a kind of kinetic, scatter-shot, nonpartisan, political-correctness-be-damned logic. But, in its manic performance, it also does something that Hollywood movies rarely do. It confronts, explores, and headlines issues. It looks at all of the major domestic problems in nineties America, the state of the union, and it tries to analyze where those problems came from and how we have to recognize them and try to fix them. It is no coincidence that, in his rap monologue, Bulworth's greatest tirade is against the unholy alliance of the politicians, the corporations, and the media. That is the evil triad of spin in the nineties.

As a result of this election eve rap triumph of reverse political spin, Bulworth is reelected to the Senate in a landslide and even receives 20 percent of the vote as a write-in candidate for president. It seems to be a great triumph for the re-ascendance of truth in American politics. But Bulworth is immediately assassinated. The greater truth is that corporate America simply can't have a president that tells the truth. In the course of his odyssey toward truth, Bulworth gains one convert, L. D. (Don Cheadle), the South Central drug king. This Fagin of the *Oliver Twist* world of the ghetto, with his distribution gangs of twelve-year-old, gun-packing, hip-hop Artful Dodgers, is reborn into the next African American politician, declaring, "I'm gonna flip this whole power shit in a whole different way." In the deconstructive world of *Bulworth*, spin is an equal-opportunity strategy for political success in the nineties.

# CHAPTER 6

# Spin Out

## The Gay Nineties

This disease will be the end of many of us, but not nearly all, and the dead will be commemorated and will struggle on with the living, and we are not going away. We won't die secret deaths anymore. The world only spins forward. We will be citizens. The time has come.

—Tony Kushner, *Angels In America*, Epilogue

One of the greatest triumphs of positive spin in nineties American culture, offsetting in part the negative manipulative spin practiced by politicians, was the decade-long effort toward explaining and positively portraying the gay lifestyle to a mainstream audience. Addressing the issues of the gay community and portraying the normality rather than the abnormality, the joy and satisfaction and love rather than the deviance, of the gay lifestyle was a mission that a whole different breed of socially and culturally conscious spin-masters pursued in the nineties decade. The Broadway success of Tony Kushner's Pulitzer Prize–winning epic drama about homosexuality and AIDS, *Angels In America* (1990), early in the decade and then the casting of America's Everyman, Tom Hanks, as a gay man suffering from AIDS in *Philadelphia* (1993) opened the door for a full decade of discourse on the issues of the gay lifestyle.

The last speech of Kushner's *Angels In America* predicts the future of America's gay consciousness quite accurately. "We are not going away," the speaker announces. "We won't die silent deaths anymore." And this speaker affirms that "the world only spins forward." Kushner's play is the centrifuge that launched the discourse of gay consciousness into the master discourse of spin of the nineties decade. But even before *Angels In America* had its Pulitzer Prize–winning impact on Broadway, academia had already embraced the theoretical spin of what would come to be called "queer theory." Based first in the Duke University English Department in the late eighties, then quickly spreading nationwide through academia, queer theory became the fastest growing intellectual niche.

Then, immediately following the success of *Angels In America*, Hollywood also entered the spin cycle and films dealing with the gay lifestyle began to appear. The prediction of the speaker in the epilogue to *Angels In America*—"We will be citizens. The time has come"—came true in the twentieth century's version of the gay nineties. Hollywood films would portray the gay lifestyle in all its variety and would become an influential discourse site on gay life in nineties America. Thus, the gay consciousness triggered by *Angels In America* proved yet another point of confluence of Hollywood and history.

The history—or more accurately, the New Historicism—of the growth of gay consciousness culminating in *Angels In America* is worth tracing simply for the evolution of its spin strategy. Most contemporary gay history is dated from the Stonewall Riots in New York in 1969 and the annual gay pride parades that followed. But even prior to those consciousness-defining events, films attempted to portray the gay lifestyle and issues in a number of diverse ways. One of the earliest positive and sympathetic representations of homosexuality was the 1961 British thriller *Victim* starring Dirk Bogarde as a gay-curious, married man who helps police catch a gang of blackmailers who prey on gay victims. The film's major targets were England's antihomosexual laws, which were subsequently repealed. In 1968 Off Broadway, *The Boys in the Band* broke the ground for the depiction of gay men on the American stage and was followed in 1975 by the Pulitzer Prize–winning musical *A Chorus Line* that would run for fifteen years on Broadway. In 1980, a much less sympathetic crime film, *Cruising*, starring Al Pacino as an undercover cop hunting a killer in the gay underground, occasioned angry protests in San Francisco. "This is the kind of movie the KKK would make about blacks," Harry Britt, a gay city supervisor, declared.[1]

Then, in 1985, Rock Hudson, the all-American on-screen heterosexual romantic leading man, died of AIDS as a result of his forty years' closeted gay lifestyle. For the first time, that deadly new disease was given a face and it was that of one of Hollywood's most popular hetero icons. Hudson's death was the first major crack in the slammed-shut and tightly locked door of *The Celluloid Closet* (1996), as a New Historicist documentary on the subject would later call it, and the first major revelation of Hollywood's *Open Secret* (1998), as David Ehrenstein's New Historicist book on the subject would call it.[2] But it was Randy Shilts's 1987 bestseller *And The Band Played On* that would be the first "queer theory" history to be adapted to the screen in the form of a HBO cable-TV miniseries (1993). These were the benchmark, pre–*Angels In America* texts (film, theater, cultural, historical) that set the centrifuge of gay nineties spin in motion. *Angels In America* dramatized all of those texts of previously repressed gay consciousness and opened wide the door of the aesthetic closet for the nineties decade.

## TV and Stealth Spin

Yep, I'm gay.

—The coming-out episode of *Ellen* (1997)

As a medium for gay consciousness, television proved to be much more problematic and controversial than either the movies or the stage. Many extracultural entities had to be taken into account: the skittishness of corporate advertisers, the venom of the Christian right, the necessity of keeping up weekly ratings, complaints from local affiliate stations, the fear of controversy in a "cool" medium. Prior to the nineties, homosexuality on television had never been portrayed in any sort of honest and upfront way. Tony Randall in the seventies and eighties in *The Odd Couple* and *Love, Sidney* had played fussy bachelor roles and Billy Crystal had been a funny effeminate younger brother on *Soap*, but none of these ambiguous TV sitcom characters had ever actually come out and declared themselves gay. Then, in 1989, in the nighttime series *Thirtysomething*, two gay men were actually pictured in bed together talking, not about sex or homosexuality or anything controversial, mind you, but they were nonetheless there, in bed, together, men. Then, in 1994, a lesbian-curious Roseanne, star of one of the nineties most popular sitcoms, kissed another woman, and her world as a "domestic goddess" slightly trembled but did not collapse.

Therefore, well into the nineties, homosexuality on television was a stealth issue. It was there, but it was virtually undetectable. That spin strategy of stealth, at first, was the approach that the creators of a new show, *These Friends of Mine* later to become simply *Ellen* (after both the show's title character, Ellen Morgan, and star, Ellen DeGeneres), took in 1992. The initial conception of the show wanted to portray Ellen Morgan as a lesbian, but the writers and Ellen DeGeneres herself decided not: "We thought (a) we wanted to make this show about a very funny woman—we didn't want to make her sexuality an issue—And (b) we thought this would be an impossible row to hoe [with the network]."[3] When the show came on the air in 1993, Ellen Morgan was simply a very witty single woman who always wore pants and had a lot of trouble dating men. These were circumstantial symptoms that did not necessarily mean that she was a lesbian ("not that there's anything wrong with that," as Jerry Seinfeld frequently noted on his show during that same time frame).

But as time passed and *Ellen* evolved as a sitcom and Ellen Morgan developed as a sitcom character and Ellen DeGeneres formed a very public, tabloid-stalked, lesbian relationship with actress Anne Heche, homosexuality on television became more and more open and accepted. In fact, by the midnineties, gay characters in supporting roles were all over TV, twenty-two in all, from *Spin City* to *Lush Life* to *Relativity* to *Mad About You* to *Party of Five* to *Friends* to *Melrose Place* to the aforementioned *Roseanne*, which had both male (Martin Mull) and female (Mariel Hemingway) gay supporting characters. "'It's become a stock character—like what blacks were on television 15 years ago,' says Rob Epstein, co-director of *The Celluloid Closet*. . . . 'It seems mandatory to have a gay sidekick.'"[4] And *Roseanne*'s 1994 lesbian kiss was the most intimate gay moment that any of these gay supporting characters participated in. Yet, until 1997, no lead character in a TV show had ever been portrayed as openly gay. Ellen Morgan (née DeGeneres), like Tom Hanks in *Philadelphia*, proved perfect for the assignment as point lesbian, "a test case for the nation's tolerance."[5]

Like Hanks, DeGeneres presents the perfect persona for the stealth spin strategy. As one commentator wrote, "If Ellen does make the historic switch of teams (one reported scenario has her falling for a lesbian writer who speaks at the bookstore), she'd be the perfect character to make homosexuality acceptable. So likeable, so adorable, so nonthreatening."[6] The motive of stealth spin is to find the most passive, nonthreatening, least controversial way to make the unacceptable (in this case, a lesbian lead character on a TV sitcom; in the case of *Philadelphia*, an AIDS-infected, gay, professional man) acceptable, and even, perhaps, funny or sympathetic. The strategy of stealth spin is to offer as the vehicle for the controversial issue (such as gay consciousness) a spokesperson so familiar, so trustworthy, so popular, and so nonthreatening that the volatility of the issue is subsumed in the attractiveness of the persona representing the issue. Thus, a television network like ABC and a TV production company like Disney Studios or a movie like *Philadelphia* can bring its gay consciousness text in under the audience's judgmental radar, or as one wag named it, "the gay-dar."[7]

In the case of DeGeneres as the groundbreaking first gay lead ever in a network TV show, this stealth spin strategy worked for a while. The coming-out episode in 1997 gained high ratings. DeGeneres won an Emmy for it and ultimately was proclaimed Entertainer of the Year by *Entertainment Weekly* magazine "because at a time when an acknowledgement of homosexuality has entered all aspects of popular culture. . . . DeGeneres allowed herself to be a poster girl—not for lesbianism, but for honesty."[8] Laura Dern, who played Ellen Morgan's love interest in the coming-out episode, put out a similar diversionary stealth spin when she argued, "The issue isn't homosexuality, but people who care about each other. [The emphasis should be] 'These two people are great together,' as opposed to 'Oh, she's with a *woman*!'"[9] But less than a year after her historic coming-out episode and all the accolades that accompanied it, *Ellen* was canceled by ABC with hardly a protest from Disney, the show's own production company. In this TV case, the stealth spin strategy only partially worked. Yes, *Ellen* got cancelled and the only gay lead character on TV was gone, but within a year another sitcom, *Will and Grace*, with an openly gay lead character would debut and go on to a long and successful run.

Why did *Ellen* get cancelled? DeGeneres pulls no punches in answering that question: "I was fired basically because I was gay."[10] But one of the show's producers theorizes that the show failed because its tone changed, because it abandoned its stealth strategy for a more aggressive, issue-driven approach: "She got heavy-handed. The very thing that made her the right person to do the coming-out episode was missing—the light touch."[11] Even DeGeneres's off-screen lover, Ann Heche, noted the change in strategy of the star of the show: "She's become an activist."[12] Nonetheless, Ellen's simply put, "Yep, I'm gay," spun out all sorts of positive shockwaves not just through the TV industry but through the

TV-watching cultural community as well. Perhaps Chastity Bono, entertainment media director of the Gay and Lesbian Alliance Against Defamation (GLAAD), best characterized the impact of Ellen's coming out: "Any time a 'first' happens it opens the door for other people to follow. . . . I'm hoping we'll look back years from now and we'll see sexual orientation as a nonissue in the TV industry."[13] For the nineties, the Pulitzer Prize–winning success of Kushner's *Angels in America* and the door-opening acclaim for Ellen Morgan's coming out on network TV were two of the three major centrifuges out of which the changes in America's gay consciousness were spun. The third, and the most powerful in terms of its mass impact, was *Philadelphia* (1993).

## Philadelphia

Alright, explain this to me like I'm a two-year-old.

—*Philadelphia*

Where better city than "the city of brotherly love" to set the first major studio motion picture about the gay lifestyle and AIDS? What better actor than Tom Hanks, America's Everyman, the movies' most positive, widely accepted, most trusted actor since Jimmy Stewart, to deliver the message that the gay lifestyle is nonthreatening and that AIDS is a terrible disease that needs to be understood? Who better than Denzel Washington, America's most popular rising matinee idol at the time, to make the point that homophobia is an American prejudice every bit as evil and damaging as racism? What better narrative structure than a compelling courtroom drama to educate the nation on the ravages of widespread prejudice and the complex social problems generated by the AIDS epidemic? What better subgenre to couch the AIDS message in than the social problem melodrama that was a staple of Hollywood filmmaking, especially at Twentieth Century Fox, in the forties and fifties? These are all the spin factors that director Jonathan Demme mixmastered into *Philadelphia*.

Without any question, *Philadelphia* is a coldly calculated film aimed at spinning nineties America's gay consciousness in exactly the opposite direction than it had taken from the mideighties when people began to become aware of the AIDS threat and its connection to the homosexual lifestyle. Without any question, it is a film that sets out to educate mass America about two subjects it feared, misunderstood, and thus regrettably hated. Without any question, it was a very risky film to make, to act in, and to publicize. But that cutting edge, no-man's-land of risk is where the spinmaster is most at home, where the fluid, creative, mysterious operation of spin works best. *Philadelphia* is a film that, from its conception, set out to change the consciousness of a nation, combat a nation's longstanding prejudice against gay people, and educate a nation out of its denial about a disease that even in the early nineties it did not understand. Ron Nyswaner, *Philadelphia*'s screenwriter, puts the film's intentions in clear perspective: "We wanted to present a simple and moral message. Homophobia is evil. I don't think it's a big goal. It's not a cure for AIDS. But it's a small and significant step."[14]

The learning curve about AIDS and homosexuality in America in the late eighties and the early nineties was quite similar to what Vietnam veterans experienced in the seventies. After the Vietnam War, American veterans of that confusing and dividing and controversial conflict were the worst victims. All America wanted to do was forget about that lost war. All America wanted to do was deny, avoid, and move on from the war that had torn the country apart. As a result, the veterans who had fought that war and came home to none of the parades that had welcomed the veterans of America's earlier winning wars were rendered invisible. No one wanted to acknowledge them, congratulate them on a job well done, or even recognize them on an equal footing with veterans of other wars. Even worse, Vietnam veterans were reviled as losers, dopers, psychos, and baby killers. Then, from 1976 to 1979, Hollywood made a string of movies about the war, about Vietnam veterans coming home, about the problems of reintegration into American society of those veterans. The movies were the mass medicine that cured the blindness of the American people. The movies were the hand that pulled back the curtain of invisibility that America had drawn over its youngest veterans. Those movies changed the consciousness of a country.[15] That is precisely what *Philadelphia* set out to do for the AIDS epidemic and the humanizing of the gay lifestyle.

In many ways, it was Hollywood's most difficult sell, even harder than the reintegration of Vietnam veterans into the country's social consciousness had been. Whereas *Angels In America* opened the discussion onstage in New York and later Ellen DeGeneres would comically and nonthreateningly continue the discussion on TV, it was *Philadelphia* that brought the issues of gays and AIDS to the mass audience of America. In their "Holiday Movie Review" issue of 1993, *Entertainment Weekly* magazine defined "The Marketing Hurdle" that *Philadelphia* faced: "TriStar will need all the good-will Hanks and Washington have earned to overcome the fear and loathing often associated with AIDS."[16] Evidently, *Philadelphia* was successful. It made $14 million its first weekend and its star won the Academy Award for Best Actor. It proved to be what one critic termed it, "a brilliantly calculated entertainment."[17] But for all its success, *Philadelphia* still had its critics, and many of those critics came from within the gay community who felt that the film portrayed neither the loving truth of the gay lifestyle nor the day-to-day tortures of living with AIDS or caring for an AIDS sufferer. And many critics couldn't get past the genre hybridization that was central to the *Philadelphia* experiment: a forties social problem film grafted to a fifties weepy grafted to a time-honored courtroom drama. As a nineties hybrid, *Philadelphia* employs all of these Hollywood-staple genres to make its didactic points.

In *Philadelphia*, Andrew Beckett's (Hanks) defense lawyer, Joe Miller (Washington), repeatedly cues his clients and witnesses to "explain this to me like I'm a two year old." That is precisely the charge that director Demme, screenwriter Ron Nyswaner, and the actors of *Philadelphia* took on in presenting a positive spin to the two complex, controversial, politically volatile, and prejudicial issues of their film: the gay lifestyle and AIDS. They turned these two issues into a heart-tugging weepy and a compelling (though not very procedurally true) courtroom drama about two extremely popular and moral men confronting an unjust and prejudicial situation. Beckett is a brilliant young lawyer in a very prestigious law firm who is fired because he is gay and has AIDS. Miller is a savvy, street-smart ambulance chaser (who is, initially, homophobic) who takes on Beckett's wrongful termination lawsuit against Wyant-Wheeler, Philadelphia's most prestigious Main-Line law firm. It is out of this basic civil rights issue that one of the film's two main themes emerges.

One of *Philadelphia's* messages is that discrimination against gays is the nineties version of racism. Hence, the first spin point: the choice to pair the gay, AIDS-stricken litigant with a flawed (actually prejudiced) yet moral and capable-of-change black litigator. Initially, Miller refuses to take Beckett's case and even admits to his wife, "Hey, I admit it. I'm prejudiced. I don't like homosexuals. . . . I think you've got to be a man to realize how disgusting that whole idea is anyway. Would you accept a client if you were constantly thinking, 'I don't want this person to touch me.'" Months pass, then one day Joe observes the chemo-ravaged Beckett working in the law library. The librarian approaches Beckett and announces for everyone to hear the delivery of a special supplement on HIV-related discrimination cases. Everyone working in Beckett's vicinity in the library flinches, and the librarian suggests, "Wouldn't you be more comfortable in a private research room?" The librarian is trying to get Beckett, with his hair loss and his lesions, out of the sight of the other library users and make him invisible. But Beckett replies, "No. Would it make you more comfortable?" Observing this whole exchange from a distance, Miller, who had definitely been made uncomfortable by Beckett earlier, suddenly feels an identification with Beckett's situation and goes over to lend Beckett moral support. In this scene, Miller doesn't like the prejudice he sees being exercised because it is too much like the racism that he has experienced. For the first time, he is able to identify with a gay man, find a common ground, and he ends up taking Beckett's case.

At the end of this library scene, the connection that *Philadelphia* is making between racism and homophobia is explicitly defined in legal terms. Beckett reads to Miller from a published court ruling: "Subsequent decisions have held that AIDS is protected as a handicap under law not only because of the physical limitations it imposes but because the prejudice surrounding AIDS exacts a social death [long sad pause]which precedes the actual one." Miller takes up the reading from over Andrew's shoulder: "This is the essence of discrimination. Formulating opinions about others not based on their individual merits but rather on their membership in a group with the same characteristics." The first spin point has been orchestrated so well that the film has actually persuaded the audience to sit still for the reading of textbook definitions of discrimination.

A second major spin point that *Philadelphia* stresses is the need for the American public to understand AIDS as a disease, like cancer, that deserves to be viewed with compassion, not revulsion. Miller's initial reaction when Beckett tells him that he has AIDS occurs as they are shaking hands. As soon as he hears the word AIDS, Miller pulls his hand away as if he's been burned and retreats across his office as a means of putting distance between himself and the disease. Through the whole rest of their conversation, Miller flinches every time Beckett touches anything on his desk. Charles Wheeler (Jason Robards), the major partner in the law firm that has fired Beckett, rationalizes the firing in a strategy session with the other partners after the lawsuit has been filed:

> *Charles Wheeler:* Bob, Andy brought AIDS into our office, into our men's room.
> He brought AIDS to our annual Cottontail Family Picnic.
> *Walter:* We ought to be suing him!
> *Bob:* Where is your compassion, gentlemen?

That last question is a good one. In *Philadelphia* that compassion comes from Beckett's totally loving family (who are much too good to be true in the eyes of some gay critics of the film) and from Beckett's life partner, Miguel (Antonio Banderas). What all these positive, compassionate characters affirm is simply that you can touch people with AIDS, you can safely be in the same room with them (even the men's room), and you can love them and comfort them and treat them with compassion, like human beings. Near the end of the first half of the movie, the screen is filled with a black-and-white video of Andy with his family in small-town Upper Merion, Pennsylvania. Accompanying the last scene of this video is the Frank Sinatra song lyric, "If you let me love you, it's for sure I'm gonna love you, all the way." This could be the theme song for any family or support group dealing with one of their member's AIDS suffering.

A third major spin point aims at showing the physical symptoms and psychological stresses of both living gay and living with AIDS. Early in *Philadelphia*, Beckett, while frantically searching for a lost file for an important court case, tells himself that "every problem has a solution." Beckett lives by that rule for life, except he has AIDS for which there is no solution except death. Beckett comes up with a number of excellent solutions to the problems he confronts in his everyday life. He hides his gay lifestyle from his employers after observing their undisguised homophobia. He conceals the symptoms of his AIDS through lies and makeup. He chooses to remain in the closet so that he can pursue his profession in a prejudiced society. For him, every problem does seem to have a solution, except AIDS. In this film, however, the "every problem has a solution" mantra of Beckett can also be applied verbally to his homophobic attorney, Miller. "You have a problem with gays, Joe," his wife charges him. "Not especially," he denies, but her cross-examination clearly defines his problem. What this film argues is that while there may not be a cure for AIDS, there are solutions to the problem of homophobia and Miller is going to be a test case for change.

The first half of *Philadelphia* sets up all of these spin points that support the two major education themes of the film about the positive aspects of the gay lifestyle and the realities of AIDS. Then, the trial begins and the second half of the film falls comfortably into the conventional format that so many educative-issue movies have chosen in the past, the courtroom drama (for example, *JFK*, 1989's *A Dry White Season*, or the tremendously successful nineties TV franchise *Law and Order*). Once the film enters the courtroom, its two social-issue themes no longer need to be shown or dramatized through characterization or dialogue or symbolic scene. Show becomes full-frontal tell. The trial becomes a vehicle for direct speechmaking about the film's two carefully defined issues. The message of the film's spin can literally be delivered as if the movie really is explaining it to the audience "as if they were a two-year-old."

The second half of the film begins with two speeches (with the actors facing the camera head-on): the opening arguments to the jury of the attorney for the complainant, Miller first, and the attorney for the plaintiff, Emily Conine (Mary Steenburgen) second. These opening gambits set the stage for the overt speechmaking of the rest of the film (most of which, procedurally, would probably never be allowed in any real civil courtroom). "Ladies and gentlemen of the jury, forget everything you've seen on television or in the movies," Miller begins his opening by quickly appealing to the media-governed sense of history of both the unseen jury and the film audience that he is full-frontally addressing. Then, in the simplistic rhetoric of numbered points, Miller ticks off the film's themes that have been established dramatically in the first half: "Point number three: His employers discovered his illness and, ladies and gentlemen, the illness I'm referring to is AIDS. And point number four: They panicked (pause) and in their panic they did what most of us would like to do with AIDS which is just get it and everybody who has it as far away from the rest of us as possible." The lawyer for the plaintiffs uses the same simplistic "explain it to me as if I was a two-year-old" rhetoric: "Fact: Andrew Beckett is dying. Fact: Andrew Beckett is angry because his lifestyle, his reckless behavior, has cut short his life." Thus, when the trial begins, these speeches turn the film into a soapbox for the rhetorical dissection of the two established themes, the gay lifestyle and AIDS, but, as the trial proceeds, the film focuses in on one important aspect of those two issues, bringing them out in the open, ushering them out of the closet so that they can be understood and perhaps even accepted in a positive and nonthreatening way.

This nineties coming-out emphasis for both the gay lifestyle and AIDS is first defined in a speech that Miller makes to the judge (Charles Napier) when he is ordered to approach the bench. As part of the meticulous calculation of *Philadelphia*, this speech has been carefully set up by two preceding scenes. In a bar with a group of lawyers, Miller watches himself giving a media interview on the courthouse steps. On the TV screen, Miller says, "We're standing here in Philadelphia, the city of brotherly love, the birthplace of freedom, where the founding fathers offered the Declaration of Independence and I don't recall that glorious document saying anything about all straight men are created equal." At this point, one of the other lawyers in the bar taunts Miller: "You're not getting a little light in the sneakers, are ya?" Miller answers sarcastically: "Yeah, I am, Phil. I'm changing." Though Miller says this mockingly and doesn't mean it at all at this point in the film, he will change before the trial is over and America will change as a result of the spin strategy that this film unleashes in its courtroom drama. In another, very similar scene, a young athletic University of Pennsylvania law student approaches Miller in a drug store, compliments him on his handling of the case, and then tries to pick him up. Miller's temper flares in homophobic panic. He explodes in a slur-laced tirade that screams, "I'm not gay," and stalks out. These two scenes in which Miller's heterosexual manhood is threatened are the setup for the coming-out speech that Miller delivers when called to the bench by the judge:

> Your honor, everybody in this courtroom is thinking about sexual orientation, you know, sexual preference, whatever you wanna call it. Who does what to whom and how they're doing it. Judge, they're looking at Andrew Beckett and they're thinking about it. They're looking at Mr. Wheeler and Miss Conine, and even you, your honor, and they're wondering about it. Trust me, I know they're looking at me and thinking about it. So, let's just get it out in the open, let's get it out of the closet, because this case is not just about AIDS, is it? So let's talk about what this case is really all about. The general public's hatred, our loathing, our fear of homosexuals.

Later, in a similar speech, Miller (going against all real courtroom rules of procedure) approaches the bench and actually berates the judge in a loud voice that the whole courtroom can hear: "C'mon. We're talking about AIDS. We're talking about lesions. Let's see what we're talking about." These speeches argue that the gay lifestyle and AIDS are two important aspects of American life that society refuses to recognize or understand. Bringing the gay lifestyle and AIDS out into the open, inviting it to come out of the closet for all the world to see, is the necessary starting point.

*Philadelphia* is the coming-out party for gay consciousness and AIDS education in the nineties. If it is a calculating spin vehicle, if it is at times "explain it to me as if I were a two-year-old" simplistic, if it is at times sentimental (as in the representation of Beckett's saintly family) or heavy handed (as in its violation of courtroom procedure) or comically intertextual (as in a jury member's comparison of gay Beckett to a "top gun," the most-watched–macho man movie of the previous decade), it nonetheless delivers its message: America must change its attitude toward homosexuals and toward the disease of AIDS. Movies sometimes take their audience places that they do not usually go or do not want to go. What *Philadelphia* argues is that, in some cases, we have to go there to watch an AIDS patient face his own death, to see how people around an AIDS patient deal with the disease, to see what a gay masquerade party is like, to confront our own fears of homosexuals and AIDS. Spin doesn't always involve misrepresentation or diversion or manipulation or exploitation of the truth. Sometimes, spin involves simply bringing the truth out into the open in both its good and bad lights. As one AIDS sufferer in *Philadelphia* who contracted the disease from a blood transfusion declares, "I don't consider myself any different from anybody else with this disease. I'm not guilty. I'm not innocent. I'm just trying to survive."

An emphasis upon simplification and straightforward messaging, then, marked the spin strategy embedded in *Philadelphia*. One critic characterized the dilemma of director Demme when "he took on the opportunity of making the first full-scale Hollywood drama about the contemporary gay life (and not just gay death). But *Philadelphia* turns out to be a scattershot liberal message movie, one that ties itself in knots trying to render its subject matter acceptable to a mass audience . . . a stop and shop instructional tour of AIDS, homophobia, and American gay life."[18] In fact, right up until its release, studio executives protested that *Philadelphia* was not really an AIDS drama, but rather "just a metaphor 'for many factors' that cause discrimination."[19] But no matter how it was publicized or how much the critics knocked its "explain it to me as if I was a two-year-old" approach, *Philadelphia* was successful as a positive spin strategy. Hanks may have won the Academy Award for Best Actor in *Philadelphia*, but Washington also deserved one for representing all the rest of us, our consciousness, the audience's consciousness by the end of the film that there are some basic changes that we all have to go through in terms of our prejudice and an understanding of this disease. "In this courtroom," the judge intones, "justice is blind to all matters of race, creed, color, religion and sexual orientation." But attorney Miller answers with the simple truth: "With all due respect, your honor, we don't live in this courtroom, do we?"

In *Philadelphia*, art and spin came together to bring out into the open and comment upon some aspects of American life that, out of fear and loathing, had been rendered invisible by prejudiced society. Other films would follow—*And the Band Played On* (TV: 1993), *The Cure* (1995), even *Outbreak* (1995), which can be read as a metaphor for AIDS—but none of them made the points or had the impact that *Philadelphia* did. In retrospect, perhaps its spin strategy to "explain it to me as if I was a two-year-old" was a good one.

In September 1995, a special issue of *Entertainment Weekly* titled "The Gay '90s: Entertainment Comes Out of the Closet" presented a progress report on the positive spin strategy aimed at the gay lifestyle and the AIDS crisis. In it, one writer declared that the "gay stream flows freely into the mainstream."[20] By mid-decade, the positive attributes of a once reviled, invisible, and certainly unprofitable gay lifestyle had been assimilated into the culture at a level of acceptance that had never been anticipated. Cynically, *Entertainment Weekly* accounted for this revolution in attitude in the most predictable commodity culture terms: "What force roiled this sea change? A mission by Hollywood to (a) eradicate all forms of bigotry and homophobia, or (b) to destroy the values upon which society rests? Not on your lifestyle. Quite simply, gay sells."[21] What this argument does, despite its denial of art and higher motives, is acknowledge that the nineties gay revolution is, indeed, a result of coldly calculated spin. It argues that "it's no accident that advertising was at the vanguard of the gaying of America as the first business to realize that homosexuals comprised a very desirable demographic."[22]

Regardless of who was responsible, be it Calvin Klein or Versace with their male underwear and "lesbian-chic" ads, or the afternoon talk shows featuring male dancers and revelations of homosexual crushes, or the popularity of openly gay or bisexual music artists like Elton John, David Bowie, k.d. lang, or Melissa Etheridge, or the proliferation of gay characters on TV sitcoms, or the integration of gay characters with straight characters on reality-TV shows like *Real People*, by the midnineties gay people, the gay lifestyle, and gay issues had totally inundated popular culture. The educational process targeting the gay lifestyle and the realities of the AIDS epidemic had come a long way in resisting and changing the embedded homophobia of mainstream American culture. American society in 1995 was still divided on the issues of homosexuality and the understanding of AIDS, but significant progress had been made.

Of all of the cultural discourse sites exploring the positive representation of the gay lifestyle and the education into compassion about AIDS, at the forefront of this cultural spin strategy was the movie industry. After *Philadelphia*, films with gay characters, gay themes, and discourse on gay issues carved a prominent niche in the yearly releases. These films represented the gay lifestyle from every angle—setting, fashion, humor, homoerotic imagery, domestic commitment—and engaged all of the important gay themes and issues—certainly AIDS, but also coming out, gay/straight relationships, so-called lesbian chic, cross-dressing and transvestitism, and even the alternative sexualities of the gay underground.

But with all of the success of positive gay spin in the early nineties, at mid-decade there were still powerful homophobic forces marshaled at negative spin positions defined by the political and the religious right. Strangely enough, one of the major cultural icons most under fire by these forces was Disney. Since the forties, Disney had been the anchor of family values and wholesome entertainment in American mass culture, but by 1995 Disney films, theme parks, and even toys were being boycotted by the religious right nationwide. Disney's crime was its endorsement of the gay lifestyle. In October of 1995, Disney extended health benefits to the partners of its gay employees and all the alarms went off. Earlier in the decade, at Disney World in Florida, an annual Gay and Lesbian Day had been welcomed as an event complete with group discount tickets featuring a pink Mickey Mouse. Finally, the religious right went after Disney's movies and TV shows, charging that they contained subliminal sex images, overt homoerotic scenes and characterizations, and undermined Christian family values. The Reverend Tim Benson, vice president of the Florida Baptist Convention, characterized the depths to which Disney had sunk in the nineties: "Here was a guy who built an entire entertainment empire on appealing to what is good, noble and moral. But Disney in the 1990s has gotten completely away from that. They've taken another step in the direction of making the traditional family meaningless."[23] It all came to a head over the Disney film *Powder* in 1995 when its writer-director Victor Salva was revealed to be a convicted child molester and the film was criticized for its homoerotic imagery.

GLAAD was formed in the 1980s in Hollywood to defend against just such attacks of homophobia toward the film industry and within the film industry. The scene in 1995's Academy Award–winning *Braveheart* in which Edward I throws his son's gay lover out of a window to his death and the nineties history of homophobia of *Braveheart*'s director and star Mel Gibson catalyzed GLAAD-organized protests against the film nationwide. Gibson himself initially responded angrily to the criticism of his film's homophobia by saying, "I'll apologize when hell freezes over,"[24] but within eighteen months Gibson was sitting down with eighteen gay writers and directors at a GLAAD-organized forum to discuss their differences. By the midnineties, the positive spin strategy toward the gay lifestyle and AIDS had made giant strides in countering the powerful homophobia of American culture and the Hollywood film industry had taken the point in this positive spin campaign. But perhaps most importantly and most entertainingly, the Hollywood gay-themed films of the nineties represented, with intelligence and humor and grace, the coming out of the gay lifestyle in America.

## Coming Out

> So let's just get it out in the open. Let's get it out of the closet. Because this case is not just about AIDS, is it? So let's talk about what this case is really about, the general public's hatred, our loathing, our fear of homosexuals.
>
> —*Philadelphia*

Of all the gay issues raised by the films of the nineties decade, the most frequently explored is the defining act of gay identity consciousness, coming out. Despite (and because of) the powerful critical and box-office success of *Philadelphia* and the Robin Williams–Nathan Lane–Gene Hackman drag opus *The Birdcage* (1996), Hollywood, in the first half of the nineties, seemed "skittish about gay films that don't fall into two relatively safe categories—cross-dressing minstrel shows or AIDS dramas."[25] But as the decade moved on, more films began to explore with both humor and style the problems, intrigues, relationships, and romance of gay life. The awkwardness of coming out was, perhaps, the one situation that provided the most entertainment value for mainstream audiences who had been introduced to gay-themed movies by *Philadelphia* and *The Birdcage* as well as for gay moviegoers who hungered for movie representations of their own lives, movie affirmations of their own emerging identities.

It all started with the wedding movies: *Four Weddings and A Funeral* (1994), *Muriel's Wedding* (1995), *My Best Friend's Wedding* (1997). What a wonderful irony that a trio of movies celebrating the most revered heterosexual ritual would double as highly popular gay-themed films. When *Four Weddings and A Funeral* vaulted to the top of the box-office charts in 1994, most of the credit was given to the script's wonderful wit and the charm of the Hugh Grant–Andie McDowell heterosexual romantic chemistry, but, for everyone who saw the film, the most touchingly romantic moment was the funeral in the title. While the four weddings were hilarious celebrations of heterosexual relationships, the funeral was a powerful moving celebration of a lifelong gay partnership that made W. H. Auden's elegiac poem the anthem of gay true love for the nineties. *Muriel's Wedding*, an overtly heterosexual Australian ensemble comedy, followed in 1995, and, to the surprise of everyone, found its most enthusiastic reception among gay audiences in America who read it as a metaphor for coming out into the urban gay lifestyle. When Rachel Griffiths, the star of *Muriel's Wedding*, asked a fan, "OK, what's with the *Muriel's Wedding*/gay man thing?" she got a clear postmodernist answer:

This guy, who was like in his early 30s, gave me this whole deconstruction of the film as a metaphor for the gay man's journey away from the small town where he's judged for not fitting in and for being some kind of a freak, like Muriel, to the big metropolis, where suddenly there's a scene that he's a part of. And he totally reinvents himself and accumulates a sort of surrogate family of friends . . . and then gets this terrible disease which . . . in gay mythology or culture, is like your best gay friend getting AIDS.[26]

Both of these foreign films paved the way for the 1997 American blockbuster *My Best Friend's Wedding* (also directed by P. J. Hogan, the director of *Muriel's Wedding*) in which Julia Roberts attempts to sabotage her true love's wedding with the help of her other, close, male friend who just happens to be gay (Rupert Everett). *My Best Friend's Wedding* participated just as powerfully as the two *Father of the Bride* (1991, 1995) films in the deconstruction of America's most sacred heterosexual ritual.

All of these wedding films also opened up the field for the other movies about the coming out experience that tilted time-honored film formats toward the particular problems and joys of the gay lifestyle. In the tradition of straight ensemble films like *American Graffiti* (1973), *The Return of the Secaucus Seven* (1980), *The Big Chill* (1983), *Peter's Friends* (1993), and *Circle of Friends* (1995), Terence McNally's *Love! Valour! Compassion!* (1997), directed by Joe Mantello, took a time-honored circle-of-friends format (beautiful old house or cars as refuge for a heterogeneous group of friends to work out their individual, mostly love, problems) and simply extracted the hetero from it.

*Love! Valour! Compassion!*'s eight gay men meet for three holiday weekends at a Martha Stewart summer home far away from the city in a film that without fanfare does what all the other gay films of the decade were afraid to do, explore not only the emotional but also the physical side of gay love (and lust). Where *Philadelphia*, *The Birdcage*, *Basic Instinct* (1991), and even *Longtime Companion* (1990) had consciously avoided (in the name of gaining cross-over mainstream acceptance) any physical representation of gay sexuality (most films even fled from showing a gay screen kiss), *Love! Valour! Compassion!* creates a world and a set of relationships where gay kissing, sleeping in the same bed, embracing, touching, holding hands, and full frontal nudity are natural, fully contextual, and in no way shocking or sensational.

Mantello and McNally foresaw and feared a real problem with the MPAA ratings board over the full frontal male nudity of the film but, much to their surprise, nothing happened. "'We didn't want to get coy about draping legs just so, but we also didn't want to flaunt it in people's faces,' says Mantello. 'Our attitude was, if you saw somebody's d——, you saw it and if you didn't, you didn't. It just seemed natural and innocent that way.'" Much to everyone's surprise, the ratings board agreed. With little discussion, the film was given an R rating (rather than NC-17) accompanied by compliments that *Love! Valour! Compassion!* was "'a really tasteful film.' We were shocked. But we said, 'Um, gee, thanks.'"[27] Where most gay-themed films debated endlessly about showing an onscreen kiss, *Love!*

*Valour! Compassion!* let it all hang out, so to speak. But because it was all justified by the writing, the acting, and the appropriateness of the context, nobody cared and the film found an appreciative critical and theater (though not completely mainstream) audience.

*Love! Valour! Compassion!* opens with a house and a passionate gay kiss in the kitchen. Before it is a minute old, the film has aligned itself with a traditional film subgenre—"I love my house," the narrator in voiceover intones to open the film. "I love to fill it with my friends. . . . Over the years, we've become like a family"—and has exorcised the bugaboo of prior gay films by presenting a passionate, steamy sexual encounter between two pajama-clad men in the dark kitchen. This opening says that the film is both the same and different, both conventional and daring, and both comfortable in its associations and intertextuality yet new and radical in the physical gay spin it is putting on the audience's expectations.

But *Love! Valour! Compassion!* doesn't stop there. The second scene is a hilarious depiction of gay road rage in which Perry, the driver, spews forth every obscene female gender slur imaginable at the offending woman driver who has cut him off on the highway. This introduces a second theme of the film. Not only will *Love! Valour! Compassion!* engage naturally the physicality of gay sexuality but it will also explore the expressiveness (quite hilariously) of gay language patterns. After the enraged Perry gets done calling the woman driver every obscene name in the homosexual book, his life partner of fourteen years, Arthur, scolds him for using that stream of insensitive, derogatory language and ends up saying, "Of course I'm right, you big fairy."

The circle of friends is composed of the married couple Perry and Arthur, both buttoned-down business types; Gregory, the choreographer owner of the house and his unfaithful blind lover from the city, Bobby; John and James Jekyll, twin brothers (dubbed James the Fair and John the Foul) with very different personalities; Ramone, the sluttish Puerto Rican dancer, much younger than the others; and the most important character in the film, Buzz (Jason Alexander), the flamboyant, Broadway show-tune singing, HIV-positive, totally out ringmaster of the complex festivities. Through these eight meticulously developed characters, *Love! Valour! Compassion!* does exactly what its title promises. It explores all of the major issues of the gay lifestyle—from coming out to falling in love to having physical sex to gay marriage to AIDS to the frightening specter of their own deaths that hangs over everyone in the gay community.

But, above all, it affirms all the same values and relationships that the straight world constantly valorizes: love, physical attraction, marriage, fidelity, caring, compassion. Except, all its characters are gay men. *Love! Valour! Compassion!* is really no different at all from the worlds of *The Big Chill* or *Grand Canyon* or *Peter's Friends*. Well, there *is* one other difference, AIDS.

*Buzz:* Alright. That's five dollars.
*John:* What?
*Buzz:* Anyone who mentions AIDS this summer, it's gonna cost them.

No true gay movie in the nineties can avoid the one issue that looms over the whole gay community as announced by *Angels In America*. Early in *Love! Valour! Compassion!*, Buzz announces everyone's desire to avoid the issue of AIDS, but, as the film unfolds, no one can. Over the course of the summer, Gregory, who is a choreographer, is planning an AIDS benefit that will feature a gay male *corps-de-ballet* dancing of *Swan Lake*. At first, all the circle of friends, except Buzz (who can't wait) and Ramone the professional dancer, resist the idea of putting on tutus and becoming hairy, some bearded, ballerinas.

> *Perry:* You've done enough for AIDS. We all have.
> *Arthur:* Nobody's done enough for AIDS.
> *Perry:* People are sick of benefits.
> *Buzz:* Especially the people they are given for.

All of their lives have been changed by the AIDS epidemic whether they have the disease or not. For them it is not so much the threat of AIDS that they fear but the hopelessness that accompanies that threat. As they sit around the dinner table in the classic circle-of-friends configuration, there are major differences because they are gay: they are outsiders in their own country, and they are helpless in the face of AIDS.

> *Buzz:* The state of the American musical has me very upset.
> *Perry:* It's the state of America that should have you upset.
> *Buzz:* It does, you asshole . . .
> *Perry:* The point is we're all sitting around here talking about something, pretending to care, because the truth is there is nothing we can do about it.

AIDS is a disease with no cure that kills. This circle of friends and the gay community that they represent feels a terrible helplessness in the face of its threat. No matter how much they want to avoid the subject of AIDS, they have to discuss it because it is the one reality that overshadows all of their lives. For John (John Glover), however, the issue of AIDS is a much more acute and personal problem:

> *John:* My brother, he wants to come over.
> *Bobby:* I didn't know you had a brother.
> *John:* Twin brother. . . . He's not well. He needs me and I don't like him.
> *Bobby:* I work with quite a few AIDS organizations.
> *John:* Thank you. They can help him find a doctor. Thank you.
> *Bobby:* It never ends.

Buzz's problem with AIDS is the most personal of all because he is HIV-positive. But then James, the twin brother, comes on the scene suffering from full-blown AIDS. Facing their disease together, the two become lovers, and the film takes the hopelessness of AIDS and spins it into the most meaningful relationship in the movie. Until James arrives, Buzz is the only one who sleeps alone in the house. He and John are two very different studies in loneliness. James arrives as a kind of angel for both of them, a catalytic figure who revives their humanity out of their hopelessness.

But AIDS is by no means the only issue that *Love! Valour! Compassion!* informs about and posits solutions toward. Perhaps because of the nature of the circle-of-friends format or, perhaps, because it was a stage play before becoming a film, *Love! Valour! Compassion!* is a very talky movie. Its scenes are set up like forums or group panel discussions on the crucial gay issues. Perry and Arthur discuss at length their fourteen-year marriage and celebrate their anniversary with their circle of friends. Ramone and Bobby discuss the problem of infidelity to their partners in relationships. John and Buzz both become caregivers for the dying James. And everyone, at one point or another in the film, contemplates their own death at a young age. The last line of the film, like the last speech of *Angels In America*, faces the sad reality of gay life in the age of AIDS. Gregory, the narrator and owner of the beautiful house, the refuge from the world that has brought them all together as an alternative family, mourns, "I bury every one of you. It got awfully lonely out here."

Ultimately, *Love! Valour! Compassion!* is a movie about a very universal situation, loneliness. That theme, as well as its honest and unabashed presentation of all the aspects of the gay lifestyle that so many other films were afraid to engage, sets it apart from all the other gay films. It brings all of these issues out of the gay film closet. In that sense, it is a coming-out film for the industry. *Philadelphia* did a good job of dealing with AIDS in an informative way for a mainstream audience, but *Love! Valour! Compassion!* deals with all the other aspects of the gay lifestyle that were considered too controversial or deviant for mainstream audiences to see. It succeeds in spinning those controversial elements in a positive way by presenting them as quite similar to the same emotions, desires, and relationship issues that straight couples and families encounter in the nineties. One of the funniest speeches of the film is delivered by Buzz on heterosexuals and capsulizes the basic spin strategy of the film: "I'm sick to death of straight people. Tell the truth, aren't you? There's just too goddam many of them. I was in a bank the other day. They were everywhere. Writing checks. Making deposits. Two of them were applying for a mortgage. It was disgusting. They're taking over." It is that kind of sly ironic humor that more of the gay films of the nineties might have exploited in their spin strategies. One other film, *In & Out* (1997), did.

While not nearly as adventurous a film as *Love! Valour! Compassion!*, whose title's defiant exclamation points brought the realistic representation of the gay lifestyle out of the prudish closet, *In & Out* still has a ripped-from-the-headlines plot premise that gives cultural credibility to its comedy. At the 1994 Academy Awards, Tom Hanks accepted his Best Actor award for playing a gay man in *Philadelphia* by thanking his high school teacher as one of the "finest gay Americans . . . that I had the good fortune to be associated with."[28] That real speech became the governing event of the film *In & Out* three years later when Howard Brackett (Kevin Kline), a popular English teacher and track coach in Greenleaf,

Indiana, who is "smart, neat and really clean" (but doesn't know that he is gay) is outed at the Academy Awards before a national TV audience by one of his ex-students.

But beyond this real-life–reel-life connection, *In & Out* also had its share of controversy. The actual event that brings Brackett out of the closet and makes him realize that he really is gay is a brilliantly conceived screen kiss between two gay men. Not since Mel Brooks had Marcel Marceau utter the only words in *Silent Movie* (1976) has casting against type been as successfully exploited as in *In & Out*'s kiss between Brackett and TV tabloid reporter Peter Malloy (Tom Selleck). The idea of super-macho *Magnum P.I.* kissing another man serves as a perfect *rapprochement* to the postmodernist self-reflexivity of the whole film. Not only is this a film about a gay man being publicly outed before millions of people and then coming out of his own naïve lack of understanding of himself, but it is also about Hollywood having fun with its own foibles and fears about making movies about gays, about showing men kissing onscreen, about bringing a much more open approach to gay lifestyle movies to a mainstream audience. Much ado was made in the press and many apprehensive hands were wrung by the studio producers over the Kline-Selleck kiss. Both actors were endlessly interviewed about it. But in the end it really signified nothing. Like coming out in general, that kiss between two famous actors symbolized the dynamics of the whole coming-out process. The fear, uncertainty, and anxiety of anticipation of a gay man leading a double life and thus contemplating coming out is, indeed, analogous to the phenomenon of a macho male actor like Selleck (or Rock Hudson) playing a gay character and kissing another man onscreen. The whole question was whether it would be accepted by a mainstream audience, and it was accepted with little fanfare. Why? Because it fit the context and the postmodernist spin of the movie perfectly.

*In & Out* did capture a mainstream audience with a vengeance. Steve Daly wrote about *In & Out* in an article titled "In The Money" with a subheadline of "Who says gay doesn't pay?" Daly noted that "the movie opened to a $15 million gross over the weekend of September 19, the second largest September opening. . . . But *In & Out*'s significance goes well beyond box office numbers. For the first time, a mainstream audience is embracing a film about a central gay character who isn't dying of AIDS (a disease mentioned nowhere in the script), nor is he a broadly drawn, drag . . . stereotype (as . . . in *The Birdcage*)."[29] Another commentator, under a subheadline that characterizes *In & Out* as "a comedy that moves homosexuality into the mainstream," captures the spin strategy of the film. Commenting upon the film's comic timing, Liza Schwarzbaum writes that it "pulls *In & Out* way up, onto a new playing field: minority gay sensibility as majority virtue."[30]

But despite its "ripped-from-the-headlines" plot premise and its surprisingly noncontroversial screen kiss, *In & Out* succeeded as an extremely popular and mainstream gay film because of its writing. It is most certainly a message movie, and its message concerns the fear and uncertainty of the coming-out experience.

But the script delivers that message with a witty, ironic comedy whose spin strategy consistently compares one of the central events of the gay lifestyle to similar events, fears, and uncertainties in the mainstream straight lifestyle. *In & Out* is a movie where, instead of the usual porno movies, Barbra Streisand in *Funny Girl* is the entertainment at the bachelor party. *In & Out* is a movie where on the altar at his wedding, instead of saying "I do," Brackett says, "I'm gay." *In & Out* is a movie where a Catholic priest in the confessional advises Brackett to have premarital sex with his fiancé to prove he's not gay. *In & Out* is a movie where when the central character is aggressively trying to have sex with his fiancé to prove that he's not gay, he looks up and sees Richard Simmons, the ultimate American flamboyant gay, shaking it on the TV screen. *In & Out* is a movie where Brackett's disappointed fiancé, Emily (Joan Cusack), after throwing herself at TV hunk Peter Malloy who advises her that he is also gay, screams out in frustration, "Is everybody gay!" *In & Out* is a movie in which a man can have a complete dialogue with an audiotape titled "Explaining Your Masculinity" in which the central proof of masculinity is that straight men "do not dance," but, while listening to the tape, Brackett cannot resist the pull of his happy feet and the tape screams at him to stop: "What are you doing? Stop dancing you bitch ballerina!" (which is an interesting intertextual allusion to the gay *corps de ballet* doing *Swan Lake* at the end of *Love! Valour! Compassion!*). Finally, *In & Out* is a Hollywood metamovie that not only has witty fun with the gay coming-out experience but also parodies itself in its hilarious send-up of the Academy Awards. The year that Cameron Duke (Matt Dillon) is nominated for playing a gay soldier in a war movie, the other nominees for best actor are

> Paul Newman for *Coot*
> Clint Eastwood for *Codger*
> Michael Douglas for *Primary Urges*
> Steven Seagal for *Snowball In Hell*

*In & Out* is a successful gay movie (and a successful movie) simply because it is consistently, self-reflexively, and postmodernly funny. Ironic wit rules and makes the film's gay theme acceptable to the mainstream, nongay audience that it is trying to reach, gay kiss and all.

The spin strategy of *In & Out* is, in fact, quite similar to that of *Love! Valour! Compassion!*. Where *Love! Valour! Compassion!* argued that its eight gay men were working through the exact relationship problems that the straights of *The Big Chill* and *Peter's Friends* were facing, *In & Out* argues that the insecurities and self-delusions of gays and straights are strikingly similar and actually matter much less than we think they do. For example, Malloy becomes Brackett's mentor in the coming-out process in *In & Out*. "I came out," Malloy tells Brackett, "to everyone—my folks, my boss, my dog. One day I just snapped. I just got tired of switching pronouns and remembering to lower my voice and I couldn't take lying to people I loved." When Brackett asks Malloy what happened, the answer is both nonchalant and predictable. Nothing really happened. "Everybody surprised me," Malloy says, "once I trusted them." What the spin strategy of *In & Out* is saying is that coming out of the closet isn't really that big a deal at all; it's only as big a deal as all of our both gay and straight fears, insecurities, and prejudices make it. *In & Out* ends with the whole town of Greenleaf, Indiana, coming out in support of "Best Teacher" Howard Brackett. The high school students, the parents, the farmers, the police officers, and the postmen all declare their gayness in support of Brackett's humanity. In this movie, not only does Brackett out himself at the altar at his wedding (the central ritual of heterosexuality) but the whole community outs itself at a high school graduation (a central ritual of heterosexual passage). *In & Out* is a deft and crafty spin movie that triumphs through its ability to laugh at itself.

One of the funniest (and postmodernist) subtexts of *In & Out* is the film's parody of Hollywood and its rituals, especially the Academy Awards. But in the nineties the coming out theme of *In & Out* became a controversial issue in Hollywood—witness the Ellen DeGeneres–Anne Heche tabloid frenzy or the tongue-in-cheek coyness of Kevin Spacey escorting his mother to the Academy Awards. Coming out of the closet in the Hollywood of the nineties was a pretty tricky business. Ellen Morgan's "Yep. I'm gay" was a remarkably straightforward way of coming out, but the reactions within the industry to DeGeneres and her lesbian lover, Heche, were anything but straightforward. DeGeneres got cancelled and industry-wide doubt was expressed as to whether Heche could ever play heterosexual roles again. Perhaps the most interesting Hollywood coming-out scenario played out around *Gods and Monsters* (1998), the biopic of openly gay thirties monster movie director James Whale. Sir Ian McKellan, who is also gay, having come out in 1988 on a BBC radio program, played Whale, the director of both *Frankenstein* (1931) and *Bride of Frankenstein* (1935), in that inside-Hollywood metamovie (a movie about making movies). He was nominated for the 1998 Best Actor Academy Award for the part. *Gods and Monsters* director Bill Condon defines how Hollywood politics were stacked against McKellan: "I showed the movie to a publicist who handles a lot of Academy campaigns. She said, 'The only problem is, there's never been a gay man who's been nominated for a gay role.' She said it right before the [1997] nominations came out, and indeed Rupert Everett didn't get nominated [for *My Best Friend's Wedding*] and Greg Kinnear did [for *As Good As It Gets*]."[31]

Other metamovies that self-reflexively touched upon the problems of coming out in the business of Hollywood, such as *Billy's Hollywood Screen Kiss* (1998) and *Love and Death on Long Island* (1997), did not receive nearly the attention generated by *Gods and Monsters*, yet dealt with the same coming-out-due-to-falling-in-love dynamic. In *Love and Death on Long Island*, John Hurt, another distinguished English gay actor playing a gay role, brings the film's whole coming-out premise to life. Ironically, over the decades, controversial gay roles have been major career-building stepping stones for many straight actors. In 1971 Peter Finch was "the first actor to receive an Oscar nomination for portraying an openly homosexual character."[32] Following Finch, Al Pacino and Chris Sarandon were nominated for *Dog Day Afternoon* (1975), Marcello Mastroianni for *A Special Day* (1977), James

Coco for *Only When I Laugh* (1981), Robert Preston and Julie Andrews for *Victor Victoria* (1982), John Lithgow for *The World According to Garp* (1982), Dustin Hoffman for *Tootsie* (1982), Tom Courtenay for *The Dresser* (1983), William Hurt for *Kiss of the Spider Woman* (1985), Bruce Davison for *Longtime Companion* (1990), Jaye Davidson for *The Crying Game* (1992), of course Tom Hanks for *Philadelphia*, and Greg Kinnear for *As Good As It Gets* (1997). All of them gained industry-wide and worldwide acclaim for playing complex gay characters, few of them actually won the Academy Awards for which they were nominated, but all of their careers benefited. So, while coming out in the business of Hollywood may be dangerous in real life, playing gay over the years has been a successful way for straight actors to demonstrate their protean skills.

This Hollywood focus upon the coming-out experience of gay people and upon its own coming-out history demonstrates a sea change in the nineties toward all aspects of the gay lifestyle, not just AIDS. Changes of public opinion and social attitude don't just happen randomly. They are defined, led out, and organized by those who have the platforms, the vehicles, the technology, and the talent to control public opinion and social attitudes. The gay acceptance spin strategy, in its evolution across the nineties, graphically demonstrates how a seismic shift in social attitude can be triggered, argued, and sustained by the mass media for the mainstream.

## The *Will and Grace* Syndrome

> The saintly gay friend is a cliché worthy of retirement.
> —Owen Gleiberman, "An Unmarried Woman," *Entertainment Weekly*

Julia Roberts in *Pretty Woman* (1990) is a Cinderella for the nineties, an updating of one of history's favorite heterosexual fairy tales, an archetype just begging to be deconstructed. Roberts in *My Best Friend's Wedding* (1997) does just that, deconstructs her own image. "Will Cinderella dance again?" one of her two best friends in the movie, George (Rupert Everett), coaxes her on her cell phone at her other best boy friend's wedding reception. But George is gay, and, as the heterosexual love of her life is going off on his honeymoon with another woman, George, magnificent in his tuxedo, leads her to the dance floor and takes her in his arms with yet another glib deconstruction, "Bond. Jane Bond." One of the most popular, offbeat, ineffectual, and tortured gay spin film subgenres of the nineties was a large group of gay/straight buddy movies that attempted to spin the need for intraorientation friendship (always verging on impossible love) between the two polarized lifestyles. While *Butch Cassidy and the Sundance Kid* (1969) may have contained suppressed homoerotic instincts and Batman's dark brooding in *Batman and Robin* (1997) may have been caused by repressed desire, the gay/straight buddy movies of the nineties attempted to put a hip postmodern spin on the classic buddy relationship and didn't convince anyone.

While so many aspects of the nineties positive gay spin strategy (toward understanding AIDS or supporting coming out) were remarkably successful, the gay/straight love relationship spin was not. Instead of succeeding in portraying gay/straight relationships in terms of celebratory buddy movies or screwball comedies, too often the couples in these films end up as sad versions of Jake Barnes and Lady Brett Ashley in Ernest Hemingway's *The Sun Also Rises*, both hopelessly impotent in their own way. The gay/straight relationship films of the nineties know that their friendship/love stories can never work, yet they argue for the fun of the hopeless chase, the desire for the process over the finished product, the value of a love relationship as game or experiment rather than the total fulfillment of romantic destiny, and still don't convince anyone.

*The Crying Game* (1992), Neil Jordan's romantic thriller, a kinked love story set against the backdrop of IRA (Irish Republican Army) terrorism, was the first and ultimately most successful of the gay/straight spin movies of the nineties. When Fergus (Stephen Rea), fleeing to London to escape his IRA roots, falls in love with Dil (Jaye Davidson), a beautiful and sexy hairdresser, the film seems to be taking a gentle right turn away from its setup as an IRA thriller toward a conventional redemption-through-love scenario. But then, abruptly and shockingly, it takes a very postmodern, sharp turn left into a whole different and previously unexplored country. After a slow, tentative, very cautious, and quite conventional courtship, Fergus and Dil steal to her room to make love for the first time. But, to the totally unsuspected, unsignaled, unimagined shock of both Fergus and everyone in the audience, Dil has a penis. It is a very postmodern twist to the conventional love story tradition.

While *The Crying Game* seems to be a gay/straight film, it really isn't. It is a very conventional film of heterosexual desire with the small exception that both love partners have a penis. Fergus is a slow, sincere heterosexual male who falls in love with an erotic, beautiful, utterly sensuous woman whose sexual orientation is outwardly and inwardly heterosexually female, except for her one problem. The interesting thing about *The Crying Game* is the direction in which Jordan and the actors take this sexual orientation dilemma. The film opts to deal with the problem rather than flee from it as so many of the gay/straight films that follow in the nineties will do. After the initial shock wears off, neither Fergus nor Dil (or the film's audience) start looking for ways to say goodbye. Instead, Fergus and Dil find a way to stay together by redefining the concept of love, by directing their feelings toward each other through the intense heat of desire into an entirely different, cooler, clearer, recognition of love as a protecting and nurturing relationship. In a sense, phoenixlike, the sexual shock of the film's pivotal love scene totally melts Fergus and Dil down and recasts them as lovers of a whole new kind, takes them through and beyond desire into a brave new world of post–sexual orientation love.

As a gay/straight film, *The Crying Game* is a noble experiment, probably the most sensitive of all the succeeding gay/straight films of the decade, yet does it succeed in terms of the very positive spin it puts on gay/straight relationships? Unfortunately, all anyone talked about at the time or remembers about the film is the shocking revelation scene at its center. For a film that sets out to decenter the audience's conventional definition of sexual desire, the power of its pivotal scene ironically served to focus upon the very phallic center that the film was trying to deconstruct. Perhaps the spin strategy of *The Crying Game* overestimated its audience's postmodernity. It is a problem that plagued all the gay/straight films of the rest of the decade. No matter what spin strategy these films take, it is almost impossible to get past the engrained importance of penises and vaginas, and the power of the desire they create. *The Crying Game* made a valiant attempt to do just this but with very little success.

Less successful in terms of gay/straight spin were the majority of the films that followed *The Crying Game*, such as *M. Butterfly* (1993) and *Farewell My Concubine* (1993), which shared both the anatomical and the political concerns of *The Crying Game*. As *The Crying Game* began with IRA intrigue in Ireland, *M. Butterfly* and *Farewell My Concubine* are both set against the backdrop of the political turmoil of Mao's China and the gender-bending aesthetic of the Beijing Opera. Again, like *The Crying Game*, both divert their focus from their historical and ideological settings to the intimate, personal worlds of tender, romantic (and sexual), gay/straight love stories. Both films, with their settings in the highly ritualized opera, have an aesthetic out (or escape hatch) that *The Crying Game* didn't have. Because most of the central characters in these two films are by profession actors, they possess the tools of their trade (makeup, costume, aesthetic tradition), which, to a degree, Dil in *The Crying Game* did as a hairdresser. These tools of cosmetic illusion allow them to create a believable illusion of gender and love that the lovers need only convince themselves to believe.

*M. Butterfly* is the story of French bureaucrat Rene Gallimard (Jeremy Irons), who falls in love with a beautiful opera diva who turns out to be a man. *Farewell My Concubine* is the story of the opera's androgynous tradition transferred from art to life through the triangular love of the homosexual Cheng (Leslie Cheung) and the straight Duan (Zhang Fengyi) and the beautiful prostitute Juxian (Gong Li). Whereas *The Crying Game* attempted a complete redefinition of romantic love as a means of breaking down the barriers to a gay/straight relationship, these two opera films embrace a spin strategy that is utterly self-reflexive. Just as the Beijing Opera has always embraced the gender-bending stylization of its characters and stories with men playing women as a rule, so too do the lovers in these two films choose the illusion over the reality. In *M. Butterfly*, Rene chooses not to acknowledge that his love object, Song (John Lone), is really a man, despite that everyone else inside the film and watching the film knows this fact much earlier than anyone knew the secret of Dil in *The Crying Game*. Similarly, in *Farewell My Concubine*, Cheng chooses to move her stage role as Duan's concubine into the realm of the real despite Duan's marriage to the prostitute. In both films (and in *The Crying Game*) one of the love partners chooses to spin either their heterosexuality (in the case of Fergus and Rene) or their homosexuality (Cheng) into an alignment that will allow them to be with their beloved despite the gay/straight difference. The choice of illusion over anatomical gender reality, of the world of the stage over the world of the streets (and all of their historical realism), make these two films, along with *The Crying Game*, affirmations of the power of simulacra whereby the acting of the gender role becomes more believable than the actual gender reality.[33]

Two other films, *Three of Hearts* (1993) and *Threesome* (1994), develop less successful spin strategies for dealing with gay/straight relationships. Both of their plots resemble the triangular love story of *Farewell My Concubine* but fail in the working out of their gay/straight relationships. At least *Threesome* possesses a modicum of believability while *Three of Hearts* never rises above its TV-sitcom premise (read: *Three's Company* made into a movie). In *Three of Hearts*, lesbian lovers (Kelly Lynch and Sherilyn Fenn) break up and one hires a male gigolo (William Baldwin) to make the other jealous and thus lure her back. Gosh, where is Mr. Roper when we need him? *Threesome*, though its premise is just as tortured, is a much more believable exploration of gay/straight sexual confusion. In a college dorm, polite and quiet (read: gay even though he doesn't know it yet) Eddy (Josh Charles) is assigned to room with Stuart (Stephen Baldwin), who is a heterosexual gatling gun primed to mow down any and every girl who wanders into his range. Enter Alex (Lara Flynn Boyle), who by mistake ends up rooming with Eddy and Stuart. Only when Alex falls in love with Eddy does Eddy figure out that he is gay and actually attracted to buddy Stuart, not heterosexy Alex. It is, once again, a TV-sitcom dilemma, but it differs in that it really involves ménage-à-trois, gay/straight sex. Heterosexuality and homosexuality do manage to find a congenial space in which to cohabit in these three likable characters' dorm room, and the audience comes away with a real sense that heterosexual and homosexual desire take much the same form and share many of the same feelings.

Of all the gay/straight films of the nineties, the most postmodernist in its style and theme is Kevin Smith's low-budget, high-intensity, hetero-boy-and-lesbian-girl-fall-in-love dramedy, *Chasing Amy* (1997). Even though it is set in the world of comic books, it is the most literary of these gay/straight relationship films because its whole focus is upon words, language, the way that talking about sexuality can mediate the seemingly insurmountable problems of increasingly complex nineties sexual relationships. Auteur Smith (writer, producer, director, and actor in this $250,000 film) is quite conscious of his academic interest in the semantics of nineties sexuality: "I like to write stuff you don't usually see on the screen. . . . The conversations you have with your friends—the frank sexual discussions—you never see that. When was the last time you remember anyone talking about going down on a woman in a movie?"[34] Verbally raunchy as Smith's films may be (1994's *Clerks* far exceeds *Chasing Amy* in its foulmouthed exchanges), in the era of Clinton, when the president of the United States is talking candidly to the nation about oral sex, Smith's focus on the language of sexuality is so appropriate that he is able to make linguistics entertaining. Just as Hollywood and history collaborated to bring postmodernist thought into the nineties mainstream, so does *Chasing Amy* become a crash course in the semantics of contemporary sexuality, one of Lyotard's more important "language games."

What do Smith's characters in *Clerks* and *Chasing Amy* do? They talk. What do they talk about? They talk about sex. What do they find so interesting about sex that entices them to spend so much time talking about it? Mostly, they talk about how to talk about sex: how to define it, describe it, what words to use in referencing it, how to play with sexual language. Smith's films are playful. At a hockey game, Alyssa (Joey Lauren Adams) says that she always cheers for the "Visitors" and then tells Holden (Ben Affleck) why:

*Alyssa:* I'm a big "Visitors" fan. Especially the kind that make coffee for you in the morning before they go. That was a joke, a little wacky wordplay.
*Holden:* What do you mean by "Visitors"?
*Alyssa:* Was I being too obscure?

Earlier in the film, Banky (Jason Lee), Holden's best friend and partner in the writing and drawing of comic strips, unreels a complete monologue on the semantics of "fucking," especially "lesbian fucking": "Fucking is not limited to penetration. To me, it refers to any sex not totally about love," he concludes his eerily proleptic argument that Clinton would later appropriate before the Starr chamber when asked to define "sex."

The literary/linguistic theme of *Chasing Amy* is evident from the very first scene. It is a book signing (comic books rather than conventional texts, but literary in a very nineties way nonetheless) in which the central attraction is Hooper (Dwight Ewell), the gay black militant gangsta author of the comic book series *White Hatin' 'Coon*, whose phony black rage lecture at the microphone turns into a critical reading of *Star Wars* as a racist epic. This whole film criticism discourse then segues into Hooper's comic regaling of Holden and Banky with an equally ingenious queer theory reading of *Archie and Jughead* comic books. This hilarious, frenetic parody of literary interpretation places *Chasing Amy* in the semidocumentary company of *This Is Spinal Tap* (1984), the ensuing Christopher Guest mockumentaries *Waiting for Guffman* (1997) about civic theaters, *Best In Show* (2000) about competitive dog shows, and *A Mighty Wind* (2003) about folk music.

Holden, as his *Catcher in the Rye* name signals, is a naïve hetero dreamer, and, in an odd way, the film that *Chasing Amy* most resembles is *The Crying Game*. Much earlier in the film than did Dil in *The Crying Game*, Alyssa drops her big, not-so-secret secret on Holden that she is a lesbian. But like Fergus when he finds out that his girl Dil has a penis (which is, indeed, different from her being a man), Holden continues to pursue and fall in love with Alyssa. Unlike Fergus and Dil who completely redefine their love in platonic terms, Holden and Alyssa talk about love conquering all but all their talk can't overcome Holden's sexual orientation insecurities. Like J. D. Salinger's Holden Caulfield, Smith's earnest Holden ventures into the tangled swamp of nineties sexual orientation and finds out that he can't save anyone. He can't save his love for Alyssa. He can't save his friendship with Banky. And he can't save himself. He ends up "Chasing Amy," caught in the dilemma (as named and defined by Silent Bob played by Smith himself) of continuing to love a woman he has pushed away because of his own inability to accept the reality and power of that love. For Alyssa, love can conquer all, but, unfortunately for Holden, it can't erase the images of her past sexual escapades from his mind's heterosexual eye.

But if *Chasing Amy* is one of the nineties' most serious explorations of the possibilities and impossibilities of gay/straight relationships, it is also the only film of the decade to exhibit and analyze the diverse semantics of gayness. The film is composed of one scene after another in which the central characters, Holden, Alyssa, Banky, and Hooper, graphically discuss every conceivable aspect of both homosexuality and heterosexuality. Hoop is a veritable walking diction-ary of every racist and homophobic slur extant. *á la* Clinton, Holden and Alyssa exchange their personal definitions of "sex" and "virginity." Banky and Holden constantly argue about what words mean and what are the proper words to use: "Don't call her a dyke, she's a lesbian," Holden corrects Banky at one point. On the telephone, one of Alyssa's lesbian friends refers to her relationship to straight Holden as "playing the pronoun game."

In *Chasing Amy*, Smith and his Lyotardian "language games" bring Holly-wood and postmodern academia into closer contact than any of the other queer theory films of the nineties. *Chasing Amy* also embraces a theme perhaps closer to the academic heart than any other: How do you represent important concepts (like sexuality) in words? How does language dictate action? How does talking something out substitute for acting something out? Unfortunately, both the gay/straight relationship of Holden and Alyssa, and the gay/straight semantic dis-course of the film, end badly. The full exposure of reality through words causes the film's characters to flee from each other. If in the gay films of the nineties, such as the kissless *Philadelphia*, the images fail the subject matter; in *Chasing Amy*, so do the words.

While, aside from *The Crying Game*, the representation of gay/straight love relationships created little more than a discourse of confusion in nineties films, one thing that the gay/straight films of the nineties accomplished was the killing off of the "saintly gay friend" cliché. They portrayed gay friends to perturbed straights as sometimes less than "saintly" and then bequeathed this whole cliché to post-*Ellen* television in the form of *Will and Grace*. *My Best Friend's Wedding* drives the nail through the heart of the gay friend cliché by making the gay friend of the film's confused heroine so incredibly tall and handsome, so Cary Grant witty, so black-tie elegant, that he completely outshines the straight man who is supposed to be the heroine's object of affection. By the end of *My Best Friend's Wedding*, no one cares that Julia Roberts loses her ex-boyfriend (Dermot Mul-roney) to another because she is dancing with clearly the best man at the wed-ding in terms of looks, intelligence, and wit, even if he is gay. As Rupert Everett himself put it, "It's a totally hip choice of hers [Roberts] to do a film where first of all, she loses her man to a younger woman, and second of all, where she ends up going off with a homosexual."[35] If the popularity of *My Best Friend's Wedding* is any indication, this significant upgrading of the gay friend cliché was enthusiasti-cally accepted by the 1997 audiences.

Not so enthusiastically accepted were the saintly gay friend clichés of *The Object of My Affection* (1998) and *As Good As It Gets* (1997). *The Object of My*

*Affection*'s screenwriter, Wendy Wasserstein, when asked, "Did you write this because of the popularity of Rupert Everett's character in *My Best Friend's Wedding*?" answered, "Honey, I started writing this when Rupert Everett was 10."[36] Though *The Object of My Affection* had been in development for ten years, it was the gay nineties and especially the popularity of *My Best Friend's Wedding* that got it made, and it was that same popularity that made it fail. While Everett's dashing gay wit was a step forward in the entertainment value of gay male friend relationships with straight women, Nina (Jennifer Aniston) and George's (Paul Rudd) relationship in *The Object of My Affection* is a step back. One critic even wrote that the "movie inevitably plays like an extension of the final scene of *My Best Friend's Wedding*."[37] When Nina finds out that she is pregnant by her obnoxious ex-boyfriend, she turns to George who has also just ended an exploitative gay relationship with an equally obnoxious partner. Nina wants George to be her surrogate husband even if he can't be her lover. Perhaps this is where Hemingway's Jake and Lady Brett might have ended up if they had been turned into sitcom characters. *The Object of My Affection* is so conventional and mainstream that, by comparison, Smith's *Chasing Amy* is a significant social document.

By the end of the decade, ironically, all of the gay/straight explorations of the brave new nineties world of gay/straight relationships actually did find a home, and it was in a TV-sitcom, *Will and Grace* (1998), that would run for more than seven years well into the new millennium. Whereas *Ellen* three years earlier had been first outed then taken off the TV screen, *Will and Grace* was welcomed with open arms causing one commentator to ask, "Is this the same country that threw a massive conniption over a little show called *Ellen*? Has the Moral Majority up and moved to Ecuador?"[38] The truth of the matter is that the road had been so well paved for *Will and Grace* that "the gay-man/hetero-gal duo has become the pop-culture relationship *du jour*, the screwball comedy match for the millennium, a safe, lucrative way to package gay characters for the heartland. . . . Gay men and straight women are to the '90s what Oscar and Felix were to the '70s."[39]

This proliferation of nineties gay/straight relationship films signaled the need for gender bridges and gave another aspect to the gay spin strategy of the decade. While the first focus of that spin strategy had been on issues, such as AIDS, homophobia, and coming out, these gay/straight films emphasized all that the different sexual orientations shared. In the early nineties, gay life was not yet fully out of the closet. AIDS fears had not yet fully been allayed. By the late nineties, these films examined the tentative reaching outs between the genders and the sexual orientations who were suddenly trying to accept each other on equal terms. Hokey as some of these films are, they represent a very necessary spin in the direction of gay/straight understanding. The early nineties was the historical epoch of the first recognitions of gay rights in the form of laws, gay marriages, gender-bending relationships, and a new media openness, and these films, albeit tentative and sometimes contrived, caught that new spirit of reaching out and spun it in some very positive and often comical ways.

Much more sinister and denigrating than the gay/straight films of the nineties were the parade of lesbian crime films that titillated (and did little else to) the decade. Like that unexpected penis in *The Crying Game*, the lesbian relationships in nineties films seemed to exist mainly for their surprise value, the "oh, so that's how it is" plot twists that recapture an audience's attention in midmovie. For example, *Basic Instinct's* (1992) lesbian relationship is never anything more than a red herring thrown into the film's murderous mix in order to include a *French Connection* (1971)-style car chase. The lesbian relationship between Sharon Stone's lethal heiress and her look-alike paramour takes place completely off stage and carries no more emotional connection or impact than the expression of one brief fit of lesbian jealousy.

Despite being crowned (after *Basic Instinct*) as the blonde sex symbol of the nineties, successor to Marilyn Monroe, Grace Kelly, Jayne Mansfield, Faye Dunaway, and Kathleen Turner, Stone brought a new lesbian-chic twist to the previous totally hetero image of the blonde bombshell sex doll goddess. Overtones of lesbianism kept surfacing in Stone's nineties films. In *The Quick and the Dead* (1995), she actually takes over a male genre as a gunslinger in chaps. Her most disturbing foray into lesbian chic, however, comes in the feminist, antipatriarchal revenge remake of the 1956 film *Diabolique* (1996).

The film opens with two women framed (enclosed) in a window looking out on the world of the posh St. Anselm's School for Boys. They are Mia (Isabel Adjani), the wife of the headmaster of the school, and Nicole (Sharon Stone), the sexy teacher who is having an affair with Mia's husband, and they are trapped together in an all-male world. While Mia's husband Guy (Chazz Palmintieri) systematically humiliates his wife in veiled sexual language—"Swallow. Swallow it for once," he commands her to eat at the headmaster's table before all the teachers at the school—and attempts to sexually dominate his mistress, the two women not only have formed a liaison to kill the sadistic husband but are also on the verge of becoming lesbian lovers. That burgeoning relationship is what provides the film's Hitchcockian twists and ultimately makes the film's two murderous, feminist, lesbians palatable to the moviegoing audience. Their crimes are misdemeanors compared to the patriarchal evil of Guy, the husband and headmaster.

Mia and Nicole are two seemingly one-dimensional stereotypes of women. Mia is utterly submissive, and Nicole is aggressive, vengeful, and hateful toward men whom she tries to control with her sexuality. In an early scene, Nicole kisses Mia's shoulders and arms and asks: "Does *he* do this to you?" This signals that, in their lesbian relationship, Nicole will be taking the dominant male role. *Diabiolique* is a *Gaslight* (1944) meets *Psycho* (1960) meets *The Trouble With Harry* (1955) pastiche of a movie that ironically resembles very little the 1956 original. Its main innovation is its plot-changing lesbian love twist. Again ironically, the two women actually fall in love with each other, and Guy and Nicole's original plot to scare the weak-hearted Mia to death (*á la Gaslight*) turns into Nicole and Mia's plot to murder Guy. After they supposedly kill the piggish husband the first time, the two women get into bed with each other and Mia says, "He'll never hurt us again," to which Nicole answers, "Fuck him, fuck them." Nicole's second dismissive epithet, of course, refers to men in general.

The one dominant imagery of *Diabolique* is the windows of the school as a framing device for the entrapment of these two women in the male patriarchal world. Two videographers, on the St. Anselm's campus to shoot a commercial for the school, see the two women in the window and speculate: "Twenty bucks they killed him. Dykes." Another visitor to the campus, the female private detective (Kathy Bates), sides with the two women. "Men," she chatters. "I don't know how they sleep at night. It's not your fault. Men. Testosterone. They should put it in bombs." As the drowned body disappears, and the detective shows up, and everyone is pointing their finger at the two women, confusion seems to have taken over the film until one thing starts to give meaning to the whole chaos. The two women start to fall in love:

> *Mia:* I'll say we are lovers.
> *Nicole:* Well, you can take the girl out of the convent.
> *Mia:* I thought we had the same reason.
> *Nicole:* We did have the same reason. I just had another one.

And with that realization Nicole kisses Mia passionately for the first time and the film arcs away from being a Hitchcockian feminist revenge thriller into a lesbian love story. *Bound* (1996) takes the same arc.

Unlike the male homosexual films and the gay/straight films of the nineties, the lesbian films are very film noirish, very femme fatale-ist, very antimale, and very feminist. Whereas the gay men films and the gay/straight films were comedies and social consciousness films, the majority of the lesbian films are dark, violent, and highly sexual, openly angry, hateful, and even murderous toward men, but always clearly feminist in their existential decision making and in their journeys to independence from patriarchal bondage. *Bound* is an excellent example. Its two lesbian heroines are utterly alienated from men before the film even begins. Corky (Gina Gershon) is a lesbian plumber who dresses in men's muscle shirts, work boots, and white jockey shorts. When she goes into her favorite lesbian bar after being in prison for five years, she tells the bartender, "I'm just here to get laid." Corky says that if "there's one thing I can't stand it's a woman who apologizes for wanting sex." Violet is a lipstick bisexual who is kept by Ceasar (Joe Pantaliano), a stupid but ultraviolent mafioso. When she sees Corky, it is love at first sight. Corky is rehabbing the apartment next door to Ceasar's and meets Violet in the elevator. Through the thin walls of the apartment, Corky hears Violet having sex with Ceasar. "What you heard wasn't sex," Violet tells Corky. "It was work." The next time Corky listens through the walls, she hears Ceasar torturing another gangster.

*Bound* has none of the reticence about graphic sexuality of the majority of the male gay films or of *Diabolique*. Its narrative is as simplistic as a porno film—sexy plumber seduces bored housewife. But after the explicit lesbian sex scenes end, the film noir begins. If *Diabolique* is a Hitchcock pastiche, then the Wachowski brothers' *Bound* is mini-Mamet as in *House of Games* (1987) and *The Spanish Prisoner* (1998). Twist layers upon twist, and metaphor layers upon metaphor.

As in *Diabolique*, the lesbian lovers hatch a plot to steal Ceasar's mob money. "I want out. I want a new life," Violet begs Corky to help her. She is talking about escaping her sexual bondage to her brutal boyfriend, but she could just as easily be talking about escaping her kept heterosexual whoredom for the heated lesbian love that Corky offers. "This is the part where you tell me that inside you is a little dyke like me," Corky mocks her. Corky and Violet concoct a perfect plan just as Nicole and Mia do in *Diabolique*, and just as in that film, it goes drastically wrong. At one point, as their plan is unraveling, Corky considers taking off with the mafia's two million dollars and leaving Violet to take the torturous consequences, but she doesn't. Just as in *Diabolique*, the plot is overcome by the two lesbians falling in love. Lesbian love, in both films, transforms the venal scheming murderers and thieves from villainesses into lovers trying to escape the bondage of violent male oppression.

"Don't quit on me Violet, and I won't quit on you," Corky whispers to her lesbian lover through the walls. When they finally confront the rabid Ceasar, he screams, "What did you do to her. That's my Violet. [then to Violet] What did she do to you?" And Violet answers, echoing Nicole's "Does *he* do this to you?" in *Diabolique*, "Everything that you couldn't." Not only can men not make these women happy or loved, but they can't fulfill them sexually either. Only their lesbian lovers can do that. As in *Diabolique*, the lesbian love relationship proves true and holds against all the pressure of the twisted film noir plots.

*Wild Things* (1998), however, does not embrace this "romance conquers all," antinoir sentimentality. In *Wild Things*, the film noir plot conquers all and no matter how steamy the lesbian love affair may be, the plot and the lure of the money takes over. *Wild Things* is *Body Heat* (1991) meets trailer-trashy Mamet meets *It's A Mad, Mad, Mad, Mad World* (1963) and then circles back to *Body Heat* again. But there is another significant difference between *Wild Things* and the other lesbian-chic love stories. Besides having more plot twists than a Philadelphia pretzel, it has major ideological differences: Though one of the lesbian lovers wins out in the end, the other is sacrificed for money. The nineties commodity culture plot overrules the lesbian love affair, which was not at all the case in either *Diabolique* or *Bound*.

The iconography of lesbian-chic plays a prominent part in *Wild Things*. Like Corky in *Bound*, Suzy Toller (Denise Richards) dresses in combat boots, works on cars, and lives in isolation on a crocodile farm on the edge of the Everglades. Kelly Van Ryan (Neve Campbell) is the lipstick lesbian Violet of this film, a member of Miami high society and the reigning Yuppie princess of the exclusive Blue Bay High School where Sam Lombardo (Matt Dillon) works as a guidance counselor and reigning, macho, sex symbol for all of the teenage girls (and their mothers). These two seemingly mismatched teens seem to team up to claim that Sam raped them. But what seems to be yet another lesbian-lovers plot revenge on a sexually oppressive male villain movie (like *Diabolique* and *Bound*) suddenly metamorphoses into a steamy ménage-à-trois legal loophole scam (like *Body Heat*) orchestrated by Sam pulling the strings on the two young women to get a settlement payoff from Kelly's rich mother. Then the twists begin as in a

David Mamet movie. Kelly's attempt to kill Suzy in a swimming pool turns into a steamy lesbian love scene. But then Sam and Kelly turn on Suzy and seemingly kill her and dump her body in the glades. Then, the detective who is investigating the case turns up naked in Sam's shower and the fourth member of the conspiracy surfaces. Then, the detective kills Kelly on Sam's boat, but then Suzy comes back to life and kills both the detective and Sam, and sails off into the sunset.

*Body Heat* is the film that has its hot noir fingerprints all over *Wild Things*. In *Body Heat*, the femme fatale ends up on a Caribbean beach sipping a *piña colada* in the sun and enjoying her money at the expense of all the men she has manipulated and the double she blew up in the boathouse to fabricate her death. In *Wild Things*, first Sam, then Suzy, replay (visually) this exact scene, sitting on a beach in the sun alone, luxuriating in the money they have just scammed out of their victims. In *Wild Things*, the lesbian wins in the end, escapes with the money, yet loses her lesbian love. Nineties commodity culture ultimately triumphs over romantic lesbian chic.

Lesbian sexual heat and lesbian patriarchal hate seems to be the message in these nineties film noirs. But that is not at all the approach that John Sayles takes in *Lianna* (1993) or that Rose Troche takes in *Go Fish* (1994). Both set out to portray lesbian life in its everyday domestic normality and both succeed triumphantly. These films may not be as chic as the lesbian noirs, but they are much more realistic and natural. As one commentator wrote, "*Go Fish* does for lesbian culture what Spike Lee's *She's Gotta Have It* (1986) did for black culture back in 1986: opens the doors and invites the entire neighborhood in for some fun."[40]

While the gay films of the nineties, in all of their variety, pushed the possibilities of spin to the limit in the pursuit of bringing gay issues (such as AIDS and coming out) and the gay lifestyle (such as gay/straight tolerance and the reality of gay sexuality) into the mainstream, perhaps the most interesting dynamic of all was the American acceptance (as demonstrated by strong box-office figures) of comic films about the alternative gay lifestyles of drag queens, cross-dressers, transvestites. As one commentator noted in 1995, "Drag went fabulously mainstream this weekend."[41] Perhaps this particular circle of the gay spin cycle proved more acceptable to audiences because it had brilliant predecessors who had paved the way for its comic extravagances. Gender-bending comedies had enjoyed huge success in the past. Billy Wilder's *Some Like It Hot* (1959) and Sydney Pollack's *Tootsie* (1982) certainly cleared the way for the highly successful comic spin into the mainstream given to a series of drag queen films in the nineties. *Some Like It Hot* and *Tootsie* were the ultimate drag queen films, but there was never any sense whatsoever in those two films that the characters who dressed up in women's clothes were gay. The mainstream drag films of the nineties started out in that same old conflicted style with *Mrs. Doubtfire* (1993), but a succession of drag films followed that under the strong pull of the gay spin strategy redefined the drag film subgenre into a statement about gay identity and gender.

*Mrs. Doubtfire* is nothing new at all. A "patchwork rip-off of *Tootsie*,"[42] one critic called it. Both movies are not about gay men who enjoy dressing up like women because it makes them feel better about themselves and confirms their true identity. Rather, both *Mrs. Doubtfire* and *Tootsie* are about failing males who take on elaborate acting roles as women in order to circumvent their failures. They are not gay men who want to be women. Rather, they are actors auditioning for roles they can't get as men. Drag is nothing more than a tool. It is certainly not a lifestyle. In sync with the more honest, open, and out gay spin of the nineties, the drag queen films that followed *Mrs. Doubtfire* would explore gay drag as a lifestyle rather than just a last resort of straight men in desperate circumstances. The drag queens of *The Adventures of Priscilla, Queen of the Desert* (1994), *To Wong Foo, Thanks for Everything, Julie Newmar* (1995), and *The Birdcage* are celebrative of their gay drag identities, joyful in their constructing (through makeup and costume) of those identities, and utterly open in their vibrant display of those identities to all who want to look. There is no sense in any of these films that drag is simply a space where straight men go slumming out of desperation. For the hero/heroines of these films, drag is a joyful, playful space where the characters want to live, not where circumstance has forced them to take up uneasy residence. These films can certainly thank RuPaul for some of their exuberant cachet.

*The Adventures of Priscilla, Queen of the Desert* and *To Wong Foo, Thanks for Everything, Julie Newmar* are essentially the same film, from their interminable titles to their drag stereotype characters to their aliens-stranded-in-a-clueless-small-town plots (reminiscent of 1982's *E.T.: The Extraterrestrial*) to their buddy road trip structures to their positivity toward the drag lifestyle and their exuberance in living it. In both films, three drag queens set out on a cross-country journey not to find themselves (they've already done that with gusto) but rather to show themselves off to the rest of the world either publicly (in terms of orchestrated musical production numbers) or privately (in terms of personal encounters with the clueless straights they meet along the way). Though these drag queens are trekking across different countries, Australia and America respectively, they are acting out their gender-bent identities in the same way and making friends (not making people uncomfortable) as they go along.

When these two films arrived in the midnineties, the critics made much of their mainstreamness. "*To Wong Foo* marks the movies' first mainstream dip into the culture of cross-dressing," one critic who clearly hadn't seen *The Adventures of Priscilla, Queen of the Desert* the year before gushed.[43] "*Wong Foo* aims at the mainstream," a Hollywood producer argued. "It won't be perceived as anything more sexually threatening than Flip Wilson playing Geraldine."[44] This excitement over the fact that something so obviously alternative (even within the gay lifestyle itself) could be spun into the mainstream says a great deal about how successful the gay spin strategy was by the midnineties. Films were no longer content just to show gay men and women trying to live out their everyday lives. The spin strategies of *Angels in America*, *Philadelphia*, *In & Out*, and *Love! Valor! Compassion!* had proven so successful that Hollywood wanted to push the envelope of gay spin even further. Charles Busch, one of Broadway's most prominent drag queen actors, mapped the new territory that *To Wong Foo, Thanks for Everything, Julie Newmar* was entering: "This is *E.T.* with falsies. . . . We've had enough of downbeat drag queens shooting up and killing themselves. It was nice seeing a family picture about transvestitism."[45]

But while these two buddy road movies were moderately successful (at the box office) in their positive, asexual, even sentimental portrayal of the gay drag lifestyle, their success was nothing compared to that of *The Birdcage*, Mike Nichols's and Elaine May's remake of *La Cage aux Folles* (1978). But *The Birdcage* does nothing new and explores no territory of gayness that *The Adventures of Priscilla, Queen of the Desert* and *To Wong Foo, Thanks for Everything, Julie Newmar* hadn't already explored. *The Birdcage* does it better with more gloss and panache. Perhaps that is why *The Birdcage* appealed so strongly to mainstream straight audiences and had so little appeal to the gay community. *La Cage aux Folles* and now *The Birdcage* has always been "a gay minstrel show, the kind of 'safe' dragqueen [*sic*] burlesque that could become an art-house crowd pleaser in an era [the late seventies] when true gay cinema remained locked in the closet."[46] Actor Hank Azaria, who plays the hilarious Guatemalan houseboy, puts the film in perspective: "We were aware of everything—the gayness of it, the politics. But the first priority was always, *Is it funny?* We weren't making *Philadelphia*."[47]

While Azaria is very conscious of genre in his perception of the film, the studio public relations brains were very conscious of spin in their marketing of *The Birdcage* to American audiences. Ironically, they embraced the same spin strategy that had been employed on behalf of *Philadelphia*:

> Still a mainstream movie about a happily settled gay couple? It's a tricky pitch, particularly in these neoconservative times. . . . The challenge, of course, was selling a gay-themed cross-dressing movie to a predominately straight audience. . . . The strategy MGM/UA ultimately came up with to market the film: Don't ask, don't tell. [echoing Bill Clinton's policy for gays in the military in the nineties]
>
> "For me it was just an exercise in not shooting yourself in the foot," explains Gerry Rich, MGM/UA's president of worldwide marketing. . . . Translated from suitspeak, that means *Birdcage*'s trailers, TV spots, and print ads pitched the film less as a gay love story and more as another wacky Robin Williams laugh riot. Even the drag angle was downplayed in the film's posters, with Lane wearing a straight-laced business suit.[48]

What both Azaria and the Hollywood spinmasters realized was that *The Birdcage* would probably never truly appeal to gay audiences precisely because it is a comedy, a farce, and the nineties is an era where gayness is demanding to be taken much more seriously, where the gay community is seeking to shed its swishy, flamboyant, neurotic, stereotypical image for a much more mainstream subdued normality. *The Birdcage* didn't fit that gay lifestyle spin strategy in exactly the same way that drag divas like RuPaul and Starina a.k.a. Albert (Nathan Lane) in *The Birdcage* don't fit the neoconservative gay image of the nineties—the Tom Hanks, Kevin Kline, *My Best Friend's Wedding* image of gay men.

*The Birdcage*'s screen scene plot, its two main characters, Armand (Robin Williams) and Albert, and its greatest triumph (getting Gene Hackman into drag), are all "the entropic principles of farce . . . of chaos emerging from order."[49] The new image of the gay lifestyle in the nineties didn't allow for the old drag queen dramatics of the past. The nineties-spun gay image was a much more serious and self-conscious image that didn't really see the farcical possibilities of the gay/straight neoconservative clash. However, what everyone involved—both the studio marketing execs and the protective gay community—forgot was that *The Birdcage* wasn't really a film about gayness at all.

Drag movies aren't really about gay identities. They are about theater and acting (as *Tootsie* was), about disappearing into a role and creating a new identity when the old one doesn't work for whatever reason. While so many of the gay films of the nineties are about finding one's gay identity and coming out, drag films are about going in to women's clothes and glamorous new identities. In *The Birdcage*, when Albert is on stage as Starina, he truly is a star, a diva, totally in control of a very glamorous image. Offstage, Albert is a neurotic, hypochondriac, emotionally unstable mess. Order lies with the gay drag image while chaos rules everyday life. Armand exudes all of the positive aspects of the neoconservative nineties gay lifestyle. As played by a restrained Robin Williams, Armand is talented, sensitive, loving, and in charge (and never in drag). Albert, on the other hand, is a walking emotional time bomb who can only find order in his life when he is not himself. Armand doesn't need to escape reality but Albert does, and drag is his ticket of passage. *The Birdcage*'s nineties message is that, in order for some gay men to come out of the closet, they first have to dress up in the clothes hanging in there.

But *The Birdcage* has an obvious political subtext as well. Armand's son by a one-time, ill-advised liaison in the distant past is getting married and wants Armand to meet the in-laws, neoconservative U.S. Senator Kevin Keeley (Gene Hackman) and his wife. They are an uptight, patriotic, politically conservative, and openly homophobic heterosexual couple who nonetheless are totally fooled when Albert shows up at the dinner party dressed like Barbara Bush. Before this whole chaotic affair is over, Albert has Senator Keeley dressed up like Margaret Thatcher or Janet Reno. Because the senator accepts Albert's drag, everything turns out alright and order is restored. The symbolism ultimately is the same as that of *To Wong Foo, Thanks for Everything, Julie Newmar*. Neoconservative America needs to see the value and utility in supporting alternative lifestyles.

But some alternative gay lifestyles were much more resistant to positive gay spin. While the comedy genre could spin cross-dressing and transvestitism into a nonthreatening domestic gay idiosyncrasy, some of the more extreme aspects of the gay lifestyle could not be so happily displayed. The gay underground of the controversial *Cruising* (1980) still existed, and no amount of positive gay spin could palliate its perverse deviance and threatening violence. *Savage Nights* (1992) could be termed the anti-*Philadelphia*. This story of a bisexual Parisian filmmaker who finds out he is HIV-positive but doesn't care is gay spin's worst nightmare. It raises the specter of the gay community as plague carriers and a threat to society. *The Boys of St. Vincent* (1994) explores the theme of pedophilia in a Newfoundland orphanage run by the renowned winemaking Christian Brothers and predicts a real crisis in the Catholic Church, the sexual abuse of children by priests, that would surface all over America in the late nineties. Director Todd Solondz's independent film *Happiness* (1998) won the International Critics Prize at the Cannes Film Festival despite its subject matter, a black comedy treatment of pedophilia in suburbia. It became an art-house hit in New York but never gained any sort of mainstream distribution because its sympathy for pedophiles was just too extreme a spin concept for American audiences to accept.

Perhaps the most acclaimed and popular film to touch upon severely troubling aspects of the gay underground is *The Shawshank Redemption* (1994). It employs the stark and brutal reality of homosexual rape in men's prisons as a reality check, as the deepest descent into the underworld, for the film's central character, Andy Dufresne (Tim Robbins). From this depth of brutal degradation and dehumanization, Andy rises to not only survive but to win the battle for personal identity in a violent underground world. In *The Shawshank Redemption*, homosexuality isn't really considered as an issue or given any sort of spin at all. It is simply there, one of the brutal realities of the antiexistential underworld of the prison.

The made-for-TV film, *Serving in Silence: The Margarethe Cammermeyer Story* (1995), addresses perhaps the most publicly debated government policy concerning gays in the nineties, the Clinton administration's decision that the best way to deal with the issue of "gays-in-the-military" is to simply ignore the issue, "don't see, don't tell." In other words, the president of the United States endorsed a military policy that forced gays who were serving their country to stay locked in the closet, to bury part of their identity underground. The TV film itself was an accurate depiction of the gays-in-the-military issue, including a lesbian kiss between the title character, Colonel Cammermeyer (Glen Close) and her lover (Judy Davis).

In both Oliver Stone's *JFK* and in the thriller *The Jackal* (1997), the remake of *The Day of the Jackal* (1973), the gay underground appears as a tool of plot. In *JFK*, the gay orgies, complete with body painting and male prostitutes held in the mansion of ultrafey Clay Shaw (Tommy Lee Jones), form a backdrop for the bringing together of some of the conspirators in the assassination. In *The Jackal*, the title character, also an assassin, uses gayness as one of his cover identities, an escape hatch when surveillance drives him underground. In the original *The Day of the Jackal*, the title character picked up a gay lover in a bathhouse. His only motive was to use the gay man's flat as a safe house when his pursuers were closing in. In *The Jackal*, the title character hustles a government employee in a DC bar, then calls him later when he needs the man's townhouse for a crash pad as he awaits his opportunity to assassinate the First Lady. In this case, the gay pickup is less than human and the Jackal (Bruce Willis) is hardly believable as gay. He kills the gay pickup in cold blood before they even touch. In *Midnight in the Garden of Good and Evil* (1997), Jim Williams (Kevin Spacey) is the Clay Shaw of Savannah, Georgia, in the mideighties. But of all the films that take the movie audience into the alternative gay underground, *Midnight in the Garden of Good and Evil* is the one most specifically interested in the subject of underground gayness. It is a true story, based on John Berendtz's nonfiction novel about a scion of Old South high society who murders a young male prostitute. Like all of the other gay underground films, gayness is only interesting if it is closeted, taboo, and against the mainstream spin of all the positive gay films of the nineties. As one critic wrote of the film about Williams's underground life in Savannah, it has "a pungent psychosexual hook . . . he's a gay man in the closet . . . his sexuality depends on its invisibility."[50] The gay underworld in these films is a discourse space for closeted gays, gays willing to keep their sexual identities secret in the service of larger rituals, such as social acceptance or advancement in the military or political action.

These gay underground films are films of another era before the positive gay spin strategies of the nineties kicked in and coming out of the closet became a good thing, a necessary existential act, rather than a threatening thing, an ostracizing decision that forced one out of a safe, secret underground into the harsh light of exposure. In the nineties, coming out of the closet isn't exposure of a grotesque underground self (like Dorian Gray's picture) but the acknowledgement of one's true, repressed self as a liberating act.

The film *Far From Heaven* (2002) signals how much things have changed from the closeted past, how far attitudes have changed under the influence of gay spin. A remake of the Douglas Sirk fifties weepy *All that Heaven Allows* (1955), which starred Rock Hudson as the heterosexual stud gardener that the widowed lady of the house falls for, *Far From Heaven* certainly raises the stakes of its fifties predecessor. In this millennial film, the gardener is black, the relationship is not only interracial but adulterous, and the lady of the house's husband isn't dead but rather has just come out of the closet as gay. *Far From Heaven* goes where no fifties weepy (or Hudson for that matter) could go in the past, and the growing power across the nineties decade of positive gay spin is one of the reasons. Gay spin changed the perspective of American society toward one of its most feared and reviled alternative lifestyles, and American film played a significant part in accomplishing that social and historical sea change.

# CHAPTER 7

# Sex and the Nineties

> Sex has always been complicated, but only until recently has it become
> synonymous with danger. On screen, getting laid is almost a sure way to get laid
> out . . . the metaphors for AIDS have kept a breakneck pace with the disease.
> —Lawrence O'Toole, "I Love You to Death," *Entertainment Weekly*

AIDS changed the whole sexual landscape and redefined sex in the nineties for both gays and straights. Naturally, gay culture needed to create an elaborate spin strategy to deal with the AIDS epidemic because homosexuality was being blamed for causing it. But AIDS had an equally powerful impact upon heterosexual culture. Straight sexual adventuring in the nineties had to make the same behavioral adjustments that gay cruising made. Those industries that fed on the prurient allure of promiscuous, illicit, deviant, erotic sexuality—the movies, the porno industry, strip joints, prostitution—had to develop elaborate spin strategies to justify their continued existence as cultural purveyors of sex in the era of sexual disease.

The nineties decade was the fourth sexual landscape of the twentieth century that had to be completely remapped because of significant social change. The post–Freudian Modernist era at the turn of the century was the first. The post-war–Roaring Twenties driven by Prohibition and burgeoning women's liberation was the second. The post-Pill sixties and seventies fueled by free love and rock-and-roll was the third. In each of these sexual epochs, people rethought their sexuality, its milieu, and its consequences as a reactionary necessity under the stimulus of major events (intellectual, historical, scientific) that changed their attitude toward their own sexuality. This was especially true of the post-AIDS nineties.

As the AIDS epidemic emerged and spread throughout the mid- and late eighties, world sexual culture slowly began to realize that the free love, polygamous, cruising, party sex, drug-induced, one-night-stand sexuality of the freewheeling sixties and seventies was no longer viable. In the eighties, sex and death converged to create a necessity for monogamy, long-term relationships, and sexual caution. This landscape of fear accomplished what all the efforts of the priests and preachers from their pulpits, all the erstwhile sex educators in their classrooms, and all the frightened parents trying to stop the momentum of the runaway sexual experimentation, promiscuity, and deviance of the sixties and seventies had failed to do. By the nineties, under the threat of AIDS, a sexual neoconservatism quite similar to that of the fifties emerged in America. The sexual revolution ended, and sexual isolationism became the new culture. Marriage, monogamy, and long-term, single-sex-partner relationships made an almost instantaneous comeback. These versions of sexuality were not resuscitated because the fifties arguments of their morality, their fulfillment possibilities in terms of relationships, or their pure human rightness finally being heeded, but rather simply because they were safe. You wouldn't die of monogamous sex. You wouldn't be infected by a sex partner who was clean and exclusive. The Woodstock Nation–fueled, take-it-to-the-streets free love of the sixties and the cocaine-driven disco promiscuity of the seventies gave way to what came to be called the "cocooning" of the nineties. Group sex, public sex, party sex, and polygamous sex quickly fell out of favor in the face of AIDS. "Safe sex" became the mantra of nineties sexual spin.

In the age of AIDS, nineties sex became masturbatory. The rule was hands off others but hands on yourself because you are the only person you know who is certifiably safe. Sex became voyeuristic rather that participatory. Again, the rule was hands-off. It was safe to watch sex, but you weren't allowed to touch. Sex went back behind closed doors, became something enjoyed only "in the privacy of one's own home" (to quote a phrase dear to the hearts of the nineties sexual spin doctors) where it was risk-free and controllable.

Hands-off sex sought mainstream acceptance and moral legitimacy simply because it was safe and you couldn't catch AIDS and die from it. Sex flooded the society, seeped into the home, drowned out the music, because in lieu of doing it, consumers substituted the masturbatory stimuli of watching it and hearing it. When hands-off voyeuristic sexuality became the safe-sex product of the early nineties, masturbation and one-dimensional sexual relationships became the sex acts of choice. And condoms, once relegated to under the counters of the drug stores, became the indispensable, most colorful, and most available fashion accessory of the new safe-sex nineties. Every new drug mart and all-purpose pharmacy sported extensive condom displays right in the middle of their busiest aisles or next to their cash registers. Gas stations sold condoms, candy bars, and cigarettes to customers on the move. And the tiny condom machines in the public restrooms of the past were replaced by dispensers covering the whole lavatory wall that sold at least three styles of condoms in assorted colors plus playing cards, temporary tattoos, and jelly beans. Though network television refused to accept condom commercials, they became a ubiquitous presence in nineties films, a sort of obligatory public service announcement placed among the scenes of sex and violence.

In fact, the movie industry became a valued ally of the sexual spin strategies that, by necessity, evolved out of the AIDS-threatened environment of the nineties. With voyeurism, masturbation, and cocooned coupling becoming the landmarks of the new VCR-furnished, "in the privacy of your own home" sexual landscape, the demand for sexual electronic visual products became overwhelming. Pornography exploded as a mainstream entertainment industry. Via videotape and cable TV, hardcore pornography entered the home where it could be viewed without any of the attendant embarrassment of being seen going into an adult theater in a sleazy part of town or buying dirty skin magazines from a matronly cashier looking askance at you over the tops of her reading glasses.

The hands-off sexual culture of the nineties vaulted strippers and strip joints back into popularity, only now they were gentlemen's clubs and the girls were dancers and the bouncers became tuxedoed doormen. These newer, bigger, fancier, topless, bottomless, totally nude strip emporiums fit the "look but don't touch" AIDS-dictated sexual spin of the nineties to a T.

Then, by the end of the decade, the exhibitionist culture of the strip clubs went mainstream via Britney Spears and the other pop divas of her generation (following, of course, in the before-her-time footsteps of Cher). The broad popularity of the barely legal, adolescent slut style of the teenage divas triggered the bare-midriff, low-cut, hip-hugging, lingerie-exposed, no-panty-line fashions of the hip-hop millennium.

AIDS did, indeed, change everything. Its threat gave a whole new spin to the sexual culture of the nineties. The films of the nineties (as they had so skillfully for the spin strategies of homosexuality) recorded, participated in. and supported the new monosexual, masturbatory, and voyeuristic sexual spin strategies. And it was only appropriate that the first major sexual blockbuster of the nineties, *Basic Instinct* (1991), would emphasize all of those various aspects of post-AIDS sexual spin.

Following the example of 1987's *Fatal Attraction* (even including Michael Douglas), as an AIDS metaphor film, *Basic Instinct* sets the tone, defines the ideology, and articulates the post-AIDS spin strategies for the sex/death obsessions of nineties film. From its very first frame, *Basic Instinct* assaults the audience with a relentless checklist of every sexual orientation, perversion, position, game, and power possibility conceivable. But what *Basic Instinct* also does is cleverly articulate all of the different sexual strategies that one could embrace to keep from getting killed by having sex.

### *Basic Instinct*

I think she's the fuck of the century.

—*Basic Instinct*

Katherine Tramell (Sharon Stone) may be "the fuck of the century," but her film (and it truly is *her* film), *Basic Instinct*, is the sexual lexicon for the nineties decade. It defines the new neoconservative approach to sexuality necessitated by the onset of AIDS. In its strange, cold, quadraphonic, sadomasochistic sexual relationship among homicide detective Nick Curran (Michael Douglas); Katherine; Roxie (Leilani Sarelle), the bisexual Katherine's lesbian lover; and psychoanalyst Elizabeth Garner (Jeanne Trippellhorn), who, at different times, is Katherine's lesbian lover and Nick's hetero lover, *Basic Instinct* creates a sex/death chemistry that articulates all of the different available nineties strategies for having or simulating sex without taking the risk of dying from it (read: AIDS).

For example, *Basic Instinct* is heavily into voyeurism, a central hands-off strategy of sexual stimulation. The film's very first frame is of a ceiling mirror above a bed of two people having sex. Throughout the film other mirror images are used to create situations of voyeuristic spying, Peeping-Tom situations. In every mirror is an image of a naked woman dressing or a naked couple copulating. Voyeurism becomes the grammar of almost every scene of the film. Nick enjoys Katherine's nakedness in the mirror as she changes clothes. The assembled interrogators enjoy looking between Katherine's legs as she answers their questions. Gus (George Dzundza) spies on her in the police car's rearview mirror. The detectives watch her take a polygraph test via a hidden camera. Nick follows her home and watches her undress from a darkened doorway. In the dance club, Katherine first teases Nick by caressing Roxie and then teases Roxie by caressing Nick. Nick and Katherine perform oral sex on each other as the movie audience watches them in the mirror above the bed. Roxie watches the whole sexual encounter between Nick and Katherine and is so disturbed that she tries to kill Nick out of jealousy.

The perverse ménage à trois between Nick, Katherine, and Roxie nails down the strong theme of voyeurism. "You like watching, don't you?" Nick accuses Roxie. "She likes me to watch," Roxie taunts Nick. Later, after Roxie has died in a car crash, Katherine sobs guiltily: "I shouldn't have let her watch us. She wanted to watch me all the time." But Nick realizes that Katherine encourages this voyeurism. It is one of the many sexual games she loves to play. "Do you like her to watch you?" Nick asks, even though he knows the answer. "She never got jealous before. She got excited," Katherine protests.

Voyeurism is a game these women play with men, a kind of foreplay for their own lesbian sexual encounters. But, as one critic notes, Joe Eszterhas's script, with its explicit sexual language coming out of the mouths of a supercool Hitchcock blonde (Grace Kelly never talked that way), and Paul Verhoeven's direction, with its full-frontal nudity, "falls right into the trap of thinking that 'more explicit' equals 'sexier.'" The same critic argues that this explicit sexual approach can't equal the perverse sexual fascination of one of the many *Basic Instinct* straight-to-video rip-off films, *Animal Instincts* (1992). That film's "portrait of a stale marriage enlivened when hubby starts watching his wife have sex on television ripples out from the VCR to address our own video voyeurism. And that's more daring than anything in *Basic Instinct*."[1] Not true. Voyeurism ripples out of almost every scene in *Basic Instinct*. Someone is always watching in *Basic Instinct* and in Eszterhas and Stone's follow-up sex film, *Sliver* (1993). In the post-AIDS sexual landscape, it may be safe and arousing to watch, but it is also frustrating.

Throughout *Basic Instinct*, Nick is trapped in a hands-off situation where he can look but not touch. He even admits sheepishly to his shrink that masturbation is his only outlet for this frustration. "My sex life is really pretty shitty . . . (holds his hand up). I've started developing calluses," Nick jokes. Later, however, when his partner catches him working on the case late at night, Gus chides him: "Ain't you got nothing better to do than come in here and jack off the damn machine?"

Masturbation is the natural complement to voyeurism. Both are solitary. Both are distanced from the object of sexual attraction. But, above all, both are safe. They give the voyeur and the masturbator complete control over their sexual environment. In *Basic Instinct*, for most of the film, Nick can't touch but everyone is touching everyone else. Nick tells another psychiatrist, "Number one—I don't remember how often I used to jerk off, but it was a lot." In the distanced and solitary world of the reluctant voyeur, masturbation is the last (but obvious) recourse. In the nineties, people didn't choose the voyeurism of pornography and strip clubs or opt for masturbation as their sex act of choice, or the condom as their primary evening accessory. AIDS propelled all these things to the foreground of the sexual landscape.

*Basic Instinct* could have been just a big-screen episode of *The Streets of San Francisco* (1972), the TV cop show that first made Michael Douglas famous, but it goes well beyond that. It does all the things that could never be done on network TV in 1991 (full-frontal nudity, deviant sex, violent sex, gay sex, starkly sexual language). But it also confronts much more serious sexual issues than TV could ever portray. It deromanticizes, dehumanizes, and desentimentalizes sexuality. *Basic Instinct* (as did 1980's *Body Heat*) is the first major nineties movie that cynically scoffs at the sentiment of love and immerses itself in the perverse power of sex. In almost her first line of the film, when asked if she was dating the retired rock star who has been found murdered, Katherine answers, "I wasn't dating him. I was fucking him." Love, in all its sentimental self-deceptions, doesn't enter Katherine's sexual equation. "Let me ask you something, Miss Tramell, are you sorry he's dead?" the obtuse and naïve cop presses her on the subject. "Yes," Katherine answers, "I liked fucking him." Later in the film, during the centerpiece interrogation scene, filmed in such a way by Verhoeven that you can't take your eyes off of Katherine, she expands on her unsentimentalized, uninvolved, icy definition of the nineties sexual ambiance: "I had sex with him for about a year and a half. I liked having sex with him. He wasn't afraid of experimenting. I like men like that, men who give me pleasure." Whenever Katherine speaks about sex, she speaks with total detachment as if it could never touch her, never penetrate her icy cool.

Nick is a different type altogether. "Sometimes I think he started banging her just to get off the hook with Internal Affairs," a detective colleague half-jokingly comments. "No. He ain't that way," Nick's partner, Gus, defends him. "He's got a heart." But Nick's girlfriend, police psychiatrist Elizabeth, after having been anally ravished by him, isn't so sure:

*Elizabeth:* You weren't making love to me.
*Nick:* Then who?
*Elizabeth:* You weren't making love.

In the nineties (as defined in *Basic Instinct* and in Tina Turner's song "What's Love Got To Do With It"), love isn't even part of the game; love is only a "second-hand emotion." Love and sex are two totally different things, and AIDS has put them both under siege. For Katherine and Nick and Elizabeth and Roxie in *Basic Instinct*, sex is a dangerous, risky game that all too often ends up in death.

*Basic Instinct*, in Hollywood-pitch speak, is Hitchcock (especially *Psycho* and *Vertigo*) meets *Body Heat* meets the AIDS-generated sexual landscape of the nineties. One small detail marks it as a central AIDS metaphor film. As Nick receives a phone call summoning him to the murder scene of his major accuser in Internal Affairs, a vampire movie is playing on his TV set. That is exactly what these ice-pick murders in *Basic Instinct* are. That is what AIDS is. They are vampiric ravishments of blood. They are the infection of death-in-life transmitted through bloody sexual contact. No wonder the nineties was so enthralled with the vampire novels of Ann Rice and the vampire movies beginning with *The Lost Boys* (1987) and Francis Ford Coppola's *Bram Stoker's Dracula* (1992) and culminating with Tom Cruise and Brad Pitt in *Interview with the Vampire* (1994). The erotic connection between sex, blood, death-in-life, and AIDS was unmistakable. Early in *Bram Stoker's Dracula*, the count (Gary Oldman) surprises Jonathan Harker while he is shaving and plucks the razor out of his hand to hungrily lick the blood off it. Any nineties audience would gasp in shock at this scene, not because it is gross, not because it is homoerotic, but because nineties audiences are indoctrinated to the death-dealing potential of another person's blood. That is why, in the nineties, AIDS is a subtext of any vampire movie. Blood kills! The nineties audience knows this and that is what vampire movies are all about. One critic described Neil Jordan's *Interview with the Vampire* as "an erotic dreamscape, a blooming midnight reverie of blood and danger and sin."[2] Sex in the age of AIDS is just that sort of nightmare—sinful, dangerous, and a terrible threat to the blood. Lestat, in the novel and in the film, is like a conscienceless carrier of the AIDS virus through the centuries, "a sexual seducer . . . for an age of erotic knowingness."[3] The nineties film audience knows that the worst crime of the new sexual landscape is the erotic act that knowingly infects the blood of the sexual partner.

During *Basic Instinct*'s filming in San Francisco and when the film was released, Queer Nation organized a persistent series of protests and tried to disrupt the filming because they read the film as guilty of a different sort of crime, homophobia. Their reading, however, missed the point of the film's commentary upon nineties sexuality. *Basic Instinct* set out to map the sexual landscape of the nineties, and voyeurism and masturbation, both forms of distanced sex, were the main points of interest on that map while AIDS was the superhighway that led to them all.

While *Basic Instinct* defined them, other films picked up the AIDS metaphor and the sexual spin that the AIDS metaphor generated. None was more disturbing than *Single White Female (1992)*. The whole film is a home invasion, a life invasion, and a sexual invasion, and, ultimately, that invasion turns deadly. When Allie (Bridget Fonda) takes in Hedra (Jennifer Jason Leigh) as her new roommate, she has no idea that she is welcoming a poisonous, many-headed viper into her life who will infect her whole world. One critic notes that "there's hardly any reference to . . . lovemaking in Single White Female that isn't demeaning, ugly or contaminated. . . . Yet, for an audience living with the threat and reality of death-by-sex, dating-death movies are cathartic—even more so on video. They act out our anxieties in the well-lighted privacy of our own homes. . . . They're escapist entertainment in a world under sexual siege."[4] By the end of 1992, it had been such a hot erotic year for sex on the film screen that *Entertainment Weekly* published a sidebar showing a red thermometer ranking, in terms of heat, the sexiest films of the year and called it "Fahrenheit '92: A Screen Fever Chart."[5] What is interesting about this take on the year's films, however, is the choice of the dis-ease language to represent it.

## Full Frontal

If there is the same type of nudity in future episodes, we probably won't air it.
—Ken Schreiber, *WTVW*, Evansville, Indiana, commenting on *NYPD Blue*, in
Casey Davidson and Frank Spotnitz, "Naked Truth," *Entertainment Weekly*

By 1993, reacting to the successes with sexual material and the strong competition from cable television where anything goes, nudity and more frequent and explicit sexual themes had become standard fare on network television. *Seinfeld*, the most popular sitcom on TV, had devoted a complete episode to masturbation. Nudity was an expected weekly bonus on the gritty cop show *NYPD Blue*, and MTV videos were flashing more skin per minute than any censor could have kept up with. "Let's talk about sex," TV observers wrote in 1993 because "the sexual content of prime time has emerged as the hottest trend on the tube."[6]

The movies were even hotter. Nudity had been a component of movies since the sexual revolution of the sixties, but not the kind of nudity that began showing up in the films of the nineties. Since the sixties, film nudity, with a few exceptions like *Body Heat*, had most often been fleeting, gauzy, romanticized, backgrounded, and rear viewed. In the nineties, film nudity went full frontal and the sexual content of films like *Basic Instinct, Interview with the Vampire*, and *Showgirls* (1995) became suddenly cynical, brutal, and exceedingly perverse. Nudity was no longer a quick glimpse of breast or a well-formed derriere disappearing through a doorway. In the nineties, nudity was top to toe, front to back, fully aroused, and relentlessly lingered upon.

Sharon Stone's leg-opening interrogation scene in *Basic Instinct* followed by the artsy full-frontal nudity of the supermodels in *Sirens* (1994) began the nineties camera's downward tilt into hitherto, off-limits areas of the nude female anatomy. A comic throwaway line in the strip-club scene in *Showgirls*—"In America everyone is a gynecologist"—captured rather well the new pubic focus of the Hollywood camera.

But women were not the only objects of the camera's affection. Bruce Willis's penis in *Color of Night* (1994) generated headlines and threatened lawsuits while sending the Motion Picture Association of America (MPAA) ratings censors into virtual meltdown. Philip Noyce's unabashed focus upon a full erection in *Angels and Insects* (1996) raised legitimate film to the same level of explicit hardcore sexuality that porno films had always inhabited. And *Boogie Nights* (1997), purportedly about the most impressive erection ever, was afraid to show it yet got a tremendous amount of publicity about it. Actress Jeanne Tripplehorn tells the story of how after refusing to do a nude scene in *Waterworld* (1995) she insisted upon picking her body double. "I'm going to pick the person representing my derriere," she recalls and when the three finalists were brought in, she said, "Ladies, drop the robes!"[7] This is eerily reminiscent of the scene in *Showgirls* where Tony Moss (Alan Rachins) instructs the Vegas revue dancer hopefuls, "OK, show me your tits!" Throughout that film, Rachins is doing an on-the-money imitation of Bert Parks, who probably never said that to the assembled Miss America hopefuls from the 1950s to the 1990s. Artsy paintings in films also became excellent excuses for the camera to linger on full-frontal still lifes of posing models in films like *Sirens*, *As Good as It Gets* (1997), *Great Expectations* (1998), and even the only nude scene in the biggest blockbuster of the decade, *Titanic (1997)*.

The one film that gave a pretty good name to the full-frontal naughtiness was the sex comedy *Sirens*, which played not only upon the worldwide nineties fascination with supermodels but balanced its voyeuristic camera obsession with every inch of their bodies by offering up the likeable, perpetually sheepish, and sexually curious Hugh Grant as its voyeur-in-residence. By 1995, questions were starting to be asked about the obsessive full-frontal nudity and the intense sexual encounters in nineties Hollywood films. "Sex sells. At least that's what the age-old marketing mantra always promised. But with the less-than-steamy receptions given to this fall's NC-17-carrying *Showgirls* ($21 million) and the atmospheric *Jade* ($9 million), a more fitting catchphrase in Hollywood these days might be *sex stalls*," one pop-culture observer wrote.[8] After the blockbuster success of *Basic Instinct* and the positive reception of *Sirens* (1994), other sexually intense films were not openly accepted in the theaters. *Sliver*, a Sharon Stone follow-up to *Basic Instinct* about obsessive voyeurism, *Showgirls* (1995), and *Jade* (1995), all written by *Basic Instinct*'s Joe Eszterhas, flopped, as did Linda Fiorentino's slutty and foulmouthed *The Last Seduction* (1994) and Bruce Willis's full-frontal exhibitionist *Color of Night* (1994). However, though these films flopped in the theaters, they didn't really flop in terms of the nineties post-AIDS sexual spin strategy that generated them. One commentator wrote, "Conservatives shouldn't start that pop-cultural victory lap dance just yet. Voyeurs may be steering clear of the multiplex, but that doesn't mean their minds aren't still in the gutter. The very same erotic thrillers that flop in theaters have consistently become video hits (often in even *steamier*, unrated versions) . . . rental video's being a cheaper thrill and, more important, a private one."[9]

The mid-nineties saw America's home-video entertainment potential reach its highest saturation as the prices of VCRs sank to their lowest ever. Buying a VCR, which in the early nineties had been a prestige and luxury item, by the midnineties was like buying a clock radio. In fact, they were on the same shelf at the discount store. And this home video saturation complemented the post-AIDS sexual spin perfectly. Watching sex "in the privacy of one's home" underlined the new voyeuristic, masturbatory spin of the hands-off nineties.

Of all the full-frontal nudity films that followed the infamous leg-crossing scene in *Basic Instinct*, *Sirens* was the most imaginatively envisioned (read: *nude supermodels*), exotically set (1930s New Zealand with *nude supermodels*), attractively cast (classily comical Hugh Grant plus *nude supermodels*), and tastefully written (about painting *nude supermodels*). Yet everyone who saw it did so for one reason. "Nudity in the movies usually arrives in teasing flashes," one commentator wrote, "but not in *Sirens* . . . yet another cozy bourgeois fable about how good it feels to cast off the shackles of Victorianism and be free, be sexy, be nude!"[10] In fact, the central premise of *Sirens*'s plot is nudity. Bearing a striking resemblance to John Fowles's novella *The Ebony Tower* (novella published in 1975; BBC TV production in 1986), the plot of *Sirens* focuses upon the controversial full-frontal nude religious-themed paintings, particularly one titled *Crucified Venus*, of avant-garde oil-paint artist Norman Lindsay (Sam Neill). Father Tony Campion (Hugh Grant) and his wife Estella (Tara Fitzgerald) are sent by the bishop to convince Lindsay to withdraw his *Crucified Venus* from the prestigious religious art exhibition. When the Campions arrive at Lindsay's Edenic (complete with a large snake who has the run of the place) painting compound, everyone is nude, from Lindsay's middle-aged wife, who is his main model and the nude Venus on the cross in his most controversial painting, to his three in-residence models, Sheela, Pru, and Giddy (Elle McPherson, Portia De Rossi, and Kate Fischer, respectively) to ultimately the prudish Estella who succumbs to the siren song of nudity before the film ends.

*Sirens* wraps its nude supermodels and actresses in a contrived veil of painterly plot, clearly elaborated myth (the siren story is told in detail by Giddy to the Campions), and smirking bashfulness (something Hugh Grant does so well and the main reason he is in the film). Supposedly, this is a film about the antidote to repressed sexuality, but it is also a very nineties film. In the thirties, sexuality may have been repressed by organized religion, but in the nineties sexuality is repressed by the threat of AIDS. In *Sirens*, when the repressed Campions meet the nude Lindsays and their entourage of supermodels, voyeurism takes over. Tony can't keep his eyes off of the voluptuous naked women, and the mousy Estella keeps spying on the nude models, envious of their sexual freedom and how much they are enjoying their bodies. At first Tony spends a great deal of time sheepishly looking away from the women's unabashed nudity and Estella flees their openness. But everywhere the Campions turn, nudity pervades the landscape. It constantly challenges their repression in the paintings, the statues, and the models swimming nude in the green idyllic landscape. The Edenic myth melds with the myth of the Sirens to create the aura of nature and seductiveness that justifies the openness of the film's relentless nudity.

But the nineties solution to enforced sexual repression—voyeurism and masturbation—are also given strong and seductive representation in *Sirens*. Obviously, the sexually repressed Campions are the voyeurs. Tony is a predictable stereotype—the minister who can't keep his eyes off of the naked models. But Estella is the much more interesting voyeur. From doorways, through lighted windows, and from behind trees, she spies on the models' nudity and open bisexuality. From the darkness outside their rooms, she spies on them playing strip poker with their vulgar sheepherder boyfriends. From behind a tree, she spies on the women swimming naked and washing each other's bodies. From a doorway, she spies on the women posing naked for Lindsay's latest painting. But Estella's voyeurism, like the models' sexual orientation, is more complex and symbolically bisexual. She spies on a blind workman as he lies in the sun naked and masturbating after a swim. The most erotic scene in the film involves not Estella's voyeuristic spying on the models but the models' voyeuristic spying on Estella. Playfully tipsy, they tie Estella to a tree and when she calls for help the blind workman answers. The three women watch fascinated as the blind man runs his hands over Estella's body and unties her. Estella's facial expression and body language clearly abets the eroticism of their voyeurism by displaying first her arousal and then her disappointment when the blind man does not sexually molest her. She spies on the same blind man modeling naked for Lindsay. It is all hands-off sex in this film, nineties post-AIDS sex, watching and not touching, or touching and not penetrating.

Masturbation becomes the film's outlet for all of this secret and repressed voyeurism. When Estella joins the models in a dress-up visit to the local pub, they all end up drunk by the riverside. When Giddy collapses spread-eagle on the sandy bank, first the other two models masturbate her, then Estella joins in, and finally husband Tony comes looking for his wife and voyeuristically spies on her first foray into autoeroticism. These initial masturbatory experiences trigger a succession of masturbatory fantasies in Estella's hitherto prudish mind. After making unsatisfying love to her husband, Tony, Estella runs to the drunkenly passed-out Giddy's room and lets the blind workman run his hands all over her body. At dinner, Estella flees when the blind workman fingers her under the table. Her masturbatory fantasies culminate in a vision of three nude women caressing her body in the water. Truly, the sirens have lured her into their power, unlocked her repressed sexuality, yet masturbation is her only recourse. The film ends comically with Estella masturbating Tony with her foot in their crowded railway compartment. There is a great deal of watching and nude sexual touching in *Sirens*, but never any penetration. It is a model post-AIDS film in its affirmation of the distanced sexual spin strategy of the nineties.

The full-frontal nudity of *Sirens* culminates in the unveiling of Lindsay's newest painting, a large rendering of the five nude women: his wife, his three models, and, in all her totally naked and full-frontal glory, Estella. Tony says to his wife, "You better have a look," expecting her to be shocked, repulsed, shamed, and angry, but she expresses none of those emotions. She takes her time, looks at herself carefully in her total nudity, and then replies meaningfully, "It is a good likeness." Estella accepts her nude representation as art, and she affirms the rightness of her nudity. The film ends with nudity, voyeurism, and masturbation triumphant as the necessary sexual strategies for an era of sexual repression.

Perhaps these supermodels, or simply the idea of a supermodel, would become the reigning sex goddess of the nineties decade, less voluptuous versions of the fifties' Marilyn Monroe, the sixties' Jane Mansfield, the seventies' Faye Dunaway, or the eighties' Kathleen Turner. But while the concept of the supermodel as the ultimate symbol of untouchable, voyeuristic sexuality evolved over the course of the decade, plenty of real flesh and blood aspirants to Monroe's ascendancy as a sex symbol came and went.

Sharon Stone was the first. In *Basic Instinct*, then *Sliver*, then *The Specialist* (1994), she created a tough-talking, no-underwear, voyeuristic, cool-as-ice, sex symbol for the nineties. By the time she did the unsexy western *The Quick and the Dead* (1995), the story goes that, at a test screening, one audience member, a woman, stood up and declared, "I'm so thankful you did not include the obligatory sex scene of Sharon Stone."[11] The nineties seemed to wear out sex symbols pretty quickly. In Stone's case, besides being overexposed, perhaps she was just too smart to be a sex symbol for very long. Her finest role of the nineties came in *Casino* (1995) as Robert De Niro's mob wife. In *Casino* she plays a bimbo on-the-make convincingly enough to garner a Best Supporting Actress Academy Award nomination.

Stone's major challenger for the status of sex symbol of the nineties, Demi Moore, ironically traced an even more eccentric career arc across the decade than Stone. Stone blazed to sexual stardom in *Basic Instinct* then slowly cooled until some real acting roles came along in *The Quick and the Dead*, *Intersection* (1994), *Casino*, the lesbian thriller *Diabolique*, and the prison film *Last Dance* (1996). Moore's sex symbol arc was more a process of alternation between sexually charged roles in *Indecent Proposal* (1993), *Disclosure* (1994), *The Scarlet Letter* (1995), and *Striptease* (1996) balanced off by the intentional deconstruction of the sex symbol image via military desexing in *A Few Good Men* (1992) and *G.I. Jane* (1997).

Other wannabe nineties sex symbols experienced quick flameouts. Statuesque Kim Basinger generated all sorts of heat in *91/2 Weeks*, *Batman* (1989), and *Final Analysis* (1992) but looked silly and miscast doing comedy in *Blind Date* (1987), *My Stepmother Is an Alien* (1998), and *Marrying Man* (1991), until she finally got the role she was born to play as the Veronica Lake look-alike prostitute in *L.A. Confidential*. Madonna as sex symbol burned out just as quickly. Literally creating herself as the sex queen of kink in her photobook *Sex* (1992) and in her sadomasochistic *Body of Evidence* (1993), Madonna (unlike Basinger) proved much more entertaining as a comedienne in *Desperately Seeking Susan* (1989) and in *A League of Their Own* (1992) than as an in-your-face sexual predator (in the vein of Katherine Tramell in *Basic Instinct*). By the end of the decade, another full-frontal pretender challenged Stone and Moore for sex symbol of the nineties when Nicole Kidman appeared totally nude on the London stage in David Hare's play *The Blue Room* (1998) and followed up with her sex-fantasizing wife in Stanley Kubrick's high-profile last film *Eyes Wide Shut* (2000). Unfortunately, *Eyes Wide Shut* fizzled as did Kidman's brief flirtation with sex symbol stardom. She went on to garner acclaim as a musical comedienne in *Moulin Rouge* (2001).

Because all these sex symbol pretenders had such checkered careers throughout the nineties, perhaps the real sex symbol of the nineties was an idealized sexual concept, the supermodel, rather than an overpowering individual sex-symbol actress. Within the sexual spin strategy of the post-AIDS nineties, the supermodel was the ultimate eye candy for the voyeur. First of all, supermodels were ubiquitously available for the nineties voyeur. In peekaboo and décolletage dresses on magazine covers, full-frontally nude in *Playboy* magazine photo spreads, unabashedly naked in films like *Sirens* and *Pret á Porter* (1994), night clubbing in the decadent, heroin-chic, tabloid scenes of New York and Los Angeles, the supermodels were everywhere. As the co-president of the Ford Modeling Agency said of one of her most famous supermodels, Elle McPherson, "This girl's body is a national treasure."[12] It is fitting, however, that the real sex goddess of the deconstructive nineties should be a sexual concept, an untouchable (hence safe) ideal rather than a flesh-and-blood and bodily-fluid-exchanging, real-live woman. In the age of AIDS, it was just safer that way.

## Strippers

The nudity will be extremely classy. This movie isn't about eroticism but about topless dancers.
> —Paul Verhoeven, director of *Showgirls*, quoted in Benjamin Svetkey,
> "Why Movie Ratings Don't Work," *Entertainment Weekly*

A funny thing happened on the way to the nineties multiplex—the guilty pleasure of sexual voyeurism that used to be dirty suddenly went legit. From the forties to the nineties, the burlesque house evolved into the strip joint, became the topless/bottomless restaurant, became the titty bar, became the Las Vegas topless revue, became the—voila!—Gentlemen's Club. Somehow, in the nineties, the sleazy, combat-zone, red-light district, wrong-side-of-the-tracks fixture of the nightworld of illicit sexuality morphed into an entertainment venue not only licit, socially acceptable, and nearly mainstream but also "gentlemanly." Between 1992 and 1995, the number of strip clubs in America doubled to three thousand. A social thermometer as sensitive as *The New Yorker* even notes this temperature change in a review of the stripper film *Showgirls*: "Verhoeven doesn't prod us into ogling, because—and this is bliss—his movie likes to suggest that all these bare-assed boys and girls and all these swirling, nipple-raising, ice-and-fire routines . . . are really rather classy."[13] Gentlemen's clubs, classy dancers, and the legitimization of something as traditionally sleazy as stripping embodies spin at its most outrageous.

But the very nature of the striptease, the topless dancer, the pole dancer, and the lap dancer fits the specifications of nineties sexual spin perfectly. In the era of AIDS, of hands-off sex, of voyeurism and masturbation, of distanced safety in one's sexual adventuring, stripping fit the bill perfectly. No wonder strip joints in the new, classier dress of the gentlemen's club made such a strong comeback in the nineties. There is no sexual risk in the simulated sex of a striptease, a pole dance, or a lap dance. The sexual heat and excitement is there, but the dangerous bodily fluids are harmlessly released. Caught up in the spin of the nineties strip-club craze, the movies offered their multiple versions of the new, reborn, classier, and, above all, safer world of nudity and voyeurism packaged for a society that needed sexual outlets that were harmless and distanced, yet stimulating. Strip clubs became the safe alternatives to the bygone whorehouses of the pre-AIDS fifties, sixties, and seventies. In the movies, strip clubs became the most popular venues for voyeuristic sex. The most prominent architect of all of these sexual spin strategies in the films of the nineties (especially the voyeurism option) was Eszterhas, screenwriter of *Basic Instinct*, *Sliver* (the most elaborate voyeurism film of the decade), and the ultimate stripper movie, *Showgirls* (1995).

Among the magnus floppus films of the nineties (which certainly include 1995's *Cutthroat Island* and *Waterworld*), the most critically trashed of all the big event films that failed was *Showgirls*. Coming from Hollywood's hottest screenwriter, Eszterhas, and one of its hottest young directors, Verhoeven, the team that had defined nineties sexuality in *Basic Instinct* (and actually welcomed its NC-17 rating for full-frontal nudity), *Showgirls* was supposed to be the first major Hollywood nudie movie to go mainstream. From its initial reception, *Showgirls* seemingly failed miserably at the box office and drew the universal scorn of the critical community. But wait. Like the old, dirty strip joints being reborn as gentlemen's clubs, *Showgirls* found a new life on video and went from being a laughable embarrassment in the multiplex to a cult classic in the home-video market. Frightened away from the theaters by its NC-17 rating and the embarrassment of being seen entering or leaving a skin flick in the multiplex, audiences rushed to rent *Showgirls* and sample its prurient, voyeuristic delights in the privacy of their own homes. In a 1995 interview, both Eszterhas and Verhoeven argue that they knew exactly what they were doing in terms of nineties sexual spin:

> *Verhoeven:* Now we have movies about strippers. Who knows why? The only thing I can say is we're moving into a much more repressive sexual climate in this country. And you can't repress sexuality.
>
> *Eszterhas:* Perhaps, to a certain degree, these movies are a response to AIDS. There's a line in *Showgirls* that explains the whole thing. Stripping is like having sex without really having sex. It's like hooking without really hooking. It's safe for the '90s. And I'm not just talking about the movies. It's a trend in general. It's sweeping the nation.[14]

Actually, *Showgirls* itself, in its themes and metaphors, works hard to capture the cultural significance of stripping in the ultra material, superficial, and degrading sex culture of Las Vegas. Yet *Showgirls* is also an old-fashioned backstage movie like *42nd Street* (1933) or *All About Eve* (1950) except topless, bottomless, full-frontal, and about lap dancers, not Broadway actresses. The first thirty minutes of *Showgirls*, its build up, focuses upon the milieu, the social function, and the sexual spin of the strip-club world. Nomi Malone (Elizabeth Berkley), new in town and broke, takes a job as a stripper and lap dancer at the Cheetah Club, an upscale gentlemen's club just off the Vegas strip. Al (Robert Davi), the Cheetah Club's owner, introduces a new girl to the assembled strippers backstage in the dressing room and, in the process, roughly articulates the whole hands-off masturbatory spin of nineties sexuality. Al introduces the new girl who says that her name is Penny, but he immediately changes her name to Hope because "they want class, dum-dum. They don't wanna fuck a Penny. They wanna fuck a Heather or a Tiffany or a Hope." Following that reflection on the new "class" image of the strip-club world, Al explains the rules of lap dancing: "It's touch and go. They touch and they go. You can touch them but they can't touch you." This simple rule defines the whole hands-off, post-AIDS sexual spin of the decade.

The showcase scene of this opening section of the film is Nomi's pole dance followed by a degrading lap dance. These two dances embody the main components of nineties sexual spin: its masturbatory emphasis, its voyeurism, its hands-off safety. Cristal (Gina Gershon), the headline dancer at the Stardust Hotel and Casino's topless sextravaganza stage show *Goddess*, brings her boyfriend Zack (Kyle McLachlan), the hotel's entertainment director, to watch Nomi strip and to humiliate Nomi by buying her for a lap dance. When Nomi begins her pole dance on stage, her first move is to play with herself, to simulate masturbation for the customers. The lap dance that follows is a three-tiered exercise in voyeurism and autoeroticism. Zack can't take his eyes off Nomi as she strips, dances, and finally sits on his lap and masturbates him with her naked body. Cristal can't take her eyes off Nomi as she snorts cocaine, watches the simulated sex taking place on her boyfriend's lap, and entertains lesbian fantasies of the naked Nomi. And James Smith (Glen Plummer), Nomi's choreographer friend, spies on her from the doorway of the club's VIP, lap-dance room and judges her harshly. When the lap dance ends and Zack and Cristal are gone, Smith censoriously aligns Nomi's lap dancing with the whole temper of the times and defines it in terms of nineties sexual spin:

> *Nomi:* I didn't fuck him.
> *James:* Yeah you did. You fucked him and her.
> *Nomi:* Are you followin' me around? I didn't fuck anybody.
> *James:* I saw you. I mean, everybody got AIDS and shit. I mean, what is it you think you do? You fuckin' 'em without fuckin' 'em.

This exchange focuses the whole issue of the nature of sex in the post-AIDS nineties. "Fuckin' 'em without fuckin' 'em" is the core of nineties sexual reality. In the age of AIDS, people have to find different and safer sexual outlets, like finding ways to make sleazy strip clubs into more palatable and acceptable sexual venues.

Later in *Showgirls*, another scene of three-tiered voyeurism, almost identical to this lap-dance scene, reinforces the sexual turn-on and the power satisfaction of the voyeuristic option. Tony Moss (Alan Rachins), the producer of the hotel's topless stage sextravaganza, auditions Nomi for a dancer's position in Cristal's show. As Cristal watches from backstage, clearly aroused, Moss first makes Nomi masturbate for him then affirms the sexual turn-on of his own voyeurism. The scene begins with Moss ordering the audition dancers to "OK, show me your tits." But, immediately, it focuses in on Nomi:

> *Moss:* You got something wrong with your nipples?
> *Nomi:* No.
> *Moss:* They're not stickin' up. Stick 'em up.
> *Nomi:* What?
> *Moss:* Play with 'em. Prick 'em a little. You want me to do 'em for ya? I'll do it.
> *Nomi:* (she masturbates her nipples)
> [Cut-away to Cristal watching excitedly]
> *Moss:* I'm erect. Why aren't you erect? Here, put some ice on 'em.

There are three voyeurs operating in this scene as Nomi is stripped, forced to masturbate, and sexually humiliated: Moss leering at her nipples, Cristal spying in lesbian desire from the wings, and the movie audience watching voyeuristically. As a film about voyeurism, *Showgirls* works brilliantly to draw its audience into the experience. It is extremely hard to take your eyes off.

This opening section of *Showgirls*, its stripper-movie section, clearly articulates the spin strategy of post-AIDS nineties sexuality. It is a strategy of voyeurism, masturbation, and sexual game playing in which the power has shifted to the passive participant who is watching but not touching. The stripper submits to utter sexual humiliation in order to arouse the voyeur. The person in power, the watcher (in *Showgirls* the voyeur's gender is interchangeable as first Zack then Cristal becomes aroused watching Nomi strip) becomes aroused by watching the stripper masturbate and simulate sex. When the setting of *Showgirls* shifts from the Cheetah Club to the elegant Stardust topless revue, *Goddess*, each sextravagant production number is one scene of simulated sex after another. Describing the elaborate sets of the Las Vegas topless revues, Owen Gleiberman notes parenthetically, "(The theme-park paraphernalia is there to make the patrons feel a little less like voyeurs.)."[15] Jean Baudrillard, who chose the American theme park as his salient example of simulacra, would feel right at home in the audience of *Goddess*. The nineties is the decade of simulacra, and simulated sexuality is one form of that phenomenon. Everyone is watching everyone else strip, and there are no rules for this form of safe sexual arousal. In this section of the film, the sexual attraction of Nomi's dancing shifts to the lesbian arousal of Cristal and their sexual game playing surveys the nineties sexual landscape just as Nomi's earlier conversation with James Smith did. Over lunch, Cristal describes her voyeuristic attraction to Nomi:

*Cristal:* You have great tits. They're really beautiful.
*Nomi:* Thank you.
*Cristal:* I like nice tits. I always have. How about you?
*Nomi:* I like having nice tits. . . . I like having them in a nice dress or a tight top.
*Cristal:* You like to show 'em off?
*Nomi:* I didn't like showing them off at the Cheetah.
*Cristal:* Why not? I liked lookin' at 'em there. Everybody liked lookin' at 'em there.
*Nomi:* Made me feel like a hooker.
*Cristal:* You are a whore, darlin'.
*Nomi:* No I'm not.
*Cristal:* We all are.

If Cristal and Nomi are whores, then they are a new breed of nineties hands-off whores who manage to get paid not for sex but for its simulacra.

If *Showgirls* is the big event blockbuster of the nineties stripper films, then *Striptease* is the big star-driven social commentary film in the decade's stripper movie pantheon. Adapted from literary novelist Carl Hiaasen's comic political novel and starring one of America's most popular mainstream stars, *Striptease* had a rather highbrow pedigree to accompany the curiosity impact of its racy title. Demi Moore was one of the few nineties actresses (perhaps Julia Roberts and Sharon Stone were the others) who could open a movie on her own. But Moore naked and strip dancing seemed a surefire attraction for nineties audiences. Ironically, Moore came to *Striptease* from one of the few flops of her nineties film forays. She moved straight from the dark Puritan clothes of *The Scarlet Letter* (1996) to no clothes at all in *Striptease*. But even though *The Scarlet Letter* was a steamy sexual take on Nathaniel Hawthorne's nineteenth-century novel, film audiences didn't take to it in nearly the numbers that queued up to see *Striptease*. Why? Because *Striptease*'s flaunting of its voyeuristic nineties take on sexuality, what one writer called Moore's "exhibitionistic behavior"[16] (including an appearance on the David Letterman TV talk show in her skimpiest stripper costume and giving Barbara Walters a bump-and-grind gyrating lesson on her TV show), hyped the film the way that she never could *The Scarlet Letter* no matter how sexy its nineties version was.

Actually, many critics speculated that the real attraction of *Striptease*'s big opening weekend was seeing a truly big star take it all off (as Julia Roberts never did and as Sharon Stone refused to do after her burst into stardom with *Basic Instinct*). While Moore's heavily hyped nudity was the main attraction for moviegoers, the main worry for the makers of *Striptease* was convincing both audiences and critics that it was not another *Showgirls*, thus giving it an identity as a serious film with a nineties social message. As one commentator noted, "to prove that its film is not *Showgirls II*, the studio's trailer sells *Striptease* as a screwball comedy . . . rather than as a sordid glimpse into the world of stripping."[17] And Phil Borach, who books films into 250 theaters in the conservative Midwest, was well aware that "the challenge will be to let people know it's not like *Showgirls*."[18]

Ironically, the popular fate of *Striptease* turned somewhat similar to that of *Show-girls*. Though moderately successful in theaters (but not nearly as successful as Moore's 1990 *Ghost* or *A Few Good Men* or 1993's *Indecent Proposal*), *Striptease* found a second, guilty pleasure life on video. Again, ironically, perhaps the most controversial aspect of *Striptease* was the hitherto unimaginable amount ($12.5 million) that Castle Rock Pictures paid Moore to take off her clothes. Certainly, neither Elizabeth Berkley nor Gina Gershon got that much for showing much more and dancing much better in *Showgirls*, but neither were they as big a box-office star or tabloid personality as Moore. "If you're making a movie called *Strip Tease* [*sic*], you'd better get one of the sexiest women in town and pay her what-ever you have to," argues producer Dawn Steel.[19]

Of all the stripper films of the nineties, *The Players Club* (1998) rode the sexual spin of the decade much better than the bigger budget films. "Who could have predicted that gangsta-rap godfather Ice Cube would write and direct a strip flick that's sexier and smarter than *Showgirls* and *Striptease* combined?" asks one commentator.[20] It is rather curious how a small independent film like *The Players Club* could actually get behind the scenes of the strip-club world whose preten-sions to class and upscale mainstream legitimacy were given an ethnic twist in the all-black production.

For its niche audience, *The Players Club* was much more credible in terms of capturing the strip-club mise-en-scène than the overglitzed *Showgirls* or the star-hampered *Striptease*. Both *Showgirls* and *Striptease* take you backstage in strip clubs and into the locker rooms with the naked strippers getting ready to go on stage. But the strip-club dressing room at the Cheetah Club in *Showgirls* plays like a group of sorority girls getting ready for a big dance while the strippers in *Striptease* are a remarkably dull lot, there to decorate the set while Demi Moore flexes in front of the mirror and her character worries about how to pay her lawyer. The backstage world of *The Players Club*, however, actually comes alive with a gritty representation of the different motives and issues of the strippers' lives. The central character, Diamond (Lisa Raye), is motivated by class values in exactly the same way that Moore's character in *Striptease* is. Both have to make money stripping in order to sustain middle-class lifestyles and protect their chil-dren or surrogate children from the realities of a degrading, exploitative world. But the world of *The Players Club* is much more believable and much more real-istic. It actually *shows* a sense of humor in its portrayal of the stripper's life and the corners the stripper has to cut to live that life and still stay human.

All of these stripper films emphasize the class theme in order to bolster their believability and make their argument that strippers are just ordinary people in our commodity culture. Strippers have to make ends meet like everyone else goes the argument, and stripping is a necessary service in the post-AIDS world of the nineties goes the spin. That service, in every case, is provided by hard-working and imaginative perfectionists desperate to either gain or maintain their social status in the middle class. In *Showgirls*, the marginalized working for a living in star-crossed Las Vegas of Nomi Malone and her starstruck seamstress room-mate is motivated by the frayed and worn-out fantasy of moving up in class and becoming a star (or dating one). In *Striptease*, the central character needs money to fight a custody battle, and in *The Player's Club*, Diamond is working out (in the most degrading of circumstances) her desire to attain the middle-class American dream. While *The Player's Club* is at least believable, none of these three films succeed in articulating the class component and how it functions as part of the sexual spin strategy of the nineties decade.

But, by far the most believable and funny stripper film of the decade of spin was one of those little British films, like *The Lavender Hill Mob* (1951) or *Doctor in the House* (1954) or *Four Weddings and a Funeral* (1994), that just does everything right, *The Full Monty* (1996). As working-class art right out of the Angry Young Men era of the fifties of Alan Sillitoe and John Braine and David Storey but with a sense of humor, *The Full Monty* outstripped (sorry!) the post-AIDS sexual dilemma and articulated a nineties spin strategy that actually made stripping an honorable and respectable way of making a living. "These things are like cultural viruses," *The Full Monty's* director Peter Cattaneo argued. "Fortunately, this is one of the good ones."[21] In a time dominated by fear of the AIDS virus, the voyeuristic promise of stripping can provide an antidote for the sexual quarantine, the loss of a center, of the decade.

In *The Full Monty*, the center that has failed to hold is the steel industry in the gritty Yorkshire town of Sheffield, England. The film opens (much as *L.A. Confidential* does) with a glitzy promotional film extolling the industrial, commercial, and entertainment virtues of early 1970s Sheffield when the steel mills were burning brightly and the nightlife was ringed in neon. But all has changed "25 years later," as the film designates its present-day time frame. That prosperous Sheffield of the promotional video is long gone. The steel mills have closed, unemployment reigns, the cityscape is gray, and the residents are desperate. Cattaneo's camera dwells on the shut-down urban landscape of Sheffield, its dark closed mills, abandoned buildings, and aging flat blocks. The decentered city is always there in *The Full Monty*, in the background of almost every shot. The depression and desperation of that formerly thriving, exciting city is the film's visual metaphor for the post-AIDS nineties. Early in the film, Dave's (Mark Addy) wife, Jean (Lesley Sharp), in the men's room during a "women only" Chippendales male strip show, says, "It's like 'ee's given up. On life, on me, on everything." How she describes her husband and his sex drive captures well the state of sexual confusion in the nineties decade as a result of the AIDS epidemic. The open sexuality of the past had to end just as Sheffield's boom economy couldn't last forever. But the result was that Sheffield's steelworkers and the world's lovers were quarantined, left confused and displaced, by the seismic social changes that the closing of the mills and the AIDS epidemic forced upon them. The desperation that hangs like a shroud over decentered Sheffield in *The Full Monty* mirrors the pall that fell over the sexual possibilities of the nineties decade due to the onslaught of AIDS.

But unlike AIDS, in *The Full Monty* there is a cure for Sheffield's urban disease and it is found in stripping. *The Full Monty's* success lies in its "less is more" approach. It doesn't try to say too much. It sets up a group of straightforward characters, all out-of-work steel men, and, as in the other stripper films, gives then simple clear reasons for their desperation and their need to turn things around. Gaz (Robert Carlyle) needs money and wants to keep seeing his son Nathan (William Snape). Dave is having intimacy problems with his wife and is overweight. He is losing hold of both his hope and his manhood. Gerald (Tom Wilkinson) is afraid to tell his wife that he's lost his job so he keeps putting on his coat and tie every day and going to a park bench. Barry (Paul Butterworth) is suicidal because he's out of work, lives with his failing mother, and is a repressed homosexual. And this visual milieu of Sheffield embodies all of these situations of quiet desperation. In the sexual spin strategy of *The Full Monty*, stripping can solve all of these problems. It is what Thomas Carlyle calls a "Morrison's Pill." Stripping cures everything: money problems, love problems, identity problems. These unemployed steelworkers pull off a classic nineties deconstruction: they become strippers, unembarassedly, to overcome worse kinds of embarrassment (unemployment, loss of manhood, divorce, depression).

*The Full Monty* is a movie about how to turn a dead end into a yellow brick road. It is a working-class spin strategy film from start to finish. The bleak reality of Sheffield hangs over every scene of the film, but these ordinary men use their imaginations to transform that bleak reality into a livable landscape. As in *The Wizard of Oz (1939)*, as in the post-AIDS sexual wasteland of the nineties, as in bleak, tough times, what is needed is a good fantasy and this working class Yorkshire version of the Chippendales provides it all the way to "the full monty." There had always been a continuous daisy chain of striploitation movies, most of the made-for-video variety—such as *Stripped to Kill* (1987), *Stripped to Kill II* (1989), *Midnight Tease* (1994), *Lap Dancing* (1995)—and strip-club scenes appear obligatorily in almost every urban film. In the Arnold Schwarzenegger spy thriller *True Lies* (1994), Jamie Lee Curtis, playing a bored housewife out for adventure, takes a job as a stripping call girl, enjoys her work, and does it well. But the no-frills, working-class *Full Monty* captures the voyeuristic necessity of nineties sexual spin better than any other.

## Whores

The idea of being a whore for a night is kind of exciting for a woman.
—Adrian Lyne, director of *Indecent Proposal,* quoted in Meredith
Berkman, "Saturday Night Fever!: How Date Movies Are
Heating Up The Box Office," *Entertainment Weekly*

If strippers were the voyeuristic, hands-off antidote for post-AIDS sexuality, were there any voyeuristic hands-on antidotes for that particularly nineties sexual dilemma? Because of AIDS, the age-old hands-on sexual outlet, the prostitute, became an extremely high-risk sexual choice in the nineties. At the least, no sane person, male or female, even considered going with a prostitute without benefit of condom, and at the most, those who might have indulged themselves with prostitutes in the seventies or early eighties gave up the habit altogether. But the films of the nineties picked up the slack. In the best spirit of post-AIDS sexual spin, the movies offered a whole spectrum of whores for audiences to watch and reminisce about the good old days when prostitutes were still relatively safe. If America was afraid to pick up its prostitutes on the street (at least at the pre-AIDS rate), then customers could find them at the movies. If it is true (as Adrian Lyne argues) that every woman would like to be a whore at one time or another, then that outrageous generalization must doubly apply to actresses in the nineties. As in every other decade in film history, there were plenty of hooker parts and plenty of actresses perfectly willing to play hookers because hooker parts (especially involving a heart of gold) have always been the stepping stones to big Hollywood careers for actresses, such as Jane Fonda in *Klute* (1971) or Elizabeth Taylor in *Butterfield 8* (1960). But the whores of the nineties proved a somewhat different breed and tended to push a safe-sex agenda that was never a concern in the past.

Julia Roberts in *Pretty Woman* (1990) is the *Ur*-whore of the nineties. Even though her film, coming early in the decade, presents her wide-smiled whore (a contemporary Cinderella) as the same old clichéd hooker with a heart and innocent little-girl hooker of the thirties and forties, Roberts's character is also very much a streetwalker of the nineties, forthrightly supportive of the safe-sex spin of post-AIDS sexuality. Early in the film, just prior to plying her trade with her princely client, she produces a veritable drugstore display of condoms out of her capacious purse for his selection and then proceeds to do an infomercial for them complete with a full description of every color, texture, and novelty attraction that they offer.

But if *Pretty Woman* was a fairy tale version of nineties whoredom, other equally clichéd yet sociologically spun versions of the hooker also appeared. Hookerness, for example, becomes a direct subject of discussion between Cristal and Nomi, the strippers of *Showgirls*. Housewife hookers were all the rage in the nineties. Not only was Luis Bunuel's *Belle De Jour* (1967) rereleased to a very creditable reception, but its premise of a bored housewife going to work afternoons in a whorehouse was no longer the epitome of erotic kinkiness that it had been in the sixties. In the nineties, housewives working in the sex business were not all that unusual. In the age of hands-off sex and masturbation as the safest sexual alternative, phone sex became a popular and highly marketable commodity, a lucrative small business that could be run by a housewife from her own home even more easily than being an Avon lady or an Amway saleswoman. Perhaps the most domesticated of all the nineties hookers is Melanie Griffiths's V in *Milk Money* (1994). Lisa Schwarzbaum places this version of the cliché right in the middle of the vortex of nineties sexual spin:

> In her way, V is the natural successor in these plague years, to Vivian, the Cinderella streetwalker so charmingly created by Julia Roberts. . . . Where *Pretty Woman* suggested that turning tricks is a way to find Mr. Right, *Milk Money* suggests that hooking is a way to find Daddy. . . . And this is what I figure: Fear is the reason. Fear of AIDS, fear of sex, fear of the ratings board, fear of offending. The fearful '90s has turned Melanie Griffith . . . into an aging Barbie doll. Of wussy PG-13

movie makers [*sic*], who wear their condoms so tight they're afraid to make a *comedy* about hookers that's really serious.[22]

In the sexual spin of the nineties, fear causes moviemakers to think twice about making movies about real whores. So whoredom must take a more domesticated form, hence the proliferation of housewife whores.

One of the more interesting of the nineties housewife whores is represented in a small film directed by Jane Campion and set in New Zealand, *The Piano* (1993). In it, Ada (Holly Hunter) becomes a whore not for money but for music, sells herself so that she can preserve her self in the degrading situation of slavery that she has been sold into by her own father. Added to her unusual motive for becoming a whore is Ada's muteness. She is a woman who chooses to be a whore for reasons of spiritual survival rather than the usual material survival, but she is also a woman without a voice, utterly degraded in a brutal man's world on the outposts of civilization. Ada is neither a cliché whore, nor a domesticated one, as are the other housewives, Cinderellas, and gold-hearted hookers. In *Dangerous Beauty* (1998), based on the life of sixteenth-century Italian poet and courtesan (read: high-class call girl) Veronica Franco, she is a whore so powerful that, in the end, the whole city stands up for her and saves her from death at the hands of the priests. The film's director claims that his intention was "to look at something that has been pushed down in our culture, the power of a woman's sexuality."[23] But *Dangerous Beauty* is as much a nineties fable as it is a sixteenth-century historical recreation. The turning point of *Dangerous Beauty* is the onset of the plague. That is quite similar to the nineties plague of AIDS that redefined the role of the prostitute in society. The AIDS metaphor resonates in all of these hooker films.

Equally vulnerable to being a cliché is naïve hooker and porn movie actress Linda Ash (Mira Sorvino) in Woody Allen's *Mighty Aphrodite* (1995), but she escapes clichéd whoredom through the wit of Allen's writing and Sorvino's brash and hilarious delivery. If *Pretty Woman* was the nineties version of the whore as Cinderella, then *Mighty Aphrodite* "is an Upper East Side variation on 'Pygmalion.'"[24] Sorvino plays hooker and porno star Linda Ash who turns out to be the birth mother of Lenny Weintrib's (Allen) adopted son. Like Vivian in *Pretty Woman*, she is a professional working girl—she greets Lenny the first time with "Hello? Are you my three o'clock?"—and also a movie star under the *nom de screen* of Judy Cum. If Vivian in *Pretty Woman* was looking for Mr. Right and V in *Milk Money* was looking for a father figure, then Linda Ash is being set upon by the most neurotic Jewish New Yorker version of Henry Higgins imaginable. Allen's very funny version of "My Whore Lady" presents a wittily believable nineties version of a hooker with a heart of gold, much more believable than the decade's *Ur*-whore, little girl Vivian in *Pretty Woman*.

And then there is the Moore-Whore. Not only does Demi Moore play the highest-priced whore of the nineties in *Indecent Proposal* (1993), after she turns her million-dollar trick, she steals the poor john's wallet, rips off every whore who has come before, and plagiarizes their scenes. If *Pretty Woman* is not about a whore finding Prince Charming, but rather is really about shopping for dresses on

Rodeo Drive, then *Indecent Proposal* sets that same shopping scenario in the fancy (and expensive), upscale boutique of a Las Vegas casino where Diana (Moore) meets her billionaire john, John Gage (Robert Redford). First, Gage offers to buy her a very expensive dress and then later he offers to buy her for the evening for one million dollars, an offer that neither she nor her struggling architect husband, David (Woody Harrelson), can refuse.

The *Pretty Woman*ish shopping scene in the casino boutique sets up the whole sexy nineties commodity culture premise of *Indecent Proposal*. The setup is all based on nineties economics. A young couple begins to build their dream house, but a recession hits, they are laid off, the banker calls in their loan, and in desperation they go to Las Vegas to try to win enough money to pay off their creditors. "A life without risk is like no life at all," husband David intones in an early voice-over, but what he doesn't understand is that this is a bad axiom for the AIDS-plagued nineties where people are dying from taking sexual risks. In *Indecent Proposal*, the sexual risk that David and Diana take infects their marriage in the same way AIDS infects the whole sexual spin of the nineties decade.

While David is gambling away their last dimes, Diana meets Gage in the casino boutique and he offers to buy her the dress of her dreams, vis-à-vis Julia Roberts and her tycoon in *Pretty Woman*. Diana refuses, but Gage coaxes, "I've enjoyed watching you. You've earned it." But Diana balks, "No I haven't. The dress is for sale. I'm not." That is how the prostitution theme of the film is rather transparently introduced. Soon after, David wins some money in the casino and he and Diana decide to make love while counting it on their hotel room bed. Their sexual encounter in that bed full of money is a scene right out of the earliest blatantly commodity culture novel to celebrate whoredom, Daniel DeFoe's *Moll Flanders*. Unfortunately, the next day they lose all the money they have been literally rolling around in, and, like DeFoe's Moll, Diana wants to get back into that bed full of money. This whole first section of *Indecent Proposal* is just like Moore's other film, *Striptease*. The Moore-Whore character must be in desperate economic straights before she will lower herself to become either a stripper or a whore.

The second section of the film, the proposal itself, is far from the offhand, playful bet situation that the audience expects. Instead, the indecent proposal of the title is truly whorish: hard-hearted, purely economic, a business deal, a ruthlessly negotiated contract for services on delivery. David and Diana even bring in their lawyer, Jeremy (Oliver Platt), to negotiate the contract for Diana becoming a whore. Here, the nineties image of the lawyer as snake or shark is superseded by the image of the lawyer as pimp.

The third section of the film is little more than a Gatsbyesque fantasy, Diana's foray into the Oz-like world of runaway nineties commodity culture. Gage, in his Gatsby suit, spirits her over the rainbow in his helicopter to his yacht where the million-dollar night of sex will take place amongst moonlight and city lights and the sly attraction of big money. Ironically, the million-dollar sex between Redford and his golden girl takes place off camera, probably quite a disappointment for Moore-Whore fans for whom "the sighting of her nudity has become a regular national event, like the launch of the space shuttle. If she completes a successful docking so much the better."[25] It seems that once the contract to be a whore has been signed, the sex that follows isn't really that important. The excitement lies in the deal, the negotiation, the closing of the sale. What this third section does is crystallize the whole issue of sex as commodity in the risky post-AIDS nineties. On the deck of his yacht, he dressed as Gatsby, she costumed as a geisha, Diana asks Gage, "Why me then?" He answers, "I bought you because you said you couldn't be bought."

The rest of *Indecent Proposal* is so eminently predictable—in fact, blatantly plagiarized (the anecdote of the girl on the ferry from *Citizen Kane*, the rain scene from *Four Weddings and a Funeral*)—and embarrassingly illogical that the film's message tends to get lost in the theft and bad writing. Ultimately, *Indecent Proposal* becomes a film about what happens when the pressures of nineties commodity culture cause people to lose their center in a world that is empty (though in this case and in *Pretty Woman* is quite well dressed). In the act of selling themselves, Diana and David become decentered, hollow men in the commodity culture heart of darkness of post-AIDS America.

In the movies of the nineties, they were not alone. In *Honeymoon in Vegas* (1992), after a high-stakes poker game, the wife (Sarah Jessica Parker) is given to the gangster (James Caan) by the lover husband (Nicholas Cage) to pay off a gambling debt. Before the weekend is over, the gangster offers the wife a million dollars (ahoy, Demi) to marry him because she looks just like his dead wife. As it turns out, not only prostitutes and ruthless corporate sharks like John Gage have a heart of gold, but, in *Honeymoon in Vegas*, so do the gangsters. In *Mad Dog and Glory* (1993), the same unbelievable do-gooder whorishness applies when a loan shark (Bill Murray) gives one of his female debtors (Uma Thurman) to a policeman (Robert De Niro) for a week then tries to sell her to him permanently. This film is most akin to *Indecent Proposal* when the woman-turned-commodity's price is negotiated down from $75,000 to $40,000.

Whores were all the rage in post-AIDS nineties films, but the one constant in their movie representation was the risk involved. Perhaps the film *Very Bad Things* (1998) summed up the risk of sexual adventuring with whores better than any other. When a bachelor party spins wildly out of control and a prostitute is accidentally killed, the AIDS metaphor significance of the film's title becomes clear: very bad things happen when you get carried away with sex (especially with prostitutes) in the nineties.

## Masturbation

*Molly:* My god, I haven't gotten laid in six months. My right hand's so tired I can't even thread a needle.
*Nomi:* Use the left one.

*—Showgirls*

If, in the sexual spin stratagems of the AIDS-conscious nineties, the voyeuristic needs of sexual searchers were satisfied by both male and female strippers and the rise of the gentleman's club and if the real streetwalkers (who were a disappearing breed) were replaced by a horde of high-visibility movie whores, still, the most hands-on sexual strategy in the hands-off and "in the privacy of your own home" nineties was masturbation. This age-old autoerotic option proved an easy and readily available solution to everyone's sexual problems. The opening of *American Beauty* (1999), the Academy Award–winning Best Picture, certainly attests to that: the camera moves slowly in on the film's voice and central character performing his regular morning masturbation in the shower. The spin upon the therapeutic value of masturbation that culminates in Lester Burnham's (Kevin Spacey) daily workout in *American Beauty* at the end of the decade first drew attention to itself in the title of a little-seen independent film early in the decade, *Spanking the Monkey* (1994). A dark comedy more about incest than about the masturbation in its title, *Spanking the Monkey* drew attention to the idea that in the absence of the erotic, the autoerotic would serve. All through the decade, in films like *The Cook, the Thief, His Wife & Her Lover* (1990) and *Like Water For Chocolate* (1993), which employ food as a way to either stimulate or relieve the erotic impulse, films like *Spanking the Monkey* were looking for "romantic substitutes"[26] for the real thing that, due to AIDS, had become too risky. *Risky Business* (1983) indeed! That early eighties Tom Cruise hooker comedy's title ironically signaled the sexual spin of the whole nineties decade.

By the end of the nineties and into the millennium, masturbation scenes had become standard fair and were even given extended coverage when women were the featured autoerotics. The masturbation scenes of the frustrated teenager Ray (Jeremy Davies) in *Spanking the Monkey* are always interrupted by the dog barking before they go very far, and Lester's morning masturbation in *American Beauty* is coyly shot through the steamed-up glass of the shower. But female movie masturbation had come a long way since Sarah Miles's then-daring brief masturbation scene in *The Sailor Who Fell From Grace With the Sea* (1976). The female autoerotics in films like *The Center of the World* (2001), *Mulholland Drive* (2001), and *Unfaithful* (2002) glory in their masturbation, extend it to great lengths in screen time, talk to others and experience elaborate fantasies while doing it, and even perform it as erotic entertainment for their voyeuristic lovers.

The two essential aids to masturbation in the nineties, one traditional and historically long-standing, the other newly conceived for the AIDS-risk spin strategy of the decade, were pornography and phone sex. The creation of print, film, and verbal texts to masturbate by became a thriving industry in the sexually at-risk nineties. Repeatedly, the films of the decade represented the powerful influence of these sexual stimulant texts. For example, the nineties became famous for making two movies almost exactly the same on the same subject. There were two volcano movies, *Volcano* (1997) and *Dante's Peak* (1997), two movies about the seventies New York club scene, *54* (1998) and *The Last Days of Disco* (1998), two Dalai Lama movies, two Steve Prefontaine movies, and two phone-sex movies, *Girl 6* (1996) and *Denise Calls Up* (1996). In other films, such as Robert Altman's *Short Cuts* (1993), while not featured, phone sex appears as a housewife's way of finding some relief from boring domestic life and making some extra money much in the spirit of Godard's *Belle De Jour*. Similarly, in *The Truth About Cats and Dogs* (1996), another of the cutesy romantic comedies that the decade of TV's *Friends* is famous for, a phone-sex scene is central to the plot. Actor Ben Chaplin, who did that scene, describes his fantasy reaction to doing it: "'Hi, honey, how was your day?' 'Oh, I masturbated.' . . . 'I can't believe I'm doing this for a living.'"[27]

The phone-sex movies are truly interesting in terms of their spin consciousness because all make the case for an otherwise sick and disgusting sexual addiction as a positive, therapeutic service to society. *Girl 6* and *Denise Calls Up* do exactly that with a vengeance:

> Discussing your sexual fantasies over the phone used to be the sort of thing that could get you shunned in polite company (if not arrested). But to judge from the recent, multimillion-dollar explosion in phone-sex services (not to mention the rise of cybersex), America no longer has much polite company. We've become a nation of heavy-breathing schmoozers—vicarious erotic fantasists who fork over piles of cash to talk about the things we don't feel safe doing. Even in intimate relationships, getting off over the phone has acquired an aura of psychodramatic chic.[28]

This national magazine description of the new service industry, however, doesn't quite analyze deeply enough the reason that phone sex spiked as an industry in the nineties. It gained its popularity because it was so well adapted to the sexual spin strategies of the decade. "Talk dirty to me" phone services had been advertised in the back pages of skin magazines for decades, but only in the nineties did they gain the cachet that took them from a homebound cottage industry to a corporate cash cow run out of high-tech telephone boiler rooms. A clearer take on the reason for the phone-sex explosion comes from the boss of the boiler room in *Girl 6* during her training session for new phone-sex telephone operators: "It's not just sex, OK. You're their friend. They're lonely. They're divorced. Their wives aren't into what they're into. . . . You are the ones who listen. Gotta listen, yes? You're the one who appreciates them. You're the one who doesn't judge them. You want 'em to like you, ladies. 'Cause if they like you, they call back, and if they call back a lot of you make lotsa cash, ladies. . . . Alright ladies, listen. This job can be a lotta fun, and you can make a lotta money, and you're safe here, very safe." Ultimately, the bottom line of the nineties sexual spin strategy is safety, especially safety from infection with AIDS.

*Girl 6*, like the Demi Moore movies, has economic desperation driving a girl into the nineties sex industry. Before she becomes a disembodied phone-sex voice, *Girl 6* (Theresa Randle) walks out of an audition with the hottest new film director (played self-referentially as a cameo by Quentin Tarantino) when he asks her to show him her breasts, loses her agent who sides with the director ("Sharon Stone spread her legs and look what happened"), takes a job passing out flyers on the street, can't pay her rent, loses her acting coach because she can't pay her, decides she can't work as either a peep-show girl or a stripper, and finally ends up in a phone-sex boiler room after convincing herself it is a form of acting.

Girl 6's first customer is a businessman masturbating at his desk talking about the million-dollar deal he just closed (as in *Indecent Proposal*). "Are you nice and hard for me? Are you touching yourself?" Girl 6 asks. When he experiences orgasm, she feels equally satisfied. "He hung up happy," her boss congratulates her. "Good job!" From the very beginning, Girl 6 realizes that the fragile phone-sex relationship she establishes with her customers is masturbatory for her, too. "I love men," she says. "My luck's for shit with 'em, but I love 'em. So I said to myself, if you can't get it in real life, you might as well get it on the job."

Later in the film, when Girl 6 is spectacularly successful at playing every role her clients request, her boss, concerned, asks her: "You comin' with 'em?" She can't give a satisfactory answer, but when her neighbor Jimmy (Spike Lee) asks her when she's going to quit "this phone-bone stuff," she answers, "I don't know because I'm startin' to like it." This fairly straightforward Spike Lee version of a Demi Moore movie makes an abrupt turn in the direction of Godard's *Belle de Jour*. Girl 6 starts having elaborate technicolor fantasies of herself as Dorothy Dandridge in *Carmen Jones* (1954), Pam Grier in *Foxy Brown* (1974), and as a phone-obsessed teenage daughter on *The Jeffersons* eighties TV sitcom. Ultimately, she sets up her phone-sex service in her own apartment and takes the nineties sexual strategy of "in the privacy of your own home" to a whole new level. Now she gets a headset to free her hands to masturbate as she talks to her callers. She is getting far too into the fantasies she creates until one day she is forced to stop masturbating when one of her callers threatens her and tells her that he knows her address. Suddenly, her hands-off, safe-sex business is no longer safe and that is when she quits.

Near the end of *Girl 6*, Girl 6's next-door neighbor, Jimmy, challenges the masturbatory view of life to which she has become addicted. "This ain't reality. I know what's real and what's not, whether you wanna believe it or not. Do you?" All Jimmy can do is throw up his hands in frustration: "You get off on this stuff, huh?" Spike Lee takes a pretty perceptive look at how the sexual spin of the nineties has settled on masturbatory simulation (*à la* Baudrillard) as the best option for minimizing risk and keeping one's sexual proclivities private, but he also realizes that masturbation is a nonprogressive option. In other words, the sexual spin of the masturbatory nineties can only keep spinning but can never go anywhere. *Girl 6* ends where it began (at an audition), and nothing has changed. Girl 6 has fled New York (and her masturbatory phone-sex addiction with its rising risk) for Hollywood and a new beginning as an actress. But in her first audition in LA, the director, once again, asks her to take off her top and expose her breasts. This time she walks straight out of the audition. Perhaps that is a progress in terms of her identity, but it really is not any sort of progress in terms of the nineties world that she is trying to survive in. Then Spike Lee throws in a final ironic coda. Girl 6 stalks out of the Hollywood Boulevard audition, walking right over Dorothy Dandridge's star on the Walk of Fame, and into a movie theater that announces on its marquee that it is showing a film called *Girl 6*. This self-reflexive bit of directorial masturbation is fitting for a film that focuses on a sexual spin strategy that is itself totally self-reflexive.

The other phone-sex film, *Denise Calls Up*, is not nearly as complex a spin analysis as is Spike Lee's *Girl 6*. In fact, *Denise Calls Up* could easily pass as a slightly racy episode of the TV sitcoms *Friends* or *Seinfeld*. Actually, it is really quite similar to the notorious masturbation episode of *Seinfeld*. It represents the nineties love affair with the cell phone and the cell phone's potential for inventive phone sex in new and exciting locales and circumstances. *Denise Calls Up* represents phone sex as both a nineties sex game and a Lyotardian "language game." For the twenty-somethings of *Denise Calls Up* who cannot escape from their own self-isolation and social alienation in the age of risk and loneliness, phone sex adds spice to their masturbatory spin strategies of survival. The film chronicles the lives of a group of New York City yuppies who have taken the "in the privacy of your own home" spin of nineties sexuality ultraseriously. They never leave their apartments, and their whole lives, all their relationships with other people, even their sexual encounters, are conducted on their cell phones. As opposed to the commodity culture professionalism of the phone-sex practitioners in *Girl 6*, this is the amateur version of phone sex, but it is equally imaginative, erotic, perverse, and masturbatory.

The other traditional texts that have always been aids to masturbation, visual and verbal pornography (especially skin magazines), also received abundant representation in the movies as part of the sexual spin strategy of the nineties. "So *this* is what happens when you shut down the adult theaters in Times Square—pornography invades mainstream culture," one commentator personifies the change in attitudes toward pornography in imperial military terms.[29] Like the transformation of strippers into dancers, of strip joints into gentlemen's clubs, of naked dancers into working moms, of whores into Cinderellas, of housewives into hookers, of masturbation into psychic therapy, the spinning of previously under-the-counter pornography into entertainment for the stay-at-home masturbating masses was a recurrent American strategy that found representation in some of the most highly acclaimed Hollywood offerings of the nineties.

Both *The People vs. Larry Flynt* (1996) and *Boogie Nights* (1997) received the highest honors from film culture (Academy Award nominations) despite the pornographic distastefulness of their subject matter. Did art triumph over the sleaziness of the material in these cases, or did the material cleverly hitch its fortunes to a burgeoning sexual spin strategy that took it on a wild ride over the rainbow into a colorful land of social acceptance? Probably neither *The People vs. Larry Flynt* nor *Boogie Nights* would ever have been made and would never have portrayed their characters in the strangely skewed positive ways that they did if the sexual spin strategy of the nineties hadn't given them plenty of encouragement.

If, in the spirit of nineties sexual spin, masturbation became the darling of the sexual options available to those unwilling to face the risks of sexual adventuring, then the greatest whitewash of the decade was Hollywood's mainstreaming of *Hustler* magazine's Larry Flynt. The critical reaction to Flynt's biopic, *The People vs. Larry Flynt*, forms an ongoing motif of spin language. From the very beginning, commentators on the film treated it as a transparent spin text:

The movie all but portrays Flynt as the Patrick Henry of porn, a First Amendment freedom fighter whose Supreme Court case helped make the world safe for democracy—not to mention crotch shots.[30]

Forman pursues his entertaining but blinkered agenda of painting Flynt (Woody Harrelson) as a victimized reprobate.[31]

Forman (*Amadeus, Ragtime*) set about polishing a reprehensible sleaze-monger into an endearing free speech hero.[32]

In perhaps the greatest absurdity of all the spin rhetoric that surrounded *The People vs. Larry Flynt* was one critic characterizing it as a Capraesque feel-good movie, "a sort of *Mr. Smut Goes to Washington*."[33] In all of these cases, the critics are analyzing the art of the film less and the obvious spin strategy of the film more.

Gloria Steinem, speaking for her feminist constituency, was not amused. "Flynt is a violent, sadistic pornographer," Steinem protests, "but this film almost portrays him as a hero. It's totally dishonest. It's the Watergate of movies."[34] While the similarity of the film's representation of Flynt and his porno empire to Watergate is rather hard to decode, Steinem's hyperbolic overstatement expresses the astonishment of so many different segments of American society—women, the religious Right, the religious Middle and Left (if there is such a group), even the Supreme Court—that Hollywood would reach this low to find a dramatic subject.

All of this commentary on *The People vs. Larry Flynt*, however, is pretty heady evidence of the distance the nineties sexual spin strategy had come. By 1997, sexual spin was so much in control of the American consciousness that no topic or persona was too controversial or negative or just plain sleazy to benefit from its positive reinforcement. After all, if spin could limo strippers out of the raunchy roadhouses into gentlemen's clubs and could bring masturbators out of their bathrooms and to the couches of their home entertainment centers, it could certainly spin pornography and an absolute sleazeball like Larry Flynt into First Amendment defenders. By middecade, it seemed that sexual spin could do anything, and *The People vs. Larry Flynt* also paved the way for the first historical epic about pornography.

Paul Thomas Anderson's two-and-half-hour-long *Boogie Nights* is the sexual spin *Birth of a Nation* (1915) of the nineties. It succeeds where *Showgirls* and *Striptease* failed in being a big-event, epic treatment of a purely sexual subject. *Boogie Nights* goes inside the seventies world of pornography and domesticates it, portrays it as a world in which a family of would-be artists try to compete with the corporate powers that rule both the movie and sex industries in America.

According to the sexual spin of the nineties, post-AIDS sexuality is not really about sex, and all the different versions of post-AIDS, hands-off, "in the privacy of your own home," nineties sexuality are not really about sex either. They are about entering the mainstream, making a decent living, having a nice house, upholding the Constitution, or simply being safe. The language of sexual spin can turn sex into any number of other, more positive things. That was certainly the case with *Boogie Nights*: "If New Line sells *Boogie Nights* as a film about sex, its director-producer-writer, 26-year-old Paul Thomas Anderson, could accuse the company of selling out what he modestly calls 'an epic.' So instead, the studio is calling attention to the film's sexier angle by relentlessly claiming that its porno setting is really beside the point. 'It isn't about porn. It's about dreams and grow-ing up in that time, and how our mores are different.'"[35] Freud would really like *Boogie Nights* because it turns a history of the seventies porno filmmaking scene into a domestic family romance. The spin strategy argues that *Boogie Nights* is really an off-beat family picture like *The Addams Family* or *The Flintstones*. Jack Horner (Burt Reynolds), the porno producer-director is the father. Amber Waves (Julianne Moore), the hard drinking, cokehead porn star, is the mother. And all the revolving teeny-bopper wannabe porno princes and princesses are the chil-dren. It is the freewheeling, cocaine-fueled seventies when the film is set, but its representation and sexual spin is pure nineties.

According to *Boogie Nights*, the porno underground is a fun-loving party place, sunlit and free, a haven for would-be artists and misunderstood youth, a place for nurturing and self-expression. In other words, and in terms of sexual spin, *Boogie Nights* is as much an idealized whitewash as *The People vs. Larry Flynt*. Where are the gangsters who force women into prostitution and pornography at gunpoint? Where are the drug dealers who tempt women into pornography after addicting them? Where are the sleazy casting couch porno producers who lure runaways into performing sex acts on film? Where are the exploiters and the perverts and the mob killers who run the porno industry?

But in the nineties, pornography is no longer the taboo, the unspeakable and perverse reality of sex. In the nineties, pornography has become a mainstream sexual aid, an acceptable aphrodisiac, sort of like oysters or ginseng. In the nine-ties, pornography even has its own Las Vegas convention and its own version of filmdom's Academy Awards. As a sidebar to the annual Consumer Electron-ics Show in Las Vegas, the adults-only technology exhibit and the *Adult Video News Awards* are the national trade show and the Academy Awards of porn all rolled into one, the pornography industry's own Baudrillardian simulacra of the mainstream film industry's big night. Perhaps this characterization of this adults-only event best describes the impact of pornography upon nineties culture and how it happened: "Fifteen years after X-rated videotapes proved to be the VCR's "killer app"—the irresistible application that introduced the VCR into Ameri-can homes—the bottom feeders are again pushing the leading edge of technol-ogy. . . . It's all part of a huge porn market . . . whose true dimensions might be four times [larger] if mail-order sales were public knowledge. . . . Not that life on porn's front lines has gotten glamorous. AIDS is still a danger, and except in gay videos, condoms seldom appear on set."[36]

Masturbation and the available therapeutic aids to masturbation (like porno videos) became the center of the sexual world of the nineties. In a masturbatory world, solipsism is both fact and necessitated desire, and masturbation is the primary sexual venue of solipsistic man and woman. A fable for this post-AIDS masturbatory culture is the fittingly titled (in more ways than one) *The Center of the World* (2001). As the stripper-whore Florence (Molly Parker) so delicately puts it at one point (mimicking Gertrude Stein), "a woman's cunt. That is the center of the world. A cunt is a cunt is a cunt." But *The Center of the World* is really like that old Jules Verne sci-fi story that its title echoes. In this nineties version, in this post-AIDS version, hands-off nonpenetrating sex is the ultimate goal of the journey to the center. In this nineties journey in the quest for sexual fulfillment, for the ability to feel, the only sex that is affirmed as true turns out to be masturbation (or sexual *simulation*). At the end of the film, when computer geek Richard (Peter Saarsgard), who has bought Florence for a sexual weekend in Las Vegas, breaks down in tears because he realizes that he can't make Florence feel anything real for him, Florence screams: "You want real? I'll show you real!" And she proceeds to masturbate in front of him, long and relentlessly intense, until she quakes in orgasm. This scene is a coda to nineties sexual spin. It declares that masturbation is the only kind of sex that is real in an age of AIDS and commodity culture. For Richard, the buyer of Florence, the sexual commodity, this masturbation scene is the revelation of the film's grail, the truth of the quest, of the journey to the center. She doesn't masturbate in front of him out of malice or anger, the motives that drove him to rape her. She does it to teach him. Hers is the most striking masturbation scene of a whole progression of such scenes in nineties films. The camera dwells on her intense masturbation like a hungry voyeur, and the scene defies the central opposition of nineties sexual spin, the power struggle of penetration verses the solipsistic fulfillment of masturbation.

*The Center of the World* brings together all of the venues of nineties sexual spin—strippers, whoredom, masturbation—and focuses their function in terms of its penetration versus masturbation thematic opposition. The film begins in a coffee shop as *Pulp Fiction* (1994) did. "I'm a stripper," Florence tells Richard and invites him to see her dance at Pandora's Box, which calls up the sexual metaphor of *Mulholland Drive*. At the strip club, Richard watches as Florence does a full-frontal lap dance for a group of men, masturbating herself with a candy sucker and then sticking it into the customer's mouth. When Richard approaches her later for a lap dance, she stresses the house rule: "I said no touching." Soon, like the characters in *Indecent Proposal* and *Pretty Woman*, Florence negotiates a contract with Richard for a weekend in Las Vegas and sells herself to him as a whore for $10,000. But it is an ironclad contract, a very nineties safe-sex contract, that clearly stipulates "No kissing on the mouth. No penetration." Like Cinderella, Florence's contract limits her hours as a whore to "10 PM 'til 2 AM each night." *The Center of the World* brings together all of the characteristics of nineties sexual spin in one neat package, then stands back like a voyeur and watches them deconstruct.

Their first night the contract holds. She puts on an elaborate, beautifully costumed and choreographed whore's performance for him. She dresses, makes up, and dances for him. The second night she strips herself, caresses herself, and does an elaborate naked lap dance for him. This time he can touch, but he cannot penetrate her. He mainly must sit in his chair and watch. The third night, neither one of them can live up to the contract any longer. She strips and begins to dance, then goes cold and breaks down in tears. He forces himself upon her, penetrates, and rapes her. She feels nothing. They can find no center in each other. As Sartre predicted, intersubjectivity is not possible. Two people cannot come together as one, especially in the nineties age of commodity culture and post-AIDS, low-risk sexual spin. At one point, in the afternoon of their second day, after a carefree shopping spree as in *Pretty Woman*, they begin to make love but she stops him: "We have to stick to the contract." *The Center of the World* is a *coitus interruptus* film that ends in an extended scene of masturbation that comments on the utterly decentered state of nineties sexuality. In the most austere Sartrean sense, people are alone. Intersubjectivity has been written out of the contract, and people can no longer come together because it is just too risky.

## Psychosex Noir

A vulnerable Fiorentino—please!
—Lawrence O'Toole, "*Jade*," *Entertainment Weekly*

Sex has always been risky, especially in the world of the film noir. The nineties version of that genre, call it "psychosex noir," defined that risk in explicit terms. As D. H. Lawrence phrased it for the Freudian teens and twenties, sex is in the head in the nineties mainly because it is too dangerous for it to reside anywhere else. The one sexual femme fatale who messed with men's heads more graphically than any other was Linda Fiorentino. "If she had been the lead in *Basic Instinct*, I'd own a copy of it,"[37] best sums up the sex symbol status of Fiorentino in the nineties. "She's screwing with your head, Nick," the cop partner warns in *Basic Instinct*, but Fiorentino far surpasses Sharon Stone in that particular sexual expertise. She is the decade's truly bad girl, the sex symbol who will get wilder, go further, and be just plain dirtier than Sharon, Madonna, or Demi would ever consider.

In *The Last Seduction* (1994), she plays Bridget who steals a drug-deal fortune from her husband then uses every sexual trick or treat imaginable to seduce a small-town rube into killing him. It is a working-class version of *Double Indemnity* (1944), but Fiorentino performs acrobatic acts of seduction that would even make Barbara Stanwyck blush. "Bridget is a monster," one critic praises Fiorentino's performance, "but it's easy to see why this movie clicked with perverse cineaste: For women, she represents a grotesquely entertaining caricature of female empowerment; for men, she's the dangerous yet tempting hotsy-totsy."[38] Fiorentino followed her monster Bridget with an equally kinky noir performance as the title character in *Jade* (1995). In this *Butterfield 8* and *Belle de Jour* rip-off, Jade is a high-class, society wife who moonlights as a high-priced call girl whose specialty is anal sex. Fiorentino's freak-show films defined the trashy psychosex noir of the nineties but were, in a sense, closer to the gaze of desire that nineties sexual spin had banned from real life. Fiorentino as sex symbol screamed "put your hands on me," flaunted every taboo, and demanded sexual penetration in some of the most public venues. In a short-lived TV series, *EZ Streets* (TV: 1996–97), she even showed up naked in the back pew of a church to seduce her gangster boyfriend as he came out of confession. Fiorentino was capable of exuding a delight in sexual adventuring that AIDS had all but banned from nineties sexual life.

But nineties psychosex noir was much more than the latest noir queen's ability to control and twist her male victims' often obtuse minds. Psychosex had its professional practitioners as well, working psychiatrists caught in the pull of nineties sexual spin. Bill Capa (Bruce Willis) in *Color of Night* and the husband and wife psychoanalysts in Kubrick's *Eyes Wide Shut* (1999) as played by Hollywood's then most glamorous couple, Tom Cruise and Nicole Kidman, are just such characters. As psychiatrists themselves, they ought to know better. Yet the allure of illicit sexual adventuring proves too strong for them to resist. In *Color of Night*, in the middle of a psychotherapy appointment, one of Capa's patients throws herself out of his office window and plummets to her death. This psychiatrist's reaction to the professional trauma is to flee to Los Angeles and immerse himself in an intense erotic relationship with a mysterious woman half his age (Jane March). Similarly, in *Eyes Wide Shut*, Cruise and Kidman play married psychologists. When Cruise begins to doubt his wife's fidelity, he flees to New York's erotic underworld and ends up at a grotesque orgy in a dark suburban mansion. None of this is very professional behavior, but it does characterize the central problem with the psychosex noir of the nineties, its lack of credibility. "Has there ever been a movie psychiatrist who behaved remotely the way real shrinks do?" asked one critic of *Color of Night*.[39] Star Willis reportedly characterized his movie more directly as a "f— fest."[40] *Eyes Wide Shut* presents similar problems of credibility. High-society doctor Cruise, unable to deal with his own sexual fantasies of his wife having sex with other men, sets out to teach her a lesson by doing exactly that himself, a leap of logic that would embarrass any real therapist. Ironically, both of these unprofessional psychosex odysseys fit the needs of nineties sexual spin. In the post-AIDS time where sex has been forced out of the physical and into the mental realm, even the shrinks need some inspiration to fuel their sexual fantasies: "*Color of Night* is yet another attempt . . . to spice up the life of the mind with some raunch and mayhem."[41]

Both *Color of Night* and *Eyes Wide Shut* were controversial sexual films before they ever hit the screen. The widely publicized censorship battle over the full frontal shots of Bruce Willis's penis and the ultrasecrecy of Kubrick's filming combined with the overheated rumors of steamy Cruise-Kidman sex scenes built high expectations in voyeuristic film audiences, expectations that both films spectacularly disappointed. While both films were surprising box-office flops (after all the media hype), both predictably found strong second lives on home video. Their dark eroticism, while too kinky and disturbing for public viewing, fit quite nicely into "the privacy of your own home" rubric of nineties sexual spin.

The psychotherapists of *Color of Night* and *Eyes Wide Shut* were contemporary Jekyll and Hyde figures (as were nineties film audiences). Professionals by day, wanderers of the sexual underworld by night, these psychotherapists found, perhaps, the most accurate representation of nineties sexuality in the Jekyll and Hyde story *Mary Reilly* (1996). Nineties movie audiences kept up their outward appearances by day and indulged their voyeuristic sexual adventuring via video in the privacy of their own homes by night. In *Mary Reilly*, Doctor Jekyll (John Malkovich) is a serious psychotherapist sincerely involved with treating the child-abuse trauma of his housemaid, Mary Reilly (Julia Roberts), which has turned her into a nearly mute wage slave. Yet he cannot control his own sexual deprivation. What Jekyll is reacting against by turning himself into Hyde, Victorian sexual repression, is a perfectly fitting metaphor for the bleak AIDS-repressed sexual landscape of the nineties. The gloomy sexual isolation of nineties life imposed Jekyll-like solipsism and Hyde-like illicit desire upon everyone. Sexuality had to find new ways to express itself and forge new identities to protect itself from social harm. Nineties sexual spin turned everyone into Jekylls and Hydes, venturing out at night to gentlemen's clubs or staying in to watch pornographic videos.

Other screen psychotherapists dealt with their own and their patients' sexual problems in less somber and sinister ways. The psychosex that surfaced in the nineties both affirmed well-known and documented sexual practices and showcased newer ingenious reactions to the limitations of nineties sexuality. The psychotherapist, Dr. Mickler (Marlon Brando), in *Don Juan De Marco* (1995) is not at all the troubled, cursed solipsist in the vein of the Willis-Cruise-Malkovich succession of Jekylls. Brando's Dr. Mickler is an almost grandfatherly psychotherapist whose sexuality, like that of the nineties decade, has been cast into a state of dormancy until he meets the Don Juan (Johnny Depp) of the movie's title. *Don Juan De Marco*, light, witty comedy that it is, also serves as a clear metaphor for nineties sexual spin. All of the women that this nineties Don Juan entices into his dream world are sexually dormant but are sexually reinvigorated by Don Juan's wit and imagination. It is as if the film is saying that, in the age of AIDS, only creative fantasy can keep the sexual appetites satisfied.

Other psychosex noirs explore much more violent, less-romantic metaphors for spicing up the dormant sexuality of nineties life. As *Don Juan De Marco* referenced the romantic sexual creativity of Lord Byron's poetic hero, both Madonna's *Body of Evidence* (1993) and Roman Polanski's *Bitter Moon* (1994) referenced the darker sexual imagination of the Marquis de Sade. One critic, comparing the punky-fresh "trampy insolence" of Madonna in *Desperately Seeking Susan* (1985), "her ruby-red smirk both a tease and a come-on—a luscious advertisement for sin," to Madonna in *Body of Evidence* (1993) might well be defining the difference between eighties and nineties sexuality: "Now, the exuberance—the sensual invitation—is gone."[42] With all of its S&M kinkiness, *Body of Evidence* is still just another AIDS metaphor movie. In the courtroom drama that anchors the plot of *Body of Evidence*, Rebecca Carlson (Madonna) is literally a femme fatale. She is charged with killing her older, heart-damaged lover with sex. Aha Watson, death by sexual intercourse! Ironically, that exact outstanding premise defined the major difference between eighties and nineties life. Like the dark psychosex of *Body of Evidence*, sex in the nineties had become dangerous, painful, and lethal. Polanski's *Bitter Moon* is equally AIDS metaphoric. The story is told in flashback by Oscar (Peter Coyote), the wheelchair-bound and angry ex-lover of Mimi (Emmanuelle Seigneur), the voluptuous and extremely kinky young woman whom he has grown to hate and whose violent sexuality has destroyed him, turned him into a dying shell of a human being. "Beware kinky sex!" these films rather puritanically warn. It leads to danger, disease, and death.

Perhaps the ultimate AIDS-warning metaphor film is *Crash* (1996) where sex and death come together nicely in the favorite action scenario of nineties filmgoers, metal-crunching car crashes. Of all the kinky fetishes that show up in the psychosex noirs of the nineties, the sex-death metaphor of *Crash* at least touches on one aspect of nineties sexual spin that the others have failed to explore. David Cronenberg's film acknowledges the nineties sexual dependence upon technology rather than real flesh-on-flesh encounters for its thrills. In a decade where some of the most prominent aids to sexual fulfillment are electronic—VCRs, vibrators, erotic music for strippers to dance to—why not bring the ultimate American sex machine, the automobile, into the vortex of sexual spin? Where before, for example, in *American Graffiti* (1973), cars were simply sexual playrooms; in *Crash* they have evolved for the torpid sexual nineties into the ultimate, most dangerous fantasy in which sex meets death at high speed. In a sexual climate where the thrill is gone and the risk is oppressive, the need to break out, to flee the sexual boredom, becomes an obsession. Historically, when Americans feel the need to break out of the narrowed margins of their lives as Jack Kerouac did, inevitably they take to their cars. In the case of *Crash* as a nineties cultural document, both sex and speed kills.

All of these kinky, outlandish, deviant, and extravagant psychosexual explorations are nothing more than substrategies within the overall sexual spin strategy of the nineties decade. They are desperate measures for coping with the isolation, the sexual dormancy, the loneliness, and the frustration of nineties sexual life. Often, these substrategies take the form of elaborate scenarios of kinky behavior or dangerous games played to stave off boredom and widen the field of limited sexual play. But the psychosex of the nineties, the attempt to make D. H. Lawrence's "sex in the head" a substitute for real and so-called normal sex, is still not enough to offset the limits set by AIDS on nineties sexuality. While psychosex sought to offset sexual solipsism with elaborate, deviant, game-playing, other forms of sexual deviance proved much more sinister, socially sicker, and physically violent.

## Predators

> She's my sister. She's my daughter. She's my sister and my daughter.
> —Evelyn Mulwray in *Chinatown*

Roman Polanski's *Chinatown* does so many filmic things so well that perhaps overlooked is the most shocking crime of all the crimes—murder, political corruption, land theft—committed in this classic film noir, incest. In its time, the seventies, Evelyn Mulwray's revelation late in *Chinatown* of her incestuous relationship with her father, Noah Cross (John Huston), evoked a gasp from film audiences; it was the kind of sudden shocker that fulfills the governing tone of all great film noir, that nothing is ever what it seems. But while the crime of incest may have shocked seventies audiences to attention, by the nineties such sexually deviant criminality had been brought by a sensationalistic tabloid media so far out of the shadows and into the light of day that it was no longer shocking. In fact, the central sex scandals of the nineties in the Catholic Church, in the workplace, and in the American family, when publicized in the media, seemed so widespread that the whole culture suffered the same sort of embarrassed shock of recognition that Jake Gittes (Jack Nicholson) experienced in *Chinatown*. How could we not have seen what was going on with the predator priests, bosses, and parents? How could this criminal deviance be so widespread yet so overlooked? In the seventies, urban police departments had vice squads to deal with the predominant sexual crimes of the culture: prostitution, homosexual solicitation, brothels, and bathhouses. But in the nineties, police departments have special sex crimes units that investigate a whole new vocabulary of sexual offenses that were always existent but not as culturally widespread or socially exposed. The new lexicon of sex crimes of the nineties was based on the concept of predation: incest, pedophilia, sexual harassment, stalking, rape.

The increased social consciousness of these predatory sexual crimes underlined the emphasis upon danger and risk that played such a dominant role in the sexual spin of the nineties decade. Where previously the most prominent sexual transgression, prostitution, had been viewed as a victimless crime and jokingly referred to as the world's oldest profession, in the new vocabulary of sexual criminality, every crime has a victim. Those victims are children and women, and they are being preyed upon by persons in traditional positions of trust: parents, priests, bosses in the workplace. The films of the nineties, always on the lookout for new villains different from the usual suspects (gangsters, terrorists, serial killers), did not hesitate to explore this particular aspect of sexual spin.

Freud's concept of the family romance found some of its most graphic representations in nineties films about incest. *Angels and Insects* (1996), based on a novel by A. S. Byatt, offered a much more graphic portrayal of predatory incest than *Chinatown*'s off-screen incest ever considered. Even the central metaphor and imagery of *Angels and Insects*, the hive and its hothouse relationships, emphasize the theme of secret predation. When Victorian entomologist William Adamson returns from the South American jungle and marries rich and lovely Eugenia Alabaster (Patsy Kensit), they settle into a quiet life of country manners and entomological studies. But the Queen Bee of this particular hive must be at the service of all the workers in the family. When her husband is engrossed in his study of the family romances of the insects in his hives, Eugenia's brother is bedding her as he has since they were adolescents. One critic says of *Angels and Insects* that "this stuff is fabulously, maturely, weirdly *dirty*."[43] If that is true, then the incest at the center of *The House of Yes* (1997) is absurdly, outlandishly, whackily dirty. In this Thanksgiving-from-hell movie, brother Marty (Josh Hamilton) and sister Jackie-O (Parker Posey), who, like the siblings in *Angels and Insects*, have a sexual history, come back together not as themselves but as Jack and Jackie Kennedy. Incest and insects, incest and assassination: what is truly disturbing about these two films is that they portray incest so graphically and so cavalierly. In *Chinatown*, incest was the original sin, the deepest secret in the heart of darkness. In these nineties films, incest is just something that happens regularly in the best of families. The moral numbing of ubiquitous sexual spin in the tabloid media can be credited with desensitizing the nineties to these previously shocking taboos.

If incest was defanged and made into little more than just another practiced fetish by the movies and the media in the nineties, pedophilia (especially involving priests) was a much more ripped-from-the-headlines issue. In the early nineties when the issue of predatory priests and the cover-up of their crimes by the leaders of the Catholic Church was exposed, it placed a high-intensity spotlight on the basic issues of crimes of predation: violation of trust, sexual exploitation of the weak, evil lurking beneath the façade of good. Hitchcock captured with gleeful relish this uneasy set of issues in films like *Shadow of a Doubt* (1943) and *Frenzy* (1972), but the films of the nineties study these particular kinds of sexual predators with a cool but equally uneasy detachment as if these criminals were some strain of space aliens, an invasion of the child snatchers, rather than the figures of trust and tradition that people deal with every day.

Of all the films of the nineties, *Happiness* (1998), directed by Todd Solondz, may expose sexual deviance more uneasily and exert sexual spin more aggressively than any other. Like Hitchcock's *Shadow of a Doubt*, Solondz's *Happiness* goes into a typical suburban world of lives hidden behind a façade of happiness and exposes them in all their sickness and, in one case, predatory criminality. But, and here is the twist: Solondz chooses to view them nonjudgmentally and even sympathetically. What really pushes the limits of sexual spin in *Happiness* is Solondz's portrayal of a married gay pedophile who molests his own son's friends. He doesn't portray this character positively, but as one critic notes, "Solondz refuses to demonize him. He finds it far more interesting to try to understand what makes him tick."[44] While *Happiness* generally received rave reviews as well as high acclaim at the Cannes Film Festival, its distributor, October Films, on orders from its corporate owner Universal Pictures, refused to distribute it due to its particular sexual spin: "'It turned my stomach,' says one executive. 'I don't need to see a movie about a pedophile.'"[45]

But *Happiness* was not the only movie of the decade about a pedophile, even if it was the only one to give its pedophilia the semblance of a positive sexual spin. Conversely, *The Boys of St. Vincent* (1992) and *Sleepers* (1996) both explored the devastating psychological effects that child molestation has upon young male victims, effects that were daily being described in the media as the pedophile priests scandal in the Catholic Church came to light. *The Boys of St. Vincent* portrays the predatory crimes of just such a priest while in *Sleepers* a priest (Robert De Niro) in Hell's Kitchen, trying to save "his boys," finds out just what put them on their paths to crime—systematic molestation by the guards in the juvenile detention facility. Other films also portrayed the problems of priests with their vows of celibacy but involved much less controversial (though equally predatory) heterosexual and adult relationships. Both *The Proposition* (1998) in which Father Michael (Kenneth Branagh), a 1930s Catholic priest, must confess his sexual secret, and *The Scarlet Letter* (1995) in which the Reverend Dimmesdale (Gary Oldman) must watch his sexual sin posted on his lover's chest, however, do not involve children. While these films are historically distanced and not involved with pedophilia, both mirror the very real crisis in the Catholic Church that was unfolding in the second half of the nineties.

But the predatory molestation of the weaker victim, the exertion of the power of position over vulnerability, wasn't limited to priests and altar boys. In the nineties, an equally visible (and long standing) predatory relationship was legislated into criminality. That was the workplace relationship between managers and their subordinates that was characterized as sexual harassment. The Michael Crichton film *Disclosure* (1994), despite its male backlash plot, became the poster film for exploring the issues of sexual harassment in the nineties workplace. "With *Disclosure* . . . Hollywood tackles one of the biggest hot-button issues of the 1990s: sexual harassment in the workplace," one magazine trumpeted.[46] "The film tackles a heavy sociological theme, the explosive issue of sexual harassment," another critic chimes in.[47] But a third critic only half-heartedly joins the chorus: "Ultimately, the sexual harassment theme, which is supposed to be the movie's selling point, recedes into the background."[48]

Ironically, the one highly visible film of the decade on sexual harassment chooses to take a reverse spin stance. That choice by author and director Crichton destroys its credibility. What is interesting (and brilliant) about *Disclosure* is Crichton's casting of the lead roles: Michael Douglas as yet another victim of a sexually aggressive woman as he was in *Fatal Attraction* (1987) and *Basic Instinct*; Demi Moore as the always aggressive yet strangely androgynous sex symbol of the decade as in her female sex roles in *The Scarlet Letter*, *Indecent Proposal*, and *Striptease* and her male roles in *A Few Good Men* and *G.I. Jane*. Despite familiar iconography, however, *Disclosure*'s sexual harassment of a male by a female boss gets all tangled up in its own unbelievability. David Mamet's sexual harassment Rubik's Cube, *Oleanna* (1994), on the other hand, explores just how intricate and sensitive sexual harassment issues really can be. In Mamet's film, the alleged harassment of a female college student by a male professor is verbal, the assertion of power by means of the intimidating weapons of words. Much more subtly than *Disclosure* ever aspired to do, *Oleanna* explores the gray areas of sexual harassment allegations, examines the power of words to be heard and interpreted in very different ways, especially if the speakers and hearers reside on different levels of power.

Sexual harassment in the workplace is one thing, but stalking is the physical, violent, intrusive escalation of the sexual harassment power predation scenario. Where workplace sexual harassment is more ambiguous in its sexual flirting and game-playing guise and much harder to prove in its actual predatory acting out, stalking is a clearly expressed threat involving overt acts of physical intimidation and invasion. Early in the nineties, two films, *Sleeping With the Enemy* (1991) and *Sliver*, set the parameters for films about the newly legislated stalking laws. In *Sleeping With the Enemy* a battered wife assumes a new identity only to find herself being stalked by her ex-husband, but in *Sliver* the stalking goes high-tech as a video voyeur pursues a vulnerable, single woman in a high-rise building. Director Noyce describes *Sliver* as "sort of a 1990s version of *Rear Window*."[49] Hitchcock, with his canon of films that study the sexual power politics of men over vulnerable women, would enjoy Noyce's reference, but the creepy video stalking and the voyeuristic invasion of privacy of this nineties version goes well beyond the romanticizing fifties playfulness of his *Rear Window* (1994).

Finally, the ultimate sexual predation and the threat that hangs over all of these films of criminal sexploitation is rape, and it too surfaced in the AIDS-redirected, new permissiveness of nineties sexual spin. Mike Leigh's *Naked* (1994) opens with a rape in a filthy urban alley that is right out of the "ultraviolent" *A Clockwork Orange* (1971). The brutal violence of rape also places the final punctuation on the sexual checklist that is *Showgirls*. Bone-crunching rape shocks the audience to attention in *Cape Fear* (1991). Gang rapists tie a woman to a bed in *L.A. Confidential* and brutalize a prostitute in a vacant lot in *Naked Lunch* (1992). And homosexual rape scenes degrade the protagonists in *The Shawshank Redemption* (1994) and *Pulp Fiction* (1994). John Schlesinger's rape-revenge thriller, *An Eye for an Eye* (1996), even revives (with a gender twist) the iconic rape scenario of Charles Bronson's four *Death Wish* films of the seventies and eighties. In *An Eye for an Eye*, the horror of rape is nineties-dated as a mother, caught in a rush-hour gridlock on an LA freeway, listens on her cell phone as her teenage daughter is raped and murdered. But by far the most controversial rape film of all, *The Accused* (1988), hung over all of these predatory rape films of the nineties. Despite all the new permissiveness toward strippers, toward pornography, toward masturbation, toward hands-off, "privacy of you own home," safe sex in the sexual spin of the nineties, the violent predation of sexuality, the criminal assertion of sexual power, still persisted on the dark side of the decade's sexual landscape.

## Viagra

Yuck. He's old enough to be her . . . co-star.
—Sidebar to David Ansen's "Dial R for Remake," *Newsweek*

But with all of the sexual backtracking into isolation that the sexual spin of the decade occasioned, one group of dormant sexual adventurers found a new vitality and, as a result, a whole new film image in the nineties. That group was senior citizens, and they gained their new lease on sexual life from a little blue pill called Viagra that could do magical things. Viagra came on the market in 1998 and helped redesign the sexual landscape. Viagra gave countless older males, or males suffering from erectile dysfunction, a new lease on their sex lives. And in the films of the nineties, there were more sexually active senior citizens exercising their newfound power than even the American Association of Retired Persons (AARP) could have envisioned.

The old boys' club of Hollywood studio heads, producers, directors, and actors have for decades historically nurtured the controlling sexual fantasy that demands the casting of much younger women with older men in the romantic pairings of their films. But, in the age of Viagra, these December–May pairings became embarrassingly ubiquitous. "Coincidence? You be the judge," one Hollywood commentator observed. "Just a couple of weeks after Viagra dominates the news, two of the '70s biggest sex-symbols-turned-*auteurs*, Robert Redford and Warren Beatty, are back in the saddle."[50] And, hardly coincidentally, both of the films these *auteurs* appear in, *The Horse Whisperer* (1998) and *Bulworth* (1998), pair the aging matinee idols with much younger girlfriends. Across the whole decade, similar sexual pairings seemed to be anticipating the coming of the magic pill. All the aging stars of the seventies—Redford, Paul Newman, Harrison Ford, Beatty, and Michael Douglas—came back to life in the films of the nineties as romantic leading men newly capable of seducing decades younger women. Redford was paired with Demi Moore in *Indecent Proposal* and Kristen Scott Thomas in *The Horse Whisperer* while Newman drew the aptly named Lolita Davidavitch in *Blaze* (1989) and Melanie Griffith in *Nobody's Fool* (1994). It was as if Butch and Sundance had come back to life. Beatty as *auteur* cast himself on the screen and ultimately in real life with Annette Bening, first in *Bugsy* (1991) and *Love Affair* (1994), and then in marriage. Harrison Ford really went young at heart with Julia Ormond in *Sabrina* (1995) and Anne Heche in *Six Days, Seven Nights* (1998). Finally, the reigning champion of the nineties for December–May sexual pairings was Michael Douglas with Sharon Stone in *Basic Instinct*, with Demi Moore in *Disclosure*, with Gwyneth Paltrow in *A Perfect Murder* (1998), and with Catherine Zeta-Jones in tabloid-stalked real life.

While December–May pairings for aging male sex symbols were common in nineties films, the more interesting Viagra-inspired rejuvenation was the decades' fascination with the Lolita legend. It surfaces first in *Poison Ivy* (1992), a little film in which the former golden-tressed, Shirley Temple–look-alike child star Drew Barrymore plays the seventeen-year-old title character who seduces a whole middle class family from the father (Tom Skerritt) to the mother to the daughter. Noting the postmodernizing of the myth, one critic writes, "What makes Ivy an up-to-the-minute variation on the traditional Hollywood Hills Lolita is that she's a post-Valley Girl, post-Madonna temptress. Her nose ring, her baby-hooker outfits, her attitude of having erotic knowingness—it has all been officially sanctioned by the media."[51] In other words, this teenaged Lolita is a direct product of media-fueled sexual spin, born out of MTV to feed the fantasies of all the middle-aged Humbert Humberts caught in the sexual doldrums of their dormant suburban lives as is Lester Burnham (Kevin Spacey) in *American Beauty* (1999), the Academy Award–winning Best Picture that looks at the same longing for youth and regeneration via young flesh, but this time from the point of view of the older man. Bernardo Bertolucci of *Last Tango in Paris* (1972) fame next took the Lolita legend out for a postmodernist spin in *Stealing Beauty* (1996). He cast Liv Tyler as "a limpid Lolita with commercial credibility . . . a solid track record in turning on adolescent boys in rock videos"[52] opposite Jeremy Irons as a dying older man primed for the seductions of youth.

It was probably that role in *Stealing Beauty* that qualified Irons to play Humbert Humbert in Adrian Lyne's remake of Vladimir Nabokov's real *Lolita* (1998). In the age of Viagra, what better film to remake than the original age-corrupts-innocence fable? Few commentators saw any Viagra connection in the December–May sexual pairing of the film but rather noted its clear contemporaneity, its participation in the media-fueled–Calvin Klein ads, and its revealing teenage fashions—sexual spin of late nineties culture. This particular version of the post-AIDS, safe-sex, hands-off, "in the privacy of your own home" sexual spin of the nineties found Nabokov's fantasy of a much older man being given new sexual life through his lustful fantasies toward a childlike seductress. One critic described Adrian Lyne's nineties version of Nabokov's story as a reticent fable for a "sexually spooked America of the late '90s."[53] Another sees Nabokov's story as finally finding its audience in late nineties culture: "For many people today, the very word "Lolita" denotes not a character in a novel but a familiar female archetype . . . and images from the fashion world have given the archetype a visual form."[54] Certainly, the provocative Calvin Klein ads, the new midriff-baring fashions, and the rise of so many aspiring Lolitas in the world of pop entertainment culminating in Britney Spears justifies the reemergence of the Lolita fantasy in the nineties, but that fantasy can also be read as the reemergence of the fantasy desires of Humbert Humbert as well. If Viagra reinvigorated the sexual desires of a whole generation of senior citizens, it could only be a matter of time until the pedophilic fantasy of the Lolita story would also reemerge. As one critic noted, "We have become a culture of soft-core Humberts."[55] The Lolita fantasy of the older man wanting to grasp, possess, and feed off of the sexual energy of youth has been around for centuries, but in the late nineties with Viagra, aged men were handed a tool that could actually give the sexual fantasy the potential to become sexual reality.

Compared to the female sex goddesses of the nineties—Sharon Stone, Madonna, Demi Moore—Jeremy Irons earned his position as the poster boy for the Viagra generation with a series of older man–younger woman roles over the course of the decade. In *Reversal of Fortune* (1990), he plays the aloof adulterer, Claus Von Bulow, who puts his wife in a coma in pursuit of a fuller sexual fantasy. In *Damage* (1993), he plays an over-fifty member of Parliament who has a torrid adulterous affair with his son's disturbed girlfriend thirty years his junior. In *Stealing Beauty*, he is once again the older man in a position to deflower a ripe, young virgin. When *Lolita* hit theaters, Benjamin Svetkey aligned both director Adrian Lyne and actor Irons with the ruling cultural fantasies of the Viagra generation. He wrote that "Lyne's new movie contains moments so borderline pervy they'd make Calvin Klein queasy" and "Lyne chose an actor with vast experience playing dirty old men."[56]

But if Irons was the decade's model for the older man finding sudden sexual invigoration in the lustful fantasy for younger women, then Jack Lemmon, Walter Matthau, and Burgess Meredith were the Viagra generation's version of the Three Stooges. And Jack Nicholson's heart attack in *Something's Gotta Give* (2003) is the punch line to the ultimate Viagra joke.

In the *Grumpy Old Men* (1993, 1995) franchise, Lemmon, Matthau, and Meredith display the hilarious, crude, and sometimes touching results of geriatric sexual reawakening plus they get to make leering passes at the likes of perpetually young Sophia Loren and Ann Margaret. It was as if the *Grumpy Old Men* movies were the decade's preparation for the Viagra revolution. They portrayed men in their seventies sexually frolicking like teenagers, displaying geriatric lustful desire, and expressing their horniness in the crudest possible terms. The audience for *Grumpy Old Men* was the only audience of the decade who never left their seats during the closing credits (thanks to Meredith's graphic and hilarious spewing of a series of filthy euphemisms for sexual intercourse).

From the evolution of strip joints into gentlemen's clubs, of strippers into dancers, of housewives into whores, of pornography into a home-video product for everyone to enjoy, of masturbation into an accepted form of safe sex, to Viagra giving a new lease on sexual life to a neglected generation, the sexual spin of the nineties found myriad creative ways to face the greatest threat to human sexuality to ever surface, AIDS. That terrible disease changed the lives of everyone in the late eighties and nineties, but sexual spin found ways to get around the barriers to sexuality that it raised. The sexual spin of the nineties didn't break down those barriers, didn't attack them head on. Instead, sexual spin found ways to redefine old sexual habits, to creatively simulate sexuality where it was no longer possible to indulge in its pleasures firsthand. The AIDS threat to human sexuality presented a powerful challenge to the resources of spin, and, over the nineties decade, those resources proved equal to that challenge.

# CHAPTER 8

# Neo-spin

[Walter Benjamin] approached the world as a collector, seeking to fathom the meaning of history by assembling its objects.
—Russell Jacoby, "The Collector," *Los Angeles Times*

The Clinton presidency, gay redefinition, and AIDS-driven sexual realignment were specifically nineties issues that enlisted the powers of spin to change the way that people view their contemporary reality (or simulacra). But these nineties issues are but three of the more sensational success stories of the decade of spin. Other issues also benefited from the prevailing force of spin in their representation and cultural navigation through the treacherous channels of nineties public opinion. Other issues (such as feminism and race) that are not nineties-specific also came under the powerful influence of spin. Each of these issues developed their own nineties-specific neo-spin strategy for reconstructing their cultural identities. In every case the movies played a prominent role in the evolving of spin strategies and the creation of simulacra to facilitate the representation of these cultural, historical, and social issues.

## Women

As if relations between men and women weren't baffling enough in the 1990's, Madison Avenue is developing a new strain of reverse-sexism advertising.
—Benjamin Svetkey, "Here's the Beef," *Entertainment Weekly*

Perhaps the two most extreme representations of the situation of women in prenineties society came in the much-seen film *Thelma and Louise* (1991) and the little-seen *Boxing Helena* (1993). In the former, the two title heroines, in the best tradition of Jack Kerouac and Neil Cassidy or Butch Cassidy and the Sundance Kid, plotted their journey of feminist identity all across the American cultural map. In the latter, the title character is a woman who allows a man to amputate all of her limbs and put her in a box. In the former, feminist empowerment careens out of control and ultimately over a cliff, while in the latter the patriarchal amputation of female identity runs wild in metaphor. Like the nineties advertising trend that has women turning men (or "hunks") into sexual objects, the central feminist spin strategy of the nineties is one of gender and role reversal as a critique of past female roles. Neither Thelma and Louise nor the disembodied Helena survived their metaphoric journeys. They did, however, define the parameters of nineties female identity as issues of both empowerment and submission. The empowerment that Thelma and Louise first longed for, then gained, and finally suicidally affirmed became the central goal of the strategies of representation that swirled around women's issues in the nineties. The total dehumanization that Helena submits to represents all the patriarchal issues of the past that nineties feminism rejects.

The gender-reversing empowerment of women found a strong and consistent voice in the films of the nineties decade, often in unexpected venues. For example, both western movies and Disney animation features took a militantly feminist spin. In both *Bad Girls* (1994) and *The Quick and the Dead* (1994), women strap on guns (akin to *Thelma and Louise*) and go up against the male gunslingers who have traditionally dominated this genre. Similarly, Belle in *Beauty and the Beast* (1991) is the first full-fledged Disney feminist heroine but not the last (of the nineties). Belle's aloof intellectual feminist identity paves the way for Disney's representation of *Pocahontas* (1995) as diplomatic historical heroine and Esmeralda of *The Hunchback of Notre Dame* (1997) as marginalized rebel. One commentator tracks this nineties Disney trend: "After Disney's feminist cartoon heroines, it's refreshing to meet [Esmeralda] the first postfeminist one."[1] But Disney pushed the feminist envelope even further in *Mulan* (1998) whose Chinese heroine first puts on men's clothes in order to take her father's place in the army and then distinguishes herself as a warrior. But these were not the only unusual movie venues in the nineties in which women went seeking empowerment and jumped gender.

*Mulan* was not the nineties' first woman warrior. Ellen Ripley (of the *Alien* series) serves as the imprimatur for a succession of physical warrior heroines. While the central metaphor of *Alien Resurrection* (1997) is the cloning of Ripley (Sigourney Weaver) from a DNA strand, a whole succession of warrior Ripleys were cloned in action films across the decade. The usual playgrounds of the superstar action heroes like Sylvester Stallone, Arnold Schwarzenegger, Steven Seagal, and Chuck Norris were usurped by buffed-up physical heroines who could fire off a gun or a martial kick with the best of the men. Meryl Streep takes on Montana whitewater and murderous men in *The River Wild* (1994) in the best tradition of Burt Reynolds in *Deliverance* (1972) or Sam Neill in *Dead Calm* (1989). "Bodybuilders may do it just to see if they can, to take it to that limit, and that's what I wanted to do on this film," Streep inadvertently compares herself to Stallone and Schwarzenegger. "I wanted to tax myself in that way, see how strong I could get."[2] Demi Moore copped the same attitude in *G.I. Jane* (1997) going even further physically by shaving her head and making her bodybuilding regimen an essential part of the film. Her Jordan O'Neill in *G.I. Jane* is the first woman ever to train with the Navy SEALS. The film is an "inspirational basic-training epic that glorifies the new power women . . . a no-pain-no-gain feminist machismo . . . film [that] says that if men and women are to be truly equal, they must embrace the outer limits of physical will in the exact same way."[3] No wonder one commentator characterized these macho superheroines as Hollywood's "women who run with the wolves."[4]

Feminist empowerment in nineties films invaded other traditionally male areas as well. Geena Davis post–*Thelma and Louise* was successively a baseball player in *A League of Their Own* (1992), a pirate queen in *Cutthroat Island* (1993), and a secret agent in *The Long Kiss Goodnight* (1996). Sandra Bullock of necessity became a kick-ass bus driver in *Speed* (1994) and a computer jock in *The Net* (1995). Michelle Pfeiffer not only played the supervillain Catwoman in *Batman Returns* (1992) but also a tough ex-Marine turned inner-city teacher—a la *Blackboard Jungle* (1955) and *To Sir With Love* (1967)—in *Dangerous Minds* (1995). Linda Hamilton and Bridget Fonda both buffed up for their Ripley-like roles in *Terminator 2* (1991) and *Point of No Return* (1993). Jodie Foster emulates the real female astronauts in *Contact* (1997). Frances McDormand plays a pregnant sheriff in *Fargo* (1996). *Meg Ryan* plays a Medal of Honor war hero in *Courage Under Fire* (1996). By the end of the decade, even as patriarchal and entrenched a franchise as the James Bond films was won over by postmodernist feminist empowerment. In *The World Is Not Enough* (2000), the daughter of a murdered industrialist takes over the building of a pipeline, and in *Die Another Day* (2002), Jinx (Halle Berry), an American CIA agent, proves a superspy match for even James Bond himself (and actually survives the film). Michael Nathanson of Columbia Pictures tries to downplay this female empowerment trend of the nineties—"Movies with women in heroic active roles won't necessarily take the place of male action movies. They'll simply add to the mix."[5]—but, nonetheless, there was no denying that the nineties was the decade that the women invaded the male action genre. One critic called it "feminist firepower,"[6] but Moore, talking about her role in *G.I. Jane*, focuses in on the empowerment theme: "It's an interesting role because it questions what is the role of a woman in the military and what are those boundaries. At this point, combat is one of the areas where women are not allowed, and that interested me a lot."[7] Or, more simply, as Penny Marshall, the director of *A League of Their Own*, put it: "After all, these women they were playing did it for real."[8] The new feminist empowerment of the nineties definitely involved the appropriation and usurpation of what had previously been male realms.

But women did not necessarily have to be isolated, loner superheroines like Ellen Ripley or G.I. Jane or Anne Bonny the pirate queen or Maggie the CIA assassin in *Point of No Return*. Another basic feminist empowerment venue of nineties film was the women's ensemble film: "There's enough female bonding on screen these days to resurrect Thelma and Louise. In fact, the fictional feminine outlaws would likely be moved to tears to see so many movies starring powerful female ensemble casts,"[9] *Entertainment Weekly* observed in 1995. It all began with films like *Mystic Pizza* (1988), *Steel Magnolias* (1989), and *Gas Food Lodging* (1992), but at mid-decade two films, *The First Wives Club* (1995) and *Waiting to Exhale* (1995), made such a huge splash that the women's ensemble film was given new definition. Going well beyond the "weepy" labels of earlier film history and the nineties "chick flick" label, these two films proselytized an empowerment in numbers, an all-for-one/one-for-all sisterhood formed for one reason—to deal with dishonest or unreliable men. In the case of *The First Wives Club*, the premise is actually a metaphor for the way the male-dominated film industry treats leading ladies over forty, passes them over for younger talent. *Waiting to Exhale*'s cachet is also metaphorical since it is the first time that a black women's ensemble film has been given the attention and exposure of the *Steel Magnolias* sort. These films' impact was greatly expanded in other women's ensemble undertakings. *Boys on the Side* (1995) inserts AIDS into the women's empowerment grid, and *Set It Off* (1996) brings an ensemble of black women together, not to deal with men, but to rob a bank. *How to Make An American Quilt* (1995) and *Little Women* (1994) are equally feminist nineties adaptations of familiar material. "It's certainly a feminist story," director Gillian Armstrong says of her new nineties version of *Little Women*, the fourth adaptation of Louisa May Alcott's 1868 novel.[10] *Fargo* actress Frances McDormand argues, "There are a lot more women in positions of power, in writing, directing and studios. Look at Jane Campion, Gillian Armstrong, and Allison Anders. They're changing the stories that are being told."[11]

Not all of the women's films of the nineties, however, followed the female empowerment paradigm. The nineties term "chick flick" embodied the *Boxing Helena* mentality of film representations of women going all the way back to D. W. Griffith's "rape and rescue" one-reelers. One definition of a "chick flick" is a film that no man would ever go see without being dragged there by a woman. But chick flicks can be more complex and insidious than that. They are often openly patriarchal in portraying women as still dependent upon men for their identities and happiness and place in the world. They often affirm heterosexual marriage as the ultimate goal for women when, in fact, it may be the most restrictive box. In this *Boxing Helena* metaphor, the persona of the nineties decade's most successful actress, Julia Roberts of *Pretty Woman*, *Sleeping with the Enemy* (1991), *My Best Friend's Wedding* (1997), and *Runaway Bride* (2000), becomes an anti-feminist model. The Roberts persona is all object, always caught in the power of the men in her world. In a completely different way, Sister Helen Prejean (Susan Sarandon) in *Dead Man Walking* (1996) is closed into a similar box. If Roberts's characters are the ultimate sexual objects of the nineties, then Sarandon's loving and compassionate nun may be the ultimate spiritual object of the decade. The problem is that in both cases the female character's identity is solely defined by her dedication and self-submission to the men who control her. What the physical feminist action heroines and the ensemble societies of sisters of nineties film are focused upon is fighting or working or thinking their way out of the boxes of chick flick objectification that have historically been the representation of women by the Hollywood patriarchy. Feminism has a history of consistently reinventing itself. In the sixties, feminism found radical definition. In the seventies, feminism focused on economic equality. In the eighties, feminism confronted domestic issues. But in the nineties, feminism was all about empowerment, and the movies provided the images and the metaphors for that female empowerment.

## Race

> One of the contemporary myths that Hollywood loves to sell is the rosy notion that blacks and whites can get along if they just drop their respective cultural luggage and accept each other as *people*.
> —Ty Burr, "Race Relations," *Entertainment Weekly*

The racial spin strategy of the nineties is much more complex than the feminist spin strategy simply because, at least in America, true diversity actually became a reality in the last decade of the millennium. In the nineties, California became the first state in which people of color outnumbered whites in the census figures. Racial issues weren't just concerned with African Americans anymore. Now Hispanics and Asians were very much a part of the racial (and racist) mix. Nineties film spun different images and focused upon different issues concerning each of these three racial groups (and their relation to whites in American culture).

The nineties vision of black/white race relations followed the most complex spin strategy. Focused on a very specific set of issues (black/white relationships, hip-hop gangsta culture, political history), the nineties saw one prominent spin-master, Spike Lee, rise above all the others in the elaboration of his vision of American racial culture. In *Jungle Fever* (1991) Lee touched off a nineties racial consciousness of black/white sexual relationships that would become a fascination in nineties film (and thus culture). Some of the most popular and surprisingly uncontroversial films of the decade involved salt and pepper love relationships or black/white work relationships that develop into something resembling true friendship. From *Jungle Fever* to *Love Field* (1992) to *Mississippi Masala* (1992) to *The Bodyguard* (1992) to *Made in America* (1993) to *The Crying Game* (1993) to *One Night Stand* (1997), interracial sexuality was represented in a surprising way, as secondary to romance and love and lust, as really no big deal.

Analyzing *The Bodyguard*, Meredith Berkman notes that "the interracial romance between Costner and Houston might have been expected to offend some people but it never became an issue. . . . Had the movie been made in the '70s, the interracial romance would probably have dominated discussion of it."[12] The film's star, Whitney Houston, made the same point: "I don't think it's a milestone that a black person and a white person made a movie together. I think for people to look at this color-blind is a milestone."[13] But sexual relationships weren't the only black/white pairings that Hollywood committed to in the nineties. The buddy movie, one of Hollywood's most dependable mainstays, also found black/white redefinition. From *Driving Miss Daisy* (1989) to the *Lethal Weapon* (1987, 1989, 1992) and *Beverly Hills Cop* (1984, 1987, 1994) franchises to *Money Train* (1995) and *White Men Can't Jump* (1992) to *Nothing to Lose* (1997), interracial partnerships became the rule rather than the exception. Whether this acceptance as represented onscreen would carry over to real-life acceptance of similar inter-racial relationships was surely questionable, but under the influence of nineties spin, it was certainly a possibility that had not existed in earlier decades.

The second major focus of nineties African American racial spin was the necessity of legitimizing hip-hop culture despite its negative gangsta connections. Hip-hop culture sorely needed positive racial spin if for no other reason than in the early nineties it quickly crossed over and was assimilated into white youth culture. In fact, the almost instant appropriation of black hip-hop by white teen-agers was almost unprecedented. Even the embrace of black rhythm-and-blues based rock and roll in the fifties didn't happen this quickly. In this case, it was the music, the street poetry, that fueled the hip-hop culture, but it was the mov-ies that allowed the black and white hip-hop nation to see the voices of rap—Ice Cube, Ice-T, Tupac—in stories from the streets that matched their poetry.

Dennis Hopper's *Colors* (1988) was the first real exploration of the gang cul-ture that would spawn hip-hop, but that film approached its subject from the perspective of two white street cops. And though Ice-T and Ice Cube were the marquee stars of *Trespass* (1993), they still had to share the film with two white firemen (Bill Paxton and William Sadler) looking for the hidden gold in the war zone of a huge abandoned factory. John Singleton's films, *Boyz N the Hood* (1991) and *Poetic Justice* (1993), however, changed all that. While *Boyz N the Hood* and the Hughes brothers' *Menace II Society* (1993) put a hard edge on the gangsta world, Singleton's *Poetic Justice* picks up from the tentatively hope-ful ending of *Boyz N the Hood* and presents a hip-hop film that moves from the violence of South Central to the open air outside the mean streets of the urban battlegrounds.

The strong impact of the spin that these hip-hop films put upon gangsta cul-ture was a result of their timing. Coming in the wake of the Los Angeles riots and in the midst of the very real gangsta rap wars, these films adopted a spin strategy that argued for love, survival, brotherhood, and even poetry and creativity in the midst of sudden, brutal, and often random, urban violence. While these films put a human face on hip-hop culture, they always had to contend with the real gangsta world that they tried to mediate. In the midst of the success of *Poetic Justice*, Tupac was shot five times in Times Square, convicted of sexual abuse, and then assassinated in what was probably a turf war between two rap record companies. One Polygram record company executive expressed the lure of the hip-hop culture: "The whole prison-poet thing is very cool to kids. These rappers are deified."[14] The representation of the hip-hop spin strategy continued across the decade in films like *Jason's Lyric* (1994) and *Fresh* (1995) that focused upon the survival of human relationships despite the surrounding urban violence, but Singleton's next film, *Higher Learning* (1995), took hip-hop into a new reality, academia, and returned to the harder edge and moral outrage of the earlier hip-hop films, *Boyz N the Hood* and *Menace II Society*. Malik (Omar Epps), a black track star on a white racist college campus, must search for ways to survive exis-tentially, emotionally, intellectually, and physically in a world where the violence, if more subtle, is equally devastating and ultimately erupts into the same free-fire zone violence that occurs regularly in South Central. In *Higher Learning* the edgy spin strategy of humanity fighting for survival in the midst of urban violence careens out of control at the end when simple violence overrules all of the film's messages. Students at UCLA where *Higher Learning* was filmed "disagree about how inevitable [racial] conflict is. But even those who find *Higher Learning* unbearably heavy-handed agree that Singleton, in the politics of diversity, has found a subject that students are anxious to debate, and whose ramifications reach beyond campuses."[15] Heavy-handed as it may sometimes be, that is exactly how spin is supposed to work.

A third focus of nineties African American racial spin is black history. But more importantly, and long overdue, it is black directors and black writers making films about black history. Lee's *Malcolm X* (1992) is the most important work of black history (in any medium) of the nineties decade. One critic, echoing ironically a 1920s description of the racist Griffith's *The Birth of a Nation* (1915), wrote that "Lee has written history with lightning"[16] and that *Malcolm X* is "the kind of history lesson white Americans shouldn't need but often do—the kind Lee loves to give."[17] Another critic noted the spin that Lee gave to his historical biopic as "a visible manifestation of the pop-culture wheel's inexorable turning . . . in a world of Public Enemy and Rodney King, the image of his [Malcolm X's] articulate impatience hits hard and naturally."[18] The most savvy of directors, Lee constantly stressed the historical accuracy of his film, relentlessly contrasted it to Oliver Stone's *JFK* in terms of its "historical rigor,"[19] and always emphasized its faithfulness to *The Autobiography of Malcolm X* upon which the script is based. The story goes, though Lee denies it, that he said black children should skip school to go see the film. While clearly building the film's credibility upon its historical significance, nonetheless in the best spirit of nineties spin, Lee created a very deconstructive representation of its title subject. There are a number of different Malcolms in Lee's film, and the ultimate Malcolm who emerges is a complex being who has literally spun himself, like Jay Gatsby perhaps, out of all the experience of his varied and colorful past. Lee's Malcolm (Denzel Washington) is a zoot-suiter, a violent criminal, a prison intellectual, a spiritual pilgrim, a cunning politician, and, ultimately (like Martin Luther King and JFK), a martyred leader of his race. There are many Malcolms, and Lee carefully set out to capture them all and place them all in dialogues with one another. In *Malcolm X*, Lee made the first film epic of black history.

Other films portraying black history were made in the nineties, but none approached the epic scope or historical significance of *Malcolm X*. Nonetheless, after *Malcolm X* (in which Lee used the press to force white director Norman Jewison off the film so that he could direct it), the films made about black historical material were directed by black directors. Lee's take-no-prisoners approach to *Malcolm X* made that a necessity. Singleton directed *Rosewood* (1997) about a racist massacre of a black settlement in the south by white neighbors, and Morgan Freeman directed *Bopha* (1994) about *apartheid* South Africa. Both focused their films on the perspectives of black characters only, which set them apart from the majority of films about black history by white directors.

Across the decade, the single most consistent articulator and spinmaster of the black experience was Lee. From *She's Gotta Have It* (1986) and *Do the Right Thing* (1989) to *Mo' Better Blues* (1990) to *Malcolm X* to *Crooklyn* (1994) to *Clockers* (1995) to *Get On the Bus* (1996) to *He Got Game* (1998), Lee's films immersed themselves in the nineties black urban experience as no other cultural voice did. Anthony Walton, in an essay titled "Heretofore Unseen," credits Lee with providing the impetus for "the New African-American cinema." He writes of *She's Gotta Have It*: "It was the first time I, or anyone else, saw in that most American of art forms, the movies, black characters who resembled black people as we saw ourselves or as we saw the people we knew and loved. This made it revolutionary."[20] *Do the Right Thing* cemented Lee's leadership position as the African American spinmaster of his time. His anatomy of one Bedford-Stuyvesant neighborhood on the hottest day of the year succeeds in capturing all the racial and generational issues that exist beneath the surface of every urban neighborhood and can be brought to the surface by the slightest catalytic event. Lee's message in what is arguably his finest film is that race is by far the most important issue in nineties culture, that race is a time bomb sitting in the midst of America's urban landscape that can be set off by the slightest spark. The Rodney King affair in Los Angeles certainly underlined the accuracy of Lee's racial message in *Do the Right Thing*.

Lee's films that followed in the nineties explored issues of African American culture with a relentless black consciousness. After his multiple-identity take on *Malcolm X*, Lee set out to make what he characterized as an "overtly nonpolitical"[21] movie in *Crooklyn*, a family story set in a Brooklyn neighborhood in the seventies much different from the Bed-Stuy neighborhood of the nineties in *Do the Right Thing*. Lee makes one telling comment about *Crooklyn* that sets it apart from all of his other nineties films and cuts to the heart of the hip-hop cultural tragedy of the nineties as represented in his film *Clockers* as well as in *Boyz N the Hood* and *Menace II Society*. *Crooklyn* depicts a time in the African American past when "we were able to have childhoods"[22] far removed from the urban violence and drug culture of the nineties. *Clockers*, set in a totally different world, followed. It takes Lee back to oppositions that were so strong in both *Do the Right Thing* and *Malcolm X*. One critic writes perceptively that *Clockers* is "a film about confusion, about a clouded murder mystery that won't clear. . . . Spike Lee wants '*Clockers*' to argue with itself, and all credit to him."[23] Lee is well aware of how meaning moves according to your perception of it or the context that one brings to it. Doing the right thing in the nineties is no longer referential to the old moralities of the past because the centers no longer hold. Of all of Lee's films (including *Do the Right Thing*), *Clockers* is his most realistic representation of life in the nineties urban nightmare, and his most deconstructive. The violence at the end of *Do the Right Thing* is almost understandable when compared to the total chaos of life in the projects of *Clockers*. Violence, drugs, gangs, white racism, murder, and family breakdown are all commonplace, accepted, in the world of *Clockers*. Teenagers are selling drugs, and cops are gleefully racist. *Clockers* is Lee's most nineties film, his take on the realities of life in a totally decentered society. The issue du jour of *He Got Game* (1998) is much less sweeping or riveting than the vision of *Clockers*. While *Clockers* and *Do the Right Thing* set out to explore the complex fragility of the urban world, *He Got Game* is little more than an unrealistic satire of the con game of college sports. Tell me, would the governor of New York really furlough a convicted murderer from prison in order to recruit a high school basketball player? It is no coincidence that *He Got Game* is a Disney movie. The real film (actually a documentary) about college sports in the nineties is *Hoop Dreams* (1994). Nonetheless, the one steady and relentlessly thoughtful African American voice of the nineties was Lee.

While Lee was the nineties version of a long tradition of African American spinmasters running from Martin Luther King and Malcolm X through Elijah Muhammad, Jesse Jackson, and Muhammad Ali, Hispanic culture in American society in the nineties was looking for a voice and trying to define the issues of its immigrant culture that needed to be spun. Before the forces of spin can go into operation for any personal agenda or set of group issues, that agenda or those issues need to be defined. In the nineties, Hispanic culture was looking at the issues of its American presence for the first time.

The most important issue, a traditional one for any immigrant group in American society, is, of course, assimilation. As one critic described the situation, Hispanic immigrants to America are "people whose homelands are tantalizingly near yet psychically far, whose adopted country both beckons them in and shuts them out."[24] Early nineties films like *Stand and Deliver* (1988) and *American Me* (1992) were both spun into existence by one of the most prominent Hispanic voices in nineties American film culture, director-actor Edward James Olmos, who portrays this Hispanic assimilation experience both positively and negatively. *Stand and Deliver*, while portraying the education issue for Hispanic children in American schools with hope and possibility, also clearly acknowledges the battle for assimilation. *American Me*, on the other hand, is a gangster film akin to *Scarface* (1983) yet much more aware of the possibility that assimilation into American life could actually change a person, could modify a Hispanic temper into a Hispanic American temperament. *American Me* follows the life of real LA gangster Santana Montoya (played by Olmos) growing up, going to prison, and selling drugs. Yet, unlike Al Pacino's brutal Tony Montana in *Scarface*, Olmos's Montoya tries to change, tries to mediate his life to the country that has both rejected him and given him unequalled opportunity. That is the ambiguity that plagues those who would try to spin the Hispanic American experience. America represents great potential for a better life for Hispanics, yet its social prejudice consistently shuts them out and makes the attainment of the potential a dehumanizing battle.

If Olmos proves too tentative a spinmaster in terms of the assimilation experience, then Pacino's Hispanic characters, Tony Montana and Carlito Brigante, serve as a measurement of how the assimilation experience has been mediated over time from the eighties to the nineties. Carlito is a very different Hispanic American than Tony. Carlito is trying to get out of the drug business. Carlito is, like Santana in *American Me*, a character who realizes that assimilation means change. New York Supreme Court justice Edwin Torres, the novelist creator of Carlito, has watched the problems of assimilation in his courtroom for over thirty-five years and realizes that the numbers are not in positive assimilation's favor: "Two guys are from the same place, one goes good, the other goes to the electric chair. Except with me, it was about 50 other guys."²⁵ What these early nineties films about Hispanic gangsters realize is that the assimilation experience can't be done the easy way, the violent way, the criminal way. Carlito realizes what way he needs to take, as does Santana, but their past histories won't allow them to take that way. So, in the early nineties, a spin strategy for Hispanic Americans was still very much in the formative stages. But all Hispanics in America are not gangsters, and other Hispanic voices realized that Hispanic Americans needed to be portrayed more realistically and less sensationally or melodramatically.

"*Mi Vida Loca* tells a different kind of LA story" reads the subheadline of an article titled "Living on Barrio Time."²⁶ By the mid-nineties Hispanic spin voices began explaining other aspects of the assimilation experience. *Mi Vida Loca* is a Hispanic youth movie presented from an American feminist perspective, but *My Family* (1995) is the first film since Gregory Nava's fine *El Norte* (1983) about Hispanics in America made completely by Hispanic Americans. There is one obvious reason why films like these found a voice by the mid-nineties, and that reason is economic. By 1995 there were 26.5 million Hispanics in America, and a Hollywood survey revealed that Hispanics bought as many movie tickets as African Americans (12 percent of the national total).²⁷ In Hollywoodese, Hispanics had finally become a player, a voice to be listened to, and those with the power to spin Hispanic issues finally had their chance. *My Family* is the one nineties film that puts the most realistic, truthful, and positive spin on the Hispanic assimilation experience. Jimmy Smits, one of the impressive list of Hispanic actors (Olmos, Elpidia Carillo, Esai Morales) who helped director Nava make the film as a low-budgeted labor of love, tells about drawing a crowd of well-wishers in San Antonio who repeatedly told him that "*My Family* says so much about my life!" Smits goes on to assess the spin impact of *My Family*: "I know this film alone is not going to do it, but I hope that industry people will now see there is a large market for movies that both are true to the Latino experience and use Latino actors. . . . After all, *My Family* is just the tip of the iceberg of Latino stories that we have to tell."²⁸

Unfortunately, as the decade continued, English-language Hispanic blockbusters did not become a trend while Spanish-language films found a very healthy niche market and Spanish-language TV thrived, especially in southern California, Arizona, and West Texas. The only really major Hispanic American mainstream production with crossover power after *My Family* was the tragic biopic of Hispanic American pop star *Selena* (1997) that catapulted Jennifer Lopez to stardom.

Selena Perez, the crossover singing sensation assassinated at age twenty-three, and Jennifer Lopez, who plays her in the film, are both potent images of the possibilities for assimilation in the burgeoning world of Hispanic American economics of the nineties. But by the end of the decade, the jury was still out on the effects of positive spin upon the Hispanic American experience. However, by the turn of the twenty-first century, politicians in certain parts of the country were speaking Spanish and counting the Hispanic vote, educational opportunities for Hispanics had expanded considerably, and working conditions free of INS fear had considerably improved. The assimilation process for Hispanic Americans was well underway, and the spin that movies had presented had somewhat helped.

In the nineties, the issue of cultural assimilation was not nearly as difficult for Asian Americans as it had been for Hispanic Americans because the Asian American vehicles of spin had been in operation longer. Early in the decade in films like *Rising Sun* (1993), American directors were still portraying Asians in the same way that post–World War II films of the forties and fifties and the post–Vietnam War films had represented them as cannon fodder or as inscrutable gangster organizations. But Stone in *Heaven and Earth* (1993) at least made an honest attempt to represent the Asian view of the Vietnam War years, the post-Vietnam situation, and the American assimilation experience. One critic described it as "the first major American movie to examine the Vietnam War from a Vietnamese perspective."[29] *Heaven and Earth* takes the point of view of a young, Vietnamese peasant woman, Le Ly Hayslip (Hiep Thi Le) whose true story covers the whole range of experiences of the Vietnam War and its aftermath. Hayslip wrote two books about her experiences[30] in the war and then in the assimilation process in southern California after the war. *Heaven and Earth* has been described as "Stone's epic simulation,"[31] yet it is very different from Stone's other films about the war and its aftermath, *Platoon* (1986) and *Born on the Fourth of July* (1989). Stone clearly set out in this film to show what he didn't show in *Platoon* (a Vietnamese perspective on the war) and in *Born on the Fourth of July* (a Vietnamese woman's perspective on postwar assimilation). No one will argue that he doesn't make an honest attempt in *Heaven and Earth*. Stone knows this material, and his track record is an ongoing search for the truth and the true representation of it. But still, like so many films of the eighties and early nineties,[32] Stone is an American filmmaker portraying the Asian and the Asian American experience.

*The Joy Luck Club* (1993) changed all of that. As the African American film community all through the nineties led by Lee and Singleton did, and as the Hispanic American film community late in the nineties with *Mi Vida Loca* and *My Family* did, so also did the Asian American film community come together to make *The Joy Luck Club*. And the spin theme of *The Joy Luck Club* is the same theme that is given such strong attention in the Hispanic American films, assimilation (its joys and perils). This collaboration between producer Janet Yang, novelist Amy Tan, and director Wayne Wang gave *The Joy Luck Club* an Asian American credibility that no other previous mainstream film could boast. Its distribution by Disney gave it a crossover potential that no other Asian American film had experienced. What was so attractive about Tan's novel was exactly its combination of the Asian and the American in portraying the assimilation experience. Tan's novel paired the experiences of Asian mothers with those of their American-born daughters in the attempt to bridge both the generational and the familial divides. Actress Rosalind Chao best describes how *The Joy Luck Club* is about "assimilating. Somebody couldn't ask me, 'Well, are you more Chinese or more American?' It's like saying 'Which arm do you want—your left arm or your right arm?' I think I would like to have both!"[33] That is a physiological metaphor for the deconstructive consciousness of *The Joy Luck Club*. The Asian American team that made *The Joy Luck Club* realized that the assimilation experience, with its constant clash between the old world and the new world, the past and the present, parents and children, is always deconstructive.

One other genre of Asian American film, the martial arts action film, faced no struggle with gaining acceptance in American culture in the nineties. Known as the Hong Kong "chop-sockees" in Hollywoodese, these crime films with their balletic choreographed violence had been popular with American audiences since the Bruce Lee films of the seventies. Run Run Lee, the Hong Kong godfather of the martial arts genre, had carved out such a significant niche in the American film market over three decades leading up to the nineties that Asian American martial arts films were not only a commonplace in American theaters but were being nominated for Academy Awards while their actors and directors were becoming crossover stars. One month Hong Kong's Chow Yun Fat would be starring in a violent martial arts epic, and the next starring in a new version of *The King and I* (2001) with Jodie Foster. One month director John Woo might be directing Jackie Chan in *Rumble in the Bronx* (1996), and the next an all-American cast in *Broken Arrow* (1999) or *Face Off* (2000), both with John Travolta. When Asian American art manages to coincide comfortably with American culture as the Hong Kong action genre films clearly did, then assimilation can be easily accomplished. The chop-sockee vision of Asian culture superimposed itself so neatly over the urban violence vision of American culture that audiences saw little difference between the two, barely noticed any racial difference between the two, and barely noticed any racial difference between Jackie Chan and Chuck Norris, between Chow Yun Fat and Steven Seagal. The two cultures converged in the subject matter and the arresting visual style. It didn't seem to matter whether it was an Asian or an American hero of these crime films as long as they could kick high, chop straight, and keep the action spinning.

# CONCLUSION

# Spinning into the Millennium

Movies do not come out of the thin air. They have a history, just as we and our society do, and the histories of film, our culture, and ourselves are intimately intertwined.

—Robert Kolker, *Film, Form and Culture*

Across the nineties decade, spin and the different spin strategies that evolved out of the particular political and cultural issues, the intellectual history and the social history, became as common and necessary as the gravitational forces that keep the planets spinning through the universe. Spin could be the servant or the bodyguard of power (as it certainly was for the Clinton presidency) or it could be a force for changing minds, for negotiating prejudice into acceptance (as it was for the gay community), or it could be the catalyst for a seismic shift in human behavior (as it was for the redefinition of sexuality under the threat of AIDS). But above all, in the decade of popular deconstruction, spin was the elemental configuration of reality.

Christopher Sharrett writes about the illusion "that American popular art is usually reverential toward the truth of historical events . . . the truth usually supported by Hollywood is one comforting to specific concepts of race, gender and class interest."[1] In other words, Hollywood movies have always participated in the spinning of cultural and social history. But Sharrett then goes on to state a curious thing: "Such renditions of American history did no disservice to our collective sense of the Real."[2] What Hollywood (especially in the nineties) understood was "how films make stories and how those stories fit into our culture."[3]

Spin (in the nineties) became the elemental force that influenced our postmodernist conception of reality. Spin actually became our way of life, our culture. Again, Robert Kolker writes,

Culture doesn't mean "high-toned" or refer to works of high art that are supposed to be good for us. Rather, culture is the complex totality of our daily lives and acts. Culture is the form and content of our subjective selves and our communal lives, our social and economic class, our entertainments, our politics and economics. Culture is the way we act out ideology. Ideology is the way we agree to see ourselves, to behave, and to create the values of our lives. . . . Culture is made up of expressions and intersections, representations, images, sounds, and stories. . . . Culture is the sum total of the intricate ways we relate to ourselves, our peers, our community, to our country, world, and universe.[4]

In the nineties decade, culture is spin. Spin is the one option for finding a new kind of order in a decentered world. When a president is flawed, when a marginalized group is demonized, when a terrible disease threatens the very basis of life, spin offers a solution and becomes a strategy for survival. Spin is not just a technique of diversion, a smoke screen or a con game. Spin is a reconfiguration of reality that can generate a positive change out of the most negative situation.

The nineties needed spin. With the threat of AIDS hanging over everyone's heads, with social prejudice (especially against gays) spreading insidiously, and with the Clinton presidency as fragile as Humpty Dumpty, the nineties needed spin to reconfigure its reality, to give its society hope, to restore the kind of confidence that would drive the stock market to its all-time high and fulfill the nation's moral potential both at home and abroad. For the nineties, spin turned out to be a very positive thing that helped culture navigate some very treacherous waters.

The other nineties discourse that spin helped to positively navigate was the relationship between history and the media. By the end of the nineties decade, spin had renegotiated the cultural apocalypse, "the dumbing down of public discourse through the influence of the media" that Neil Postman had prophesied in the mid-eighties.[5] By the end of the nineties, the media of culture, especially the movies, had so refined their spin strategies that their cultural and historical representations were able to "transform discourse into a medium of power."[6] Never was this negotiation between history and film so sexy as in January of the new millennium.

In the first month of 2000, history, Hollywood, and spin converged with a vengeance. All of the negative critics concerning the Hollywood version of history that had surfaced in the media discourse surrounding films like *Mississippi Burning* (1988), *The People vs. Larry Flynt* (1996), *A Civil Action* (1998), *Boys Don't Cry* (1999), *Amistad* (1998), and *The Insider* (1999) swirled up once again in "the ugly media battle over the movie's veracity"[7] that surrounded *The Hurricane* (1999). Armyan Bernstein, producer of *The Hurricane*, complained, "If this controversy taints our film then we'll have to rethink *Ghandi*, *Lawrence of Arabia*, *Silkwood*, *All the President's Men* and a lot of great movies. It's like someone has suddenly raised the bar on how a drama is supposed to deal with the truth."[8] Ironically, Bernstein's comment captures the acceptance that spin had garnered over the course of the nineties decade. What the historical accuracy debates of the late nineties exposed was the basic disagreement between traditional historicism (with its illusion of objectivity and realism) versus the New Historicism (with its cultural consciousness). After any historical event has occurred, the reality of the event immediately begins to evaporate into the simulacra of that event. Spin can enter the equation in both types of historical simulacra. As Hayden White, among others, has argued,[9] political, cultural, and sociological spin can be emplotted equally in traditional reconstructions of history as in New Historicist representations.

What one critic characterizes as the fulfillment of Neil Postman's doomsday prophesy of dumbed-down history in terms of "middle-brow embellished history"[10] had become, by the end of the nineties, the norm rather than the exception, and it was not a negative thing at all. Hollywood, by the end of the nineties, after the historical discourse generated by *Primary Colors* and *The American President*, by *Philadelphia* and *In & Out*, by *Basic Instinct* and *Showgirls*, had come to the realization that motion pictures (including those dealing with real historical events and people) were active participants in the cultural discourse of spin. Perhaps the best example, coming right at the turn of the millennium, was the reaction to *Erin Brockovich* (1999). A Hollywood representation of a true story with its title character played by one of Hollywood's biggest marquee stars (just as *The Hurricane* had been), *Erin Brockovich*, though it took a number of liberties with the facts, conflated characters, and even introduced new characters who never existed in the historical reality (just as *The Hurricane* had done), garnered none of the negative attacks from the traditional historicists. Why? Perhaps the real Ed Masry (Albert Finney) put it best: "If they want to do a true movie, it can only help. It can't hurt."[11] That is the gravitational field that spin had established for itself as a discourse not only of power but for ideals like good and truth. At the turn of the millennium, and at the very apogee of the decade of spin, prior to the violent leveling and global decentering of 9/11, the strategies for the spinning of reality had become so refined in their skill, so powerful in their impact, that the concepts of spun reality had actually superseded the failed historical attempts to traditionally reconstruct reality.

## Y2K

Better get down with the 2K. . . . History gonna start right here, right now.
—*Strange Days* (1995)

By the end of the nineties decade, an apocalyptic dis-ease flared up in the now global consciousness. The portmanteau watchword for all of these futurist fears was the computer abbreviation Y2K. The year 2000, the millennium, took on a personality of utterly decentered threat, of looming chaos, of technological breakdown followed by economic collapse culminating in global disorder so complex that only the most isolated aborigine would be unaffected. In other words, as the century came to an end, Y2K was "slouching toward Bethlehem"[12] and the whole world was holding their breath in expectation, waiting to see if time would stop and the center would cease to hold.

Y2K wasn't just an abbreviated date. It was a fear, a technological fantasy, an entry through a black hole in time into a future (the twenty-first century) that threatened to begin in a timeless void. The real digital threat of Y2K was rather simple, really. When the millennium came on December 30, 1999, there was the possibility that all the computers' clocks in the world would fail to turn over, that time literally would stop, causing a technological breakdown unprecedented in history. Like geek SWAT teams, every computer programmer in the world was mobilized to combat Y2K. The ultimate time bomb was ticking.

Y2K was an extremely potent metaphor, and it certainly caught the attention of everyone as the end of the decade of spin, the millennium, loomed. It was a metaphor for all the doubts about the unstable virtual world that spin had created. It was a metaphor for an age of metaphor, an age that had taken reality and had spun it into realities, simulacra, and virtuality. Again, the movies proved a credible historical text.

In portraying the decade of spin as it approached the millennium, the movies not only captured all the fear and paranoia, they actually envisioned the potential breakdown and actually tried to predict what might really happen. If the end of the world was going to come on New Year's Eve 1999, then Hollywood was going to be its limo driver. As early as 1995, in the film about a simulacra-seduced world,[13] *Strange Days*, Hollywood was already predicting the global scenario of Y2K.

*Strange Days* best captured the ambiance of the end of the century. The whole social history of the nineties decade is summed up in the very *Blade Runner*-like, verging-upon-apocalypse, virtual-reality-seduced Los Angeles of *Strange Days*. This Y2K film is about a world that has been spun so fast that it has careened out of control. Ironically, *Strange Days* is also a movie about history (it says so itself in the epigraph to this section), but that history chronicles how nineties spin has taken reality to the point of utter social dysfunction so acute that it has brought the world to the verge of apocalypse. *Strange Days* takes place on one day, the last day of the century, but in LA it seems like the end of the world.

Lenny (Ralph Fiennes) is a sleazy, leather-clad dealer, not in drugs but in the new hallucinogenic high of the coming millennium, virtual reality. LA, on the verge of Y2K, is a kind of exercise in parallel universes. Its dark urban reality of riots, fascistic police brutality, and impending apocalypse exists in parallel with a world of seductive simulacra, of people paralyzed in the dreams and fantasies of virtual reality. But the problem with virtual reality "play back" is that it is every bit as addictive as the heroin, cocaine, and other drugs of the twentieth century. As Jean Baudrillard argues, simulacra ultimately replaces the reality from which it is derived because it is more controllable, can be called up on demand, and can be enhanced. Perfectibility becomes part of the illusion of virtual reality.

But Lenny's LA world of New Year's Eve 1999 is a far cry from perfectibility. As Lenny sets out to peddle his virtual reality wares, the call-in disc jockey on the car radio announces, "December 30, 1999, the last day of the whole damn century." *Strange Days* is a film of digital clocks, digital calendars, digital watches, a film about time and its total dominance over our lives, all leading up to Y2K, the moment when time stops, perhaps even disappears.

Because "the streets are a war zone," the DJ's voice is a last outpost of order in a world where reality is no longer real, where virtuality and simulacra rule. Conversely, Lenny is the commodity culture prophet of flight from the war zone, escape from the self, and immersion in virtual reality. Lenny's argument is that simulacra is safer, more exciting, and more fulfilling than reality. Lenny's millennial world has been totally seduced by spin, by the manipulation of reality. It is a world vulnerable in its lack of substance. The era of spin, of simulacra, of virtual reality, has to come to an end, and global society has to come back to reality. Y2K looms for these characters as a false alarm, but it served as a symbolic pressure point for the decade of spin. As history would prove, the survival of Y2K would only be a temporary reprieve, a warning that the virtual reality world created by the power of spin cannot last.

Other films near the end of the century exploited the apocalyptic warning of Y2K. The title of the James Bond film *Tomorrow Never Dies* (1997) offers a millennial vision of a "New World Order." The film creates the first fully postmodernist Bond villain, William Carver (Jonathan Pryce), a media mogul like Ted Turner or Rupert Murdock who wants to control the world by taking over all of its TV signals. "All power is in words," Carver preaches, and only James Bond, a man of few words, can stop the world war that Carver is orchestrating as the prime attraction on his global network of spin. *Entrapment* (1999) is a much less ambitious Y2K film than either *Strange Days* or *Tomorrow Never Dies*. It is an old-fashioned caper movie with a simple Y2K twist. A wily bank robber (Sean Connery) sees an opportunity to exploit by computer the virtual reality of the global monetary system. He programs a way to transfer eight billion dollars from a huge bank in Kuala Lumpur to his private account during the thirty-second Y2K time rollover at midnight on New Year's Eve. For all of these movies, Y2K and its temporary suspension of time served as a moment of vulnerability for the century.

But worse, Y2K became a symbol of all of the dysfunction, the loss of connection with reality, and the set-adrift, unanchored uncertainty of the world at the turn of the twenty-first century.

By the end of the nineties, as Don DeLillo expressed it, "the idea was to live outside the given limits, in a chip, on a disk, in whirl, in radiant spin, a consciousness saved from void."[14] But reality loomed just off screen. When Y2K passed uneventfully, no one suspected that the disaster that Y2K might have been, the disaster that would throw the whole world out of synch, that would stop time and outdistance spin, would drop the bottom out of the world's economic markets, and would undermine everyone's sense of their own safety, would come some nineteen months later. Y2K was but a simulation, a trial run for 9/11.

## The End of the Decade of Spin

*Stanley:* How can you justify all this?
*Gabriel:* It's the greatest good.
*Stanley:* How about 10 innocents?
*Gabriel:* Now you're getting it. How about 100? How about 1,000?
*Stanley:* You're no better than any other terrorist.

—*Swordfish* (2001)

Overshadowing the steady escalation of terrorist events throughout the eighties and nineties,[15] the attack on the World Trade Center ended the free-form virtuality of American life in the nineties. September 11, 2001, brought the "over-the-rainbow" world of the Clinton nineties and the technology-driven bull stock market to a shuddering fall. In the aftermath of 9/11, Americans tried to build a protective wall around themselves, their personal worlds, and their country. After 9/11, Americans were afraid: afraid certainly of the threats of further terrorism, afraid to invest in the stock market in such unstable times, afraid of irrational violence suddenly raising its head in the form of crazies with guns at home as well as terrorist attacks from abroad. Movie distributors were even afraid to release new films that portrayed any sort of terrorist action. Filmmakers realized that the obsessive voyeurism that the news coverage of the 9/11 attack created with its repeated images of exploding airplanes and toppling buildings was acceptable as real-life news but wouldn't be acceptable as fiction.

In an interview in early October 2001, legendary film director Robert Altman reflected upon what had happened one month earlier: "The movies set the pattern, and, these people have copied the movies. Nobody would have thought to commit an atrocity like that unless they'd seen it in a movie. How dare we continue to show this kind of mass destruction in movies? I just believe we created this atmosphere and taught them how to do it."[16] Altman's theory that the over-the-top action movies of the nineties served as a training manual for the 9/11 terrorist attack on the World Trade Center in New York goes well beyond Oscar Wilde's "life imitates art" decadence and echoes Dominick LaCapra's "instruments of diffusion" theory of postmodernist life.[17]

Ironically, eighties and nineties films actually had come close to predicting the 9/11 terrorist attack. *Die Hard*'s (1988) plot involves the terrorist hijacking of a skyscraper. In *Independence Day* (1996), the symbolic buildings of Washington DC are blown up. But perhaps the film that came closest to prophesying the 9/11 attack was the cyber thriller *Swordfish* (2001). It is a highly self-reflexive film that, while cast as the portrayal of a terrorist event, actually delivers a discourse upon how the western world (read: the United States) should retaliate and take its revenge for terrorist acts—in other words, wage a "war on terrorism."

*Swordfish* opens with a very Baudrillardian monologue delivered by its superterrorist central figure, Gabriel (John Travolta):

You know what the trouble with Hollywood is? . . . Realism. Not a pervasive element in today's modern American cinematic vision. . . . Now what if, in *Dog Day*

*Afternoon*, Sonny really wanted to get away with it. What if, now this is the tricky part, what if he started killing hostages right away? No mercy. No quarter. Meet our demands or the pretty blonde in the bell bottoms gets it in the back of the head. Bam! Splat! What? So there's no bus. C'mon, how many innocent victims splattered across the window would it take to have the city reverse its policy on hostage situations? And this is 1976. There's no CNN. There's no CNBC. There's no Internet. Now fast forward to today. Present time. Same situation. How quickly would the modern media make a frenzy over this? In a matter of hours it would be the biggest story from Boston to Budapest. Ten hostages die. Twenty. Thirty. Bam! Bim! One after another. All caught in high-def, computer-enhanced, tele-connected, you can practically taste the brain matter. All for what? A bus? A plane? A couple of million dollars that's federally insured?

Though this is Gabriel, an *über*terrorist in a movie, speaking in the ultrahip voice of Travolta, it could be Osama Bin Laden describing his millennial terrorist strategy as he sits on a rug in front of a video camera in a cave in Afghanistan in the year 2000. The concepts of "no mercy" and "no quarter" of a "modern media . . . frenzy" could well be close to the rhetoric of the al-Qaida planning for the 9/11 attacks.

Like Graham Greene's novel *The Quiet American* (1954), *Swordfish* is an eerily prophetic film. After Gabriel's opening speech, it goes on to predict the events and effects of 9/11 in some frighteningly imagistic ways: a helicopter flying a bus into a skyscraper, terror in the streets after a devastating explosion, a "cyber criminal task force" monitoring the airports electronically, an all-out "war on terrorism" in retaliation. But the very idea that drives the plot of *Swordfish* is, perhaps, the most prophetic aspect of the film. When Stanley (Hugh Jackman), the cyberhacker forced by Gabriel into the terrorist plot, asks the inevitable "Why?" Gabriel answers,

> *Gabriel:* Because wars cost money.
> *Stanley:* War? Who are we at war with?
> *Gabriel:* Anyone who impinges on American freedom. Terrorist states, Stanley. Somebody must bring their war to them. . . . Our job is to make terrorism so horrific that it becomes unthinkable to attack Americans.

It is a cleverly deconstructive tune that *Swordfish* dances to—the *über*terrorist orchestrates a huge terrorist event in order to get enough money to fight a war against all the other terrorists. If it weren't for the fact that Gabriel is a total monomaniac like Jack D. Ripper (Sterling Hayden) in Stanley Kubrick's *Dr. Strangelove* (1964), his arguments for financing an all-out war on terrorism sound a lot like President George W. Bush's rhetoric in the aftermath of the 9/11 attacks.

But, by far, the most frightening prophetic image of *Swordfish* is that of a helicopter hoisting a bus into the air and flying it into the side of a skyscraper. This scene includes footage of the helicopter and the bus flying into the building, the helicopter imbedded in the side of the building explodes in a ball of flames, people in business suits and dresses inside the building run for their lives when the helicopter hits, glass shatters, walls cave in, floors give way, bodies plummet. This sequence ranks right up there with the nuclear plant accident in *The China Syndrome* (1979) as one of the scariest and most accurate film prophesies ever made. Maybe Altman is right, that the terrorists get their ideas from the movies, that fiction really can fuel fact, that the movies do actually participate in the making of history.

In so many ways, 9/11 brought America down out of the vortextual spin, the ever-changing reality of the Clinton nineties. But that decade had been an invigorating, highly profitable joyride for a long time, a wheeling, spinning, careening thrill ride through all manner of virtual realities. Every nineties social issue, every nineties historical event or public figure, every nineties political or economic or social argument, and every nineties film representation of American life existed in a centrifuge of perpetual, postmodernist motion and was caught in the decade's passionate love affair with spin.

# Notes

## Preface

1. This is a term used by Dominick LaCapra to describe the many different kinds of texts that disperse contemporary versions of history to the masses in the late twentieth century. See Dominick LaCapra, *History and Criticism* (Ithaca, NY: Cornell University Press, 1985), 18–19.
2. Quoted in William H. McNeill, "What It All Means: Why Jacques Barzun Is America's Greatest Teacher," *Los Angeles Times*, May 21, 2002, Books section.
3. Margot Norris, *Writing War In The Twentieth Century* (Charlottesville: University of Virginia Press, 2000), 2.
4. The two books preceding this one in my trilogy of social histories, *The Films of the Seventies: A Social History* (Metuchen, NJ and London: Scarecrow, 1987) and *The Films of the Eighties: A Social History* (Carbondale: Southern Illinois University Press, 1993), are part of this movement to map and analyze the representation of contemporary social history in films that the following books also study: Tom O'Brien, *The Screening of America* (New York: Continuum, 1990); Mark Crispen Miller, *Seeing Through Movies* (New York: Pantheon, 1990); Marsha Kinder, *Playing With Power in Movies, Television and Video Games: From Muppet Babies to Teenage Mutant Ninja Turtles* (Berkeley: University of California Press, 1991); Ruth Vasey, *The World According to Hollywood* (Madison: University of Wisconsin Press, 1996); Gary Crowdus (ed.), *The Political Companion to American Film* (Chicago: Lake View, 1998); Joseph Natoli, *Hauntings: Popular Film and American Culture: 1990–1992* (Albany: State University of New York Press, 2001); and Robert Brent Toplin, *Reel History: In Defense of Hollywood* (University Press of Kansas, 2001).
5. Jay Parini, "Delving Into the World of Dreams by Blending Fact and Fiction," *Chronicle of Higher Education*, February 27, 1998, B4.
6. All these statements are quoted in Jan Breslauer, "History With a Head and Heart," *Los Angeles Times*, May 14, 2000, Calendar section.

# Chapter 1

1. Dominick LaCapra, *History and Criticism* (Ithaca, NY: Cornell University Press, 1985), 18.
2. See Jean-François Lyotard, *The Postmodern Condition: A Report on Knowledge*, trans. Geoff Bennington and Brian Massumi (Minneapolis: University of Minnesota Press, 1984), 15, 31–41.
3. See Hayden White, *Metahistory: The Historical Imagination in Nineteenth-Century Europe* (Baltimore: The Johns Hopkins University Press, 1974).
4. The popularization and mass diffusion of postmodernist thought in the nineties was the natural evolution of the postmodern sensibility. The growth of postmodernist thought in academia in the seventies and eighties finally found public expression in the nineties when postmodernist thought finally entered the public domain from the protective covering of its academic breeding ground. If the seventies ushered in the first definitions of postmodernist thought via the study of such theorists as Jacques Derrida, Michel Foucault, Mikhail Bakhtin, Giles DeLouze, Hayden White, Walter Benjamin, Jean-François Lyotard, Jean Baudrillard, and many others; such critics as J. Hillis Miller, Dominick LaCapra, Clifford Geertz, Stephen Greenblatt, Jonathan Culler, Frederick Jameson, Frank Lentricchia, and Stanley Fish; and if the eighties adapted these philosophical ideas of these thinkers not only to the reading of texts but to the reading of culture and society as well, then the nineties, through the "instruments of diffusion" of the mass media, turned this arcane, heavily jargoned, highly theoretical, academic obsession into pop culture.
5. Stephen Greenblatt, *Shakespearean Negotiations: The Circulation of Social Energy in Renaissance England* (Berkeley: University of California Press, 1988), 1.
6. Quoted in "Spielberg Lauds Power of Film," *Gannett News Service* to *Lafayette Journal and Courier*, February 26, 1994, A2.
7. "Jim Mullen's Hot Sheet," *Entertainment Weekly*, February 11, 1994, 8.
8. Quoted in "*Natural Born Killers*: The Director's Cut," *Entertainment Weekly*, August 2, 1996, 66.
9. Quoted in Eric Slater, "Gene Siskel, 53, film critic, dies," *Los Angeles Times*, February 21, 1999.
10. For example, see the headline of James P. Pinkerton's commentary column in *Newsday*, January 10, 1999, which reads, "Real-life collides with reel-life."
11. The concept of "panopticism" is defined in Michel Foucault's *Discipline and Punish*, trans. Alan Sheridan (New York: Vintage Books, 1979), 195–228.
12. "Skirting: The Question," *Entertainment Weekly*, April 15, 1995, 47.
13. The passing of the torch from the American Film Institute (AFI)'s *American Film* to *Entertainment Weekly* as the Hollywood-insider magazine in the nineties is an interesting history in itself. The AFI was created in 1967, and in 1975 *American Film* magazine was established, under the leadership of George Stevens Jr., "to roam through the highways and byways of communications, and ever under the surface will be root questions on the role of film and television in American life" (quoted in *American Film*, July/August 1988). For thirteen years the AFI produced the journal under the masthead "Magazine of the Film and Television Arts." In 1988 *American Film* was sold to Billboard Publications and the masthead changed to "Film, Video and Television Arts." But the journal still remained affiliated with the AFI. In November of 1988, the editorial offices of *American Film* moved from New York to Los Angeles and called for its readers "to notice some of the design and editorial

changes we have already started to make" (*American Film*, November 1988). Then, in March of 1989, *American Film*'s new editor announced that "our own offices, here on Sunset Boulevard, have lately been fraught with epic churning. Next month, look for a complete redesign of the magazine, with a new, enlarged format." In April 1989 the Billboard Publications sister magazine, *Hollywood Reporter*, was incorporated into *American Film*. While all of this was going on at *American Film*, Time-Warner Publications was simultaneously designing *Entertainment Weekly* with a Hollywood review and business insider mission and format that almost exactly mimicked that of *American Film*. *Entertainment Weekly* debuted in February 1990, and within nine months *American Film* was putting together its final double issue. The new weekly had put the less-popular monthly out of business. For the purposes of this book, while *American Film* had been the major review and Hollywood-industry source for *The Films of the Seventies: A Social History* and *The Films of the Eighties: A Social History*, *Entertainment Weekly* became the most valuable source for review perspectives and insider industry quotes.

14. Quoted in Benjamin Svetkey, "Flirting With Disasters," *Entertainment Weekly*, May 17, 1996, 8.
15. Quoted in Svetkey, "Flirting," 8.
16. Quoted by Bruce Fretts, "1990s," *Entertainment Weekly*, February 14, 1999, 97.
17. Mike Lopresti, "McGwire makes Maris history," *Gannett News Service* to *Lafayette Journal and Courier*, September 9, 1998.
18. Jonathan Yardley, "History's field of dreams allows each generation its own home run chase," *Washington Post*, September 9, 1998.
19. Ian Jarvie, *Movies and Society* (New York: Basic Books, 1970), 124.
20. Linda Chavez, "Paranoia from the Hollywood Left," *Gannett News Service* to *Lafayette Journal and Courier*, May 6, 1995.
21. Quoted in *Lafayette Journal and Courier*, September 23, 1997.
22. LaCapra, *History*, 18–19.
23. Karen J. Winkler, "History in Hollywood: The Way Films Present the Past," *Chronicle of Higher Education*, December 15, 1995, A10.
24. Quoted in Winkler, "History in Hollywood," A11.
25. Winkler, "History in Hollywood," A11.
26. Quoted in Winkler, "History in Hollywood," A11.
27. Quoted in Jessica Shaw, "Very Special Explanations," *Entertainment Weekly*, April 5, 1996, 16.
28. Quoted in Suna Chang, "The Reel Truth," *Entertainment Weekly*, January 15, 1999, 7.
29. Ibid.
30. Thomas Doherty, "World War II in Film: What Is the Color of Reality?" *Chronicle of Higher Education*, October 9, 1998, B4.
31. Douglas Brinkley, quoted in Doherty, B4.
32. Doherty, "World War II," B4.
33. Quoted in Michelle Ephraim, "Fiction and the Holocaust: Must Realism Be Paramount," *The Chronicle of Higher Education*, July 31, 1998, B5.
34. Arline R. Thorn, "Letter," *Chronicle of Higher Education*, May 22, 1998, B3.
35. Ibid.
36. John M. Roberts, "Oliver Stone's Films: Fact or Fiction?" *Chronicle of Higher Education*, March 7, 1997, B11.
37. LaCapra, *History*, 17.

38. Susan Wloszczyna, "'Canyon' echoes the era," *USA Today*, January 22, 1992, 5D.
39. Stuart Klawans, "In Memory of Movies as Grand but Futile Gestures," *Chronicle of Higher Education*, February 19, 1999, B9.
40. Michael Medved, "Has Hollywood Gone Too Far," *USA Weekend*, March 27, 1992, 4.
41. Lisa Schwarzbaum, "No Shame, No Gain," *Entertainment Weekly*, December 31, 1994, 64.
42. Dana Kennedy, "The Young and the Reckless," *Entertainment Weekly*, December 26, 1993, 24.
43. Quoted in Dana Kennedy, "Downey Goes Down," *Entertainment Weekly*, December 19, 1997, 8.
44. Quoted in Dana Kennedy, "The Days of Wine and Noses," *Entertainment Weekly*, January 14, 1997, 28–29.
45. Rebecca Ascher-Welsh, "Death of a Hollywood Bad Boy," *Entertainment Weekly*, February 2, 1996, 15.
46. Quoted in Jess Cagle, "Craze the 'Titanic,'" *Entertainment Weekly*, September 13, 1996, 14.
47. Anne Thompson, "Tempest In An Egg Cup," *Entertainment Weekly*, June 21, 1996, 13.
48. Dave Karger, "Coppola Bucks," *Entertainment Weekly*, July 24, 1998, 10.
49. Daniel Fierman, "Brawl Over 'Beloved'," *Entertainment Weekly*, October 16, 1998, 20.
50. Gregg Kilday, "Hollywood Squeeze," *Entertainment Weekly*, August 21, 1992, 27.
51. Gregg Kilday, "Springtime For Hitless," *Entertainment Weekly*, May 20, 1994, 38.
52. Anne Thompson, "The $100 Million Question," *Entertainment Weekly*, September 23, 1994, 16.
53. Jess Cagle, "Marquee Marks," *Entertainment Weekly*, February 7, 1997, 32.
54. Gregg Kilday, "Feast Or Famine?" *Entertainment Weekly*, May 9, 1997, 25.
55. Benjamin Svetkey, "Box Office Bingo," *Entertainment Weekly*, September 5, 1997, 17–18.
56. Andrew Essex, "What a Bummer," *Entertainment Weekly*, July 24, 1998, 22.
57. Benjamin Svetkey, "Has Hollywood Lost It?" *Entertainment Weekly*, March 14, 1997, 29.
58. Robert Sklar, "Taking Hollywood By Storm: Behind the Triumph of Independent Films," *Chronicle of Higher Education*, March 14, 1997, B7.
59. Steve Daly, "Midas 'Touch,'" *Entertainment Weekly*, October 9, 1998, 25.
60. Steve Daly, "Brush Up Your Hitchcock," *Entertainment Weekly*, March 15, 1997, 28.
61. Chris Nashawaty, "Deja View," *Entertainment Weekly*, December 6, 1996, 8.
62. Quoted in Nashawaty, 9.
63. Hutcheon first defined her concept of "historiographic metafiction" in the preface to the paperback edition of *Narcissistic Narrative: The Metafictional Paradox* (New York: Methuen, 1980), xi-xviii.
64. Terrence Rafferty, "Culture Clash," *Gentleman's Quarterly*, December 1997, 93.
65. Ibid., 93, 96.

## Chapter 2

1. The two books preceding this one in my trilogy of social histories, *The Films of the Seventies: A Social History* and *The Films of the Eighties: A Social History* are part of this movement to map and analyze the representation of contemporary social history.

2. Eric Harrison, "Truth Isn't in the Details," *Los Angeles Times*, February 8, 2000, Calendar section, 2.

3. Quoted in Susan King, "Films Seen Through History's Lens," *Los Angeles Times*, February 6, 2000, Calendar section, 16.

4. Harrison, "Truth Isn't in the Details," 73.

5. Quoted in Randy Harvey, "Griffith Could Have Used a Real Hurricane Warning," *Los Angeles Times*, January 21, 2000, D2.

6. Godfrey Cheshire, "You Can't Break Oliver Stone," *Talk*, November 1999, 90.

7. Ibid., 91.

8. Lawrence Suid, "WWII at Sea, as Fought on the Screen," *Los Angeles Times*, April 25, 2000, F4.

9. Quoted in Lori L. Tharps, "Dive and Conquer," *Entertainment Weekly*, December 1, 2000, 28.

10. Quoted in Gregg Kilday, "They Did Their Homework," *Los Angeles Times*, May 7, 2000, Calendar section, 106.

11. Ibid.

12. Lisa Schwarzbaum, "News of the Whirl," *Entertainment Weekly*, November 28, 1997, 57.

13. Owen Gleiberman, "Bios Debatable," *Entertainment Weekly*, January 8, 1993, 32.

14. Owen Gleiberman, "Misty Beethoven," *Entertainment Weekly*, January 20, 1995, 34.

15. Quoted in Tim Appelo, "Of False Notes And A Nut," *Entertainment Weekly*, January 20, 1995, 35.

16. Ty Burr, "Mete the Beatles," *Entertainment Weekly*, September 30, 1994, 66.

17. This ascendance of the New Historicist consciousness and the application of New Historicist theory to the analysis of film and film history is defined and historically located in Chapter 1 of *The Films of the Eighties: A Social History*, titled "The Holograph of History."

18. Owen Gleiberman, "Shipwrecked," *Entertainment Weekly*, October 16, 1992, 56.

19. Owen Gleiberman, "Lost at Sea," *Entertainment Weekly*, September 4, 1992, 53.

20. Terry Catchpole, "Rebel Hell," *Entertainment Weekly*, April 1, 1994, 59.

21. Owen Gleiberman, "Native Son," *Entertainment Weekly*, September 25, 1992, 42.

22. Ken Tucker, "Over the Texas Borderline," *Entertainment Weekly*, June 21, 1996, 47.

23. Warren Goldstein, "Bad History Is Bad for a Culture," *Chronicle of Higher Education*, April 10, 1998, A64.

24. Anne Thompson, "Making History," *Entertainment Weekly*, January 21, 1994, 14.

25. Ibid., 20.

26. Ibid., 16.

27. Ibid., 20.

28. Owen Gleiberman, "Dark Victory," *Entertainment Weekly*, December 17, 1993, 44–45.

29. Tim Appelo, "Oskar Winner," *Entertainment Weekly*, January 24, 1994, 24.

30. Gleiberman, "Dark Victory," 46.

31. Jessica Shaw, "Things That Go 'Gump,'" *Entertainment Weekly*, February 3, 1995, 9.

32. Jeff Gordinier, "Mr. Gump Goes To Washington," *Entertainment Weekly*, February 10, 1995, 28.

33. Ibid., 20.

34. Quoted in Glenn Kenny, "Politically Indirect," *Entertainment Weekly*, May 5, 1995, 76.

35. Jeff Gordinier in "Tom Hanks," year-end special issue, *Entertainment Weekly*, 1998, 17, argues that "Tom Hanks may just be the last man on the silver screen who conveys a sense of decency. He tires of the terms: Average Joe, Boy Next Door, Mr. Nice Guy."

36. Jean Baudrillard writes about the nature of "counterfeit" reality in the modern world in *Simulations*, trans. Paul Foss, Paul Patton, and Phillip Beitchman (New York: Semiotext[e], 1983), 97–101.

37. Linda Hutcheon first defined her concept of "historiographic metafiction" in the preface to the paperback edition of *Narcissistic Narrative: The Metafictional Paradox* (New York: Methuen, 1980), xi–xviii.

38. Quoted in Jonathan Alter, "The Long Shadow of Slavery," *Newsweek*, December 8, 1997, 60.

39. Baudrillard, *Simulations*, 151–52. See Baudrillard's definition of the relationship between "art and reality" and throughout Lyotard's *The Postmodern Condition: A Report on Knowledge* and "Answering the Question: What is Postmodernism?"

40. David Ansen and Allison Samuels, "Amistad's Struggle," *Newsweek*, December 8, 1997, 67.

41. Alter, "Long Shadow," 60.

42. Quoted in Kevin Cullen, "'Amistad' author: Spielberg film not truthful, but helpful," *Lafayette Journal and Courier*, January 20, 1998, C2.

43. Quoted in Alison Schneider, "A Career Studying the Amistad Rebellion," *Chronicle of Higher Education*, January 9, 1998, A12.

44. Eric McKitrick, "JQA: For the Defense," *New York Review of Books*, April 23, 1998, 53.

45. Jeff Gordinier, "Mutiny and the Bounty," *Entertainment Weekly*, December 12, 1997, 27.

46. Ibid., 25.

47. Cullen, "'Amistad' author," C2.

48. Alter, "Long Shadow," 60.

49. Anthony Lane, "Great Scot," *New Yorker*, July 25, 1998, 94.

50. David Ansen, "Witnessing the Inferno," *Newsweek*, July 27, 1998, 57.

51. Quoted in Jon Meacham, "Caught In The Line Of Fire," *Newsweek*, July 13, 1998, 49.

52. Ibid., 47.

53. Owen Gleiberman, "The Killing Field," *Entertainment Weekly*, May 26, 1995, 61.

54. Quoted in Jeff Gordinier, "Message in a Battle," *Entertainment Weekly*, July 24, 1998, 29.

55. Owen Gleiberman, "Shell Shock," *Entertainment Weekly*, July 24, 1998, 46.

56. Lyotard, *The Postmodern Condition*, 38.
57. Owen Gleiberman and Lisa Schwarzbaum, "Winter Takes All," *Entertainment Weekly*, January 8, 1999, 44.
58. Owen Gleiberman, "Sunken Treasure," *Entertainment Weekly*, December 19, 1997, 49.
59. Ibid., 49–51.
60. Ibid., 50.
61. Degen Pener, "Deep Thoughts," *Entertainment Weekly*, January 23, 1998, 29.
62. Paula Parisi, "Goodbye, Mr. Ship," *Entertainment Weekly*, May 15, 1997, 22.
63. Benjamin Svetkey, "In the Wake of *Titanic*," *Entertainment Weekly*, February 6, 1998, 23.
64. Paula Parisi, "*Titanic*: Man Overboard," *Entertainment Weekly*, November 7, 1997, 30.
65. Pener, "Deep Thoughts," 28–29.
66. Kristen Baldwin, "Dawson's Crypt," *Entertainment Weekly*, April 24, 1998, 12.

## Chapter 3

1. Owen Gleiberman, "Dark Side of the Moon," summer double issue," *Entertainment Weekly*, 1995, 78.
2. Ibid., 79.
3. Jeff Gordinier, "Ground Control to Major Tom," *Entertainment Weekly*, June 23, 1995, 17.
4. Quoted in Gordinier, "Ground Control," 17.
5. These lyrics are from the song "That Old Black Magic." Music by Harold Arlen. Lyrics by Johnny Mercer. RCA Records, 1942.
6. Jean-François Lyotard, "Answering the Question: What is Postmodernism?" in *The Postmodern Condition: A Report on Knowledge*, trans. Regis Durand (Minneapolis: University of Minnesota Press, 1984), 74–75.
7. Jean Baudrillard, *Simulacra and Simulation*, trans. Sheila Faria Glaser (Ann Arbor: University of Michigan Press, 1994), 42.
8. Ibid., 7.
9. Ibid., 108.
10. Jean-François Lyotard, *The Postmodern Condition: A Report on Knowledge*, trans. Geoff Bennington and Brian Massumi (Minneapolis: University of Minnesota Press, 1984), 10, 17.
11. Ibid., 15.
12. Baudrillard, *Simulacra*, 42.
13. Ibid., 41.
14. Ibid. See also Stewert Ewen, *PR! A Social History of Spin* (New York: Basic Books, 1996) and Larry Tye, *The Father of Spin: Edward L. Bernays and the Birth of Public Relations* (New York: Crown, 1998).
15. Christopher Shea, "How Corporations Won the Hearts and Minds of America," *Chronicle of Higher Education*, October 9, 1998, A16.
16. "The 100 Greatest TV Moments of the 1980s," *Entertainment Weekly*, February 19, 1999, 94.
17. Alanna Nash, "Fashion Victim," *Entertainment Weekly*, January 16, 1998, 38.

18. Lawrence Buell, "In Pursuit of Ethics," *PMLA: Publications of the Modern Language Association* 114, no. 1 (January 1999): 11.

19. Bradley Butterfield, "Ethical Value and Negative Aesthetics: Reconsidering the Baudrillard-Ballard Connection," *PMLA: Publications of the Modern Language Association* 114, no. 1 (January 1999): 64.

20. Ibid., 72.

21. Lyotard, *The Postmodern Condition*, 37.

22. See Hayden White's *Metahistory* (Baltimore: Johns Hopkins University Press, 1973), 40–41, where he writes, "But historical thought had no need of a Marx to project it into its third, or crisis, stage. The very success of the historians of the second phase was sufficient to plunge historical consciousness into that condition of Irony which is the true content of the 'crisis of historicism.'"

23. Lyotard, *The Postmodern Condition*, 40.

24. Ibid., 41.

25. Ibid., 61.

26. Lyotard, "Answering the Question," 74–75.

27. Ibid., 76.

28. Quoted in Scott Heller, "Professor Sees Influence of Edgar Allan Poe in 20th-Century Literature and Cryptography," *Chronicle of Higher Education*, April 4, 1997, A13.

29. "'Wag the Dog' ads try to take real life by the tale," in *Lafayette Journal and Courier*, 30 January 1998, D3, reprinted from *Los Angeles Times*.

30. Daniel Fierman and Jeff Jensen, "A Star Is Reborn," *Entertainment Weekly*, November 27, 1998, 8–9.

31. Suna Chang, "Bond of Gold," *Entertainment Weekly*, November 28, 1997, 10.

32. Owen Gleiberman, "Agent of Change," *Entertainment Weekly*, December 13, 1996, 53.

33. Shirley Fung, "Hollywood U," *Entertainment Weekly*, September 19, 1997, 8.

34. Quoted in Simon Frith, "John Keats vs. Bob Dylan: Why Value Judgements Matter," *Chronicle of Higher Education*, March 14, 1997, A48.

35. Ibid.

36. Baudrillard, *Simulacra*, 2.

37. Ibid., 7.

38. Ibid., 8.

39. Ibid., 13.

40. Ibid., 11.

41. Ibid., 16.

42. Lyotard, *The Postmodern Condition*, 24.

43. Ibid., 26.

44. Spin serves the consolidation and expansion of power (Foucault). Spin embraces the dialogic, decentered discourse of reality (Derrida). Spin explores the many marginalized voices, races, genders, classes of reality (Bakhtin). Spin often views the *simulacra* of reality as reality itself (Baudrillard). Spin is the dominant language game (Lyotard) that has replaced illusory reality. Spin exposes the emplotted agendas of traditionally accepted versions of reality and reexamines those versions from new perspectives (New Historicism). Spin studies new sources of reality that were previously ignored (cultural studies).

45. John LeCarre, *Our Game* (New York: Alfred E. Knopf, 1995), 21.

46. Quoted in Peter Monaghan, "Notes From Academe: Australia," *Chronicle of Higher Education*, December 20, 1996, B2.
47. Quoted in Karen Winkler, "Oliver Stone Wins Some Converts at a Meeting of Historians," *Chronicle of Higher Education*, January 17, 1997, A18.
48. Quoted in "Focusing on Women," *Chronicle of Higher Education*, December 13, 1996, B76.
49. J. Hillis Miller, "What Is the Future of the Print Record?" *Profession 95: Publications of the Modern Language Association*, 33.
50. Ibid.
51. Lyotard, *Answering the Question*, 71.
52. Owen Gleiberman, "Gorilla Filmmaking," *Entertainment Weekly*, January 8, 1999, 49.
53. Ginia Bellafante, "Claws Out, Girls," *Entertainment Weekly*, November 6, 1998, 91.
54. Lisa Schwarzbaum, "Antz," *Entertainment Weekly*, October 2, 1998, 58.
55. Benjamin Svetkey, "'Bright' Light," *Entertainment Weekly*, October 16, 1998, 77.
56. Ibid.
57. Lisa Schwarzbaum, "Fame Dropper," *Entertainment Weekly*, November 20, 1998, 92.
58. Ibid., 94.
59. Lyotard, *The Postmodern Condition*, 9.
60. Quoted in A. J. Jacobs, "You've been a great audience! Good night!" Special *Seinfeld* issue, *Entertainment Weekly*, May 14, 1998, 6.
61. Owen Gleiberman, "Choose to Accept It," *Entertainment Weekly*, May 31, 1996, 40.
62. Ty Burr, "'Mission' Implausible," *Entertainment Weekly*, November 15, 1996, 79.
63. Owen Gleiberman, "Cheese Whizzes," *Entertainment Weekly*, 24 February 1995, 86–87.
64. Glenn Kenny, "Poly Wannabes," *Entertainment Weekly*, July 21, 1995, 70.
65. Brian Lowry, "'Big Brother's' Watchers See Everything but Privacy," *Los Angeles Times*, February 11, 2000, A52.
66. In "Hot Type," *Chronicle of Higher Education*, February 27, 1998, A20.
67. See both Mikhail Bakhtin's *The Dialogical Imagination*, trans. Caryl Emerson and Michael Holquist (Austin: University of Texas Press, 1981) and *Problems of Dostoevsky's Poetics*, trans. Caryl Emerson (Minneapolis: University of Minnesota Press, 1984).
68. Sean Mitchell, "Our movies, ourselves," *USA Weekend*, March 6, 1992, 10.
69. Quoted from Louis Menand, "The Trouble With Spielberg," *New York Review of Books*, September 24, 1998, in the "Melange" section of *Chronicle of Higher Education*, October 9, 1998, B12.
70. Quoted in Kate Meyers, "The Triumph of the Bill," March 19, 1993, 24.
71. Lisa Schwarzbaum, "Parallel Whirls," *Entertainment Weekly*, May 1, 1998, 36.
72. Ibid., 37.
73. Ty Burr, "The Spanish Prisoner," *Entertainment Weekly*, October 9, 1998, 75.
74. Lisa Schwarzbaum, "Knotty by Nature," *Entertainment Weekly*, April 10, 1998, 44.
75. Quoted in Elizabeth Gleick, "Yes, Mamet," *Entertainment Weekly*, June 5, 1998, 19.
76. Mike D'Angelo, "Read This Later!" *Entertainment Weekly*, January 23, 1998, 64–65.

77. Ibid., 65.

78. *Chinatown* is the focal text of *The Films of the Seventies: A Social History*, thus its kinship to *L.A. Confidential* is yet another link to the evolving of the neo-noir of the seventies and eighties (such as *Body Heat*) into the spin-noir of the nineties with *L.A. Confidential* being the salient example.

79. Owen Gleiberman, "Lost Angeles," *Entertainment Weekly*, September 19, 1997, 54.

80. Palmer, *The Films of the Seventies*, 128–36.

81. Gleiberman, "Lost Angeles," 55.

# Chapter 4

1. Fred Goodman, "Eyes Wide Shut," *Los Angeles Times*, March 12, 2000, Book Review section, 1.

2. Jonathan Alter, "The New Powers That Be," *Newsweek*, January 18, 1999, 24.

3. Quoted in Dennis Camire, "Graham claims Clinton sought to destroy Lewinsky," *Gannett News Service*, December 10, 1998.

4. Quoted on *The Today Show*, first broadcast January 28, 1998, by NBC.

5. James P. Pinkerton, "James and the Giant Impeach: Hollywood's revenge coming soon," *Newsday*, January 3, 1999.

6. Jill Lawrence, "'Wag the Dog' revisited," *Gannett News Service*, January 15, 1998.

7. Owen Gleiberman, "Con Aired," *Entertainment Weekly*, January 16, 1998, 40.

8. See Jean Baudrillard's theory of simulacra in *Simulations and Simulacra*.

9. Quoted in Jess Cagle, "The Godfather," *Entertainment Weekly*, August 19, 1994, 30.

10. Quoted in Gabriella Montell, "A Professor Challenges the Press," *Chronicle of Higher Education*, January 15, 1999, A11.

11. Ibid., A11.

12. John LeCarre, *The Tailor of Panama* (New York: Alfred E. Knopf, 1996), 332.

13. Bruce Fretts, "Spin City," *Entertainment Weekly*, January 6, 1998, 6.

14. Ibid.

15. Terrence Rafferty, "Helter Skelter," *New Yorker*, April 4, 1994, 106.

16. Glenn Kenny, "Shooting From The Hip," *Entertainment Weekly*, January 27, 1995, 56.

17. Quoted in Francine Russo, "Welcome to the Jungle," *Entertainment Weekly*, September 9, 1994, 36.

18. Ty Burr, "Newshound of Hell," spring double issue, *Entertainment Weekly*, 1998, 118.

19. Lisa Schwarzbaum, "Broadcast Noose," *Entertainment Weekly*, November 14, 1997, 52–53.

20. George Blooston, "Press Here For Ridicule," *Entertainment Weekly*, November 15, 1996, 48.

21. Quoted in Suna Chang, "Great Exhalations," *Entertainment Weekly*, January 16, 1998, 72.

22. Owen Gleiberman, "The Fabric of Life," *Entertainment Weekly*, October 1, 1993, 38.

# Chapter 5

1. Neal Gabler, "In the Serial of America, President Is the Star," *Los Angeles Times*, May 21, 2000, M2.
2. Ibid.
3. Ibid., M6.
4. David Germain, "White House remains hot Hollywood topic," *Associated Press*, November 5, 2000.
5. See Jean Baudrillard's discussion of reality in *Simulacra and Simulation*, 1, 2, 3, 5, 6 ("When the real is no longer what it was"), 7, 13 ("the fact that the real is no longer real"), 19 ("The impossibility of rediscovering an absolute level of the real"), 20, 21, 22 ("a last glimmer of reality"), 23, 28 ("the frisson of the real"), 30 ("the mutation of the real into the hyperreal"). See also Jean-François Lyotard's discussions of reality in *Answering the Question: What is Postmodernism*, where he examines the "task of derealization" and "the discovery of the 'lack of reality' of reality, together with the invention of other realities" (73–79).
6. See Lyotard, *The Postmodern Condition: A Report on Knowledge*, xxv, 10 (where "language games" are defined), 15, 17, 20, 33, 36.
7. Quoted in Germain, "White House," E1.
8. Ibid., E1.
9. Mike Feinsilber, "JFK: Separating myth from reality," *Associated Press*, January 12, 1998.
10. Kerry Temple, "Introduction," to "Person and Persona: The Presidential Balancing Act," *Notre Dame Magazine*, Spring 1999, 1.
11. Robert Schmuhl, "All the Presidents' Mien," *Notre Dame Magazine*, Spring 1999, 37.
12. Ibid., 38.
13. Lyotard, in *The Postmodern Condition*, writes, "in the computer age, the question of knowledge is now more than ever a question of government" (9).
14. Schmuhl, "All the Presidents'," 38.
15. Gabler, "In the Serial," M6.
16. The Bakhtinian carnivalesque is articulated in Mikhail Bakhtin's *Rabelais and his World*, trans. Helene Iswosky (Bloomington: Indiana University Press, 1993) and in his four lectures collected and translated as *The Dialogic Imagination*. Bakhtin derives his conception of the carnivalesque from his study of the fiction of Rabelais.
17. Lisa Schwarzbaum, "It's A Mad, Mad, Mad World," *Entertainment Weekly*, June 2, 1995, 36.
18. Tim Appelo, "The Stars Rain Down On Washington," *Entertainment Weekly*, June 11, 1993, 23.
19. Dominick LaCapra, *Rethinking Intellectual History: Texts, Contexts, Language* (Ithaca, NY: Cornell University Press, 1983), 52.
20. Chris Nashawaty, "Hail to the Chiefs," *Entertainment Weekly*, June 14, 1996, 20.
21. Quoted in David Hochman, "Beverly Hills Billy," *Entertainment Weekly*, September 4, 1998, 11.
22. Clarissa Cruz, "Flashes: Book 'Em," *Entertainment Weekly*, October 2, 1998, 12.
23. Benjamin Svetkey, "The Faking of the President: 1998," *Entertainment Weekly*, March 27, 1998, 30.
24. William J. Palmer, "The Holograph of History," in *The Films of the Eighties: A Social History* (Carbondale, IL: Southern Illinois University Press, 1993), 1–15.

25. Dan Balz, "'*Primary Colors*': Good fodder for talk, but unlikely to impact Clinton much," *Washington Post*, March 23, 1998, B3.
26. Lisa Schwarzbaum, "Prez in the Flesh," *Entertainment Weekly*, March 27, 1998, 45.
27. Svetkey, "The Faking," 24.
28. See title of Steven E. Schier's *The Postmodern Presidency: Bill Clinton's Legacy in U.S. Politics* (Pittsburgh, PA: University of Pittsburgh Press, 2000).
29. Owen Gleiberman, "Political Party," *Entertainment Weekly*, December 10, 1993, 53.
30. Both quoted in Scott Brown, "The West Wing," in 2000 year-end special issue, *Entertainment Weekly*, 25.
31. Quoted in Jeffrey Wells, "An 'American' Defector," *Entertainment Weekly*, October 21, 1994, 9.
32. See Baudrillard, *Simulation and Simulacra*, where he writes, "Simulation corresponds to a short circuit of reality and to its duplication through signs. It is always the goal of the ideological analysis to restore the objective process, it is always a false problem to wish to restore the truth beneath the simulacrum" (27).
33. Don DeLillo, *Libra* (New York: Penguin, 1988), 384.
34. Owen Gleiberman, "A Checkered Life," *Entertainment Weekly*, December 22, 1995, 46.
35. Owen Gleiberman, "The Best Wing," *Entertainment Weekly*, December 15, 2000, 41.
36. Patrick Goldstein, "A Test of Wills, Take 2," *Los Angeles Times*, January 30, 2000, Calendar section, 82.
37. Quoted in Goldstein, "A Test of Wills," 82.
38. Ibid., 84.
39. Lisa Schwarzbaum, "War Takes A Holiday," *Entertainment Weekly*, July 12, 1996, 37.
40. Gerald Ford, "More Fun Than My Administration," *Entertainment Weekly*, February 13, 1998, 73.
41. Owen Gleiberman, "Executive Action," *Entertainment Weekly*, July 25, 1997, 48.
42. Quoted in David Hochman, "The Plane and Simple," *Entertainment Weekly*, August 1, 1997, 20.
43. Rose Martelli, "Grumpy Old Presidents," *Entertainment Weekly*, December 6, 1996, 51.
44. Owen Gleiberman, "It Takes A Thief," *Entertainment Weekly*, February 14, 1997, 40.
45. Michel Foucault, *Discipline and Punish: The Birth of the Prison*, trans. Alan Sheridan (New York: Vintage Books, 1979), 195–229.
46. Lisa Schwarzbaum, "Trail to the Chief," *Entertainment Weekly*, April 25, 1997, 47.
47. Lisa Schwarzbaum, "Unrapt 'Present,'" *Entertainment Weekly*, August 12, 1994, 37.
48. Tom Russo, "The Getaway," *Entertainment Weekly*, August 16, 1996, 42.
49. Ty Burr, "Capitol Offenses," *Entertainment Weekly*, April 30, 1993, 60.
50. Gleiberman, "Running on Empty," 51.

## Chapter 6

1. Quoted in James A. Martin, "Pacino's 'Cruising' Takes a Bruising," *Entertainment Weekly*, February 13, 1998, 80.
2. *The Celluloid Closet* is reviewed by Anne Thompson and Dave Karger in the 1996 spring double issue of *Entertainment Weekly*, and David Ehrenstein's *Open Secret* is

reviewed in Steve Daly's "Closet Cases," *Entertainment Weekly*, October 2, 1998, 65.

3. Quoted in A. J. Jacobs, "Out?" *Entertainment Weekly*, October 4, 1996, 23.
4. Ibid., 21.
5. Jess Cagle, "As Gay As It Gets?" *Entertainment Weekly*, May 8, 1998, 28.
6. Jacobs, "Out?" 23.
7. Ibid., 20.
8. Lisa Schwarzbaum, "Ellen DeGeneres {Entertainer of the Year}," in 1997 year-end special, *Entertainment Weekly*, 18.
9. Quoted in Kate Garner, "Laura Dern is not a lesbian (but she plays one on TV)," *Entertainment Weekly*, April 25, 1997, 38.
10. Quoted in Cagle, "As Gay As It Gets," 28.
11. Ibid., 30.
12. Ibid., 31.
13. Jessica Shaw, "Outward Bound," *Entertainment Weekly*, July 25, 1997, 10.
14. Quoted in Rebecca Ascher-Walsh, "The Road To 'Philadelphia,'" *Entertainment Weekly*, January 28, 1994, 31.
15. See William J. Palmer, *The Films of the Seventies: A Social History* (Metuchen, NJ and London: Scarecrow Press, 1987), 179–230.
16. "Awesome Auteurs," *Entertainment Weekly*, November 19, 1993, 36.
17. Lawrence O'Toole, "Ribbons and Blues," *Entertainment Weekly*, June 17, 1994, 54.
18. Owen Gleiberman, "Pride and Prejudice," *Entertainment Weekly*, December 24, 1993, 34.
19. Pat H. Broeske, "Grim Tidings," *Entertainment Weekly*, October 15, 1993, 9.
20. Jess Cagle, "America Sees Shades of Gay: A Once Invisible Group Finds the Spotlight," in "The Gay '90s: Entertainment Comes Out of the Closet" special issue, *Entertainment Weekly*, September 8, 1995, 22.
21. Ibid.
22. Ibid., 24.
23. Quoted in Benjamin Svetkey, "Disney Catches Hell," *Entertainment Weekly*, December 15, 1995, 43.
24. Quoted in Degen Pener, "Gibson's GLAAD Handing," in 1997 spring double issue, *Entertainment Weekly*, 26.
25. A. J. Jacobs, "Are Gay Movies Still in the Closet?" *Entertainment Weekly*, August 9, 1996, 16.
26. Quoted in Kathleen Craughwell, "A Great Reception," *Los Angeles Times*, April 5, 2000, F5.
27. Quoted in Steve Daly, "Love! Valour! Costanza!" *Entertainment Weekly*, May 23, 1997, 21.
28. Quoted in Steve Daly, "Mr. In The Money," *Entertainment Weekly*, October 3, 1997, 20.
29. Ibid., 21.
30. Lisa Schwarzbaum, "What, Me Gay?" *Entertainment Weekly*, September 26, 1997, 50.
31. Quoted in Dave Karger, "A Knight To Remember," *Entertainment Weekly*, November 13, 1998, 40.
32. Michael Sauter, "OUTrageous Fortunes," special Oscar guide, *Entertainment Weekly*, March 1998, 80.
33. See Jean Baudrillard, *Simulations*.

34. Quoted in Benjamin Svetkey, "Getting The Girl," *Entertainment Weekly*, April 11, 1997, 25.
35. Quoted in Dave Karger, "The Best Man," *Entertainment Weekly*, July 11, 1997, 32.
36. Quoted in Rebecca Ascher-Walsh, "Boy Meets Girl, Boy Meets Boy," *Entertainment Weekly*, April 24, 1998, 40–41.
37. Owen Gleiberman, "Straight, No Chaser," *Entertainment Weekly*, April 24, 1998, 56.
38. A. J. Jacobs, "When Gay Men Happen To Straight Women," *Entertainment Weekly*, October 23, 1998, 20.
39. Ibid., 22.
40. Lisa Schwarzbaum, "Women In Love," *Entertainment Weekly*, June 17, 1994, 34.
41. "Getting the 'Wong' Idea," *Entertainment Weekly*, September 15, 1995, 63.
42. Owen Gleiberman, "Skirting Issues," *Entertainment Weekly*, November 26, 1993, 46.
43. Anthony Lane, "Style Wars," *New Yorker*, September 15, 1995, 96.
44. Quoted in Anne Thompson, "Women (Sort Of) On The Verge," *Entertainment Weekly*, August 5, 1994, 7.
45. Quoted in Degen Pener, "All The 'Wong' Moves," *Entertainment Weekly*, September 8, 1995, 50.
46. Owen Gleiberman, "Swish Fulfillment," *Entertainment Weekly*, March 15, 1996, 45.
47. Quoted in Benjamin Svetkey, "Tickled Pink," *Entertainment Weekly*, March 29, 1996, 24.
48. Ibid., 20, 21.
49. Terrence Rafferty, "Seeing Straight," *New Yorker*, March 18, 1996, 110.
50. Owen Gleiberman, "The Killer Elite," *Entertainment Weekly*, November 28, 1997, 48, 53.

## Chapter 7

1. Ty Burr, "Copycat Killers," *Entertainment Weekly*, October 16, 1992, 82.
2. Owen Gleiberman, "Stately Vein Manner," *Entertainment Weekly*, November 18, 1994, 75.
3. Ibid.
4. Lawrence O'Toole, "I Love You to Death," *Entertainment Weekly*, January 29, 1993, 61.
5. "Fahrenheit '92: A Screen Fever Chart," year-end special issue, *Entertainment Weekly*, 1992, 58.
6. Ibid., 6.
7. Quoted in Stephen Schaefer, "Bottoms Up," *Entertainment Weekly*, July 15, 1995, 12.
8. Chris Nashawaty, "Is T&A DOA?" *Entertainment Weekly*, November 10, 1995, 6.
9. Ibid., 7.
10. Owen Gleiberman, "Bawdy Beautiful," *Entertainment Weekly*, April 22, 1994, 39.
11. Cindy Pearlman, "Stone Cold," *Entertainment Weekly*, February 10, 1995, 12.
12. Quoted in Dana Kennedy, "Bodies Count," *Entertainment Weekly*, March 25, 1994, 16.
13. Anthony Lane, "Starkness Visible," *New Yorker*, October 9, 1995, 95.

14. Quoted in Benjamin Svetkey, "GIRLS! GIRLS! GIRLS!: Hollywood Catches Flesh-Dance Fever with *Showgirls*," *Entertainment Weekly*, September 29, 1995, 30.

15. Owen Gleiberman, "The Way of All Flesh," *Entertainment Weekly*, October 6, 1995, 41.

16. Jennifer Kornreich, "S'Moore of the Same," *Entertainment Weekly*, July 12, 1996, 18.

17. Chris Nashawaty, "Demi Goes Undercover," *Entertainment Weekly*, April 26, 1996, 6.

18. Quoted in Benjamin Svetkey and Susan Spillman, "Clash of the Titans," *Entertainment Weekly*, January 26, 1996, 8.

19. Quoted in Anne Thompson, "Moore Money," *Entertainment Weekly*, March 10, 1995, 11.

20. Bruce Fretts, "*The Players Club*," *Entertainment Weekly*, March 16, 1999, 76.

21. Quoted in Andrew Essex, "A 'Monty' Haul," *Entertainment Weekly*, November 7, 1997, 16.

22. Lisa Schwarzbaum, "Cinematic Pros and Cons," *Entertainment Weekly*, September 23, 1994, 48.

23. Quoted in Lisa Schwarzbaum, "Whore and Peace," *Entertainment Weekly*, March 13, 1998, 50.

24. Anthony Lane, "Scarlet Women," *New Yorker*, October 15, 1995, 112.

25. Ibid., 114.

26. Ty Burr, "New World Ardor," *Entertainment Weekly*, August 19, 1994, 65.

27. Quoted in Lisa Schwarzbaum, "'Truth' And Consequences," *Entertainment Weekly*, May 10, 1996, 54.

28. Owen Gleiberman, "Called Into Action," *Entertainment Weekly*, April 5, 1996, 55.

29. Dave Karger, "Porn Again," *Entertainment Weekly*, September 20, 1996, 10.

30. Benjamin Svetkey, "Porn On The Fourth Of July," *Entertainment Weekly*, January 31, 1997, 18.

31. Ira Robbins, "Love Gets Real," *Entertainment Weekly*, June 6, 1997, 71.

32. Ibid., 70.

33. In "News & Notes: Festivals," *Entertainment Weekly*, October 25, 1996, 24.

34. Quoted in Svetkey, "Porn On The Fourth of July," 22.

35. Rebecca Ascher-Walsh, "The Naked and the Dread," *Entertainment Weekly*, April 25, 1997, 26.

36. Dana Kennedy, "Flouting Convention," *Entertainment Weekly*, January 21, 1994, 27–28.

37. Quoted in Glenn Kenny, "The First Seductions," summer double issue, *Entertainment Weekly*, 1995, 107.

38. Ibid.

39. Owen Gleiberman, "Couched in Mystery," *Entertainment Weekly*, September 9, 1994, 58.

40. Quoted in Frank Spotnitz and Jeffrey Wells, "Into the Night," *Entertainment Weekly*, April 15, 1994, 10.

41. Gleiberman, "Couched in Mystery," 59.

42. Owen Gleiberman, "American Hot Wax," *Entertainment Weekly*, January 22, 1993, 38.

43. Lisa Schwarzbaum, "House of Buggin'," *Entertainment Weekly*, February 2, 1996, 42.

44. David Ansen, "A Comedy of Cruelty," *Newsweek*, October 18, 1998, 87.

45. Ibid., 87.
46. Benjamin Svetkey, "He Said. She Said." *Entertainment Weekly*, December 16, 1994, 24.
47. Owen Gleiberman, "Boardroom Eyes," *Entertainment Weekly*, December 16, 1994, 42.
48. Terrence Rafferty, "Woman on Top," *New Yorker*, December 11, 1994, 107.
49. Quoted in Jess Cagle, "Chopped Sliver," *Entertainment Weekly*, May 21, 1993, 21.
50. "The Mane Event," *Entertainment Weekly*, May 1, 1998, 55.
51. Owen Gleiberman, "The Nasty Girl," *Entertainment Weekly*, May 8, 1992, 38.
52. Ken Tucker, "Liv a Little, Love a Little," *Entertainment Weekly*, June 14, 1996, 43.
53. Ken Tucker, "Little Girl Lust," *Entertainment Weekly*, July 31, 1998, 53.
54. Susan Bordo, "True Obsessions: Being Unfaithful to 'Lolita'," *Chronicle of Higher Education*, July 24, 1998, B7.
55. Ibid., B8.
56. Benjamin Svetkey, "Girl Trouble," *Entertainment Weekly*, August 9, 1996, 28.

## Chapter 8

1. Owen Gleiberman, "Towering Achievement," *Entertainment Weekly*, June 21, 1996, 44.
2. Quoted in James Greenberg, "The Perils of Meryl," *Entertainment Weekly*, October 7, 1994, 24.
3. Owen Gleiberman, "Bald Ambition," fall double issue, *Entertainment Weekly*, 1997, 105–6.
4. Dana Kennedy, "Women Who Run With The Wolves," *Entertainment Weekly*, February 11, 1994, 17.
5. Quoted in Bronwen Hruska, "Make Her Day," *Entertainment Weekly*, June 11, 1993, 7.
6. Owen Gleiberman, "Gun Crazy," *Entertainment Weekly*, April 2, 1993, 30.
7. Quoted in Richard Natale with Shirley Fung and Cindy Pearlman, "Top Girls," *Entertainment Weekly*, October 20, 1995, 12.
8. Quoted in James Kaplan, "Geena Davis Always Plays To Win," *Entertainment Weekly*, July 24, 1992, 18.
9. Lisa Schoenfein and Jessica Shaw, "Women's World," *Entertainment Weekly*, November 9, 1995, 12.
10. Quoted in Rebecca Ascher-Walsh, "Uncommon Women," *Entertainment Weekly*, August 12, 1994, 34.
11. Quoted in Lisa Schwarzbaum, "Women of a Certain Rage," *Entertainment Weekly*, October 11, 1996, 21.
12. Meredith Berkman, "Pregnant Pause," *Entertainment Weekly*, February 5, 1993, 20.
13. Quoted in Berkman, "Pregnant Pause," 20.
14. Quoted in Robert Seidenberg with Havelock Nelson and Dan Snierson, "Bullets Over Broadway," *Entertainment Weekly*, December 16, 1994, 7.
15. Christopher Shea, "Higher Learning," *Chronicle of Higher Education* (January 1995): A37.
16. Anne Thompson, "'I'm for Truth,' Malcolm X said, 'No matter who tells it,'" *Entertainment Weekly*, November 27, 1992, 33.
17. Ibid., 31.

18. Ty Burr, "Malcolm A to Z," *Entertainment Weekly*, July 23, 1993, 62.
19. Thompson, "I'm for Truth," 35.
20. Anthony Walton, "Heretofore Unseen," *Notre Dame Magazine*, Winter 1997–98, 31.
21. Quoted in Patricia Sellers, "Do The Light Thing," *Entertainment Weekly*, May 20, 1994, 24.
22. Ibid., 24.
23. Anthony Lane, "Cracking Up," *New Yorker*, September 15, 1995, 108.
24. Ty Burr, "Viva la Diferencia!" *Entertainment Weekly*, September 4, 1992, 75.
25. Quoted in Tim Appelo, "Judge of Character," *Entertainment Weekly*, November 12, 1993, 41.
26. Owen Gleiberman, "Living on Barrio Time," *Entertainment Weekly*, July 22, 1994, 33.
27. Richard Natale with Gregg Barrios and Ken Miller, "The Latin Factor," *Entertainment Weekly*, May 12, 1995, 14.
28. Jimmy Smits, "Home Is Where the Art Is," *Entertainment Weekly*, June 2, 1995, 41.
29. Nisid Hajari, "Stone Angel," *Entertainment Weekly*, November 19, 1993, 42.
30. *When Heaven and Earth Changed Places* (1989) and *Child of War, Woman of Peace* (1993).
31. Hajari, "Stone Angel," 42.
32. See William J. Palmer, *The Films of the Eighties: A Social History* (New York: St. Martin, 1993), especially the chapter on the Reagan administration spinning of the Vietnam War.
33. Quoted in Nasid Hajari, "'Luck' Is What You Make It," *Entertainment Weekly*, September 24, 1993, 34.

## Conclusion

1. Christopher Sharrett, "Conspiracy Theory and Political Murder in America: Oliver Stone's *JFK* and the Facts of the Matter," in *The New American Cinema*, ed. John Lewis (Durham, NC: Duke University Press, 1998), 220.
2. Ibid.
3. Robert Kolker, *Film, Form and Culture* (Boston: McGraw-Hill, 1999), iii.
4. Ibid., xvi–xvii.
5. Neil Postman, *Amusing Ourselves to Death: Public Discourse in the Age of Show Business* (New York: Penguin, 1985), quoted in David F. Bell, "A Moratorium on Suspicion?" *PMLA: The Publications of the Modern Language Association* 117, no. 2 (May 2002): 488.
6. Bell, "A Moratorium," 489.
7. Patrick Goldstein, "Will This Fight End With a TKO?" *Los Angeles Times*, February 8, 2000, Calendar, F1.
8. Quoted in Goldstein, "Will This Fight End With a TKO?" F8.
9. In *Metahistory* (Baltimore: Johns Hopkins University Press, 1973), Hayden White analyzes the rhetorical concept of emplotted ideology in historical argumentation: "Providing the 'meaning' of a story by identifying the kind of story that has been told is called explanation by emplotment (7) and how it is "a means of characterizing the different kinds of explanatory effects a historian can strive for on the level

of narrative emplotment" (10). All of this leads to the realization that "there does, in fact, appear to be an irreducible ideological component in every historical account of reality" (21).

10. Howard Rosenberg, "Embellished History? Hey, It's TV," *Los Angeles Times Calendar*, 11 February 2000, F1.

11. Quoted in "Will Hollywood Do Justice to Reality This Time?, *Los Angeles Times Calendar*, 12 March 2000, 1.

12. From William Butler Yeats, "The Second Coming."

13. Jean Baudrillard in *Simulations*, trans. Paul Foss, Paul Patton, and Phillip Beitchman (New York: Semiotext(e), 1983), writes: "Abstraction today is no longer that of the map, the double, the mirror or the concept. Simulation . . . is the generation by models of a real without origin or reality: a hyperreal (2). . . . It is rather a question of substituting signs of the real for the real itself (4). . . . the whole system becomes weightless, it is no longer anything but a gigantic simulacrum—not unreal, but a simulacrum, never again exchanging for what is real, but exchanging in itself, in an uninterrupted circuit without reference or circumference" (10–11).

14. Don DeLillo, *Cosmopolis* (New York: Scribner, 2003), 206.

15. See the chapter on terrorism in Palmer, *The Films of the Eighties: A Social History*.

16. Quoted in "Film director blames movies for terrorist attacks," *Associated Press* to *Lafayette Journal and Courier*, October 18, 2001.

17. Dominick LaCapra, *History and Criticism* (Ithaca, NY: Cornell University Press, 1985), 18–19.

# Index